The New Economic Diplomacy

Decision-Making and Negotiation in International Economic Relations

NICHOLAS BAYNE and STEPHEN WOOLCOCK
The London School of Economics and Political Science

With Case Studies by:

COLIN BUDD
PHIL EVANS
MATTHEW GOODMAN
PATRICK RABE
IVAN MBIRIMI
NIGEL WICKS
RICHARD CARDEN

ASHGATE

Published by
Ashgate Publishing Limited
Gower House
Croft Road
Aldershot
Hampshire GU11 3HR
England

Ashgate Publishing Company
Suite 420
101 Cherry Street
Burlington, VT 05401-4405
USA

Ashgate website:http://www.ashgate.com

British Library Cataloguing in Publication Data
The new economic diplomacy: decision-making and
    negotiation in international economic relations. -(The G8
    and global governance series)
    1. International economic relations 2. Diplomacy 3. Economic
    policy
    I. Bayne, Nicholas II. Woolcock, Stephen
    337

Library of Congress Cataloging-in-Publication Data
The new economic diplomacy: decision-making and negotiation in international
economic relations / Nicholas Bayne and Stephen Woolcock.
    p.cm. -- (The G8 and global governance series)
    This book is based on the 2000-2001 course given at the LSE's International Relations
    Dept.
    Includes bibliographical references and index.
    ISBN 0-7546-1832-3
    1. International economic relations. 2. International cooperation. 3. Commercial policy.
    4.Negotiation in business. 5. Decision making. I. Bayne, Nicholas, 1937-II. Woolcock,
    Stephen.III. Series

    HF1359.N4685 2003
    337--dc21   2002027785

ISBN 0 7546 1832 3 (hardback)
ISBN 0 7546 4318 2 (paperback)

Reprinted 2004

Printed and bound in Great Britain by Antony Rowe Ltd., Chippenham, Wiltshire

THE NEW ECONOMIC DIPLOMACY

The G8 and Global Governance Series

Series Editor: John J. Kirton

The G8 and Global Governance Series explores the issues, the institutions, and the strategies of the participants in the G8 network of global governance, and other actors, processes, and challenges that shape global order in the twenty-first century. Many aspects of globalisation, once considered domestic, are now moving into the international arena, generating a need for broader and deeper international co-operation and demanding new centres of leadership to revitalise, reform, reinforce, and even replace the galaxy of multilateral institutions created in 1945. In response, the G8, composed of the world's major market democracies, including Russia and the European Union, is emerging as an effective source of global governance. *The G8 and Global Governance Series* focusses on the new issues at the centre of global governance, covering topics such as finance, investment, and trade, as well as transnational threats to human security and traditional and emerging political and security challenges. The series examines the often invisible network of G8, G7, and other institutions as they operate inside and outside established international systems to generate desired outcomes and create a new order. It analyses how individual G8 members and other international actors, including multinational firms, civil society organisations, and other international institutions, devise and implement strategies to achieve their preferred global order.

Also in the series

New Directions in Global Economic Governance
Edited by John J. Kirton and George M. von Furstenberg
ISBN 0 7546 1698 3

The New Transatlantic Agenda
Edited by Hall Gardner and Radoslava Stefanova
ISBN 0 7546 1780 7

Guiding Global Order
Edited by John J. Kirton, Joseph P. Daniels and Andreas Freytag
ISBN 0 7546 1502 2

Shaping a New International Financial System
Edited by Karl Kaiser, John J. Kirton and Joseph P. Daniels
ISBN 0 7546 1412 3

Hanging In There
Nicholas Bayne
ISBN 0 7546 1185 X

The G7/G8 System
Peter I. Hajnal
ISBN 1 84014 776 8

New Directions in Global Political Governance
Edited by John J. Kirton and Junichi Takase
ISBN 0 7546 1833 1

The G8's Role in the New Millennium
Edited by Michael R. Hodges, John J. Kirton and Joseph P. Daniels
ISBN 1 84014 774 1

Governing Global Trade
Theodore H. Cohn
ISBN 0 7546 1593 6

Contents

v

List of Tables

List of Figures

Preface and Acknowledgements

Economic diplomacy, as presented in this book, is the brainchild of the late Mike Hodges, Senior Lecturer in the International Relations Department at the LSE. In 1997 he had the idea of bringing together the analytical skills of academics with the experience of policy practitioners, to examine how states organise and conduct their international economic relations. He approached Nicholas Bayne, then recently retired from the British Diplomatic Service, and they planned a series of graduate seminars in Economic Diplomacy at the LSE in 1998-1999, at which pairs of academics and practitioners would share the platform. This was intended to be the forerunner to a full graduate course, to begin the following year. But tragically Mike died in June 1998, before he could bring his plan to fruition.

Stephen Woolcock had then just become a Lecturer at the LSE's International Relations Department. He joined forces with Nicholas Bayne to continue what Mike Hodges had begun. The seminar series went out as planned. It was followed, in 1999-2000, by a full graduate course, in which academic lectures, by Bayne and Woolcock, provided the framework for a sequence of lectures by practitioners, drawn from government, international institutions and the private sector. These practitioner lectures are an integral part of the course, which has now completed its third year.

This book, *The New Economic Diplomacy*, is based on the course as we gave it in its second year, 2000-2001, with each chapter corresponding to an academic or practitioner lecture. Though the book is meant to be read as a whole, individual chapters can also be taken on their own. Each chapter is therefore meant to be self-contained, at the cost of some repetition. As a multi-authored work, this book inevitably shows some variations of emphasis. For example, Woolcock's chapters make more use of theory, as compared to Bayne's that are more anecdotal, while each practitioner author has his own viewpoint. But we believe that, overall, the book conveys a consistent message.

In producing this book, we have incurred many debts and take this opportunity to express our thanks to the many people who have helped us both with the book and with the course itself. Our first debt of gratitude is to our colleagues at the LSE, who have welcomed and encouraged this innovation, spoken at lectures and seminars and helped us in manifold ways. They include Charles Goodhart, Christopher Hill, Graham Ingham, Daphne Josselin, Richard Layard, Hilary Parker, Razeen Sally, Julius Sen, David Stasavage, Paul Taylor, Heidi Ullrich, Andrew Walter, William Wallace and Michael Yahuda.

Second, we thank most warmly all the practitioners who have agreed to speak for us, in seminars and lectures. Our greatest debt is to those who, in addition to lecturing, have contributed chapters to this volume, as follows:

- **Sir Colin Budd, KCMG** is British Ambassador to the Netherlands. From 1997 to 2001 he was Director for European Union and Economic Affairs at the Foreign and Commonwealth Office and British 'Sous-Sherpa' responsible for G8 summit preparations.
- **Phil Evans** is Chief Policy Adviser to the Consumers Association.
- **Matthew Goodman** was Executive Director and Head of Government Affairs for Goldman Sachs International while this book was being written. From 1992 to 1997 he was Financial Attaché and Treasury Representative at the US Embassy in Tokyo.
- **Patrick Rabe** is Administrator in the International Affairs Unit of the Directorate General Environment, European Commission.
- **Ivan Mbirimi** is Chief Programme Officer in the Economic Affairs Division of the Commonwealth Secretariat.
- **Sir Nigel Wicks, KCB, CVO, CBE** is Chairman of the Committee on Standards in Public Life and of CRESTCo Ltd, the UK share settlement company. From 1988 to 2000 he was Second Permanent Secretary (Finance) at HM Treasury, after being Principal Private Secretary to the Prime Minister (1985-88) and UK Executive Director to the IMF and World Bank (1983-85).
- **Richard Carden, CB** is Director-General for Trade Policy at the Department of Trade and Industry. The copyright for his chapter is held by the British government.

In addition, we are most grateful to all the other speakers, both practitioners and non-LSE academics, who have contributed to the series from the beginning: Celso Amorim, Michael Arthur, Robert Chote, the late Huw Evans, David Fisk, Andrew Fraser, Michael Grubb, Tony Hutton, Sylvia Jay, Emyr Jones-Parry, Julian Lob-Levyt, Matthew Lockwood, Ann Pettifor, Stephen Pickford, Alan Rugman, Garry Sampson, George Staple, Nicholas Stern and Gunnar Wiegand.

Third, we are indebted to everyone who has taken part in the lectures and seminars and contributed to the development of our ideas on economic diplomacy. These have included not only LSE students, but also members of British government departments, thanks to the encouragement given by Charles Bridge, Creon Butler, Jon Cunliffe and Richard Manning.

Finally, we would like to thank all those involved with bringing this book into its published state: John Kirton (Series Editor for Ashgate's *The G8 and Global Governance Series*) and Madeline Koch from the G8 Research Group of the University of Toronto; our four anonymous reviewers; Kirstin Howgate and her colleagues at Ashgate; and Christine Hunter, for her skill in converting our inconsistent and rambling scripts into presentable 'camera-ready-copy'. Thanks to them, the ideas that we have been developing and testing in the laboratory of the LSE can reach out to a wider audience.

Nicholas Bayne
Stephen Woolcock

List of Abbreviations

ACP	African, Caribbean and Pacific associates of the EU
AFTA	ASEAN Free Trade Area
AIDS	Acquired Immune Deficiency Syndrome
APEC	Asia-Pacific Economic Cooperation
ASEAN	Association of South-East Asian Nations
Bank	Short for World Bank, incorporating IBRD, IDA and IFC
BATNA	Better Agreement Than No Agreement
BDA	Bundesverband der Deutschen Arbeitsgeber
BDI	Bundesverband der Deutschen Industrie
BEUC	Bureau of European Consumers
BIAC	Business and Industry Advisory Committee (of the OECD)
BIS	Bank for International Settlements
BIT	Bilateral Investment Treaty
BSE	Bovine Spongiform Encephalopathy (mad-cow disease)
CAP	Common Agriculture Policy (of the EC)
CBC	Commonwealth Business Council
CBI	Confederation of British Industry
CDU	Christian Democratic Union (of Germany)
CFSP	Common Foreign and Security Policy (of the EU)
CHOGM	Commonwealth Heads of Government Meeting
COMESA	Common Market for Eastern and Southern Africa
COREPER	Committee of Permanent Representatives (of the EU)
CSD	Commission for Sustainable Development (of the UN)
CSU	Christian Social Union (of Bavaria, Germany)
DFID	Department for International Development (of the UK)
DG	Directorate General (of the European Commission)
DTI	Department of Trade and Industry (of the UK)
EBRD	European Bank for Reconstruction and Development
EC	European Community
ECJ	European Court of Justice
ECOSOC	Economic and Social Council (of the UN)
ECSC	European Coal and Steel Community
ED	Executive Director (of Fund or Bank)
EEC	European Economic Community
EFTA	European Free Trade Area
EMU	Economic and Monetary Union
EP	European Parliament
ETUC	European Trade Union Congress
EU	European Union

FATF	Financial Action Task Force
FCC	Federal Communications Commission (of the US)
FCO	Foreign and Commonwealth Office (of the UK)
FDA	Food and Drug Administration (of the US)
FDI	Foreign Direct Investment
FTA	Free Trade Agreement
FTAA	Free Trade Area of the Americas
Fund	International Monetary Fund (see also IMF)
GATS	General Agreement on Trade in Services (in the WTO)
GATT	General Agreement on Tariffs and Trade
GDP	Gross Domestic Product
GMOs	Genetically Modified Organisms
GNP	Gross National Product
G5	Group of Five (finance ministers)
G7	Group of Seven (summit, finance ministers and other groups)
G8	Group of Eight (summit and other groups)
G10	Group of Ten (finance ministers and officials in the IMF)
G20	Group of Twenty (on new financial architecture)
G24	Group of Twenty-four (developing countries in the IMF)
G77	Group of Seventy-Seven (developing countries in the UN)
HIPC	Heavily Indebted Poor Countries
HST	Hegemonic Stability Theory
IBRD	International Bank for Reconstruction and Development
ICC	International Chamber of Commerce
ICFTU	International Confederation of Free Trade Unions
IDA	International Development Association
IEA	International Energy Agency (linked to OECD)
IEC	International Electrotechnical Committee
IFC	International Finance Corporation
IFF	Intergovernmental Forum on Forests
IGC	Inter-Governmental Conference (in the EU)
ILO	International Labour Organisation
IMF	International Monetary Fund, also known as the Fund
IMFC	International Monetary and Financial Committee (of the IMF)
IPCC	Intergovernmental Panel on Climate Change
IPE	International Political Economy
IPF	Intergovernmental Panel on Forests
IPR	Intellectual Property Rights, see TRIPS
IR	International Relations
ISO	International Standards Organisation
IT	Information Technology
ITA	International Tin Agreement
ITC	International Trade Commission (of the US)
ITO	International Trade Organisation
LSE	London School of Economics and Political Science
MAI	Multilateral Agreement on Investment (in OECD)

MEA	Multilateral Environmental Agreement
METI	Ministry of Economics, Trade and Industry (of Japan)
MFA	Multi-Fibre Agreement (for textiles in GATT)
MFN	Most-Favoured-Nation treatment (in GATT and WTO)
MNC	Multi-National Company
MOSS	Market Oriented Sector Selective talks between US and Japan
NAFTA	North American Free Trade Agreement
NATO	North Atlantic Treaty Organisation
NEPAD	New Partnership for Africa's Development
NGO	Non-Governmental Organisation
NIEO	New International Economic Order
NTB	Non-Tariff Barrier
OAU	Organisation for African Unity
OECD	Organisation for Economic Cooperation and Development
OEEC	Organisation for European Economic Reconstruction
OFTEL	Office of the Telecommunications Regulator (in the UK)
OPEC	Organisation of Petroleum Exporting Countries
PBEC	Pacific Basin Economic Council
QMV	Qualified Majority Voting (in the EU)
Quad	Quadrilateral - of trade ministers (US, EC, Japan, Canada)
RIIA	Royal Institute for International Affairs, also called Chatham House
RSPB	Royal Society for the Protection of Birds
RTA	Regional Trade Agreement
RTAA	Reciprocal Trade Agreements Act (of the US)
SADC	Southern Africa Development Commission
SDR	Special Drawing Right (in the IMF)
SEM	Single European Market
SII	Structural Impediments Initiative (between US and Japan)
SMEs	Small and Medium-sized Enterprises
SPD	Social Democratic Party (of Germany)
SPS	Sanitary and Phyto-Sanitary agreement in the WTO
TABD	Trans-Atlantic Business Dialogue
TEC	Treaty Establishing the European Community
TEU	Treaty Establishing the European Union
TRIMS	Trade-Related Investment Measures agreement of WTO
TRIPS	Trade-Related Intellectual Property Rights agreement of WTO
TUAC	Trade Union Advisory Committee (of the OECD)
UK	United Kingdom
UN	United Nations
UNCED	United Nations Conference on Environment and Development
UNCTAD	United Nations Conference on Trade and Development
UNEP	United Nations Environment Programme
UNFF	United Nations Forum on Forests
UNICE	Union of European Industry and Employers' Confederations
US	United States of America
USSR	Union of Soviet Socialist Republics - also Soviet Union

USTR	United States Trade Representative
WEOG	West Europe and Others Group (in the UN)
WHO	World Health Organisation
WMO	World Meteorological Organisation
WSSD	World Summit on Sustainable Development
WTO	World Trade Organization

INTRODUCTION

Chapter 1

What is Economic Diplomacy?

Nicholas Bayne and Stephen Woolcock

This is a book about how states conduct their international economic relations at the start of the 21st century: how they make decisions domestically; how they negotiate with each other internationally; and how these two processes interact. While states are at the centre of this study, it also includes non-state actors, whose influence on decision-making is growing. In general, this book is about the methods and process of decision-making and negotiation, ie about economic diplomacy, rather than about the content of policy. It is not intended to be a manual for negotiators, but rather to explain why governments (and other actors in economic diplomacy) behave in the way they do.

We call this book *The New Economic Diplomacy* to emphasise how much this activity has changed in the 1990s and early 2000s. Through most of the period since World War II, economic diplomacy was dominated by governments and, within them, by permanent officials. It was shaped by the constraints of the Cold War. Now, with the end of the Cold War and the advance of globalisation, there are far more non-government players; ministers and heads of government are active alongside their officials; and a single economic system covers the entire world. Economic diplomacy is concerned not only with measures taken at the border, but increasingly operates 'within the frontier'. Finally, Cold War political impulses are being replaced by worries about globalisation and, since 11 September 2001, the fight against terrorism. All these themes will shape this book.

Most of this book, including the first seven chapters, is written by Nicholas Bayne and Stephen Woolcock of the LSE. But economic diplomacy is not just a subject for academic study. It is an activity pursued by state and non-state actors in the real world of today. In some respects economic diplomacy is like sex: easier to describe if you have practised it yourself. So an integral part of this book is provided by a series of chapters, starting at Chapter 8, written by experienced practitioners of economic diplomacy. These practitioner chapters will provide case studies and illustrations of how economic diplomacy works.

This opening chapter covers the following:

- It begins with a broad definition of economic diplomacy;
- It briefly identifies the theoretical approaches relevant to economic diplomacy;
- It sets out the main analytical framework used throughout the book, based on three tensions and eight questions;

- It explains the multi-level nature of economic diplomacy, which is the principal theme of Part II of the book.

The chapter concludes with a brief review of the structure of the book and how the academic and practitioner chapters fit together.

Why Study Economic Diplomacy?

It is worth asking why economic diplomacy deserves attention. There are four main reasons.

First, economic diplomacy is about **process** rather than **structures.** Academic studies in International Political Economy (IPE) normally focus on the structural factors that shape economic relations between states. These will include international structures, such as the relative power of different nation states in the economic system, or the structures of influence within national economies, in which different sectoral interests compete in determining policy. Likewise IPE discusses the main political causes of the evolving structure of the international economy, and the implications of this structure for national policy choice. Associated studies of international business take firms as the focus of attention, rather than government, although government policy obviously affects international business.

This book is different in being concerned with process, ie with decision-making processes in governments and international institutions. The relative importance of process over power structures in determining policy choices will vary. When there are major differences in economic power and influence, these are likely to be the shaping factor in any policy outcome. But when power relationships are more balanced, the process of negotiation is likely to be more important. As Professor John Odell points out in his book *Negotiating the World Economy* (Odell 2000), outcomes vary between cases when structural features are the same, which suggests that process is important. Hence a study of decision-making processes in international economic relations fills a gap in the field.

Second, economic diplomacy is becoming **more important**. During the Cold War international relations were dominated by security concerns and the study of international relations reflected this. Economic diplomacy was going on the whole time, of course, but it did not have the same prominence as it has gained since the end of the Cold War. After the Cold War security factors play a reduced role and economic relations have assumed a greater importance. The terrorist attacks against the United States on 11 September 2001 have placed security once again in the forefront of debate. But economic diplomacy remains relevant to efforts aimed at tackling some of the root causes of terrorism, such as poverty and marginalisation.

Third, governments need to be **efficient** and pursue the aims of enhancing economic welfare in a global economy. To a far greater extent today than in the

1970s or 1980s, national economic performance is dependent on international factors. With the advance of globalisation, governments need to choose policies that shape the interaction between the domestic and the international economy. In order to deliver results in terms of economic welfare at home, governments have to pay more attention to foreign economic relations and thus engage in economic diplomacy.

Fourth, at the same time, governments are under increased pressures of **accountability**. They have to ensure that their decisions in economic diplomacy are accountable to the growing number of constituencies affected (or disaffected) by globalisation. This requires a better understanding of decision-making processes and how they might be improved. But these processes have in the past been based on policy elites. This means that a 'democratic deficit' has grown, which has been reflected in the criticism of established channels of democratic accountability by civil society. Some of this has found expression in the streets of Geneva, Seattle, Washington, Genoa and even Gothenburg. Transparency and accountability are now the watchwords in the debate on globalisation. These issues relate directly to decision-making by governments in response to globalisation and are reflected in today's economic diplomacy.

Defining Economic Diplomacy

Diplomacy and its stereotypes

'Economic diplomacy' is the term chosen to describe the subject of this study. This has the advantage that 'diplomacy' is a broad and elastic term. But precisely because it admits of wide interpretation, some further definition is needed, to make clear what is and is not included in this book about economic diplomacy.[1]

The classical concept of diplomacy defines it as:

> The conduct of relations between states and other entities with standing in world politics by official agents and by peaceful means.[2]

A more recent definition says that:

> Diplomacy is concerned with the management of relations between states and between states and other actors.[3]

To do justice to *economic* diplomacy, it will be necessary to stretch these definitions and dispose of some misleading stereotypes associated with the term diplomacy, as set out below.

The first stereotype is that diplomacy is conducted only by diplomats, ie by people from foreign ministries.

The second stereotype is that diplomacy applies to informal negotiation and voluntary cooperation, but not to rule-based systems and legal commitments. For example, Professor John Jackson contrasts what he calls "the negotiation and diplomacy approach" with "the rule-oriented approach" in his analysis of the dispute settlement mechanism of the World Trade Organization (WTO).[4]

The third stereotype is that diplomacy is a weak and imprecise activity, where conciliation leads only to meaningless compromises.   British Prime Minister Margaret Thatcher once said at an international meeting:

> Everyone knows I am no diplomat; we have more than enough of them.[5]

The fourth stereotype is that diplomacy is elitist, conducted by an establishment of privileged officials.   The reference to 'official agents' in the classical definition already quoted rather implies this.

The fifth stereotype is that diplomacy is secretive and opaque. Diplomats, it is said, prefer to strike deals shut away in smoke-filled rooms, emerging only to announce agreement.

None of these stereotypes apply to economic diplomacy, as covered by this book.   As the following sections will show, the scope and content of economic diplomacy is much broader and more purposeful.

Government and other actors

Economic diplomacy is mainly concerned with what **governments** do. But it goes much wider than foreign ministries.   In this book we consider all government departments, ministries and agencies which have economic responsibilities and which operate internationally to be engaging in economic diplomacy, though they might not describe it as such.   Within government, economic diplomacy is less and less the preserve of closed circles of officials.   Not only ministers and heads of government but also parliaments, independent agencies and sub-national bodies are all making their influence felt.

A wide range of **non-state actors** engage in economic diplomacy, both by shaping government policies and as independent players in their own right.   Non-governmental actors have always been present in economic diplomacy to some extent.   In the past, **business** tended to be the most active interest, working both on detailed and more general questions of economic diplomacy.   Now **civil society NGOs** have assumed centre stage, questioning the merits of globalisation and staging sometimes violent demonstrations at major economic meetings.

International organisations are very important as a forum for negotiations. But this book does not treat them as independent actors.   Instead it focuses on how governments make use of these organisations and integrate them into their own decision-making processes.

International and domestic

Economic diplomacy is concerned with **international economic issues**. In principle, this should simplify the analysis. But it is becoming increasingly difficult to draw any clear line between what is 'domestic' and what is 'international'. The growth of economic interdependence since the 1950s, which has accelerated in recent years, means that what was previously considered to be domestic (or European) is now subject to international negotiation.

The Bretton Woods system of international economic institutions was based on what John Ruggie has called 'embedded liberalism'.[6] This meant that the system developed rules for economic relations between states, but left national economic autonomy largely untouched. As long as national policies did not have negative impacts on others, governments could pursue whatever employment, tax or industrial policy they wished. For example, when the General Agreement on Tariffs and Trade (GATT) was formed in 1948 - as described further in Chapter 6 - there was a clear understanding of what was a trade issue, and thus potentially subject to GATT rules, and what was a non-trade issue. Provided national regulation or policies did not discriminate between imported and local national goods, GATT rules provided no constraint on national policy autonomy.

But increased economic interdependence, now called 'globalisation', has put an end to such tidy distinctions between what is national and what is international policy. The implication of this process for economic diplomacy is to make it much more complex, covering more and more issues and including more and more actors.

Instruments and issues

Economic diplomacy, as defined in this study, uses a full range of **instruments**. We take economic diplomacy to embrace the whole spectrum of measures from informal negotiation and cooperation, through soft types of regulation (such as codes of conduct), to the creation and enforcement of binding rules or regimes. The implications and relative merits of these differing degrees of constraint on national policy autonomy are key questions to be examined in this book.

In economic diplomacy progress is usually made by persuasion and mutual agreement, rather than by the confrontation that Thatcher liked. But economic diplomacy is often confrontational and can go right to the brink of conflict. This happened, for example, in the fisheries dispute between Canada and the European Union in 1995. Economic diplomacy can include punitive economic measures taken in the pursuit of political goals, such as sanctions, and some scholars use the term only in this sense. But we prefer Baldwin's term 'economic statecraft' for sanctions and related policies, which are only covered in passing in this book.[7]

We regard economic diplomacy as being defined not by its instruments but by the economic **issues** that provide its content. Economic diplomacy is sometimes used as a synonym for trade diplomacy - the negotiation of trade agreements in bilateral, regional or multilateral contexts. Our definition includes trade diplomacy, but goes much wider. We follow the same definition as used by Odell in determining the scope of economic negotiation. This covers:

> Policies relating to production, movement or exchange of goods, services, investments (including official development assistance), money, information and their regulation.[8]

This is a very wide range of issues. A single volume could not cover them all and, of necessity, this book is selective, as revealed by the range of practitioner authors and their case studies. It concentrates on the central issues of trade, finance and the global environment. These are topics of high political profile, which arouse strong popular concern and bring out well the interplay between different actors in economic diplomacy.

This book also has to make choices between the countries studied. Much of it is about economic diplomacy as practised by the major powers of Western Europe, North America and Japan that come together at the G7/G8 summits. These are the most influential countries in the international economic system and their practices in decision-making and negotiation are relatively open and easy to study. But it would be wrong to ignore the rest of the world, at a time when more and more developing and ex-communist countries are becoming active internationally and when the problems of the poorest countries attract growing concern. So the later chapters of the book deal with issues of concern to rich and poor countries alike.

There are also some limits on the treatment of the European Union. The development of common external positions in the EU, for example in international trade, is regarded as economic diplomacy. But agreeing common internal positions, for example on monetary union, is not. The distinction is a bit arbitrary; but it means that the viewpoint is always from inside Europe looking outwards.

The impact of markets

A distinctive feature of economic diplomacy, as opposed to political diplomacy, is that it is sensitive to **market developments**. Increased economic integration, has made markets for production and investment global, with the result that virtually any national regulatory policy could have an impact on the relative competitiveness of different locations. Market developments will thus shape the actors involved in any issue, influence the negotiating positions and possibly offer alternatives to a negotiated solution. This means economic diplomacy will only succeed if the market does not offer a ready alternative acceptable to one side. Markets can also punish national policies which are not in line with market expectations.

As Odell puts it, markets can be endogenous to economic diplomacy, in that they form an integral part of the process. Foreign policy analysis is about decision-making processes and therefore has certain parallels to economic diplomacy. But it seldom sees markets as shaping the decision-making process in the way economic diplomacy does.

Is There a Theory of Economic Diplomacy?

Theoretical aspects of economic diplomacy are the subject of Chapter 2 of this book. But it is important to make clear at the outset that there is no single theory of economic diplomacy that is able to predict outcomes in any given international economic negotiation. In the absence of such a theory, an analytical framework is needed to do two things:

- *First*, to bring some order to the examination of the complex process of decision-making in economic diplomacy; and
- *Second*, to enable some generalisations to be made on the nature of economic diplomacy, drawing on the case studies examined later in this book.

Theory has two main uses. It can provide answers on how states, under given circumstances, will conduct policy. Such a theory is concerned with the prediction of outcomes and it must be possible to test whether the theory is correct or not. Inevitably, theories of this kind make significant simplifications, for example, by regarding states as unitary actors, which have clearly defined and stable policy preferences. Such a theory is not much help in economic diplomacy, which is concerned with the interaction between international and domestic factors and economic and political concerns. It makes no sense to assume that states are unitary actors, that negotiators have full knowledge of national policy preferences or that these preferences will be steady and not affected by market developments.

The alternative use of theory is in helping to identify which questions to ask. A theoretical framework of this kind will help in sorting out the complex factors that shape the policy process. Purists will argue that this is not really theory, but only an analytical tool; so be it. The aim is to identify the main explanatory factors and then consider which of these is most important in a range of case studies.[9]

The development of this framework can, of course, draw on the existing literature on international economic cooperation or IPE in general, which considers the systemic, societal and state centred factors shaping national policy preferences. This literature, as noted, looks predominantly at structures of interest and power and how these shape economic policies. The existing literature allows for different levels of analysis of economic relations between states, as follows:

- *Systemic*. In systemic theories, the international system is regarded as decisive in explaining events. Realist theories, for example, put much weight on the relative economic power of states. Hegemonic stability theory, much used in IPE, argues that economic cooperation only comes about when there is a dominant state able to ensure that it happens. Regime theory provides insights into how and why states cooperate, whether this takes the form of formal institutions or more informal processes in which shared values and norms help develop confidence in the mutual benefit of cooperation. There are other 'structural theories' which see national economic policies as dependent on the wider global capitalist system; these include dependency theory and world systems theory.[10]

- *Domestic.* In contrast to systemic theories, which concentrate on relations between states as single entities, domestic theories look within the state for explanations of international behaviour. At the national domestic level there are societal and state centred theories, which divide as follows:
    - Societal theories see policy as the outcome of interaction between different interest groups, with government officials acting as agents in negotiations. Societal forces such as interest groups can also operate across borders as transnational actors.
    - State centred theories focus more on the role of institutional structures and the interplay of interests between different government departments. Here the interaction between national parliaments and the executive branches of government is seen as important, as are bureaucratic decision-making approaches.
- *Ideas and individuals.* Some theories argue that ideas, like political ideologies, or individuals have a determining impact on policy. This impact can be felt both domestically and internationally.
- *Interaction between levels.* There are also theories or approaches which seek to capture the interaction between these different levels of analysis. The two-level game model developed by Professor Robert Putnam is of particular interest in economic diplomacy because it puts the negotiation process at the core of analysis.[11]
- *Theories of negotiation.* Negotiation theory, as developed for negotiations between private parties, as in industrial relations, is being applied more and more to international economic negotiations. It can provide some valuable insights into negotiating strategies. Odell applies elements of negotiation theory to economic diplomacy.

To recapitulate the discussion of theory, the aim is not to identify a parsimonious theory that could be used to predict the outcomes of negotiations. This might be an interesting academic study, but would not be able to interpret what happens in practice. Instead, the objective is to formulate a middle range framework of analysis that will help in understanding the factors at work in economic diplomacy and reaching some broad conclusions based on the evidence provided by practitioners.

In Chapter 2 of this volume we shall discuss in more detail some of the mainstream international relations and international political economy theories or analytical frameworks that help to inform our study of economic diplomacy. For the purposes of this volume the approaches which explain the interaction between the different levels of analysis will be most helpful.

The Analytical Framework of this Book

The main analytical framework adopted in this book draws on the theoretical strands identified in the last section. But it combines these with observation of how economic diplomats themselves behave, as illustrated in the later case studies.

The main argument of this book is that governments are trying to reconcile three types of tension, so that policies become mutually reinforcing rather than conflicting with each other. These tensions are:

- *First*, the tension between politics and economics;
- *Second*, the tension between international and domestic pressures;
- *Third*, the tension between governments and other actors, such as private business and NGOs.

Taken together, these three tensions generate eight distinct questions, to be defined below, which provide the principal lines of enquiry for this book.

Tension Between Economics and Politics

The first major tension is between international economics and international politics. In an ideal and tidy world, states would be able to keep politics and economics apart. But the world is not tidy and states are political entities rather than economic ones. So politics constantly encroaches on economics in the pursuit of international objectives. Governments strive to reconcile politics and economics so that they do not conflict but mutually reinforce their chosen policies - and this gives rise to the first two questions. In analysing this first tension, systemic theories are most relevant.

1. How to reconcile economic and political objectives?

States use the instruments of economic policy to pursue political objectives as well as economic ones. These objectives may not be compatible; how can governments make them so? In the period following World War II, the United States launched the Marshall Plan, a major economic initiative. This had the essentially political aim of helping Europe resist communist encroachment and the Americans adjusted their economic aims accordingly.[12] On that occasion politics and economics strongly reinforced each other. In the present day there are both economic reasons for rich countries to assist poor countries, such as trade expansion, and political reasons, such as conflict prevention and - since 11 September 2001 - the fight against terrorism. But there has been less success, so far, in making these objectives reinforce each other, so as to prevent poor countries falling further behind.[13]

2. How to reconcile economic and political methods?

When governments are choosing policies, they often find that those which make most sense to economists come up against political difficulties. For example, most economists argue that countries gain economic benefit by removing barriers to external competition, whatever other countries may do. But the people who lose the protection provided by these barriers agitate louder than those who gain advantage from their removal. This creates a political obstacle; how can this be overcome, so as to unlock the economic benefits? One technique that has been developed is to negotiate away trade barriers by reciprocity.[14] Countries find this politically easier, if economically sub-optimal, because they visibly get something in return for whatever they may put on the table.

Tension Between Domestic and International Pressures

The second major tension is between domestic and international pressures in economic policy-making. This fundamental tension underlies all economic diplomacy. The international penetration of domestic economies, by trade, direct investment and financial flows, has been growing steadily since the end of World War II. This is the dominant trend of the age. It has accelerated since the Cold War ended, over ten years ago, and has been labelled 'globalisation'. The effort to resolve this tension leads to four more questions. In this area domestic, state centred theories are most relevant, combined with those models like Putnam's that explain the interaction between the domestic and the international.

3. How do governments reach common decisions internally in economic diplomacy?

In political diplomacy, foreign ministries clearly dominate decision-making. In economic diplomacy other departments often have the lead, like finance or trade ministries, and foreign ministries may struggle to get their word in. As more economic issues get international exposure, more government departments and agencies become involved in economic diplomacy: environment departments involved in international environmental negotiations; competition authorities seeking to regulate international market distortions; even ministries of home affairs concerned with money laundering and terrorist finance. As a result, bargaining to achieve a common agreed view within a national government is the first step in economic diplomacy. How can all these different interests be reflected in a way that still enables the government to act decisively?

4. How best to reach international decisions compatible with the position agreed at home?

Each government sits down in international negotiations with interlocutors that have gone through internal bargaining that is parallel to its own. Each will want an international outcome which meshes with its domestic process. But economic diplomacy is a dynamic and iterative process in which domestic positions will generally have to be modified in order to reach an internationally agreed result. National policy positions are based on balancing the interests of different sectors or groups. But linkages in international negotiations often mean that concessions in one policy area are needed to achieve policy objectives in others. The original position may have to be changed and this calls for a sounding of domestic views by the chief negotiator. This process will be shaped by domestic institutional arrangements, which may be laid down in law or in national constitutions, or may be the result of precedent. But how far should the various economic and other domestic interests have a say in the redefinition of international negotiating objectives?

5. Which is more effective in economic diplomacy - voluntary cooperation or
systems based on rules and legally binding commitments?

Rule-based systems appear more predictable, more durable and a better protection against abuses. If markets are global, that argues that the rules governing markets should also be internationally agreed. Rule-based systems require governments to surrender some of their sovereignty, but the international penetration of their economies may have undermined their sovereignty anyway. However, the articulation of national policy preferences is still primarily a domestic function. If policy preferences change, international rules may not be able to accommodate this, so that they are no longer regarded as legitimate. In such circumstances the less demanding but more flexible technique of voluntary cooperation appears preferable. How can the choice be made?

6. How can governments satisfy democratic legitimacy for their positions and
reconcile efficiency and accountability?

Governments may be convinced of the economic benefits of opening up to international competition. But their legitimacy depends on the support of their electorates. How do they persuade their electorates, who have instinctive anxieties about being vulnerable to forces outside their control? Economic rules or agreements may derive from international institutions. But how can national governments make sure these decisions are understood and accepted by their parliaments? In short, how can economic diplomacy be democratic? The advance of globalisation and the growing number of constituencies touched by developments in the international economy has generated growing pressure for greater democratic accountability of decision-makers. But this can lead to a conflict between efficiency and accountability, when international agreement can only be secured by modifying the domestically agreed position. Does greater accountability require the legislative branch of government to be included in the redefinition of national interest? If so, how can one ensure that politicisation of the process will not lead to deadlock?

Tension Between Governments and Other Forces

The questions formulated so far concern governments only, defined to include both executive and legislature. The third major tension in economic diplomacy is between governments and other forces. The penetration of international factors into domestic economies, a major aspect of globalisation, is led not by governments but by private sector agents - traders, investors and financiers. As globalisation advances, other groups and social movements become involved in economic diplomacy. Their activities can go beyond seeking to influence national governments; they can combine so as to operate transnationally, as global civil society does.   In consequence, some scholars go so far as to argue that globalisation is removing any role for the nation-state and for national governments.[15]   This book does not endorse that view; but it argues that governments have to operate in a different context than before, as the two remaining questions show. For this tension, domestic societal theories are relevant, as well as analyses like Odell's that incorporate the role of markets.

7. How can governments best react to the growing influence of the private sector and of markets?

Much of the prosperity of the last 50 years has been stimulated by government giving more opportunities to private business and by transferring power to them: by the removal of trade barriers, deregulation and privatisation. What are the consequences of this transfer of powers for economic diplomacy?   What responsibilities should governments keep, what should private business undertake and how can government and business work together? This is linked to a second question: how do governments deal with market pressures? Decisions taken by a government, in fiscal, monetary or regulatory policies, will affect how markets view the credibility of that government. Effective market regulation is considered a prerequisite for attracting foreign investment and ensuring that the domestic economy is internationally competitive.   If markets perceive that regulation is either too lax or too strict, investment may go elsewhere.

8. How should governments best respond to pressures from NGOs for more transparency and more involvement?

Many issues in economic diplomacy, like the environment and world poverty, stimulate highly motivated and articulate private groups.   Some of these are constructive and well informed and have a lot of expertise to offer government. But others are destructive and anarchistic, gathering hostile crowds at international economic meetings. Some aspects of the growth of civil society represent efforts of interest groups to bypass national governments, because the interests concerned no longer have confidence in the formal lines of democratic accountability. This leads NGOs to argue for more transparency and to claim that their involvement makes the process more democratic. But should governments accept these views uncritically? How can they answer their negative critics, but cooperate with constructive NGOs in ways that allow each side to retain their independence?

That completes the list of questions for study. Together they provide an analytical framework that will be used in later chapters throughout this book. Table 1.1 sets the tensions and questions out in consolidated form.

Table 1.1   **Tensions and Questions in Economic Diplomacy**

Tension Between Economics and Politics

How to reconcile economic and political objectives?
How to reconcile economic and political methods?

Tension between International and Domestic Pressures

How do governments reach common positions internally?
How can internally agreed positions be deployed internationally?
Which is better - voluntary cooperation or binding rules?
How to ensure democratic legitimacy and accountability?

Tension between Governments and Other Forces

How do governments deal with private business and markets?
How should governments respond to NGOs?

The Multi-level Nature of Economic Diplomacy

Both the academic literature and our own analytical framework distinguish between the international and domestic levels of decision-making and examine the links between them. But within domestic decision-making there is a hierarchy of actors - government and non-government, national and sub-national - that interact among themselves; these are examined in Chapter 3. In international negotiation there is comparable interaction between the multiple levels available in economic diplomacy - the bilateral, the regional, the plurilateral and the multilateral. These different levels, and the interaction between them, provide a framework for analysis in the second part of this book, from Chapter 10 onwards. These chapters also look briefly at unilateralism, which might be considered the 'zero option'.

At first sight unilateralism would seem to be irrelevant to economic diplomacy, as it does not involve negotiation. Unilateral action, for example in trade liberalisation or protection, is a domestic policy decision. But unilateral liberalisation or protectionism clearly has an impact on other economies, by expanding or restricting access to the market concerned for investors or exporters from other countries. This can lead to a political response, in the form of imitation or retaliation. In some cases governments deliberately adopt unilateral measures in order to bring about changes in other countries' policies, as with the aggressive unilateralism of the trade policy adopted by the United States in the 1980s.

Bilateralism. Bilateral relations still form a major part of economic diplomacy, whether this consists of informal dealings between countries on a range of issues, or formal bilateral trade or investment treaties. Bilateral economic diplomacy is still the simplest technique, which makes it easy to explain to domestic interests.

But it gives advantages to the stronger partner and can easily become confrontational. Bilateral deals also contribute to building up more complex agreements on a regional or global level. Bilateralism can be important in determining how regional or multilateral rules should be interpreted, for example in economic disputes between the US and Japan.

Regionalism. The regional dimension in economic diplomacy is of growing importance. Regional economic agreements, although often politically motivated, also offer a more rapid way of opening markets. Liberalisation may be easier for national interests to accept when it occurs within a regional grouping of countries with broadly the same levels of development and similar policy preferences. For business interests, access to a larger regional market may be seen as a substitute for wider markets, or as a stepping stone to international competition. Regional agreements may even involve the pooling of sovereignty in order to have a greater impact in international negotiations or over the power of global markets. Whatever the motivation, regional agreements are clearly a growth industry.

Plurilateralism. The plurilateral level of economic diplomacy attracts less attention than either regionalism or multilateralism. But plurilateral bodies, like the Organisation for Economic Cooperation and Development (OECD), the G7/G8 and the Commonwealth, serve two important purposes in economic diplomacy. First, they can provide a forum where national governments seek to reconcile domestic and international economic objectives, by a process of voluntary cooperation. Second, they enable like-minded governments to develop agreed positions which they can then advance in wider multilateral contexts. The OECD has been the forum for the preparatory work in a wide range of subjects, which has, for example, provided the foundation for agreements on services and agriculture in the GATT and WTO.

Multilateralism. Finally, multilateral economic diplomacy provides for the involvement of all countries, though this makes it cumbersome. It incorporates regimes such as the WTO, the International Monetary Fund (IMF) and World Bank and the economic work of the United Nations, as well as a wide range of specialist organisations. Multilateral economic diplomacy is well suited for rule-making and there were great advances here in the 1990s, especially in the trade and environmental fields. But this has led the multilateral institutions into controversy: NGOs attack them as opaque and undemocratic; developing countries complain that the multilateral system puts them at a disadvantage; even developed countries find it hard to come to terms with the increasing encroachment of international rules into domestic policy. So while the prizes are high in successful multilateral economic diplomacy, the risks are high also.

Interaction between levels

The multi-level nature of economic diplomacy means that governments take advantage of the interaction between levels. This can be seen in various ways.

First, countries may identify different levels as suitable for specific policy issues. For example:

- Regional agreements will suit neighbouring countries seeking the benefits of integrated markets for trade and investment;
- Plurilateral understandings will suit policy issues, such as export credit policy, which cannot command the support of enough countries for multilateral rules to be agreed;
- Multilateral treaties are used, for example in global environment issues, where the involvement of all countries is necessary.

Second, different countries may use different levels for the same subject. In the trade negotiations between the European Union and Mexico, the EU negotiated at the regional level, Mexico bilaterally.

Third, the availability of different levels means that governments, as well as non-state actors, will shop between them, seeking to make progress wherever it looks most promising. For example, states and business interests seeking a more predictable environment for investment have sought all of the following:

- Bilateral investment treaties (BITs);
- The inclusion of investment in regional agreements, such as that agreed in the North American Free Trade Agreement (NAFTA);
- Plurilateral agreements, such as in the unsuccessful Multilateral Agreement on Investment (MAI), which built on earlier work in the OECD;
- Multilateral agreements, such as in the provisions of the General Agreement on Trade in Services (GATS) that cover right of establishment. Investment is also on the agenda for the new WTO round agreed at Doha in November 2001.

An analysis of economic diplomacy in a policy area such as investment will also show how norms or models developed at one level can find application in the others. For example, the OECD's work in investment formed the basis for regional agreements such as NAFTA. The regional agreements will generally take the principles developed within the OECD further, both in terms of the coverage and the binding nature of the agreements. Regional agreements have in turn provided the model for multilateral agreements. Regional agreements may also set regulatory norms or standards that have an influence beyond the region itself, for example, regional standards of food safety in North America or Europe. In short, agreements reached at one level will have implications for other levels of policy-making. Seldom do negotiations occur in a vacuum. There are normally models or precedents that can be found in other agreements.

The Structure of This Book

After this introductory chapter, the first part of the book - Chapters 2 to 9 - examines **The Nature of Economic Diplomacy**. Chapter 2 looks in detail at the relevant theoretical approaches. Chapter 3 analyses the growing ranks of actors in economic diplomacy, divided between national state actors, national non-state actors and transnational actors. Chapter 4 considers how governments approach domestic decision-making and international negotiation. Chapter 5 examines the new demands placed on economic diplomacy today, as a result of the end of the Cold War and the advance of globalisation, and the new strategies introduced in response to these demands.

These general chapters are illustrated by four case studies, two historical and two contemporary. The new economic diplomacy, with which this book is concerned, has its roots in the development of the international economic system since World War II. This development is illustrated by the historical case studies in Chapters 6 and 7. Chapter 6 examines how decisions were made and agreements negotiated at the creation of the multilateral trade regime in the 1940s, compared with the conclusion of the Uruguay Round in the 1990s. Chapter 7 analyses the evolution of the G7 economic summits of the 1970s, which proved to be precursors of the new economic diplomacy. These themes are picked up in the two practitioner chapters that follow. Their authors represent the state and non-state actors in economic diplomacy. Colin Budd of the British Foreign and Commonwealth Office, representing government, provides a contemporary assessment of the G7/G8 process in Chapter 8. Phil Evans, of the Consumers Association, analyses in Chapter 9 multilateral trade politics as seen by a representative NGO.

The second half of the book - Chapters 10-17 - examines **Multi-level Economic Diplomacy**, depending on whether it is pursued bilaterally; through regional groupings, especially the European Union (EU); or through plurilateral or multilateral institutions. Chapter 10 looks at the pros and cons of bilateral economic diplomacy, arguing that bilateralism is particularly attractive to the United States (though much less to its neighbour Canada). This is illustrated by the case study in Chapter 11, by Matthew Goodman from Goldman Sachs, on the complex economic relationship between the United States and Japan. Chapter 12 examines regionally based economic diplomacy, with special reference to the European Union. Patrick Rabe of the European Commission complements this with Chapter 13, analysing how the EU constructs and deploys its international environment policy.

The use of international institutions, both plurilateral (like the OECD) and multilateral (like the World Bank), is the subject of Chapter 14. This is supported by three case studies: Ivan Mbirimi of the Commonwealth Secretariat writes in Chapter 15 on developing countries in economic diplomacy; Nigel Wicks, late of the British Treasury, reflects in Chapter 16 on international financial institutions; and Richard Carden, from the Department of Trade and Industry, examines the world trading system in Chapter 17. While these chapters analyse international institutions such as the IMF and the WTO, they focus not so much on the institutions themselves, as on the use which states make of them in pursuing their national objectives.

Conclusion

Economic diplomacy is an elusive subject. New questions are always coming to the surface and the context can change abruptly. The year 1999 began with the world financial system still in turmoil, after the Asian, Russian and Brazilian crises, but the trading system looking robust. Twelve months later, the financial system had calmed down, while the trading system was reeling from the disastrous WTO meeting at Seattle. The terrorist attacks of 11 September 2001 have raised fresh questions about the likely direction of economic diplomacy. Despite this volatility, however, some trends have emerged which help to illuminate the questions chosen for study. Thus the final chapter of this book, Chapter 18, draws some conclusions about where economic diplomacy is going, in the first decade of the 2000s.

Notes

1   Marshall 1999, pp. 7-8, distinguishes six different meanings of diplomacy.
2   Bull 1977/1995, p. 156. He notes two other narrower uses of the term.
3   Barston 1997, p. 1. This is the first sentence of his book.
4   Quoted from Jackson 1998, p. 60.
5   From a speech to an Anglo-German (Koenigswinter) conference in spring 1990 - Nicholas Bayne's notes. Her reservations about diplomats are also strongly expressed in Thatcher 1993.
6   See Ruggie 1982.
7   Van Bergeik 1994 uses 'economic diplomacy' in this narrow sense. 'Economic statecraft', however, is the more usual expression, as in Baldwin 1985 and Hanson 1988.
8   Quoted from Odell 2000, p. 11, slightly edited.
9   Odell 2000 uses this classification which he attributes to Stanley Hoffman.
10 Susan Strange developed a concept of structural power to help in making assessments of power in various fields, such as security, production, finance and knowledge. See Strange 1996, especially pp. 25-30.
11 The classic exposition of the model is in Putnam 1988. He developed it from his observation of the Bonn G7 summit of 1978, when he was serving in the White House - see Putnam and Henning 1989.
12 For a vivid practitioner's account of the Marshall Plan, see Marjolin 1989.
13 This has been a recurrent objective of the G8 summits of recent years. For example, the Kananaskis summit of June 2002 adopted an Africa Action Plan to underpin the New Partnership for Africa's Development (NEPAD), in a way that has parallels with the Marshall Plan. But this project is still at its early stages - see Chapter 18 below.
14 Reciprocity is one of the basic principles on which the GATT was founded - see Chapter 6 below.
15 Held and others 1999 divides attitudes to globalisations between 'hyper-globalisers', 'sceptics' and 'transformationalists'. Examples of hyper-globalisers, who believe that

globalisation undermines the state, are Ohmae 1992 and Strange 1996. For sceptics, see Chapter 5 below. The authors belong to the transformationalist school.

References

Baldwin, D. A. (1985), *Economic Statecraft*, Princeton University Press, Princeton.

Barston, R. P. (1997), *Modern Diplomacy*, 2nd edition, Longmans, London and New York.

Bull, H. (1977/1995), *The Anarchical Society: A Study of Order in World Politics*, 1st edition 1977, 2nd edition 1995, Macmillan, London and Basingstoke.

Hanson, P. (1988), *Western Economic Statecraft in East-West Relations: Embargoes, Sanctions, Linkage, Economic Warfare and Détente*, Royal Institute of International Affairs, London.

Held, D., McGrew, A., Goldblatt, D. and Perraton, J. (1999), *Global Transformations: Politics, Economics and Culture*, Polity Press, Cambridge.

Jackson, J. H. (1998), *The World Trade Organization: Constitution and Jurisprudence*, Royal Institute of International Affairs, London.

Marjolin, R. (1989), *Architect of European Unity: Memoirs 1911-1986*, Weidenfield and Nicholson, London, translated by William Hall from *Le Travail d'une Vie*, Robert Laffont, Paris 1986.

Marshall, P. (1999), *Positive Diplomacy*, Palgrave, Basingstoke.

Odell, J. (2000), *Negotiating the World Economy*, Cornell University Press, Ithaca and London.

Ohmae, K. (1992), *The Borderless World: Power and Strategy in the Interlinked Economy*, Routledge, London.

Ohmae, K. (1995), *The End of the Nation State*, HarperCollins, London.

Putnam, R. D. (1988), 'Diplomacy and Domestic Politics: the Logic of Two-Level Games', *International Organization*, vol. 42, no. 4, pp. 427-460.

Putnam, R. D. and Henning, C. R. (1989), 'The Bonn Summit of 1978: A Case Study in Coordination', in Cooper, R. N. and others (eds.), *Can Nations Agree? Issues in International Economic Cooperation*, the Brookings Institution, Washington.

Ruggie, J. G. (1982), International Regimes, Transactions and Change; Embedded Liberalism in the Postwar Economic Order, *International Organization*, vol. 36, pp. 379-415.

Strange, S. (1996), *The Retreat of the State: the Diffusion of Power in the World Economy*, Cambridge University Press, Cambridge.

Thatcher, M. (1993), *The Downing Street Years*, HarperCollins, London.

Van Bergeik, P. (1994), *Economic Diplomacy, Trade and Commercial Policy; Positive and Negative Sanctions in a New World Order*, Edward Elgar, Aldershot and Brookfield, Virginia.

PART I

THE NATURE OF ECONOMIC DIPLOMACY

Chapter 2

Theoretical Analysis of Economic Diplomacy

Stephen Woolcock

The purpose of this volume is to bring together academic and practitioner views of the decision-making processes in economic diplomacy. We seek to provide the reader with a better understanding of how decisions are taken in the field of economic diplomacy and introduce him or her to some of the central problems and issues that characterise decision-making in economic diplomacy at the beginning of the 21st century. This cannot be done in a vacuum or simply as a series of case studies without any theoretical analysis. There is a large volume of literature in international relations, international political economy and other fields, such as negotiation theory, which provides valuable analytical and theoretical guidance to any study of economic diplomacy. Unfortunately for the reader there is no one theory of economic diplomacy. Nor is there likely to be one. Some theoretical or analytical approaches will be more useful than others. Readers will also have their own preferences and prejudices in terms of what they think drives economic diplomacy.

In the first section of this chapter we provide an overview of some of the existing literature which students of economic diplomacy may wish to explore more deeply. The central section considers a number of approaches which focus on the process of decision-making and are therefore of special interest and value. The concluding section creates a simple matrix to classify the factors that can be used to explain decision-making and negotiation in economic diplomacy.

The Mainstream IR and IPE Literature

Much of the literature on international relations (IR) is relevant to our interest in the decision-making process, even if much of this literature tends to emphasise structures of interest or power rather than processes. International political economy (IPE), which has grown since the 1970s and now constitutes a considerable volume of literature and theoretical material, is of particular interest to students of economic diplomacy. Most of the substance of economic diplomacy is covered by IPE. The core of IPE is the interaction between political and economic factors and between national and international levels of policy.[1] As Chapter 1 suggests this is also at the centre of any discussion of decision-making in

economic diplomacy. Much of the IPE literature therefore provides useful insights
into the interaction between these different levels of analysis.

Fortunately there are analyses of existing IR and IPE literature that have
discussed its relevance to economic diplomacy, or foreign economic policy-
making. Much of this is of American origin. For example, Ikenberry has
considered the systemic, society centred and state centred approaches to explaining
foreign economic policy-making.[2] Putnam and Odell also draw on many elements
of IR and IPE theory in developing their analytical frameworks.[3] The factors that
shape economic diplomacy in the first part of the following analysis draw heavily
on Ikenberry, but are followed by some additions from other aspects of IPE
literature.

Systemic Theories

Systemic approaches look at how government officials (such as economic
diplomats) respond to opportunities or constraints posed by the position of the
country in the international system at any moment in time.[4] Systemic approaches
tend to abstract from domestic factors in shaping policy.

Realism

For example, the realist school of thought will tend to argue that national policy is
determined by relative power relationships. Diplomacy is therefore about
maximising the power of one's own nation state in relation to others. Realists do
not discount economic issues or domestic factors, but tend to see them as
constraints on the pursuit of known national interest or preference. Crudely
speaking realists would expect the relative power of nation states to shape the
outcomes of negotiations. A realist approach would therefore expect negotiators to
be concerned about relative gains, or whether one party gains more than the other.
In many instances in economic negotiations there will be a question of the
distribution of the economic gains from an agreement. In so far as the distribution
of economic gains shapes relative (political) power, realism will be relevant to
economic diplomacy. In many if not most cases of international economic
negotiations all the parties to an agreement can benefit. For example, in a round of
trade negotiations each party makes concessions in order to achieve more open
markets that benefit all countries. But we must still be conscious of the
distribution of such benefits. Odell distinguishes between different negotiating
objectives in economic diplomacy, value creation in which both or all parties to an
agreement benefit and value claiming, in which one party sets out to achieve the
greatest possible gain for itself. When a national government pursues
predominantly value claiming strategies, it is behaving as realists would expect.[5]

Realist approaches are helpful in that they remind us that negotiations will be
shaped by relative power. For example, negotiations between large powerful
economies such as the United States, European Union, Japan and to a lesser extent
Canada (often called the 'Quad') and poor developing countries will be shaped by
the power of the richer countries. The leverage of controlling access to large

markets or to financial resources can stack the cards in favour of the powerful. But there are a number of weaknesses in the realist approach, which limits its usefulness. Realist approaches tend to neglect domestic factors, whereas our premise is that economic diplomacy is very much about reconciling domestic preferences and international obligations.[6] There is a preponderance of opinion favouring approaches to foreign economic policy which account for domestic as well as systemic or international factors.[7]

Power is clearly a factor that cannot be neglected, but it is a notoriously difficult property to define and measure. Sometimes it may not be possible to determine relative power until one knows the outcome of a negotiation. For example, there is a tendency to argue that country 'x' gained more from any given negotiation because it was able to bring its power to bear and shape outcomes. In other words there is a danger of tautology, or using power to explain outcomes when one can only define relative power once one knows the outcome. Strange helps in this respect by identifying four major components to power - security, production, finance and knowledge.[8] This approach may help in defining power more accurately. In the example of the EU and US, the US may have an advantage in relative power thanks to its strength in the military/security component of power, even if in economic terms the EU is its equal.

Even if we could determine relative power in any given instance, this still leaves us with a problem of explaining how it is that negotiations between the same countries can result in different outcomes even though the relative power relationship remains the same. Odell argues, for example, that the outcomes of negotiations between the US and Japan over exchange rate policy in the 1970s and 1980s differed, not because of differences in relative power, but because of the different negotiating strategies adopted by the parties.

Hegemonic stability

Hegemonic stability theory (HST) seeks to apply realist views on the influence of power to develop a theory of international relations and international political economy. By theory here we mean, of course, something that can be used to predict outcomes or answer questions.[9] HST argues that a hegemon - a leading power able to shape outcomes - is needed if international economic cooperation is to succeed. Without the coercive power of a hegemon it would not be possible to ensure effective compliance with any regime established. Hegemonic stability theory has in particular been applied to help explain how the international economic order was established after World War II under American hegemony. This was in contrast to the chaos of the inter-war period, when Britain was no longer able to fulfil the role of a hegemon and the United States was not willing to provide such a role.

In so far as economic negotiations and the establishment of regimes will be shaped by strong economic powers providing leadership, then hegemonic stability theory may well provide insights in our study of economic diplomacy. But in the current period it is debatable as to whether any single country fulfils the role of the hegemon. The United States remains the sole military super power, but even during the period of stable economic growth during the 1990s, one can still challenge the view that the US was an economic hegemon.

If one sets aside the debate about the role of a single hegemon maintaining 'the' international system, it is possible to see how major economic powers fulfil functions similar to hegemons within regional settings. Thus the United States has arguably shaped the regional economies in the western hemisphere in its image and the European Union has done the same within Europe. At this regional level the major economic powers clearly fulfil many of the functions that have been ascribed to hegemons, such as access to markets, liquidity and stable currencies, for the region at least.

HST also has short-comings in the sense that it cannot explain why international economic cooperation continued even after the demise of the US hegemony. Elaborations or qualifications of the theory have addressed this and other criticisms of the theory and argued, for example, that hegemons are needed to establish regimes but that the regimes, once established, can continue to function after the hegemon has lost its potency. Once the regime exists it reduces transactions costs, for example, by providing a common set of norms or standards that are accepted by all parties and do not have to be re-negotiated on every occasion.[10]

Other systemic theories

There are also other systemic theories, such as world systems theory and dependency theory, which seek to explain economic events and decision-making with reference to the relative power in the international economy. In essence such theories argue that those states shaping the capitalist world economy can dictate the rules of the game to the others. When we look at economic diplomacy we cannot neglect the imbalance between the powerful (northern or industrialised) countries and developing countries. Dependency theory also argues that an elite in developing countries may favour agreement with the more powerful developed economies, which might help to explain why developing countries sign up to agreements which benefit their northern economic partners more than developing economies. Although dependency theory has declined in popularity since the early 1970s, when it helped provide the intellectual foundations for developing country demands for a New International Economic Order (NIEO), one cannot deny the fact that some countries, such as those that belong to the G7, do form the core of the international economic system. Countries, such as much of sub-Saharan Africa, could probably be defined as peripheral and not benefiting from the growth in world trade and investment.

But dependency theory in particular was developed to help explain under-development. This is not our main interest in this book. Exponents of the theory also tended to place too much emphasis on systemic or international factors that might condemn certain countries to under-development and underplayed or neglected the importance of domestic political and economic factors in the countries concerned. In Chapter 16 Ivan Mbirimi discusses the economic diplomacy of developing countries and tends to confirm the view that many developing countries, especially the least developed, lack either the power or resources to have much influence. This impotence may account for the apparent absence of any clearly articulated policy aims. If the country has no influence it may not be worthwhile developing sophisticated policy aims.

International institutions or regimes

Systemic factors need not be realist in nature but may also take the form of international institutions or regimes that reflect cooperation between states or anchor such cooperation in international regimes. International regimes are consensually defined as 'sets of implicit or explicit principles, norms, rules, and decision-making procedures around which actors' expectations converge in a given area of international relations'.[11] Regime theory argues, for example, that states cooperate when there is cross border economic activity extending beyond territorial states that requires rules or norms of behaviour. For this reason the first regimes were identified in policy areas such as transport and international telecommunications. Regime theory assumes that a range of different factors and interests shape policy in any given policy area, not just unitary states. Regimes encompass both formal cooperation, such as in institutional structures, but also less formal forms of cooperation based on shared interests and experiences.

In economic diplomacy today international institutions play an important and arguably more important role, than in the past. Over the past fifty years the Bretton Woods institutions have evolved and been subject to new pressures, but they have remained. In the case of the trading system the World Trade Organization has assumed the form of a more rules-based organisation, in which national governments have accepted constraints on their freedom to act. In the liberal paradigm of world order relations between states are not simply shaped by the relative power of states but by a complex interdependence which calls for cooperation between states, especially in the field of economic relations.[12] Neoliberal institutionalism, for example, explains cooperation between states in international institutions by showing how these can reduce transaction costs for those negotiating in international economic issue areas. For example, there may be much debate in the WTO over how to apply principles of non-discrimination to new policy areas such as services or investment, but there is no need to establish the desirability of non-discrimination.[13] International institutions can take the form of multilateral institutions, such as the IMF, WTO or World Bank, covering a wide range of issues. They can be more specialised, such as the United Nations Environment Programme (UNEP), with its set of multilateral environment agreements, or other specialist organisations such as in standards. In addition to the multilateral institutions there are plurilateral organisations (such as the OECD, G7 or Commonwealth) and regional regimes, such as the EU or other less integrated regional organisations. Equally, international regimes may take the form of private or semi-public independent bodies.

Society Centred Approaches

If one of the central features of economic diplomacy is reconciling domestic and international interests, we must clearly consider the importance of domestic factors in shaping decision-making.   Again we can find a volume of literature in international relations and international political economy covering the role of domestic interests.   For simplicity's sake one can distinguish between societal and state centred theories.

According to society centred approaches national interest groups compete to shape national policy on trade, money and other topics.   Government officials tend to be seen as agents for these interest groups or principal interests.   For example, trade policy is shaped by the balance between free trade and protectionist forces.[14] Another example would be the debate within the UK over membership of the Euro, in which there is competition between the interests of small and medium sized enterprises (SMEs) and larger international companies.   The majority of SMEs favour staying out because they have limited international business and wish to retain national policy autonomy.   This is because they believe that the national government or central bank has the autonomy to respond to the immediate needs of the national or local economy.   Companies operating on international markets have, to date, been more likely to favour joining the Euro, because it ensures a more predictable environment, ie fixed exchange rates and stable macroeconomic policies, which facilitates long term investment planning across economies.

Societal models can clearly include all types of interest groups, so that they can accommodate the growing role of NGOs and explain how these balance or do not balance the interests of international business.   Such models have the great advantage of illustrating the importance of competing interests in any policy decision.   Chapter 3 discusses the general categories of interest groups and actors, but interests will be policy dependent.   In other words it is important to identify the relevant interests for each policy issue.   But societal models tend to assume that the government is the agent, ie follows the balance of pressures from interest groups in order to maximise some utility, which is usually taken to be re-election.   What is more, societal models tend to see the government as a unitary actor.   As many authors have pointed out, government is often divided, both between the executive and legislature as well as between the various ministries within the executive, or indeed between different committees in a legislature.   As we shall see in the following chapters, economic diplomacy is shaped by divisions within executives, such as between ministries representing different interests.   For example, environment ministries will not share the same views on international environmental regulation as ministries of the economy or trade.

Governments clearly also have views of their own.   Many aspects of economic diplomacy are technical in nature, so that experts in the responsible ministries can have a significant bearing on outcomes when there are few people who understand the ramifications of any decision.   In a world in which civil society NGOs are becoming more and more active and have the benefit of considerable resources, even such technical aspects of economic diplomacy may now be becoming more transparent.   But the point here is that governments are seldom pure agents.   They also have their own agendas and will seek to influence the content of negotiations accordingly.

State Centred Approaches

State centred approaches to explaining economic diplomacy can therefore help us to understand how the apparatus of the state can shape outcomes. The focus of state centred approaches is on the institutional structures of decision-making in foreign economic policy or economic diplomacy. For example, the degree of autonomy or discretion granted to the executive branch (ie economic diplomats) will be important. At the time the US was building international economic systems in the 1940s and 1950s the State Department had extensive autonomy, but, as Chapter 6 suggests, this has changed considerably since. Congress has reclaimed much of its power over commercial policy and what remains with the Administration is shared between the US Trade Representative (USTR), and the Departments of Commerce, Treasury, Agriculture, etc. Chapters 12 and 13 show how within Europe there is the question of how much autonomy from national governments the EU negotiators have in any negotiation. If negotiators have more discretion, or negotiating slack as many American writers call it, this will influence their approach to bargaining. If negotiators have little discretion or slack, it clearly makes the range of potential outcomes narrower. This issue of the scope for negotiators to exercise discretion is one of the central issues addressed in the main models of negotiations discussed below. The scope for discretion is intrinsically linked to the degree of democratic accountability and perceptions of democratic control over decision-making.

Strong and weak states

The degree of centralisation of decision-making may also be a factor. For example, Katzenstein described strong and weak states depending, in part, on the degree of centralisation. Thus the United States was seen to be a relatively weak state in trade policy, because authority was fragmented between government departments, Congress (a series of committees in both houses) and other regulatory bodies (like the International Trade Commission (ITC) or Food and Drug Administration (FDA)). In the current trade agenda, one must add state governments to this list and thus further fragment US trade policy. State governments decide on investment, government purchasing and regulatory policy issues, such as the regulation of the insurance sector, which are all the subject of economic diplomacy. In other words the United States may be a weak negotiator even though it has considerable economic power.

Consider also the position of the European Union. The EU's economic power has grown considerably over the past 30 years, but decision-making in European economic diplomacy is 'fragmented' in that it requires a consensus or qualified majority of 15 - soon to become 20 or more - Member States.[15] There is also fragmentation within 'Brussels' between the European Commission, Council of Ministers and European Parliament, not to mention the European Central Bank.

Within each of these institutions there are also differing 'sponsoring departments' such as trade, environment, social affairs and external relations, which will also have different views. Does this inevitably mean that the EU is a 'weak' actor in economic diplomacy?

In the 1970s Japan was seen to be a relatively strong state, because decision-making was and remains relatively centralised. During the 1980s Japan also became an economic power, even if recent economic performance has not matched that of the United States. Does this mean that Japan is a relatively strong negotiator compared to the US and EU?

One question which any study of economic diplomacy must address is whether all states are becoming 'weak' in the sense that the degree of centralisation or control over policy-making by a relatively small core of central government is being undermined by globalisation, as the more intrusive nature of economic diplomacy at the beginning of the 21st century leads to fragmentation of decision-making.

In other words, the state centred approach helps us to identify these differing interests within the government and within the various branches of government. It may also provide some hypotheses concerning what we might expect with, for example, differing degrees of centralisation. The degree of centralisation in policy-making will vary between issues. As Krasner pointed out a long time ago, monetary and exchange rate policy is more insulated from political and populist pressures than trade policy.[16] Environmental issues have become populist issues. Today hundreds of thousands of British pensioners subscribe to the Royal Society for the Protection of Birds (RSPB), which also happens to be a major lobby in international environmental negotiations, because of its concern for habitats. Friends of the Earth and Greenpeace are major transnational actors, with many members internationally.

Established domestic regulatory practices or cultures

The IPE literature cited may not fully account for what might be called established domestic regulatory cultures or practices. Economic diplomacy is increasingly concerned with regulatory issues, whether in the shape of regulatory norms for capital markets, environmental regulation or food safety. In such policy areas domestic political debate and the impact of domestic interests have generated a specific set of legislative measures and regulatory practice. These regulatory measures have then shaped the patterns of interest. Over time the accumulation of legislation and practice can come to be seen as a distinct regulatory culture. Society based approaches which identify the interests in any issue might cover this point, but it may be helpful to distinguish between the shorter and longer term issues and be careful of cultural differences as explanations for disputes. The important point here is that regulatory cultures are more enduring than shorter term interests. The national approach can sometimes come to be seen as immutable or part of the national 'culture'. In such circumstances the national interest is already set, in the shape of the existing regulatory approach or structure, and economic diplomacy becomes a process of either trying to sell this approach to the rest of the world, or finding ways of accommodating the divergent approaches to regulation whilst maintaining open markets. In seeking to convince the rest of the world of the merits of the 'domestic approach' economic diplomacy may employ a multi-level strategy. For example, the national approach may be first employed in regional or bilateral agreements and then in plurilateral agreements in the hope that these will provide models for wider multilateral agreements. As shown in Chapter 1 this is the strategy that has been used in investment policy.

Ideology and Ideas

The extensive literature on economic cooperation has also included the role of ideas or ideology in shaping national policies. Ideology has been added to the literature because the structures of interests and institutions have not been able to explain all policies. For example, Goldstein argues that the continued support for liberal trade in the US is based on underlying ideological norms.[17] It is ideological support for an open international economic order that has helped keep US policies relatively liberal, in the face of what would otherwise have been a protectionist coalition of interests.

Ideology can also shape economic diplomacy in the sense that a shift in the underlying paradigm that helps shape our view of the world economy will also influence negotiations. For example, the view of the world in the late 1940s was of a system in which nation states retained a high degree of autonomy over national economic policies, but which cooperated in international institutions to ensure certain principles prevailed, such as non-discrimination. There was also a belief in most countries of the need for state intervention to promote economic development. Consequently many governments pursued import substitution policies and intervened actively in seeking to manage macroeconomic cycles. During the 1970s and 1980s such Keynesian orthodoxies and interventionist industrial/development and trade policies gave way to liberal ideas. The end of the Cold War also brought an end to the extended period during which capitalism and state planning competed as alternative models. This general shift towards a liberal paradigm during the 1980s and 1990s has also been, in part, the result of the influence of a prevailing set of ideas or ideology, as well as the perceived failure of an ideology based on a more interventionist state. This liberal orthodoxy has subsequently been challenged by the backlash against globalisation.

Individuals

The role of individuals and their preferences and prejudices has been included in the study of foreign policy, though it does not feature to the same degree in international political economy (IPE). In the past individuals probably played a more important role in economic diplomacy, because the number of people involved was smaller and the issues less complex, so that an individual might be expected to have some sway over negotiations. Cordell Hull, the US Secretary of State in the 1940s with a firm conviction in the need for a liberal trading system certainly had influence. Negotiations on the Bretton Woods institutions - the IMF, IBRD, GATT and ITO - were also shaped by a relatively small group of individuals, and some of these, such as Keynes, played a shaping role.

In economic diplomacy in the 21st century one must expect individuals to play a smaller role because of the greater number of actors involved and the greater complexity of the subjects. However, individuals may play a role in certain instances, especially when the person concerned has considerable power. For example, differences between different departments of government will have to be resolved by 'pushing them up to the highest level', ie to the head of government. While most civil servants will seek to avoid this, there may be occasions when it is the only way to resolve divisions within an executive.

A powerful political figure with considerable political capital may also help to resolve divisions between the branches of government. For example, a popular US president may use political capital to push legislation through Congress that might otherwise remain blocked. One example of this might be President Clinton's success in gaining ratification of the NAFTA and GATT Uruguay Round negotiations. Heads of state and government also meet in the G7/G8 forum, which is further examined in later chapters of this book. Although G7/G8 coordination has to a greater or lesser extent been integrated into the mainstream bureaucracies of the countries concerned, there may still be occasions when the views or persuasive powers of heads of government play a role in negotiations with their peers.

It is not only powerful individuals that have an influence. In complex economic negotiations, in which different policy objectives are balanced and agreements take the form of complex texts, other individuals may play a role. If economic diplomacy is technocratic in nature, detailed knowledge of technical material can shape outcomes. Such knowledge normally resides a fair way down the bureaucratic hierarchy, so that technical experts at lower levels can have a real impact on outcomes. Therefore their motivations may well be a factor in shaping outcomes.

Multi-level Analysis and Models of Negotiating Processes

So far we have shown that a range of approaches exist that may be helpful in illuminating how decisions are taken and negotiations conducted in economic diplomacy. These approaches can be said to be located in different levels of analysis. The realist and international institutional approaches are concerned with international factors, as are the other systemic explanations such as dependency theory. Societal and state centred approaches are mainly concerned with domestic factors. Yet others, which have not been discussed here, look at transnational issues, such as the role of multi-national enterprises (MNEs) or transnational civil society. Chapter 3 discusses the role of such transnational actors.

As well as identifying the various levels, the existing literature includes efforts to integrate these different levels of analysis so as to understand IPE.[18] A number of theories, or rather analytical frameworks, have been developed to help understand the process of interaction between levels.

Two-level and Multi-level Games

One model that may be particularly helpful is the Putnam Two-Level Game Metaphor, because this seeks to organise the interaction between domestic and international factors in the process of negotiations.[19] Its central concern is with explaining the negotiating processes, rather than accounting for national preferences, like some of the other models, such as Milner's, although she seeks to develop a general theory for the impact of domestic factors on foreign economic and trade policy.[20]

Putnam developed his metaphor of two-level games after observing the G7 process, as well as the process of trade negotiations in the US. Domestic 'level II' games involve negotiators seeking to maximise their support among national interest groups or institutions. International 'level I' games involve negotiators seeking to maximise their ability to satisfy domestic interests, while minimising the adverse international consequences (ie maintaining good political relations with one's negotiating partners).

Putnam assumes a single chief negotiator, who sits at both tables. (This may be a limiting factor, given the fragmented nature of the executive branches of government today.) By strategic interplay between the two games he or she can change either the domestic or the international balance of preferences and reach an agreement acceptable to both sides. In other words the structural factors are not simply taken as a given. Putnam envisages that these can be modified through negotiation. Putnam breaks down the process into two phases, negotiation and ratification. In essence negotiation is the level I game and ratification is the level II game. But, as he points out, the two are intrinsically linked in practice. Ratification does not just mean a vote in the legislature but acceptance by the legitimate power - for example, Congress in the US, Member States in the EU, with the European Parliament (EP) and national parliaments, or the party apparatus in China.

Determining the size of the win-sets

Putnam's metaphor visualises negotiations between two parties, each with its domestic 'win-set'. (A win-set is defined as all the possible outcomes at level I that could secure ratification at level II.) If these win-sets overlap then agreement is possible, if not there will be no agreement. The larger the win-set, the greater the scope for agreement. But Putnam suggests that a small win-set may give a negotiator a stronger negotiating position on level I. The negotiator may say: 'Unless you give me what I want on intellectual property, Congress will not ratify this agreement,' or 'Unless you back off on agricultural liberalisation, the Council of Ministers will not accept the outcome of the Uruguay Round'.

The Putnam model is very helpful in studying economic diplomacy, because it provides the vital dynamic link between domestic and international levels, but it is not always easy to apply. For example, how can one define the size or range of a given win-set? Putnam recognizes this problem and makes a number of suggestions concerning the factors shaping the size of win-sets. In so doing he draws heavily on and incorporates much of what the existing literature has included in its list of factors shaping outcomes.

Domestic interests and preferences are clearly a key element in defining the win-set. For example, Putnam suggests that the balance between interests will shape the size of the win-set. Clear divisions between, for example, hawks and doves or free traders and protectionists, will enable the negotiator to identify the scope of the win-set. A more heterogeneous structure of domestic interests will provide the negotiator with more scope to find allies and to play level I against level II, but also make it harder to identify his or her win-set. It will, for example, be possible to balance opposition to an agreement from one sectoral interest with measures that favour another sector.

Echoing Krasner's view that monetary policy-making is more insulated from political pressures, Putnam also argues that level II games tend to be more complex in trade than in monetary issues, because there are more active players in trade and the issues are more populist. Putnam also incorporates the concept of linkage, which has figured in many analyses of policy-making since Rosenau.[21] In two or multi-issue games there will be linkage between the issues. Linkage means for example, that a chief negotiator can overcome opposition to a particular policy on level I by offering compensatory benefits in another issue area. For example, if there is broad opposition to further trade liberalisation among the established trade lobbies, a negotiator might add services to the agenda in order to get support from the service industry, because a new round will open export markets. This will help tip the domestic balance of interest in favour of new liberalisation. This is in effect what the US Administration did during the Uruguay Round negotiations on trade in the 1980s, and may be one of the reasons for the EU seeking a comprehensive agenda in the WTO negotiations at the beginning of the 2000s. Perhaps an opposite case is where NGOs linked environmental, food safety and labour standards issues, in order to get a critical mass sufficient to tip the balance against a new round of trade negotiations in the late 1990s.

Putnam also incorporates important elements of the state centred approaches by suggesting that the scope of win-sets will be shaped by the structure and power distribution in domestic institutions. For example, a two-thirds majority is required in the US Senate to ratify a treaty, such as the International Trade Organisation (ITO), but other agreements require only a simple majority. This is one reason why the US was able to support the General Agreement on Tariffs and Trade (GATT) which was not an international treaty establishing an international organisation, but not the ITO, which was. As Chapter 6 shows, the result of this institutional feature of the US was that the international trading system operated under the much looser GATT, while the monetary system was anchored in a fully-fledged international institution in the shape of the IMF. One can equally look at the institutional structure and voting patterns in Europe to help define the size of the EU win-set. For example, the European Parliament must gives its assent by simple majority to any agreement which touches on an issue agreed 'domestically' within the EU by co-decision-making. In other words, in this procedure the Council of Ministers (national governments) and European Parliament (EP) share power, with the EP having a de facto power of veto; see Chapter 12. On some trade issues, however, the EP has no power at all and the decision turns on a qualified majority vote in the EU Council of Ministers. However, in practical terms the EU Member States tend to seek a consensus, which means a narrower win-set and less negotiating leeway for the European Commission, where it is the EU negotiator.

The size of the EU win-set will also be influenced by the need to ensure that sub-national as well as national governments and players are involved. The Länder in Germany, the regions in Belgium or other sub-national levels of government have become important actors in decision-making. The role of such bodies is also of growing importance in the debate about the democratic legitimacy of the EU. This growing importance of sub-national levels of government has led to the introduction of the concept of multi-level governance, to describe the situation when the nation state is no longer able to monopolise policy.[22] The concept of multi-level governance might clearly be applied to the process of economic diplomacy. Indeed, this volume addresses the bilateral, regional, plurilateral and multilateral levels. But in the analysis in this volume governments are using these different levels to further their national policy objectives. Although sub-national government clearly plays a role in economic diplomacy, such as in seeking to attract foreign direct investment, the assumption here is that national governments remain at the centre of policy-making.

Putnam argues that in general the greater the autonomy of the negotiator the larger the win-set. As noted above, this is relevant to a central issue in economic diplomacy - the tension between efficiency and accountability. This contrasts *efficiency* in concluding negotiations with the *democratic accountability* of the decision-making process. It is a reasonable hypothesis that greater accountability results in less autonomy for negotiators. Putnam suggests that, as decision-making becomes more accountable, this reduces the size of the win-set and thus the prospect of concluding agreements that will find domestic support. However, once agreement has been reached at level I it is less likely to be vetoed at the domestic level II.

Exploiting and overcoming domestic resistance

If a smaller win-set means less flexibility, it may also mean a stronger negotiating position. Therefore Putnam suggests that negotiators may use strategies aimed at reducing the size of the domestic win-set. For instance, they may encourage debate or votes on issues which would harden domestic positions. One example might be to encourage legislation that would significantly limit the discretionary powers of the executive branch to act. The Gephardt Amendment in the US Congress, while not promoted by the Administration at the time, no doubt had the effect of narrowing the win-set on trade policy and thus strengthening the position of the American negotiators in their trade negotiations with Japan and other trading partners. The USTR can bring the threat of potential legislative action to the attention of its negotiating partners and say: "If you do not reach an accommodation, this is what you can expect". Clearly this has the significant negative side effect that it may make it harder for the negotiator to get the outcome negotiated on level I ratified back home.

Negotiators may offer side payments to domestic interests in order to shape the size of the win-set. Such side payments may or may not be part of the same policy area. For example, the NAFTA agreement negotiated by the Bush Administration in 1992 had not been ratified by Congress. The incoming Clinton Administration reopened the NAFTA negotiations and added two so-called 'side agreements' on environment and labour. These were side payments to the environmental and labour interests in the country and Congress were concerned about NAFTA lowering environmental and labour standards in the United States. Side payments can also literally take the form of payments. The European Union made payments to Portugal under the European structural funds in order to gain Portugal's support for liberalisation of textiles and clothing trade at the time of the mid-term review of the Uruguay Round in November 1988. More generally, interests or regions negatively affected by international agreements can be given adjustment assistance.

In addition to softening domestic resistance to an agreement, negotiators may also target particular constituencies in the other countries, by offering positive inducements in the form of, for example, tariff reductions or threatening sanctions. In such instances the negotiator is trying to increase the size or nature of the other party's win-set. The use of the so-called carousel retaliation by the United States against cases of countries not complying with trade rules is an example of such a strategy. For example, in the beef hormone case the United States took retaliatory action and imposed trade restrictions against exports into the US of cashmere woollens from the Scottish borders, because this could influence swing votes. In this case it was a question of influencing the Scottish trade minister, with a constituency in the area, to get the UK to vote in the European Council of Ministers against the continuation of the ban on the sale of hormone-enriched beef in the EU, which kept out US exports of such beef.

Negotiators may also seek to engage in the domestic debate in other countries. This might be done by commissioning reports from research organisations or consultancies, to show that the position adopted by the country concerned is less than optimal or damaging to certain interest groups. Negotiators can also monitor as closely as possible how the debate is developing in the level II negotiations of the other party. This will enable the negotiator to have a better idea of the domestic pressures acting upon his or her negotiating partner. Gathering this kind of information is an important part of the job of the economic diplomats attached to embassies in other countries.

Putnam (like others modelling negotiators) accepts that negotiators are working in conditions of *bounded rationality*, in other words they do not know everything. Negotiators may be misinformed about the level II games in other countries, which means that they cannot assess accurately whether the positions they are putting forward are within or outside the win-set of their negotiating partner.

Putnam also addresses the issue of the shape of the win-sets. Are they linear, or do they have other shapes? He makes the point that negotiators must often try to convince their opposite numbers in other countries that their win-set is 'kinky', ie not a smooth curve or linear. In other words the position they are putting forward will be ratified but a position slightly more favourable to their negotiating partner will not.

In sum, the Putnam metaphor provides a useful means of linking domestic and international level factors and focusing discussion on the negotiating process, which is what we are interested in doing. Many of the variables shaping outcomes that are discussed in the IR and IPE literature also find a place in his metaphor. (It is not claimed to be a theory hence the use of the term metaphor.) One limitation of the Putnam metaphor is that it is not a predictive theory. This accounts for recent efforts to develop a more rigorous theory.[23] Another difficulty is that it is quite difficult to define win-sets in practice, even with the help of the various factors discussed above.

Negotiation Theory

There is a body of literature developed for negotiations between private parties, such as in industrial relations, which can and has been applied to international economic negotiations. Putnam draws on this in developing his metaphor, but others such as Odell have taken it a little further.[24] This literature may help us in identifying how different negotiating strategies affect outcomes.

Zones of agreement and resistance points

Odell produces an extensive framework linked to empirical cases. Compared with Putnam, he identifies a *zone of agreement*, rather than win-sets. This zone of agreement, in any bilateral negotiation, is determined by what he calls *resistance points*. Odell sees the resistance points as being determined by, for example, the point at which no agreement is preferable to a bad agreement. This is also called the BATNA (best alternative to negotiated agreement) point. The worse the alternative to an agreement the lower the resistance point. Odell argues that thinking in terms of BATNAs is better than thinking in terms of bargaining power, since bargaining power is even more difficult to determine.

BATNAs still have to be seen as judgements on the part of negotiators, who have to balance welfare gains for the national and international economies, political relations with other countries and domestic policy objectives in deciding when an agreement is better than no agreement. Such judgements may vary over time. In other words the model is also based on bounded rationality. For example, at a time of tense transatlantic political relations, EU and US negotiators may place greater importance on positive outcomes for political reasons and thus compromise on sensitive economic issues. Or a government facing an election may place domestic electoral concerns ahead of concerns about the health of the international economy or international economic system. Odell argues that the resistance point defines the minimum that a negotiator must achieve but not the potential scope of what can be achieved.

Odell also illustrates the joint gains that can be made if the parties to a negotiation are not preoccupied with relative gains and if they are informed of the potential mutual gains from greater cooperation. Figure 2.1 shows the possibility frontier for a negotiation between states 'A' and 'B'. This shows that there are a range of options up to the possibility frontier where cooperation can result in gains for both even if the distribution of benefits may not be even. For example, at points 1 and 2 in Figure 2.1 state 'B' would benefit more than state 'A' although both benefit. If 'B' is willing to make further concessions, both 'A' and 'B' could gain more with the benefits being more evenly distributed. Point 4 however, is beyond the possibility frontier because one or both of the states are unwilling to make such far-reaching concessions of commitments.

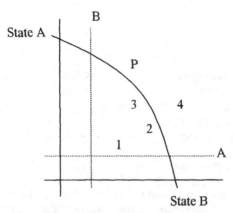

Figure 2.1 The Possibility Frontier and the Zone of Agreement

Source: Odell 2000

Value claiming, value creating and mixed strategies

Borrowing from negotiating theory, Odell suggests that the structures of interests only account for part of the picture. One must also consider how the *strategies* adopted by negotiators affect outcomes. Indeed he gives illustrations of how different negotiating strategies have had different outcomes, even though the basic structural variables have remained constant. Strategies may be distributive/value claiming or integrative/value creating in nature. *Distributive or value claiming strategies* are those that place little or no stress on mutual gains or on benefits the negotiating partner may have from a negotiation. Odell gives the Nixon shock of 1971 as an example of such a strategy, in which the US Administration imposed a 10% tariff and told its Japanese and European allies that the US would retain this tariff until they agreed to a revaluation of their currencies. Odell contrasts this with the US negotiating strategy in the mid 1980s negotiations on currency alignments when it pursued a more mixed strategy. *Integrative or value creating strategies* are those that stress joint gains. These are more common in economic diplomacy than distributive strategies. Integrative strategies seek a common solution to the problem at hand.

In practice, one is usually concerned with a spectrum from value claiming to value creating, with most governments pursuing *mixed strategies*, that combine elements of coercion as well as cooperation. Odell defines mixed strategies as consisting of the following elements:

- Efforts to discover the real nature of the issues concerned through an exchange of views and ideas;
- A joint search for potential solutions;
- Some trading of positions;
- No ruling out of concessions ab initio;
- But delay in making concessions until the shape of the final trade-offs is clear.

Such features occur regularly in economic diplomacy, thus illustrating the prevalence of mixed strategies.

The *linking* of policy issues also forms part of the Odell model. Linkage may be negative and value claiming, such as in the case of the US imposing tariffs in 1971 in an effort to force its negotiating partners into a devaluation they were reluctant to accept. In this case the US changed the BATNA for negotiating partners in the sense that the status quo became less acceptable for them than it was for the US. In other words the BATNA for Germany and Japan was shifted to a point at which agreement became more likely. Linkage can also be value creating. This applies, for example, to the measures taken by the European Union to open markets for least-developed countries with the aim of inducing them to support a broad agenda for the new WTO round of negotiations launched at Doha in November 2001. Such a strategy could be said to be value creating if one assumes that greater trade liberalisation leads to more trade and economic growth for all.

Most trade negotiations tend to be characterised by mixed strategies and linkage is adapted accordingly. For example, in the Uruguay Round the United States in particular pressed for the inclusion of international standards of protection of intellectual property. The US argued that this was value creating, in that better protection of intellectual property rights was beneficial for all. But most developing countries saw this as benefiting only the developed, technologically advanced countries. They would only agree to it in return for the liberalisation of trade restrictions on textiles and clothing exports from developing countries introduced under the Multi-Fibre Arrangement dating from 1973. Thus the linkage of two value claiming strategies produced a mixed result bringing benefit to all.

Odell draws on negotiating theory in discussing the dynamic between negotiators in order to illustrate how expectations and strategies can result in different outcomes with given structures of power and interest. For example, he suggests that negotiators are more likely to pursue value claiming strategies when they expect their negotiating partners to resist change or to exploit value creating strategies so as to achieve higher relative gains. If you expect your negotiating partner to exploit any moderation or concession on your part, without offering reciprocal concessions, then you will adopt a tough stance: value claiming. If, on the other hand, you expect concessions on your part to be reciprocated, you are more likely to adopt a conciliatory or value creating approach. Past experience and the institutional setting may well influence such strategies. For example, if the negotiation at hand follows previous negotiations in which value claiming strategies predominated, then there would be an expectation that value claiming would be the norm. Equally, if the negotiations take place within an institutional setting in which the parties have a long record of cooperation, such as in the OECD, one could also expect value creating strategies to prevail. In this respect it may be possible to link the Odell negotiating strategy approach with what one would be led to expect from regime theory. The point we seek to make here however, is simply that the beliefs and expectations of negotiators will have an effect on negotiations as well as the underlying structures of economic and political interests and power.

The strategy and effectiveness of a negotiator will also be affected by the level of domestic support. A negotiator who adopts a tough negotiating stance only to find this undermined or eroded by a lack of domestic support will lose credibility. Thus Odell suggests aggressive value claiming strategies require the credibility of strong domestic support. The threat of trade sanctions is a case in point. If negotiators make such threats, only to find that domestic interests do not support the position, perhaps out of concern for possible retaliation, they will find their credibility undermined and thus their ability to use value claiming strategies in the future.

One example of such a case can be found in US sanctions against the Soviet Union in the early 1980s. The US Reagan Administration initiated trade sanctions against the Soviet Union following the Soviet invasion of Afghanistan. When European governments failed to fully support such sanctions, the US Administration threatened trade sanctions against European and Japanese companies that delivered equipment for oil and gas pipelines to the Soviet Union. The policy of these secondary sanctions was undermined, in part because US international companies were concerned that the precedent set in forcing companies to revoke existing contracts would undermine the confidence needed to conduct international business. Major US companies shifted to oppose the position of the Reagan Administration and therefore undermined the credibility of the US position.

A counter example, where there is sufficient support, can be found in the case of the US position on European Union bans against genetically modified products. The United States has adopted a tough position on food safety and trade, arguing that the EU cannot ban imports of food or food products because there is a potential, but not scientifically proven, risk to consumers. In this, it draws support from the Sanitary and Phyto-Sanitary (SPS) agreement negotiated during the Uruguay Round and from WTO dispute settlement cases that have upheld that view. The threat of trade sanctions against the EU if it continues to ban GM foods is real, because it is backed by the major agricultural exporters, the biotechnology industry and all US exporters who wish to avoid arbitrary 'protectionist' measures taken against their exports on the basis of unsupported consumer fears. But to date US consumers have not figured much in the US debate. If US consumers begin to question the safety of GM crops or the way in which they have been regulated, then the credibility of US threats could be weakened.

Models of negotiation, such as those developed by Odell, also recognise psychological factors that may shape negotiators' views. In this he goes further into the 'individual level' than Putnam. For example, he draws on negotiation theory to show that negotiators may retain an initial position, even if this is untenable, or even raise the stakes in a negotiation rather than accept that they made an error of judgement. Clearly, the scope for this sort of behaviour will depend on how much autonomy the negotiator has.

The use of these insights into negotiation theory therefore provide further depth to the Putnam approach, which seeks to integrate relevant elements of established IR and IPE understanding of the interaction between the international and national levels of decision-making into a dynamic model which brings together domestic and international levels.

In summary, Odell seeks to go a little further than Putnam in suggesting a number of hypotheses that can be applied in economic diplomacy:

- If the market offers an alternative to agreement then the resistance point will be high and the likelihood of agreement lower;
- Credibility is important in pursuing value claiming strategies;
- A negotiator is less likely to choose value creating if opposition is expected from negotiating partners;
- There should be a means of compensating for the biases of negotiators, if one wishes to optimise negotiating performance;
- An increase in the institutional slack (ie increase in the negotiator's autonomy) increases the risk of an agreement not being ratified;
- Mixed strategies will tend to be more productive.

Conclusions: Factors Relevant to Decision-Making and Negotiation

This chapter has provided an overview of the theoretical and analytical approaches to international economic relations offered by international relations and international political economy. The overview is not complete and cannot do justice to the depth of analysis, but it clearly shows that there are a number of existing theories that are of relevance to economic diplomacy.

Figure 2.2 provides an overview of how these existing theoretical or analytical approaches fit into a two by two matrix.

As Chapter 1 pointed out economic diplomacy is concerned with the interaction between the international and domestic levels. So the theories that are of most relevance to our study of decision-making are those that focus in this interaction. These are theories or rather analytical frameworks such as the Putnam two level game and the Odell negotiation theory approaches.

	Economic	Political
International	International organisations International regimes	Realist theories eg hegemonic power
Domestic	Society centred approach eg interest groups	State centred approaches eg bureaucratic politics and domestic institutions

Figure 2.2 The Existing Theoretical Framework

The following chapter looks at the actors involved in economic diplomacy and in so doing shows in greater detail what actors or factors are at work at the international and domestic levels. Chapter 4 discusses how governments make decisions in economic diplomacy and thus falls generally within the bottom right hand quadrant, in other words the state centred or bureaucratic model of how decisions are reached. Subsequent chapters look at different case studies in economic diplomacy, illustrating the relevance of the theories and analytical approaches discussed in this chapter.

Notes

1 See Frieden and Lake 2000.
2 See Ikenberry, Lake and Mastanduno 1988.
3 See the discussion of the Putnam and Odell frameworks in this chapter.
4 Ibid.
5 See Odell 2000.
6 See Katzenstein 1978.
7 See Moravscik in Evans, Jacobsen and Putnam 1993 and Milner 1997.
8 See Strange 1993.
9 Hegemonic stability theory can also take more liberal, institutionalist forms, such as when the hegemon is benign and not concerned about relative gains. In such circumstances others may benefit more from the economic order provided than the hegemon responsible for providing such an order.
10 See Keohane 1984.
11 This is the definition of regimes accepted by most writers, see Krasner 1983, especially pp. 1-21.
12 See the general literature on globalisation and international relations, for example, Baylis and Smith 1997.
13 See Keohane 1984 for an example of this approach.
14 See Milner 1997.
15 A qualified majority requires 62.5% of the votes, with Member States of the EU holding differing voting weights depending on their size.

16 See Krasner 1983.
17 See Goldstein 1993.
18 See Moravscik in Evans, Jacobsen and Putnam 1993.
19 Putnam 1988 is the original source, from which this analysis is drawn.
20 See Milner 1997.
21 See Rosenau 1969.
22 See Marks and Hooghe 2001.
23 See Milner 1998.
24 See Odell 2000, especially Chapters 1-3, from which this analysis is drawn.

References

Evans, P., Jacobsen, H. K. and Putnam, R.D. (eds.) (1993), *Double-Edged Diplomacy: International Bargaining and Domestic Politics,* University of California Press, Berkeley.
Frieden, J. and Lake, D. A. (eds.) (2000), *International Political Economy: Perspectives on Global Power and Wealth,* 4th edition, Routledge, London and New York.
Goldstein, J. (1988). 'Ideas, Interests, and American Trade Policy', *International Organization,* vol. 42, no. 1, pp. 179-217.
Grieco, J. (1990), *Cooperation Among Nations; Europe, America and Non-Tariff Barriers to Trade,* Cornell University Press, Ithaca and London.
Ikenberry, G. J., Lake, D. A. and Mastanduno, M. (eds.) (1988), *The State and American Foreign Economic Diplomacy,* Cornell University Press, Ithaca and London. See also *International Organization,* vol. 42, no. 1.
Katzenstein, P. (1978), *Between Power and Plenty: Foreign Economic Policies in Advanced Capitalist States,* University of Wisconsin Press, Madison and London.
Keohane, R. O. (1984), *After Hegemony: Co-operation and Discord in the World Economy,* Princeton University Press, Princeton.
Krasner, S. (1983), *International Regimes,* Cornell University Press, Ithaca and London.
Marks, G. and Hooghe, L. (2001), *Multilevel Governance and European Integration,* Rowman and Littlefield, Boulder, Colorado.
Milner, H. (1997), *Interests, Institutions and Information: Domestic Politics and International Relations,* Princeton University Press, Princeton.
Milner, H. (1998), 'Rationalizing Politics: The Emerging Synthesis of International, American and Comparative politics', *International Organization,* vol. 52, no. 4, pp. 759-786.
Moravscik, A. (1993), 'Introduction' in Evans, P., Jacobsen, H. K. and Putnam, R.D. (eds.), *Double Edged Diplomacy: International Bargaining and Domestic Politics,* University of California Press, Berkeley.
Odell, J. (2000), *Negotiating the World Economy,* Cornell University Press, Ithaca and London.
Putnam, R. D. (1988), 'Diplomacy and Domestic Politics: The Logic of Two-Level Games' *International Organization,* vol. 42, no. 3, pp. 427-460.
Rosenau, J. (1969), *Linkage Politics: Essays on the Convergence of National and International Systems,* Free Press, New York.
Strange, S. (1988), *States and Markets: an Introduction to Political Economy,* Pinter, London.

Chapter 3

State and Non-State Actors

Stephen Woolcock

The aim of this chapter is to identify the universe of actors who could potentially shape decision-making in economic diplomacy in any given case. As Chapter 2 showed, economic diplomacy will be influenced by the institutional framework within which actors operate. This chapter seeks to provide a general grounding in the way actors are organised in the public and private sectors. In any specific case study, like those in later chapters of this book, it will be necessary to consider the details of the countries and sectors concerned.

As shown in Chapters 1 and 2, the more intrusive nature of economic negotiations between countries in recent years has meant that more and more interest groups are affected by and interested in the decision-making process. Within governments, a much greater number of departments are now becoming involved in international negotiations than was the case before the growth in economic interdependence during the 1980s and 1990s. New non-governmental actors have also become more interested in decision-making, including 'civil society'. As a result, the traditional role of business lobbying has now been augmented by lobbying or advocacy by a wide range of non-governmental organisations (NGOs).

This expansion of the actors engaged in economic diplomacy provokes a number of general questions, such as what impact do these growing numbers have on decision-making and what is changing if anything in terms of the relationship between the old and new actors?

What impact does this growth in the number of actors involved in economic diplomacy have on the decision-making processes? Does an increase in the number of actors make decision-making less effective, because the interests seeking to influence decisions is more heterogeneous? Or does a larger number and range of interests facilitate decision-making by providing negotiators with more information? Perhaps a larger number of actors provides an opportunity for the negotiator to play some off against the others and thus create more scope and discretion in negotiations, as the models of negotiation discussed in Chapter 2 would suggest. Involving more actors may also make economic diplomacy more democratic and accountable.

The growth in the number of actors, especially non-state actors, also leads to the issue of how established decision-makers or negotiators should treat these new actors. In the age of 'globalisation', one could argue that negotiators or governments should actively seek input from a wide range of actors in order to address the real or perceived democratic deficit in economic diplomacy. Should they engage the new actors directly in decision-making, to ensure policy is responsive to a wide range of interests? Or should they seek to maintain some distance, in order to insulate themselves from pressure and potential capture?

All these questions will be picked up in the following chapters of this book. But first it is necessary to understand more about the actors involved in modern economic diplomacy. The main part of this chapter examines the principal actors, classified as in Table 3.1.

Table 3.1   Principal Actors in Economic Diplomacy

National State Actors

The Executive Branch
The Legislative Branch
    Political Parties
Provincial, State and Local Government
Regulatory Agencies

Non-State Actors

Business Interest Groups
    Confederations of Industry
    Sector Trade Associations
Trade Unions
Consumer Organisations

Transnational Actors

Global Civil Society
International Business
International Organisations
Epistemic Communities

National State Actors

States or governments are the major actors in economic diplomacy still, but, as was pointed out in earlier chapters, we cannot assume that governments are unitary actors. There are different branches of government and the potential for different views on any given topic within the different branches of government. As noted in the previous chapter, negotiators are often negotiating on two fronts, the foreign front and the domestic front. We shall look first at the two main branches of government - the executive and legislative branches.

The Executive Branch of Government

Models of economic diplomacy sometimes consider the tension between the executive and legislative branches as being a key feature shaping economic diplomacy. Divided government is then generally seen as the divide between the executive and legislative branches of government, or 'polyarchy',[1] which affects the interaction between the executive, legislature and other non-governmental actors. The models tend to be built on the need for the executive branch to get any agreement ratified by the legislature. This may be a suitable simplification for assessing two-level games, but in economic diplomacy we are also interested in how the executive comes to define the national interest. In an increasing number of policy areas this takes the form of a complex inter-departmental or inter-agency debate.

An example from multilateral trade negotiations illustrates how the executive branch of any government must find a consensus among a wide number of different government departments. Trade negotiations in the Uruguay Round (1986-1994) were led by the USTR in the United States and DG Trade of the European Commission, in consultation with the EU Member States, in the case of the European Union. But many other departments were involved:

- *Departments of agriculture* were closely associated with the negotiations, because of the centrality of negotiations on reductions in agricultural support. Ministries of agriculture also regulated food safety standards in many countries, so they were likewise involved in the negotiations of an Agreement on Sanitary and Phyto-Sanitary (SPS) measures.
- *Departments of industry, enterprise or the economy* were involved in the negotiations because of their interest in sponsoring a wide range of industrial sectors. As the negotiations touched not only on tariff levels but also on non-tariff measures, such as quotas for textiles and clothing or tighter WTO control over the use of national subsidies, these departments played a central role.
- *Ministries of science or technology* were also concerned with the control of national subsidy programmes as well as the negotiations on Trade Related Intellectual Property Rights (TRIPS).
- *Finance ministries* were involved in the negotiations because tariff reductions resulted in reduced government revenue and because the negotiations on services covered financial services, which had been the jealous preserve of finance ministries or treasuries for many years.
- The services negotiations also involved ministries responsible for *transport, telecommunications, health and other public services*, which were all subject to negotiations and some liberalisation commitments.
- Even *ministries of the interior or home offices* were concerned with the services negotiations because they covered the free movement of people and thus touched on immigration and migration issues.

Towards the end of the Uruguay Round, the environment began to figure as a major potential issue. Labour standards were also proposed as a topic that should be added to the WTO agenda, at the time of the completion of the Uruguay Round. This meant that *ministries responsible for environmental standards and regulation* were involved in the negotiations, as were *employment or labour affairs departments*.

The fact that the number of government actors has grown can be shown by a few simple quantitative measures. In 1950 there were some 70 independent countries with over 830 departments of government, by 1975 there were 140 independent countries with over 2500 government departments. The current figures are in the order of 180 independent states with well in excess of 2500 government departments. So there are many more state actors involved in economic diplomacy.

Levels of authority

Within government departments, it is also important to consider the different levels of authority. Ministers will have more political authority and will be concerned about the implications of their decisions for the prospects of them or their party retaining power. In this sense the decision may well approximate to the dictates of maximisation of the utility (re-election) as suggested in rational choice literature. Ministers will have ultimate responsibility, but senior civil servants may well have a considerable impact when issues are of a more technocratic than political character. This was, for example, the case in many trade and investment negotiations until fairly recently.

Civil servants are likely to be motivated by somewhat different concerns. Except where senior civil servants are political appointees, it will be civil servants who will have the responsibility of implementing decisions taken by politicians who may well move on to other posts or lose elections. Civil servants will therefore tend to be more concerned with the practicality of implementing decisions. They may also provide a long term institutional memory. For example, the officials representing Member States in the EU's Article 133 Committee, which deals with many trade policy issues, tend to be in post for a longer period than the responsible ministers. Recently, one official retired having represented his country in the Article 133 Committee for more than 10 years. This means that civil servants will know of previous cases and precedents which bear on any policy debate. Continuity within the executive branch of government will vary from country to country. For example, many European officials may remain in place for a period that extends beyond the life of one government, whereas in the United States senior trade officials are political appointees whose term in post coincides with that of the administration.

Even senior civil servants will not be able to retain details of all negotiations because of the highly technical nature of some economic diplomacy. For example, in negotiating on international standards issues or technical aspects of rules of origin, national experts will play an important role in shaping policy. In some cases these will be drawn from within government and, when this is the case, specialists can have a real impact on outcomes. In other cases governments use private sector or academic experts, as in the technical committees of the international bodies setting standards for food safety or digital mobile telephony.

The Legislative Branch of Government

The role of parliaments will vary from country to country, and from region to region in the case of the European Parliament. Generally speaking, the legislative branch of government is involved mostly in the ratification of agreements. Links between negotiation and ratification are close, as work by Putnam and Milner, among others, has shown.[2] Thus a credible power of veto by the legislature will oblige negotiators in the executive to ensure that the legislature is fully informed to the point that the latter could be said to be engaged in the negotiations itself. But much economic diplomacy is still technical and negotiations are not always easy to follow for parliamentarians, who do not sit in on the negotiations with other countries.

There is therefore a question concerning the effectiveness of parliaments and legislatures in providing scrutiny of economic diplomacy. For a range of reasons, parliamentarians may find it difficult to keep close control over the negotiators, with the result that there may be a democratic deficit. The criticism by civil society NGOs, the pressure to enhance access for non-government bodies to negotiations and the calls for greater transparency are all due to the perception of such a democratic deficit or lack of accountability in many aspects of economic diplomacy. Governments have responded by seeking to engage civil society in a dialogue on policy, and increasing cooperation in international organisations.

The legislative branch of government nevertheless still plays an important role, as it will often be the ultimate ratifying body. The institutional arrangements for ratification of any agreement will tend to involve voting procedures in parliaments. The voting provisions, the practice and thus the roles of legislative branches will vary, however, from country to country and case to case. For example, the US Congress has constitutional powers in the field of commercial policy while the powers of the European Parliament are heavily subscribed. For this reason the US Congress plays a role in agenda-setting, negotiation and ratification phases of any negotiation. For any negotiation, the US Administration requires authority from the Congress, which thus has the ability to shape the agenda of the negotiations.

This is not the case in Europe. The agenda for any trade negotiation is largely set by the Member State governments in the Council of Ministers, acting on a proposal from the European Commission (see Chapter 12). National and European parliaments can only really have an indirect impact. They do not, for example, have to give negotiating authority. Whilst national and European parliaments may have to ratify an agreement, they do so only once it has already been concluded by the national governments in the Council. In short, the veto power is not credible and therefore parliaments have not been taken all that seriously by European trade negotiators. National legislatures will also tend to have less control over monetary policy than trade or other policies, especially following the shift towards the greater acceptance of independent central banks.

Political parties

Governments will also be influenced by party policy or doctrine and the desire for re-election at a party level. Parliamentary systems with strong discipline within a governing party will find it easier to ratify an agreement than a system in which there is weak party discipline or coalition government. In the former potential renegades, who risk exclusion from the party or at least exclusion for senior posts in the future, can more easily be brought into line. In such circumstances the position of the party on any international agreement becomes more important. If a governing party supports ratification of an agreement then even unpopular agreements can be ratified in the name of the greater good of the whole platform represented by the party. This does not preclude the domestic level II game in a Putnam two-level game model, but it may change the dynamics of the domestic game.

This contrasts with situations in which there is less party discipline, as in the US Congress, or where governments tend to be coalitions. In the case of the former, party affiliation is less important. In the case of the latter, heated negotiations may take place within the various factions within the coalition.

In economic diplomacy politicians must balance the medium or long term benefits of increased economic growth from greater international cooperation, with the short term political and economic costs of any agreement. In this calculation there may well be imbalances in electorate representation that skew the outcome. For example, rural or agricultural constituencies are often over-represented, in terms of the number of electors, because of the relatively sparse populations in the countryside and the slow pace of electoral reform to adjust boundaries. This helps to explain why the agricultural sector has benefited from greater support and protection in many countries in Europe, Japan and elsewhere.

Agriculture also provides an example of how short term party political factors can shape economic diplomacy. Because rural constituencies pack more political clout in Europe than urban constituencies, agricultural reform has been frustrated for many years. In Germany the coalition of the Christian Democratic Union (CDU) and the Christian Social Union (CSU) under Helmut Kohl of the late 1980s and early 1990s depended on rural votes in Bavaria, where the CSU is based. Concessions in agricultural trade negotiations, which would have resulted in fewer subsidies for the small and relatively inefficient Bavarian farmers, could have led to lost votes for the CSU, which would have undermined the coalition government. So Germany opposed reform of the Common Agricultural Policy (CAP) and any concessions in the agricultural negotiations in the Uruguay Round. It was only when reform of the subsidy programme provided compensation or side payments to the smaller farmers in Bavaria that the German Federal government was able to support concessions in the negotiations. That facilitated the preparation of the so-called Dunkel text in late 1991 that formed the basis of the final agreement on agriculture.

Once the Dunkel text had been tabled, however, the French socialist government was not willing to accept concessions on agricultural trade during 1992 because it was seeking ratification of the Maastricht Treaty on the European

Union by a referendum in November 1992. The government won the referendum by a margin of only 2% and argued, with some conviction, that concessions on agriculture could have cost it that margin of votes. Here one has a clear case of policy linkage with European integration. Even after the referendum the French government continued to oppose concessions on agriculture, because there was a general election in March 1993. Japan provides a similar illustration of how political structures operate. The Liberal Democratic Party's (LDP) strongholds in rural constituencies have ensured that the Japanese government has persistently opposed concessions on rice imports.

Provincial, State and Local Government

Our consideration of government actors must include state and local government. Economic diplomacy now includes issues, such as investment and the regulation of insurance and other financial services, as well as health and safety regulation, which come under the competence of sub-national government. For example, 70% of public procurement is accounted for by sub-national or sub-federal level government. So any serious effort to introduce multilateral rules governing this activity, which can account for anything up to 10% of GDP, would be only partial if they did not include sub-national government.

This issue is particularly important in federal systems, such as the United States, Australia, Canada and Germany where sub-national units even aspire to pursue economic diplomacy at their own level. In some instances this economic diplomacy can be ambitious, such as when the US state of Massachusetts' seeks to impose sanctions against Myanmar (Burma) on human rights grounds. More generally, provinces, states and local authorities compete to attract inward investment. It has been argued, for example by Strange, that the role of the state in the global economy is becoming more one of competing to attract economic activity rather than competing with other states for market share.[3] When it comes to attracting inward foreign direct investment (FDI) it is regional and local governments that are competing with each other, rather than national states. FDI inflows are thought to be influenced by 'clusters' of economic activity. Where suitable infrastructure and human capital resources are available, foreign investment occurs. Once a number of companies have established a presence, this enriches the human capital provision. In other words, the companies contribute to a pool of skilled labour and this attracts further inward investment. In this way clusters can lead to dramatic developments in the economic activity in a region. So it is the regions, sometimes in different countries and sometimes in the same country, that are competing for investment, not the sovereign states.

Independent or Quasi-Independent Regulatory Agencies

Regulatory agencies have been described as the fourth branch of government (after the executive, legislature and judiciary). In modern economies such agencies appear to be playing a more and more important role. Such bodies include: central banks; financial market regulators; competition and anti-trust authorities; and agencies regulating food and drug safety, access to telecommunications markets and sometimes even trade measures (ie the ITC in the United States). All of them influence access to national markets and all engage, to a greater or lesser degree, in international negotiations.

The use of such agencies is long established practice in the United States, where limitations on government intervention have meant that 'independent' regulatory agencies have been used to correct market failures.[4]   In Europe and elsewhere governments have, in the past, been more willing to intervene directly to correct market failures.   But the trend towards privatisation and growing support for independent regulatory agencies has meant that more and more countries are making more and more use of such agencies.   This relieves government of the direct responsibility for regulating sectors of the economy and is seen to be best practice because it removes government from the day-to-day operation.

The importance of such regulatory bodies can be illustrated in many sectors. For example, in 2000 there was an important debate concerning the conditions for access to public telephone networks for mobile digital telephony and the standards to be set for the next generation of mobile technology.   Both issues were central to the question of market access in this sector.   In most countries it was regulatory agencies, such as the Federal Communications Commission (FCC) in the US, OFTEL in the UK or the Directorates General (DGs) for Information Society and Competition in the European Commission, that determined the terms and conditions for competition between the existing (monopoly) common carriers and the new mobile suppliers.   Such regulatory bodies therefore figure as actors in economic diplomacy and will do more as governments seek to delegate the detailed technical regulation to specialist bodies.

In some cases the negotiation of rules and regimes is not done by public agencies but is left entirely to private sector groups.   For example, standards for mutual recognition of drug testing in the pharmaceuticals sector were negotiated between American, European and Japanese pharmaceutical companies in the framework of an international agreement of the early 1980s.   The International Federation of Stock Exchanges, the International Council of Securities Associations and the International Accounting Standards Committee provide a private sector framework for cooperation between stock exchanges and capital markets.   Similarly, mutual recognition agreements, such as between the European Union and the United States involve negotiation between professional bodies on the mutual recognition of qualifications.   These examples of the part-privatisation of economic diplomacy lead naturally to the consideration of non-state actors.

Non-State Actors

That, therefore, concludes the main review of the different aspects of the national state as actor in economic diplomacy.   The next main section of this chapter focuses on non-state participants.

Business Interest Groups

Business can impact policy directly via lobbying, either at company, sector association or confederation level, or indirectly via market decisions. The two are often inseparable. For example, a business organisation may approach its national government with the argument that, if the regulatory or tax burden on its business is not eased, investment, jobs and economic prosperity will move elsewhere. Government will have to assess whether this threat is real or simply being used to reduce costs.

The private business actors can take various forms:

- Confederations of industry, which seek to represent wide sections of business;
- Industry or sector trade associations;
- Individual firms lobbying governments directly.

Companies will tend to use all three levels of lobbying, depending on which is most suitable and effective. For example, on issues on which there is a general business interest, such as opposition to a social clause to promote core international labour standards, confederations will be used. Sector associations will tend to be used to seek protection from import competition or promote market liberalisation abroad. Individual firms will lobby themselves on issues when they cannot get broader support, or when the issue is company specific, such as subsidies for civil aircraft production.

Confederations of industry

Confederations of industry tend to represent national positions, although there is cooperation between the national confederations. One of the most powerful confederations has been the Japanese Keidanren. The corporatist nature of much of Japanese business in the past enabled the Keidanren to provide a coherent focus for Japanese industry. European confederations of industry have also been important, with the German Bundesverbund der Deutschen Industrie (BDI) and Bundesverbund der Deutschen Arbeitgeber (BDA), Confindustria in Italy and the British Confederation of British Industry (CBI) being perhaps the most important. At a European level, UNICE (Union of European Industry and Employers' Confederations) includes all national confederations of the EU Member States, as well as other Europeans.

In the United States the weaker corporatist tradition has meant that formal federations are relatively less influential than in Europe or Japan. Certainly there is the National Association of Manufacturers (which represents the larger industrial companies), the Chamber of Commerce (which represents the smaller companies) and long established organisations such as the US Council for International Business. But much of the lobbying power in Washington comes from more ad hoc coalitions of companies. These coalitions may be more or less institutionalised. They tend to have a more focused agenda than the standing confederations and can also be more flexible. As they are not as inclusive as the large federations and can focus on specific issues, their lobbying pressure is not as diffused as it sometimes is with larger groupings. The coalitions can be short lived, being formed to address a specific issue, or longer-term, such as the Business Round Table or the Coalition of Service Industries.

There are clearly differences here in terms of the degree of centralisation or focus in lobbying. The larger confederations must find a broad consensus among their members and will therefore tend to be slower in developing positions and less able to deal with detail. The smaller coalitions, sometimes made up of a few large companies with clear lobbying objectives, can be much more focused. These coalitions also tend to be more pro active and this is reflected in US business lobbying, which has often criticised European business for not being pro active enough. Some coalitions of companies have been established in Europe, such as the European Round Table of Industrialists, in order to try to provide a more dynamic and less institutionalised representation of industry. The European Round Table brought together chief executives of companies, which contrasted with the federations and confederations, where the officials of the associations tend to play a greater role.

Sector trade associations

Each country also has a large number of sector trade associations with varying degrees of influence, from the heavy hitters, such as steel and agriculture, to cuddly toys. In fact toy manufacturers have an important role to play with regard to the adoption and implementation of safety standards for toys and also lobby on trade and other policy issues.

To give an indication of the number of sector associations, the Brussels directory of interest groups lists over 600 trade associations. This contrasts with 22 chambers of commerce (such as the American Chamber of Commerce, which has an important role in monitoring what is going on in European legislation); 24 national confederations; 100 representations of regions of the EU and other regions including 15 American states; and 19 trade union organisations. Some of these organisations will be just a Director General and a secretary, often providing little more than a source of basic material on developments in the EU. Others will be substantial organisations with a capacity to closely monitor and lobby on a wide range of issues.

Trade Unions

In organised labour the national umbrella organisations similarly bring together various sector unions and seek to represent the interests of all the sector unions on general issues. Some national union organisations are clearly more cohesive and stronger than others, although union membership has declined in most countries since the 1970s, due to falling industrial membership and lower levels of organisation in the newer service sectors and the new economy. The strength of national unions, and thus to a greater or lesser extent international union organisation, has declined with the decline of major industrial unions. Generally speaking, the service sector that accounts for more and more economic activity is less unionised than the old heavy industries. Corporatist approaches to decision-making that include trade unions have also gone out of fashion in most countries. In continental Europe the corporatist tradition has perhaps remained stronger, such as in Germany, and has found expression in some elements of social dialogue at an EU level.

Consumer Organisations

Almost all countries have some form of consumer representation, although the strength of these varies. Some consumer organisations are quite close to the state but most are independent non-governmental bodies. In the developed countries there are usually between 4 and 10 consumer organisations. For example, Consumers International, which represents over 260 consumer organisations in 120 countries has 5 consumer groups in the US affiliated to the organisation. In the European countries there are generally about four or five consumer organisations. It is worth noting that European consumer organisations, like business and industry associations, are more institutionalised and centralised. In other words the national consumer groups support BEUC (the Bureau of European Union Consumers) in developing a common position. This cohesion is helped by the fact that the European institutions, such as the Commission and Parliament, take the views of EU-wide bodies more seriously than sector or national organisations. This also helps to encourage all interest groups seeking to influence EU legislation to cooperate and produce a common position for all the equivalent sectors or other interests across the EU. Consumer organisations in the US tend to be less centralised and operate as other interests do in competing to shape opinion. In Europe consumer organisations are more likely to be integrated in the policy process. Most developing countries have some form of consumer organisation although this can sometimes be weak and fragmented. There are for example, 18 consumer organisations in India that are members of Consumers International. This is due in part to the federal structure of India. Australia has ten consumer organisations for similar reasons.[5]

Transnational Actors

Global Civil Society

All the actors considered so far can be linked to an identifiable national base, though often actors from the Member States of the European Union combine to operate as a single unit. But these national links are less evident for global civil society, whose rise in recent years has been one of the important developments in terms of actors in economic diplomacy. Civil society in the modern sense consists of non-governmental organisations, which are not market actors, but which make a deliberate effort to shape policy or the shape of regulation or markets.[6] With the advent of globalisation and the establishment of a dimension to production, investment and policy process which is free from territorial constraints, there has also been a growth of global civil society, or organisations that form part of civil society which operate beyond the constraints of territory previously shaped by the strong nation state.

The moving forces behind the growth of global civil society

In recent years there has been a growth of global civil society in part as a positive response to the globalisation of markets. In other words consumers, environmental groups and other organisations such as bodies promoting development have moved to develop policies on global issues through cooperation beyond national boundaries. This type of activity of global civil society could be seen as the beginnings of political organisation beyond the nation state.

Much of the motivation for global civil society activity, however, has been more negative and could be seen as part of a backlash against globalisation of markets.[7] Global civil society opposed to globalisation has been called 'the movement'[8] because of the difficulty identifying any specific structure to the opposition. There are however, clearly different motivations behind the opposition to globalisation. First, at a very general level, there is the opposition to the prevailing liberal paradigm that has shaped economic diplomacy throughout the 1980s and 1990s. This takes a more concrete form with regard to each of the different interests concerned.

Organised labour coordinates its position in International Confederation of Free Trade Unions (ICFTU), which is based in Brussels but represents unions from around the world, not just from developed countries. Cooperation within the labour movement has suffered in the past from ideological differences. Not only was there a division between the communist unions and the unions in non-communist countries (which came together in the International Confederation of *Free* Trade Unions), but differences existed between those unions that adopted a cooperative approach to capital, (such as in Germany and the Netherlands) and those that adopted a more class conflict-based approach (France, Italy and the UK until recently). Compared to business, there are much fewer resources available to the labour movement, which has also limited cooperation.

Organised labour has fewer links with international institutions than business, so has much less to lose if the global civil society challenges existing channels of democratic accountability. Organised labour is represented in the ILO and the Trade Union Advisory Council (TUAC) of the OECD, but the latter has provided little by way of influence. Unions feel aggrieved because privatisation and downscaling of production in the industrialised countries has undermined their negotiating clout. This goes hand in hand with the perception that jobs are being lost as investment flows to countries where labour costs are lower.

In the face of globalisation organised labour has overcome some of the ideological divisions that existed between national unions that believed in cooperation with employers and the more radical national unions, and pressed a 'social clause' that would link trade with labour standards for many years but with little success. The unions also seek to shape outcomes at regional as well as the plurilateral and global levels through the Social Chapter of the European Treaties and the North American Agreement on Labour Cooperation, which was a side agreement to the North American Free Trade Agreement (NAFTA).

Organised labour's efforts to promote international labour standards, was however, also helped by its association with other civil society groups in 'the movement'. The interests of *development NGOs* were to some extent consistent with those of labour in the sense that both pointed to the inequalities created by globalising markets and the poverty that continued in many developing countries. The development NGOs, such as Actionaid, Christian Aid, Oxfam and Save The Children, came to the view that the project-based approach to development aid was insufficient by itself and that they had to advocate the interests of developing countries more widely in international organisations such as the IMF and WTO. The development NGOs therefore began to challenge the conventional wisdom of the 'Washington Consensus' that argued for market liberalisation as the best strategy for development. The failures of Russia, Indonesia and Argentina were also perceived as providing support for more revisionist views of the liberal paradigm.[9] So there was some common cause between the labour and development NGOs, even if they also differed on issues such as the use of trade sanctions to ensure international labour standards were enforced.

An important element in 'the Movement' challenging globalisation was the *environmental NGOs*. Environmental NGOs were equally if not more powerful than organised labour and the development NGOs and could draw on broad and growing support for sustainable development among public opinion and political parties, especially in the developed economies. The creation of global civil society in the field of the environment was driven by the need to protect global commons, such as the ozone layer, biodiversity and endangered species. In the field of the environment, global civil society mounted a direct challenge to the orthodox norms of liberal economics, which was seen as failing to adequately address the environmental externalities resulting from existing forms of development. The call was for 'sustainable development'. Environmental civil society also facilitated research into the effects of new products and technologies on the environment. This showed that existing scientific knowledge on the environmental impact of industrialisation was far from certain and embodied a set of values which were, in the view of civil society, skewed towards growth per se rather than the environment. As with the labour movement, environmental civil society has also been successful in establishing regional cooperation, such as within Europe. Extending this to global cooperation became relatively easy.

Another important group of interests that go to make up international civil society are *consumers*. Consumer groups have stronger institutional structures and formal channels of representation, similar to the confederations and trade associations in the business sector. At an international level Consumers International has represented national organisations since 1960 and is governed by a Council elected by the national organisations. Consumer groups have been drawn more and more into the debate on globalisation as a result of issues such as food safety issues. Consumer organisations had sought to promote 'sustainable consumption', for example through the use of labelling schemes that empower consumers and enable them to choose products with knowledge of their impact on the environment or whether child labour has been used in their production. But trade disputes over beef hormones and the use of genetically modified crops in food have heightened awareness of how international trade, and in particular the rules governing international trade, impinge upon consumer choice.[10] Consumer confidence in established, science-based food safety regulation was also shattered by the fiasco of BSE (mad cow disease) and by other cases in which 'sound science' appeared to get it wrong. Consumer groups and environmental NGOs therefore shared a common critique of the established practices and value systems that governed environmental and food safety regulation.

In other words, global civil society was challenging the value systems on which the regulation of markets had come to be based. The science-based approaches, which included liberal economics, were seen to be loaded in favour of growth and as not reflecting the value systems supported by labour, development, environmental and consumer-based civil society movements. If these value systems had been developed by democratically elected governments, this highlighted the inadequacies of the existing national political or party systems in reflecting the values of civil society. Civil society therefore had to act directly and not rely exclusively on the existing channels of democratic accountability.

Not surprisingly, therefore, global civil society saw the existing decision-making processes as opaque and undemocratic. This led to the calls for greater transparency and participation of civil society NGOs in the decision-making processes. Existing decision-making, whether it was in the OECD discussions on the Multilateral Agreement on Investment, the World Trade Organization or the IMF, was seen as less than fully accountable, even though decisions were ultimately the responsibility of elected politicians, who were accountable to the electorate. Such formal democratic accountability was seen by the NGOs as being too remote to be effective. What was needed, they claimed, was the direct involvement of NGOs that had the ability to provide more effective scrutiny. But this argument about democratic accountability can be turned back against the NGOs themselves. When they call for changes in the WTO that would place sustainability and core labour standards before wealth creation, do they reflect genuinely global concerns of civil society, or the interests of a self-selected group of well-funded Northern NGOs?

There are however precedents for NGO participation in international organisations. For, environment NGOs have been actively involved in the work of UNEP and the UN Commission on Sustainable Development (CSD). Consumers International has long had representation or at least access to the work of UN bodies such as the Codex Alimentarius Committee of the Food and Agriculture Organisation that develops food safety standards. Stakeholders, such as environmental NGOs and economic stakeholders have also initiated joint actions to address issues in sustainable development. Environment groups have observer status in the discussions on implementation of the Montreal Protocol on the reduction of the production of ozone-depleting substances. The IMF and World Bank have also begun to engage stakeholders in the development of programmes with a view to ensuring that local stakeholders have a sense of 'ownership' of the programme of development. This contrasts with the absence of any NGO participation in the WTO, where member governments, especially from developing countries, have been adamant they should not have a direct role. Having said this the WTO has also begun to promote consultations with NGOs, beginning with the March 1999 consultation on trade and development.

International Business

Business is organised at an international level in different forms. In terms of global membership organisations, there are organisations such as the International Chamber of Commerce (ICC). Established in 1919 the ICC brings together individual companies, sector level trade associations as well as national confederations. The ICC represents some 800 national chambers of commerce in over 130 countries. The main functions of the ICC are to promote open markets through the scrutiny and lobbying of national governments and international organisations, and the development and promotion of voluntary codes of conduct or rules for businesses. With regard to the former the ICC draws on a large number of specialist working groups and experts (over 500 experts) and has access to discussions in the UN and other international organisations.[11]

Business organisations are also organised at the plurilateral level. For example, the Business and Industry Advisory Committee to the OECD has for many years provided business views and input into the deliberations of the OECD. BIAC consists of the leading confederations of business or industry in the OECD countries. In some cases these are bodies specialising in international business or commercial issues, such as the US Council for International Business in the US, in other cases they are the national confederations. The impact of the various BIAC committees has varied, depending on the issues under discussion and the quality of participants on the committees. On issues such as the development of OECD work on investment policy, the BIAC has played an important role.

In addition to the formal organisations there are coalitions of businesses that come together to pursue specific aims. In some cases these coalitions may be broad and in some cases regional or sector specific. Perhaps the most well known coalition of companies coming together is the World Economic Forum (WEF), which was formed in 1971 with a meeting of European companies in Davos. Since then the WEF has expanded into a global organisation with over 1000 companies supporting it. It has the aim of creating 'partnerships between member companies and political, intellectual and other leaders to discuss and advance key issues on the global agenda'.

In terms of regional or bilateral coalitions perhaps the most important and the model for a range of other coalitions has been the Transatlantic Business Dialogue (TABD) which was established in 1995, first as a group of chief executives on each side of the Atlantic discussing the agenda for transatlantic commercial relations. Subsequently expert groups were added to seek common approaches of positions on some fairly detailed but important aspects of transatlantic commercial relations. These expert groups sometimes negotiate compromises between US and EU approaches to market regulation. In this sense the TABD engages directly in economic diplomacy and represents a partial privatisation of economic diplomacy in the areas covered. In recent years there has been a general growth in the application of this approach to bilateral commercial relations between countries or regions, so that there are business dialogues associated with many bilateral agreements between countries.

Business interests also form sector level coalitions at an international level in order to further business interests in a range of sectors. For example, there is a network of coalitions of service industries that has grown up since the 1980s to provide effective business input into the negotiations on trade in services in both multilateral negotiations in the GATS and in bilateral negotiations. The pharmaceutical sector has been active in international coalitions in both promoting common approaches to such issues as clinical testing and common positions in the TRIPS negotiations within the GATT/WTO.

Multinational companies (MNCs) with a global reach can clearly also be seen as transnational actors in their own right, and pursue their interests without reference to any formal organisations. The number of MNCs is growing all the time with increased internationalisation of production and cross border mergers and acquisitions. MNCs account for a very large share of international trade and investment. There can be little doubt that MNCs are a major factor in the international economy, but there is some debate about whether they represent a truly global economy, which is largely beyond the influence of individual national governments and national policies. It can be argued that MNCs retain a national character and must be seen as reflecting the interests of their home country, for example, through links between the MNC and its home government.

General trends in business representation are difficult to identify. There would appear to be a growth in the use of international business dialogues, whether global in nature such as the WEF or bilateral or regional in nature, such as the TABD and its followers in other bilateral relationships. This growth may have had the effect of undermining some of the more formal institutional arrangements between national confederations of business. In other words globalisation is also having the effect of shifting the relative focus of business lobbying from national confederations to bodies which rely on the direct support of companies operating in global markets.

International Organisations

All the national actors discussed earlier in this chapter have channels through which they interact at an international or transnational level. In the case of states, there are the recognised international organisations. At the latest count there were 309 international organisations, ranging from large organisations like the IMF, World Bank and ILO, through medium sized organisations like the WTO to smaller specialist bodies such as the International Standards Organisation (ISO).

International organisations may assume the role of actors in their own right. For example, the staffs of the IMF and World Bank can clearly have an impact on policy development, even if final decision-making power rests with national governments. In the case of the WTO, the secretariat is more constrained in what it can do directly. For example, all policy proposals come from WTO member countries, not from the secretariat. But the secretariat can and does play a role in brokering compromises between conflicting positions.

Generally speaking, the officials employed by international organisations will not play a central role in policy-making. But international civil servants may shape policy in a number of ways. For example, they may help to clarify the potential scope of any agreement and help coordinate the flow of information. An important early phase in any negotiation is the exploratory phase, which can be inhibited by the general lack of information on many issues in economic diplomacy. Without sufficient information on the impact of an agreement on their national economies, national negotiators may adopt defensive strategies. Clarification of the impact of possible agreements therefore plays an important role in preparing the ground for negotiations. This is the work that international civil servants often coordinate. For example, the OECD, together with an epistemic community (see below), played an important role in drawing attention to the costs of national agricultural programmes. By measuring the level of subsidies inherent in a range of national agricultural programmes the OECD initiative paved the way for agreement on agricultural trade policy issues during the Uruguay Round. International civil servants may also help to broker compromises between different positions. If the negotiations are taking place within an international organisation, such as the WTO or UNEP, civil servants employed by these organisations have an interest in finding compromises. Therefore we must include the interests of such actors in our assessments.

Epistemic Communities

If one looks at the structure of interests and power it is possible to lose sight of the fact that national interests are not always easy to define. For example, when discussions began on the inclusion of services in international trade rules, few governments had much of an idea what impact multilateral rules governing services would have on their economies. National interests may also change as new information is assimilated. In the above case the US was initially the protagonist (or demandeur) in calling for a General Agreement on Trade in Services (GATS) and France was one of the main opponents. But after the inputs of an epistemic community, information and understanding on what trade in services consisted of improved and it emerged that France had one of the largest trade surpluses in services. As a result the French became important proponents of the GATS, and the US became more sceptical.

Another example of how improved knowledge has had a major impact on policy outcomes is global warming. For many years a range of governments resisted international cooperation to reduce greenhouse gases because there was no consensus on the fact of global warming. This led to the creation of the Inter-governmental Panel on Climate Change (IPCC), an international group of scientists brought together by the UN Environment Programme (UNEP) and the World Meteorological Organisation (WMO) to assess the evidence for global warming and make recommendations to governments.   The evidence produced by successive IPCC reports has obliged the more sceptical governments to take notice.

By collecting information that is of direct relevance to policy-making, epistemic communities can therefore shape policy outcomes.   Haas defines an epistemic community as a 'network of experts with recognised expertise and competence and an authoritative claim to policy relevant knowledge in the issue concerned'.   He also argues that they have to have a common set of values and objectives, even if their means of achieving these objectives may vary.[12]

When it comes to interpreting technical issues policy makers will turn to experts.   When these experts communicate with each other across national borders, they can clearly shape national policy preferences and have an impact on policy.   There are many cases in which one can identify epistemic communities.   The measurement of Producer Subsidy Equivalents in agricultural trade issues and the consensus on the need for action to combat global warming are examples of when epistemic communities have had an impact.   Another older case is the Bretton Woods agreement to establish the post-war international monetary system, which was assisted by the fact that the economists who drew up the blue prints shared broadly similar views on what was needed.

The existence of international regimes also provides scope for epistemic communities to operate.   As we considered when we discussed negotiating tactics, much economic diplomacy takes the form of integrative or mixed strategies.   An important element in such negotiations is the fact-finding or technical work that is undertaken in preparation for any negotiation.   Technical discussions within international regimes can therefore provide a means of identifying joint gains from negotiations and thus facilitate success.

Conclusions

This chapter has set out to identify the key actors in economic diplomacy today, rather than provide a comprehensive treatment of each actor.   It confirms the position taken in the introduction, that there are today ever more actors in economic diplomacy.   This leads to the following broad conclusions:

- Not only are there more states and more bureaucratic actors within each of the nation states or regional bodies, but there are also growing tensions between different departmental interests that economic diplomacy must reconcile.   This reconciliation within the executive branches of government cannot be neglected in any study of decision-making.
- Legislative branches of government have generally played a lesser role in economic diplomacy in part because of a desire to 'keep politics out of international economic policy-making'.
- But the increased scope of economic diplomacy is creating real pressures for greater democratic accountability, as more and more interest groups see their domestic policy preferences influenced and in some cases undermined by international negotiations and agreements.

- Globalisation and the growth of global business representation and global civil society have also added a further dimension to decision-making in economic diplomacy that did not exist as late as the mid 1990s. Unless there is a general reversion to national policy autonomy, such 'global' or transnational actors are likely to continue to play a role.

The increased number of actors, the conflicts between different interests and the tensions between 'smooth', efficient decision-making, within a largely bureaucratic process, and the growing pressure for greater democratic accountability and transparency, all go to make the new economic diplomacy of the 2000s a more difficult and complex process.

Notes

1   See Milner 1992 for a discussion of this point.
2   See especially Putnam 1989, Milner 1997.
3   See Strange 1994.
4   See Woolcock 1998.
5   See the Consumers International Website for details of these organisations. www.consumersinternational.org.
6   See Scholte 2001.
7   See Klein 2000.
8   Green and Griffith 2002 distinguish between different types of global civil society body. Some are actively anti-globalisation. Others are more inclined to accept the market but seek to reform regulatory patterns to ensure it serves their purpose.
9   The point here is not to argue whether globalisation or domestic policy failings were more important in these cases, but to argue that the failures led to a perception that the liberal model was not the only answer.
10 In these cases European consumers saw the international trade rules developed in the Uruguay Round as blocking efforts to ban the use of certain products in food.
11 See the ICC website www.iccwbo.org.
12 See Haas 1992.

References

Green, D. and Griffith, M. (2002), 'Globalisation and its Discontents', *International Affairs*, vol. 78, no. 1, pp. 49-68.
Haas, P. (1997), *Knowledge, Power and International Policy Coordination*, University of South Carolina Press, Columbia, SC. See also *International Organization*, vol. 46, no. 1 (1992).
Klein, N. (2000), *No Logo*, Vintage Canada, Toronto.
Milner, H. (1997), *Interests, Institutions and Information: Domestic Politics and International Relations*, Princeton University Press, Princeton.
Putnam, R. D. (1988), 'Diplomacy and Domestic Politics: The Logic of Two-Level Games', *International Organisation*, vol. 42, no. 3, pp. 427-460.

Scholte, J. A. (2001), 'Global Civil Society' in Woods, N. (ed.), *The Political Economy of Globalisation,* St Martin's Press, New York.

Strange, S. (1988), *States and Markets; an Introduction to Political Economy,* Pinter, London.

Woolcock, S. (1998), 'European and American Approaches to Regulation; Continuing Divergence?' in Van Scherpenberg, J. and Thiel, E. (eds.), *Towards Rival Regionalism? US and EU Economic Integration and the Risk of Transatlantic Regulatory Rift,* Stiftung Wissenschaft und Politik, Eberhausen.

Chapter 4

The Practice of Economic Diplomacy

Nicholas Bayne

Building on the treatment of actors in Chapter 3, this chapter goes deeper into the practice of economic diplomacy, concentrating on what is done by national governments. It starts by analysing the activities of permanent officials or bureaucrats. These are still the people who conduct most international negotiations in economic diplomacy; and while formal decision-making powers may rest with ministers or legislatures, these powers are usually exercised on the basis of preparatory work done by officials. But as the chapter proceeds, it traces the interaction of bureaucrats with other state and non-state actors.[1]

The chapter begins with the story of the fifth International Tin Agreement (ITA) - an old story now, but a true one. Though an anecdote from the old economic diplomacy, it illustrates well both how different tensions operate within government and what methods are used to resolve them. The main body of the chapter is divided into three parts:

- The first goes through the sequence of **domestic decision-making** in government;
- The second analyses the process of **international negotiations** and relates this to the domestic sequence;
- The third examines strategies used in such negotiations that illustrate the interaction between domestic and international levels.

The conclusions relate both decision-making and negotiation to the tensions of economic diplomacy identified in Chapter 1.

The Story of the Fifth International Tin Agreement

The International Tin Agreement (ITA) came up for renewal for another five years in 1982.[2] The aim of the ITA was to iron out short term fluctuations in the world price of tin by the use of a buffer stock. The buffer stock manager sold tin if the price rose too high, bought tin if it fell too low and had a fund for this purpose. The intervention prices were set by the International Tin Council, composed of major producers and consumers of tin. The United Kingdom had always been a member of the Council. The key difference for the UK in 1982 was that policy towards the ITA had to be agreed unanimously within the European Community (EC).[3]

In 1982 Britain had separate Departments of Trade and of Industry, as is still the case in France and Canada; policy on the ITA fell to the Department of Industry. The officials concerned took the view that the UK should not join the new agreement. They argued that the effect of the Agreement over the years had been to keep the price of tin artificially high. This was bad for British industrial users of tin, who had to pay too much and were forced to seek substitutes. It was bad for the operators of British tin mines, who saw their market shrinking. Industry officials foresaw that upward pressure on the price would cause the ITA to collapse within three years.

Officials in the Foreign and Commonwealth Office (FCO) strongly disagreed with Industry and argued that Britain should join the new ITA, just as it had joined all previous tin agreements.[4]   The FCO was not convinced by Industry's economics. The Agreement had served its purpose well over 20 years, which suggested a fair balance of supply and demand. The FCO relied on political arguments in favour of joining. If Britain decided not to join, then the EC as a whole could not join; and with such a large group of consumers absent the Agreement could not survive. This would alienate the other Member States of the EC, most of whom wanted to join; it would alienate developing countries, who attached importance to this and other commodity agreements; in particular, it would alienate Malaysia, the largest tin producer. Britain had already had several rows with Malaysia in the early 1980s - Prime Minister Mahathir Mohammed had just come to power - and did not want another. FCO officials had firm instructions on that from Peter Carrington, then British Foreign Minister.

The Department of Industry and the FCO reached deadlock. So they looked for allies in other departments. The Department of Trade supported the FCO, as they were responsible for the UN Conference on Trade and Development (UNCTAD), which encouraged commodity agreements.[5] But the Treasury supported Industry, as they did not want Britain to pay money into an agreement that might collapse. So there was still an equal balance of forces.

As officials could not agree, the problem went to a Committee of Ministers, which brought in yet more departments. The Minister of Agriculture and his officials were against the tin agreement, as they did not like those commodity agreements that covered agricultural products.[6] But the Minister of Defence, like his officials, favoured joining it, as they hoped for defence sales to Malaysia. So both ministers and bureaucrats were split down the middle and there was still no decision.

In these conditions the problem had to go to the Prime Minister, then Margaret Thatcher, for her to arbitrate. She was known to be inclined against the Agreement, largely because the Americans, under President Ronald Reagan, had decided they would not join. But before she made a decision, she and Carrington went off to an Anglo-German summit, to meet Helmut Schmidt as Chancellor and Hans Dietrich Genscher as Foreign Minister.

The risks were high for the FCO at this summit, as Germany was the only other EC Member State that had doubts about the International Tin Agreement. If Germany should decide not to join, that would undermine the FCO's case, while strengthening Industry's position. Both Genscher and Schmidt were undecided when the summit began. In the event, Carrington persuaded Genscher that the right course was to join; Genscher then persuaded his chancellor Schmidt; and Schmidt persuaded Thatcher. Britain and Germany endorsed an EC position in favour of the new agreement, which was duly adopted and entered into force.

This episode reveals unusually starkly the tensions in economic diplomacy: between the Department of Industry's economic case and the FCO's political case; and between the FCO's international arguments and Industry's domestic ones. (As this was back in 1982, governments were still the only players. There was no requirement to involve other actors.) The episode also reveals how heads of government get involved, both as domestic arbiters in decision-making and as players on the international scene. Carrington's manoeuvre is also an admirable example of skilful two-level game diplomacy.

Was joining the Agreement the right decision? Here the passage of time provides the basis for a clear judgement. Three years later, the buffer stock fund overspent and became insolvent. The Fifth ITA collapsed, just as forecast, with heavy losses to the subscribing countries.

Decision-Making in Government: the Domestic Sequence

This part of the chapter looks generally at the process of decision-making by governments in economic diplomacy. It analyses the process as a sequence of six stages, mainly based on what happens in the British government, but noting significant differences with other countries where they are relevant. The six stages are:

1. Identifying the lead department.
2. Three levels of consultation:
   - Internal;
   - With outside forces;
   - Inter-departmental.
3. Political authority.
4. Democratic legitimisation.
5. International negotiation.
6. Ratification of agreement.

This sequential treatment is deliberately simplified, in two respects. First, some of the stages may happen simultaneously, in practice, not in succession. Second, the sequence may have to be repeated, in whole or part, as decision-making proceeds, either because of new domestic developments or because of its interaction with international negotiations. Economic diplomacy is rarely a linear process; it is an iterative and cyclical activity, which may go round the same course several times.

1: Identifying the lead department

The first stage in the domestic sequence is to identify the lead department for the subject in question. This is the department whose spokesmen will conduct international negotiations, whose minister will answer in the legislature and whose budget will bear any costs. In political diplomacy the lead department is almost always the foreign ministry. In economic diplomacy in developed countries this happens in the minority of cases. Usually the lead goes, by precedent and tradition, to a home department. Usually too the choice is obvious and well-established: the finance ministry leads on international finance, the agriculture ministry on external agricultural issues, the environment ministry on the global environment. The recent growth in the subject-matter of economic diplomacy does not affect this basic principle. This growth is usually the result of a domestic policy subject, like employment or education, becoming the subject of greater international pressure. This means that a home department is already available to take the lead.

This general principle requires some important qualifications, however, in relation to the role of foreign ministries and the treatment of international trade. In developed countries, when the foreign ministry gets the lead in economic diplomacy, it is usually for two reasons. One is where economic relations have an unusually high political content, so that economic diplomacy is mainly concerned with reconciling the first tension, between international economics and international politics. This applied in the past to economic relations with Communist countries and still largely applies to Russia. The other reason is where the subject covers a very wide range of external interests, with none predominating. Thus, while G8 economic summits cover trade and finance and the environment and other issues, the lead department, in Britain and most other member countries, is the foreign ministry. In developing countries, on the other hand, foreign ministries often have much greater authority in economic as well as political diplomacy and the power of home departments (except for finance ministries) is less developed.

International trade negotiations, being on the borderline between external and domestic policy, get varying treatment in different countries. Some favour the domestic aspects, others the international ones. In Britain, for example, the lead ministry is a large home department, the Department of Trade and Industry (DTI), that contributes to the formation of EU trade policy. The same applies in Germany, where trade negotiations fall to the Economics Ministry, and in France, where they are handled by part of the Finance Ministry. In Japan, however, the Foreign Ministry has the lead, not the Ministry for Economics, Trade and Industry (METI).[7] In Canada, Australia and New Zealand, responsibility for foreign affairs and international trade is integrated in a single department. Finally, in the United States and European Union (the two largest players in trade negotiations) responsibility is given to a separate body: the US Trade Representative (USTR), an agency of the White House; and the Directorate General (DG) Trade, recently detached from the DG External Affairs.

The lead department can be changed, though rarely. This can happen, for example, when governments change and redistribute Cabinet responsibilities. Up to 1997, the lead department for the British 'Know-How Fund', which provided technical assistance to Russia and other Central and East European countries, was the FCO. When the new Labour government came in, it promoted the department responsible for overseas aid, the Department for International Development (DFID), to full Cabinet status and transferred lead responsibility for the Know-How Fund to this department.

2: *Three levels of consultation*

The lead department then proceeds to consultation, on three levels: within the lead department itself; with outside forces; and with other departments. In practice these may all happen simultaneously and interact on one another.

Internal consultation. The lead department has to decide internally its negotiating objectives and tactics. Even in quite a small department there are likely to be opposing views; in large departments there can be serious differences. In the British DTI, the division responsible for preparing for a new round of international trade negotiations in the WTO will be keen to see trade barriers come down. But the division responsible for the textile industry may want to keep the barriers up, so that there is tension between international and domestic pressures. In Canada, as noted, foreign affairs and international trade are handled by the same department, so that international politics and economics have to be reconciled. The department must also resolve differences, indicated in Chapter 3, between the experts in the technical issues, who may regard their chosen subject of overriding importance, and more senior figures who are less expert but more aware of how the subject fits into the department's wider objectives.

Consulting outside forces. The lead department is likely to consult with a wide variety of forces outside central government. Sometimes the influence of these outside forces can become so strong that departments - whether deliberately or not - become dependent on them or even 'captured' by them. These other actors have already been analysed in Chapter 3. So this section contains only a brief review of their interaction with officials.

In economic diplomacy departments usually consult *business* interests, to get the views of those whose livelihood is affected by the activity concerned and to test how their policy ideas would be regarded by the markets. The pressure from business may be in conflicting directions. Small firms may have different interests from large firms. Ministries of agriculture listen to farmers, who want prices high, but also to the food-processing industry, who want their input prices low.

Departments increasingly consult *non-governmental organisations - NGOs.* In many fields, such as development, debt relief, environment, food safety, NGOs are powerful and articulate. NGOs usually become active because they are not content with the line being taken by government - and they are often opposed to business interests as well. It is a hard decision for government to judge how far to yield to them. They may be very vocal and committed, but only represent a minority view in the country at large.

Departments consult *expert opinion*, including academics. Issues in economic diplomacy are often very complex and technical and departments cannot carry all the necessary expertise in-house. Academic experts can be very influential. For example, the ideas behind the conversion of the GATT into the WTO essentially came from Professor John Jackson, an academic at the University of Michigan.[8]

In many subjects, integrating the position of *public bodies outside central government* is becoming an essential part of the consultation process. In international finance, central banks have always been involved. Now other regulatory authorities, eg for securities and insurance or for food safety, are becoming influential. Sometimes the responsible bodies are at sub-national level in federal systems. So state insurance regulators in the US and food safety authorities in the German Läender get involved in economic diplomacy.

At this stage the lead department will also consider how to involve the *media*, since consulting outside forces may have brought the issues into the public domain. This is another tricky decision for government. On the one hand the support of the media will be very important later on, to get popular backing for any international agreement reached. So it is worth preparing the media in advance. But if the government's position becomes publicly known at this early stage, it may be harder to change it later in the course of negotiation. So the usual practice is to brief trusted parts of the media 'unattributably'. That means the media gets the information and can publish it, but should not attribute it to the government or present it as a fixed government position.

Consultation between departments. The third level of consultation seeks to get a view agreed across the whole of government. As Chapter 3 showed, a comprehensive round of trade negotiations can involve almost every government department. But even before a more limited negotiation, for example on climate change, the British Department of the Environment,[9] in the lead, would consult the DTI, the Treasury, the FCO and the DFID. Each would have their departmental instincts: the DTI looking for the opportunities and costs for British business; the Treasury wanting to get value for money; the DFID concerned for the position of developing countries; the FCO seeking consistency with wider foreign policy. Each ministry would have their own contacts with outside forces - business, NGOs, academics and others. The energy industries, for example, would be closer to the DTI than to the Department of the Environment.

In a straightforward case, the lead department can get the assent of others by correspondence. Where there are conflicting views, these will be resolved at meetings of officials, called and chaired either by the lead department or by a neutral body. In Britain the Cabinet Office, under the Secretary to the Cabinet, often serves as neutral chair and secretariat in economic diplomacy, especially in European Union matters. Most other governments have comparable bodies.

If the departments concerned reach agreement on the negotiating position, this will typically be a compromise position. No department will obtain all its objectives, but each will have to adapt or abandon some. It is important that, once agreement is reached, departments give up those ambitions which are not covered by the agreed position, so that all parts of government say the same thing. This singleness of purpose is very important in effective international economic diplomacy, because it gives strength to a negotiating position. It is an aspect of economic diplomacy where Britain is generally thought to be very efficient. Geoffrey Howe, the British Foreign Secretary from 1983 to 1989, records in his memoirs the envy of his European colleagues: "Your British people", they would say, "are like the Kremlin. They all always say the same thing."[10]

But singleness of purpose of this kind has its downside. If agreement has been reached only with difficulty on a position which all can defend, it may become very hard to adjust it during negotiation. This is particularly evident in the European Union, where often the strain of producing an agreed position among 15 countries exhausts any possible negotiating flexibility.

3: Political decision

In the account given so far, permanent officials have driven the process. The next stage raises the process to the political level and involves ministers. This can be broken down into three distinct activities.

In the minimum requirement, officials submit their work to ministers for *endorsement*, to give it political authority. If officials have agreed a position, then usually simple ministerial endorsement can be obtained by the lead minister writing to his colleagues or reporting in Cabinet. Each meeting of the European Union's Council of Ministers, for example, begins with decisions taken without discussion, called 'A Points'.

The second activity for ministers involves *settling disputes*. Officials may be unable to agree; or ministers may not agree with their officials' advice. In that case ministers themselves have to meet and most governments have formal or informal machinery for this purpose. In Britain there is an established system of Cabinet Office ministerial committees; the problem could go to one of them or to a smaller, ad hoc group of ministers. Ministers will have somewhat different criteria for judgement than their officials and will be more responsive to parliamentary and popular pressures.[11] Where disagreement persists, even after ministerial discussion, then the head of government gets involved, to resolve matters and act as arbiter. Prime ministers' and presidents' time is precious, however, and departments will always try their utmost to settle matters without involving the head of government.

The third activity consists of ministerial *initiative*. This chapter has concentrated on ongoing economic diplomacy, when ministerial authority is sought only after the treatment of an existing issue by officials. But ministers may decide to launch new policies and intervene themselves much earlier in the sequence. In particular, heads of government can use their authority to drive forward issues, not waiting to be invoked as arbiter. Heads of government can increasingly draw on their own staffs - in the White House, the Elysée, the Federal German Chancellery and even No 10 Downing Street under Blair - and are using them in the place of lead departments, rather than entrusting the subject to a Cabinet colleague. This development of ministerial initiative is an aspect of the new economic diplomacy that will be explored further in the next chapter.

4: Legitimisation

In non-democratic governments, a decision by ministers or the head of government settles the matter. But in democracies a further process is required, to give the government's agreed position democratic legitimacy and to satisfy its accountability to its electorate. This normally involves a report to the elected legislature and possibly endorsement of the government's decision by a vote. In Britain this usually comes quite late in ongoing economic diplomacy. But elsewhere the elected bodies, especially the US Congress, could be involved much earlier. The report to parliament will usually be accompanied by formal statements and briefing material intended to be published in the press or other media. At this time the government announces its position formally and takes responsibility for it.

Both to the press and to parliament the government may not want to go beyond a general statement, without too much detail, so as to retain some flexibility in the later negotiation. The reaction of parliament and the press will have a stronger impact on ministers than on officials. So forces outside government, like business and NGOs, will try to influence government decisions through parliament and the media too, in addition to direct contacts with officials.

5: International negotiations

This completes the domestic decision-making sequence to prepare for an international negotiation. The actual negotiation can be left on one side at this stage - it will be considered later in the chapter. For the moment, the assumption is that the negotiation has run its course and international agreement has been reached.

6: Ratification of agreement

Once agreement is reached, a number of stages in the earlier domestic sequence are repeated. The lead department negotiator reports to the other departments concerned and seeks their concurrence. The lead department minister briefs other ministerial colleagues, to re-confirm the earlier political authority. The agreement is reported to parliament and, if necessary, legislation is introduced so that the government can meet the commitments it has taken. The government launches a media campaign to ensure the agreement wins public acceptance.

No government wants to find that the agreement it has struck internationally comes apart at this ratification stage. So governments take precautions in advance to avoid this danger. Sometimes these may be formal precautions, as when the US Administration seeks 'fast-track' authority from Congress, which means that Congress can either endorse or reject an agreement - it cannot amend its provisions. Most often international negotiators will adjust their tactics in anticipation of any problems with ratification. Even with these precautions, however, all negotiators are taking a gamble when they return to seek ratification for what they have agreed. These risks will vary from country to country, depending both on the general structure of government and the strength of the particular administration in power. This determines the size of the win-set available to the negotiator, as Putnam's analysis makes clear.

International Negotiations

This review of the domestic sequence in decision-making has deliberately left on one side what happens in international negotiations. It is now time to examine the international sequence and how it meshes with the domestic one. International negotiations can also be analysed in five distinct stages, which can sometimes be linear but will more often be iterative and cyclical, like their domestic counterpart. The stages are:

I.   Agenda-setting.
II. Mandating.
III. Negotiating to agreement.
IV. Adoption of agreement.
V.   Implementation.

I. Agenda-setting

Before any negotiation there will be an agenda-setting phase, which identifies what should be subject to international treatment. This phase can be lengthy - for example it took four years' preparation before the GATT was ready to launch the Uruguay Round. During this phase governments have usually not committed themselves to firm positions, as it coincides with the 'consultation' stage in the domestic sequence. This provides opportunities for outside forces, such as business and NGOs, to get their favoured subjects accepted on the agenda. It is often the occasion for the international epistemic communities described in Chapter 3 to establish an intellectual basis for the discussion, before the hard bargaining sets in. Once the negotiation proper begins, however, these outside forces usually have to withdraw, leaving only governments at the table.

An example of how business and academic experts may seek to influence agenda-setting relates to the Commonwealth Heads of Government Meeting (CHOGM) in Durban, South Africa, in late 1999. The CHOGM was held shortly before the world's trade ministers met in Seattle, aiming to launch a new trade round in the WTO. If the Commonwealth, with over 50 members, could decide a common line for Seattle, that should have quite an impact on the agenda to be agreed there. The Commonwealth Business Council (CBC), representing private business in Commonwealth countries, wanted the heads of government to agree at Durban on specific proposals for the new WTO round. The CBC commissioned a report from their academic advisers, who were Razeen Sally and Stephen Woolcock (co-author of this book) of the International Relations Department of the LSE. The CBC report was well received at Durban, and Commonwealth trade ministers were active at Seattle, though the meeting was a disaster for other reasons.

II. Mandating

Once the decision has been taken to launch the negotiations and the agenda is defined, the government representatives involved need a mandate to negotiate. This is provided by completing the later stages of the domestic sequence, to secure inter-departmental agreement, political authority and democratic legitimisation.

As the domestic decision-making procedures vary very widely between countries, so will the mandates given to negotiators. They will especially determine how much negotiating flexibility or 'slack' they will have. Negotiators from the United States and the European Union will normally have a tightly defined mandate, reflecting the complexity of their domestic decision-making. This will limit their win-set, in Putnam's terms, and make them hard negotiators. But negotiators from developing countries are often given much greater freedom of action and may be quite detached from the domestic process. Economic diplomacy is more often handled by foreign ministries and less integrated into domestic policy. Representatives of developing countries may operate independently of their capitals and take decisions on their own initiative.[12]

III. Negotiating to agreement

This is the core of the international process. Negotiating strategies are considered in more detail in the next section. But throughout this process the negotiator and his team, at least those from developed countries, will be checking the likely acceptability of the emerging results at the domestic level. For a delegation with only limited negotiating slack, this will be a constant, iterative process.

For example, European negotiators operating in Washington, eg at the IMF or World Bank, or in New York, eg at the United Nations, will take advantage of the difference in time zones. The domestic team in the lead department will receive at the start of the working day, in Brussels, Berlin or London, the negotiators' report and request for guidance sent overnight. They will have the morning to consult other parties, by telephone and e-mail or in informal meetings, before sending a reply out before the working day begins in the United States. Such activity will usually be confined to bureaucratic contacts. Consulting ministers or outside forces usually takes a little longer.

IV. Adoption of agreement

The negotiations, if successful, will conclude with an agreement. Before the participating governments will commit themselves to such an agreement and be ready to submit it to ratification, there is usually a more formal procedure than happens while the negotiations are in progress. There is often a pause between reaching agreement on a text (which may be **initialled** by the official negotiator) and giving formal assent to it (which may involve **signature** by a minister).

Depending on the subject, there will be different thresholds of adoption. Informal understandings on familiar subjects, based on voluntary cooperation, may not need to go beyond official level. But any agreement involving a formal commitment or a new departure in policy will usually require political authorisation by ministers. In some countries, such as the United States, the government may consult the legislature before adopting an agreement, to be sure that the subsequent ratification process will go smoothly.

V. Implementation

Once an agreement has been negotiated internationally and ratified domestically, then it has to be implemented. All governments taking part in an international agreement have an interest in seeing that other parties respect the agreement as faithfully as they do. The effectiveness of this will depend on the structure of the agreement and the institutions sponsoring it. For example:

- Agreements based on voluntary cooperation often rely on peer pressure to ensure implementation. In compact institutions like the OECD this can be effective, but in wider, more diffuse bodies like the UN commitments are easily evaded.
- Some voluntary agreements are self-regulating, especially where funds are involved. Countries following IMF programmes are not obliged to observe them - but they will not receive the desired finance if they fail to do so.
- Other agreements are based on formal rules and legal obligations. Failures of implementation are subject to dispute settlement procedures. These can apply bilaterally, in regional agreements (the EU or NAFTA) or multilaterally, especially in the WTO.

Implementation is thus a major factor in deciding between voluntary cooperation and formal rules - one of the key questions for this book.

Table 4.1   How Domestic Decision-Making and International Negotiation Fit Together

Domestic	*International*
1. Identifying the Lead Department	
2. Three Levels of Consultation	I. Agenda-Setting
3. Political Authority	
4. Legitimisation	II. Mandating
5. Negotiation	III. Negotiating to Agreement
	IV. Adoption of Agreement
6. Ratification	
	V. Implementation

After this analysis of both the domestic and international sequences, Table 4.1 illustrates how they fit together.

International Negotiating Strategies

This section returns to the actual process of international negotiation and examines some of the strategies used, especially those that try to take advantage of the domestic process in other negotiating parties.   This analysis of negotiating strategies is picked up again in Chapter 14, in the examination of international economic institutions and what governments want from them.   The strategies considered here are the following:

1. Bargaining among lead negotiators:
   - Value claiming bargains;
   - Value creating bargains;
   - Package deals.
2. Exploiting divided counsels.
3. Intervention by outside forces:
   - Direct intervention;
   - Indirect intervention;
   - Collective intervention.
4. Political intervention - playing the head of government card.

1. Bargaining among lead negotiators

Negotiators from the lead departments (who may have people from other departments at their elbows) come to the international table with a double aim: to maximise the area on which they can agree with the other parties; and to demonstrate the benefits of the agreement reached to their partners in the domestic process. As explained in Chapter 2, negotiations can be divided into two methods: distributive or value claiming bargaining - when party A gains, party B loses; and integrative or value creating bargaining, where everybody gains.[13]

Value claiming. It is instinctive to think of negotiators bargaining so as to gain advantage at the expense of the other parties; a gain for me means a loss for you. Popular opinion - like parliaments and the media - often looks at negotiations in this way. But if negotiators only concentrate on their gains, this is not likely to be a fruitful approach to economic diplomacy.   An agreement is unlikely to be concluded where one or more parties are clearly the losers. Such an agreement is unlikely to be ratified back home and, even if it were, the losing side would always look for ways to escape or overturn it. The US Administration fell into this error in its approach to a new round of negotiations in the WTO at Seattle in late 1999; it proposed an agenda which brought obvious gain to the United States but did not offer enough to anyone else.

Value creating. So the skilful negotiator looks for value creating deals where all parties can regard themselves as having benefited. The problem here is that simple deals of this kind are difficult to identify. For example, in climate change negotiations, it appears as though everyone would benefit from the reduction of emissions of greenhouse gases worldwide. But developing countries point out that this is in fact an unequal bargain, as reducing emissions inhibits their growth more than it does for mature industrial countries. So they have resisted such commitments without some compensation from rich countries.[14]

Package deals. In practice, many value creating agreements turn out to be packages of a number of value claiming deals. In each individual deal, some countries gain more than others, but the total package adds up in such a way as to provide something for everyone. So in the initial agreements to create the European Economic Community, the French feared that the common commercial policy would benefit German industry too much and insisted on provisions in agriculture and help for their ex-colonies as well. One consequence of this is that international economic negotiations quite often proceed by large package deals. For example, negotiating rounds in the WTO consist of a 'single undertaking', so that nothing is agreed until everything is agreed.[15] This strategy increases the chances of there being something for everyone, as well as the adverse consequences for a government that causes such a deal to collapse.

2. Exploiting divided counsels

It may be that the ingenuity of negotiators in constructing value creating bargains and package deals is not enough to close the gap. So governments look for ways to take advantage of the domestic processes in other parties. Each government in the negotiations knows that the others have been through a comparable process of consultation and political decision. A skilful negotiator looks for ways to exploit evidence of divided counsels in other governments.

One method is to play on known departmental rivalries. In some cases officials may feel closer to their colleagues from the same ministry abroad, whom they see as allies, than to officials from other ministries at home, whom they regard as rivals. Normally the Japanese government is very cohesive, but there is an interesting opportunity to use this tactic in trade negotiations, because the Foreign Ministry has the lead, rather than the Ministry of Economics, Trade and Industry (METI), which may therefore feel left out. The British Department of Trade and Industry (DTI) has close links with its sister ministry the METI and may find it more responsive than the Foreign Ministry to its arguments to get the Japanese position changed.

Even where there are no built-in rivalries, it is normal that the agreed position of a government is more limited than individual departments would prefer. In principle, departments should abandon their wider objectives and rally behind the agreed position. But many departments in practice cannot or will not abide by this discipline. They let it become known that they could accept or even prefer a different position. The British, as noted, are usually very disciplined internally and so are the French. Other countries are more given to fighting out their inter-departmental battles in public or at the negotiating table - such as the Americans and the Germans. This makes them obvious targets for others to exploit these divided counsels.

The same tactic can also be practised against the collective negotiating position of the European Union when the common purpose of the Member States is fragile. When Canada, in 1995, had a bitter dispute with Spain about fishing in the North Atlantic, the Spanish expected solid European support for their position, because the EU operates a Common Fisheries Policy. But within the EU, Britain and Ireland had the same complaints about Spanish over-fishing as the Canadians had. They ensured that the EU and Canada struck a deal which increased the discipline over everyone's fishing practices.

3. Intervention by outside forces

While governments try to take advantage of domestically divided counsels to move international decisions in their favour, outside actors - business, NGOs and others - may do the same. This too is part of economic diplomacy and three methods can be identified.

Direct intervention. With this method, a group outside government in one country tries to influence the government in another. An example of this happened in 1998 during negotiations before the Birmingham G8 summit on debt relief for low-income countries. Christian Aid, a leading British charity in the Jubilee 2000 Campaign that was lobbying for generous debt relief, correctly identified Germany as the main obstacle to agreement. It issued its supporters with postcards addressed to the German finance minister, printed with a text in German urging a more generous approach. 15,000 such postcards flooded into the German finance ministry, while a second wave targeted Federal Chancellor Helmut Kohl and the leader of the opposition, Gerhard Schroeder. It is rare for a direct approach of this kind to be effective immediately and the Kohl government did not change the German position while it was in office. But after Schroeder and the German Social Democrats (SPD) won the election of late 1998, one of their earliest acts in office was to reverse the stance on debt relief.[16]

Indirect intervention. The second method is where forces outside government in one country mobilise supporters outside government in another. For example, European and American insurance companies were very frustrated in the 1990s by the barriers to access to the insurance market in India, which was a government monopoly. Direct appeals to the Indian government had little impact. But the Western insurers learnt that Indian industry was equally frustrated, because it wanted better quality insurance cover than the government monopoly could offer. So Western insurers provided Indian industry with arguments to press their case with the authorities - with the effect that in December 1999 the new Indian government passed a law opening up the insurance sector to competition. A similar manoeuvre was tried at the Doha WTO meeting of November 2001, when the Indian trade minister was holding up agreement. The head of the British Confederation of British Industry (CBI), who was at the meeting, contacted his counterpart in India, pointing out that a failure to agree would hurt Indian business and urging that local pressure be brought to bear on the minister - though it is not clear if this had any effect.

Collective intervention. In the third method, groups outside government combine to exert pressure on governments together. For example, the WTO's negotiations on financial services twice came near to collapse, in 1993 and 1995, largely because of differences between the US and the EU negotiators. The US wanted too much, while the EU would settle for anything. Then a group of American and European financial service firms came to realise that they had a joint interest in a good result from the negotiations. So they exercised collective pressure on the European and American negotiators to work together - with the result that the negotiations concluded with an agreement in 1997.

Collective intervention is increasingly practised by the NGOs active in global civil society. This may include concerted lobbying of the staffs of international institutions, such as the World Bank. It may also manifest in the form of public demonstrations at the time of major international meetings, like European Councils or G8 summits.

4. *Political intervention - playing the head of government card*

The international strategies examined so far have been initiated by government officials or by outside forces. However, even in negotiations conducted by officials, ministers often intervene, though they are not themselves at the table. Internationally heads of government may try to break the deadlock when this persists at lower levels, just as they act as arbiters nationally. Now that heads of government, like Tony Blair and George Bush, often talk on the telephone, such intervention is becoming more common. This chapter therefore concludes with a few examples of intervention by the British Prime Minister.

These interventions range from the simple to the more ambitious. A simple intervention took place in 1999 when Blair telephoned his French counterpart, Lionel Jospin, over the French attempt to maintain a national ban on sales of British beef after a Europe-wide ban had been lifted. Blair appealed to Jospin for help, because of the political difficulties which the French move was causing him. (Jospin apparently replied that, if he helped Blair, he would have worse political difficulties of his own and the ban has remained in force.) In 2000 Blair intervened with US President Clinton to get British exports of cashmere taken off the list of products subject to American retaliatory trade barriers because of the EU policy on bananas. Blair argued to Clinton that the US was alienating its most likely ally in the European trade debate. He tried a similar approach to Bush in 2002, before the US imposed new tariffs on steel imports, but this was to no avail.

A more ambitious intervention took place early in 1999, again over debt relief for the poorest. Britain has always been a keen advocate of this policy, while Germany was initially reserved. As noted earlier, after Schroeder replaced Kohl in office, the Chancellor himself announced a reversal of policy on debt relief, taking a much more forthcoming approach.[17] However, the finance ministry was still the lead department for this subject in the German government and they continued to drag their feet.

At some point Blair contacted Schroeder to draw his attention to this, knowing that Schroeder was not on very good terms with his finance minister, Oskar Lafontaine. The result was that Schroeder removed the lead responsibility for this subject from the finance ministry and transferred it to his own department, the Federal Chancellery. The Chancellery moved the subject along much faster, and the Cologne summit produced a substantial agreement. This was another example of an advanced 'two-level game' move in economic diplomacy, comparable with Carrington's tactic described at the start of this chapter.

Conclusions

This chapter has analysed the methods adopted by governments today, in decision-making and negotiation, to reconcile the three tensions of economic diplomacy, as set out in Chapter 1. The main focus has been on the second tension - between domestic and international pressures.

The **domestic sequence of decision-making** is initially concerned with how governments reach common positions internally - the third question in Table 1.1. It provides both for the allocation of responsibility, at official and ministerial level, and a series of techniques for reaching agreed views, right up to the use of the head of government as arbiter.   This aspect mainly relates to the **efficiency** of government.   But as the domestic sequence proceeds, it increasingly focuses on **accountability** - the sixth question in Table 1.1 - by involving political authority, democratic legitimisation and ratification.

In the process, however, domestic decision-making also addresses the other two tensions, as follows:

- The task of reconciling the first tension, between international economics and politics, falls particularly on foreign ministries. They are regular players in the consultation process, though seldom in the lead except when external political factors are unusually strong.
- To reconcile the third tension, between government and other forces, outside actors, especially business, NGOs and the media, have to be integrated into the decision-making process, so that wider domestic pressures can be satisfied. Outside actors are involved not only in confidential consultations with officials but also in the more public lobbying of ministers and parliament. This is a growing trend, which will feature in future chapters.

In **international negotiations**, economic diplomacy looks for ways in which domestically agreed positions can be deployed successfully in international contexts - the fourth question in Table 1.1. The negotiators seek to maximise the scope of agreement in ways that will satisfy not only their own domestic backers but also domestic interests in their negotiating partners, since without that, the agreement will fail to secure the necessary ratification. They therefore look, in the first instance, for solutions which provide something for everyone. If such solutions are not readily attainable, negotiators look for ways in which the domestic processes in their partners can be turned to their advantage.

While much of this activity takes place among the circles of officials concerned with the negotiations, it can go wider and bring in the other strands of economic diplomacy:

- Ministers, and especially heads of government, try to advance agreement by introducing additional political arguments;
- Outside forces, like business, NGOs and epistemic communities, also seek to intervene directly, indirectly or collectively to change the course of the negotiations;
- The implementation of international agreements is relevant to question 5 in Table 1.1 - whether voluntary cooperation or formal rules work better.

Many of the practices involving officials described in this chapter, though still valid today, derive from the 'old economic diplomacy'. The next chapter focuses on the pressures acting on economic diplomacy in the 1990s and early 2000s and the strategies adopted in response to them. It looks at the rising involvement of ministers, non-state actors and international institutions and thus will provide a fuller analysis of the 'new economic diplomacy'.

Notes

1 This chapter, and this book generally, follows the European (and Japanese and Canadian) usage of 'ministers' and 'officials', rather than the American terms 'politicians' and 'bureaucrats'.
2 For an account of the operation of commodity agreements generally, see Spero and Hart 1997, Chapter 7.
3 On decision-making in European trade policy, see Woolcock 2000 and Johnson 1997. The common EC regime for commodity agreements, called 'Proba 20', was only agreed in early 1982, so that it did not apply when the ITA had last been renewed in 1977, even though the UK was already in the EC by then.
4 The author was the official mainly concerned in the FCO.
5 The rise and decline of UNCTAD is covered in Spero and Hart 1997.
6 At the time these covered cocoa, coffee, tropical timber and wheat.
7 The more familiar name for this ministry is the 'MITI' - Ministry for International Trade and Industry. The new name was only introduced in 1999.
8 The ideas in Professor Jackson's paper *Restructuring the GATT System* (Jackson 1990), especially pp. 93-94, were taken over almost exactly in the design of the WTO.
9 Since June 2001, this department's name has been the Department of the Environment, Food and Rural Affairs, replacing the Department of the Environment, Transport and the Regions. Before the Blair government took office in 1997, it was simply known as the Department of the Environment.
10 See Howe 1994, p. 447.
11 For a perceptive analysis of the differences between ministers and officials, see Aberbach, Putnam and Rockman, 1981.

12 This is illustrated in the case studies by Patrick Rabe (Chapter 13) and Ivan Mbirimi (Chapter 15).
13 For further analysis, see Odell 2000, pp. 31-34. Odell prefers the terms 'value claiming' and 'value creating'.
14 The absence of commitments by developing countries in the Kyoto Protocol of 1997 was one of the main reasons for American opposition to it, first in Congress and then by the Bush Administration that took office in 2001.
15 For the single undertaking in the Uruguay Round, see Croome 1995 and Preeg 1995. The single undertaking is also part of the mandate agreed for a new WTO round at Doha in 2001.
16 For details of what happened at Birmingham, see Bayne 1998.
17 This was done in an article in the *Financial Times* on 21 January 1999.

References

Aberbach, J., Putnam, R.D. and Rockman, B. (1981), *Bureaucrats and Politicians in Western Democracies*, Harvard University Press, Cambridge, Mass. and London.

Bayne, N. (1998), 'Britain, the G8 and the Commonwealth', *The Round Table*, no. 348, pp. 445-457.

Croome, J. (1995), *Reshaping the World Trading System: A History of the Uruguay Round*, World Trade Organization, Geneva.

Howe, G. (1994), *Conflict of Loyalty*, Macmillan, London.

Jackson, J. J. (1990), *Restructuring the GATT System*, Royal Institute of International Affairs, London.

Johnson, M. (1998), *European Community Trade Policy and the Article 113 Committee*, Royal Institute of International Affairs, London.

Odell, J. (2000), *Negotiating the World Economy*, Cornell University Press, Ithaca and London.

Preeg, E. (1995), *Traders in a Brave New World*, University of Chicago Press, Chicago.

Spero, J. and Hart, M. (1997), *The Politics of International Economic Relations*, 5th edition, St Martin's Press, New York.

Woolcock, S. (2000), 'European Trade Policy' in Wallace H. and Wallace W. (eds.), *Policy-Making in the European Union*, 4th edition, Oxford University Press, Oxford.

Chapter 5

Current Challenges to Economic Diplomacy

Nicholas Bayne

This chapter seeks to identify the new demands made on economic diplomacy, as a result of developments at the close of the 20th century and the start of the 21st. It analyses the strategies devised in response to these demands, which form part of 'the new economic diplomacy'. It looks forward to the initial set of case studies, in Chapters 6-9, as well as the treatment of multi-level economic diplomacy in Part II of the book.

The chapter is structured as follows:

- *First,* it analyses two powerful forces shaping economic diplomacy - the end of the Cold War and the advance of globalisation;
- *Second,* it distinguishes the good side of globalisation from its darker side and looks at the efforts made by governments to manage globalisation;
- *Third,* it sets out four distinct strategies for economic diplomacy, developed in response to the new challenges.

In conclusion, this analysis will aim to show how the new strategies endeavoured to reconcile the three basic tensions in economic diplomacy identified in Chapter 1: between politics and economics; between domestic and international pressures; and between governments and other actors.

Forces Shaping Economic Diplomacy: The End of the Cold War

Impact in Europe

The end of the Cold War and the collapse of communism in Europe came with bewildering speed. In the space of twelve months, from mid-1989 to mid-1990, all the countries of Central and Eastern Europe threw off communism, without provoking any intervention from the Russians. The Berlin Wall came down on 10 November 1989, opening the way for the two halves of Germany to be reunited. The Soviet Union itself survived for only another 18 months, till the end of 1991; then it crumbled apart into its component republics. They too threw off their communist regimes and became independent states.

Governments in the West were completely taken by surprise by this. But when they grasped the scale of the historic changes taking place, there was a strong desire to help the countries escaping from communism to put in place working democracies and market economies. Western governments concluded that the collapse of communist regimes marked the victory of the open economic system over the rival centrally planned system. So they looked for a means of transition for ex-communist countries, to convert them to the sort of economic system they themselves practised.

The institutional innovations were fairly modest. The European Bank for Reconstruction and Development (EBRD) was created, especially to build up the private sector in all ex-communist countries of Europe and the former Soviet Union. These countries all joined the IMF and World Bank and the IMF created its Systemic Transformation Facility to help them. The European Union (EU) rapidly offered economic agreements to all these countries and began preparing to admit its Central European and Baltic neighbours to membership. This process proved much longer than was expected at the time. It took the entire decade, till the European Council at Nice in December 2000, for the EU to reach the decisions necessary to enable these new members to be admitted later in the 2000s. Even so, the Central European and Baltic countries, having gone down as a result of the collapse of communism, were all on the way up again by 2000. The prospect of EU membership, though deferred, remained an economic incentive.

But EU membership was not available to Russia or to the rest of the former Soviet Union outside the Baltic States. The conversion of Russia into something approaching a market economy proved much more difficult. Some other parts of the former Soviet Union were even worse off. Very large sums of money were provided to Central and Eastern Europe, especially Russia, over the 1990s. Some have even argued that this flow of finance was comparable in scale to the Marshall Plan, though this is hard to substantiate. Most of what went into Central Europe was well used, but a lot of what went into Russia was wasted.[1]

For much of the 1990s, the countries of former Yugoslavia were largely left out of account, while they were being torn apart by civil war. But from 1999 they became beneficiaries of a new Stability Pact for South-Eastern Europe, which was even extended to include Serbia, once President Milosevic was removed from power. So all the ex-communist countries entered the 2000s with prospects of hope and support, though some started from a very long way down.

International consequences

The consequences of the end of the Cold War spread much wider than Europe. Up till 1989 there had been two opposing poles of attraction in the international economic system: the open regime of the West and the centrally planned system of the East. Many developing countries tried to position themselves between the two, advocating the 'New International Economic Order'.[2] With the collapse of communism in Europe, however, there was no longer a real alternative to the open competitive system favoured by the West. All governments engaged in international economic relations had to learn to play by its rules.

Up till then the major international economic institutions had not had worldwide membership. Many communist countries stayed out of the IMF, World Bank and GATT. Major developing countries, like Mexico, stayed out of the GATT too. Now these institutions all became truly global, like the United Nations. By the early 2000s, even China and Taiwan had gained access to the WTO, though Russia still had further to go.[3]

As a result of all this, 'interdependence', which had prevailed in the West in the 1970s and 1980s, was extended over the whole world and was recognised as 'globalisation'. This will be analysed in the next part of this chapter. But one more consequence of ending the Cold War needs to be registered: its complex impact on the balance between international politics and economics.

In many respects the impact was beneficial. Helping ex-communist countries into the international economic required that the system itself be in good repair. This factor helped to bring the Uruguay Round to its eventual conclusion and contributed to the good result from the 1992 environment conference at Rio. Other effects were less helpful, when concern with its enlargement to the East distracted the European Union from its wider international responsibilities.

More generally, as economic contacts expanded and became more complex with globalisation, the scope for economic disputes expanded also. In some ways these disputes became harder to resolve. While the Cold War was on and the West faced a security threat from a hostile super-power, unity was at a premium and economic disputes were not allowed to endanger it. There were some serious economic disputes during this period , but they were kept within limits.

With the Cold War over, this restraint on the pursuit of economic disputes was removed. In the mid-1990s, the United States threatened sanctions against European firms doing business in Cuba, Libya, and Iran. The peaceable Canadians forcibly arrested a Spanish fishing-boat in international waters. The list of trade disputes between the US and Europe continued to lengthen. It seemed as though removing the pressure of a common external threat made it harder for the Western countries to agree among themselves.

The Advance of Globalisation

The end of the Cold War, as already recorded, greatly accelerated the advance of globalisation. This was not something new or sudden. It had been gathering pace ever since the end of World War II. But the Cold War, while it lasted, had distracted attention from it. Now the advance of globalisation became the dominant economic current of the age.[4]

Since the 1940s, but especially in the 1990s, governments have progressively removed the barriers to external competition: sometimes as a result of international negotiation; but just as often by unilateral action, as they recognised the benefits of the open system. First the barriers come down to trade across borders, so that trade grows faster than output. Then restrictions on direct investment are removed, so that foreign firms, including multinationals, become embedded in the economy. Foreign direct investment grows faster than trade. Then controls are lifted on foreign exchange transactions and capital flows. These grow fastest of all, outstripping the direct needs of trade or investment while being extremely mobile. During the 1990s, world trade grew about twice as fast as world output; flows of foreign direct investment grew twice as fast as trade; and foreign portfolio investment grew twice as fast as direct investment - though of course growth varied from year to year.[5]

International activities thus come to occupy more and more of a country's economy. This brings greater efficiency but greater scope for friction with other countries.   The process is stimulated by new technologies - aviation, telecommunications and information technology. These shrink distances, speed up transactions and accelerate the pace of change.

Globalisation shifts economic power from governments towards the private sector. Private firms, which can operate internationally, enjoy advantages denied to governments, whose powers derive from their national electorates. Firms spread their operations around the world, wherever they can find the best competitive conditions of capital, technology and qualified people.

Governments in turn do all they can to create competitive conditions in their countries. This affects mainstream economic policies, by requiring tight budgets and low inflation. It also affects areas which had hitherto been immune from outside pressures, like social policy and education. Governments themselves adopt many practices of the private sector - to the point of privatising many activities formerly under state control. In this way governments become more efficient; but they erode yet further their powers and resources.

The net effect of all these changes through the 1990s was some great advances in wealth and prosperity. The star performers, in different ways, were the United States and the countries of East Asia, including China but not Japan. Governments sought to create the conditions for growth and then let the private sector get on with it - which they did: cutting costs, improving quality and choice, generating new investment, developing new markets and creating new jobs - though often destroying other jobs in the process.

The Good Side of Globalisation

The features described so far provide the basis for what might be called the good side of globalisation. This delivered some striking achievements in the early 1990s. These can be perceived in retrospect, though the decade began with a mild recession in the G7 countries and with much more friction between the United States and Europe than anyone expected.

International trade

The first major achievement was the conclusion of the Uruguay Round of trade negotiations in the GATT, which should have finished at the end of 1990.[6] In fact they dragged on for three more years, mainly because the US and the EU could not agree on agriculture. The Round was finally concluded on 15 December 1993. The agreements concluded were ratified over the year ahead and came into force in 1995. During the extra three years most ex-communist countries were absorbed into membership and developing countries became much more active than before. The outcome was a richer crop of agreements, both for the substance and the structure of the multilateral trade system.

The Uruguay Round agreements converted the weak GATT into the strong WTO. The key points were:

- Whereas the GATT applied mainly to trade in manufactures, the WTO agreements covered all areas of trade, including agriculture and services.
- Whereas the GATT only applied selectively to developing countries, WTO agreements applied equally to all members.
- The WTO embodied a much stronger mechanism for the settlement of trade disputes than the GATT had. Its judgements were binding on the disputants and could not be evaded.
- The WTO provided for a regular schedule of ministerial meetings and a system for periodic evaluation of its members' trade policies.

The Uruguay Round was, if anything, too successful for its own good. It brought international disciplines deeper than ever before into politically sensitive areas like agriculture. This sharpened the tension between domestic and international pressures. Its dispute settlement mechanism became the only judicial process operating in the international economic system and got dragged into disputes that were not really about trade at all. These factors created problems that will be considered later in this chapter.

Environment

The global environment regime was a second area of achievement dating from the early 1990s. A lot of issues came together at the UN Conference on Environment and Development (UNCED) at Rio in June 1992. The Rio Conference concluded binding international agreements on climate change and biodiversity; to these were added an earlier agreement on preserving the ozone layer and later ones on deserts and on oceans. Global environment issues of this kind needed agreements in which all countries participated. These were only possible in conditions of globalisation, after the Cold War was over. However, converting the broad commitments made at Rio into agreed policy actions proved harder and took longer than had been expected.

Economic growth and stability

The good side of globalisation largely prevailed for the first three-quarters of the 1990s. In its Economic Outlook published in the spring of 1997, the IMF gave one of its most optimistic forecasts ever. It foresaw buoyant prospects for growth everywhere, with inflation very subdued and 'no dangerous tensions in the world economy'.[7] Growth would be well spread around the world, averaging 3% in industrial countries, over 6% in developing countries and 5% even in sub-Saharan Africa. It looked as if globalisation was bringing benefits to everyone.

The Dark Side of Globalisation

This happy picture was shattered on 2 July 1997, the day on which Thailand ceased to defend its exchange rate. The Thai currency and economy collapsed and the crisis rapidly proved contagious, dragging down Korea and Indonesia as well. The IMF had to launch huge rescue operations, mobilising a total of $115 billion for those three countries. Other economies in East Asia were also affected, such as Malaysia and Hong Kong, and there was widespread economic hardship. Once the crisis in Asia seemed to be under control, the contagion spread further. The rouble collapsed in August 1998 and Russia defaulted on its government debt. In October 1998, Brazil needed a massive bail-out from the IMF.

These financial crises were not without precedent. Mexico had also suffered a currency collapse in late 1994. But the Mexican crisis, like earlier international financial crises, had been caused mainly by the mistakes made by the government. The 1997 Asian crisis was the first to be caused by the mistakes of the private sector; by imprudent domestic borrowers and irresponsible foreign lenders. That was the critical difference; and it introduces the dark side of globalisation.

These are some of the darker features of globalisation:

- International financial markets develop on a scale that outstrips the ability of governments or central banks to control them. By 1995 the estimated daily turnover in the foreign exchange markets had risen to $1 trillion, far in excess of the reserves held by central banks. In 2000 it was estimated at $1.3 trillion. So financial crises, when they happened, easily became contagious.
- The removal of economic barriers, which benefited the honest citizen, created opportunities for the criminal too. Crime thus became an international business and had to be added to the agenda of economic diplomacy, whether it concerned drug trafficking, money laundering or, most recently, the financing of terrorism.
- Globalisation is a Darwinian process. Those who succeed are rewarded; those who fail or make mistakes are punished, whether firms or governments. As the IMF concluded: "The pressures of globalisation ...have served to accentuate the benefits of good policies and the costs of bad policies".[8] Here small, poor countries were at a great disadvantage. A few profited from globalisation, including populous countries like China and India; but many did not, especially in Africa, and these risked falling yet further behind.
- For all these reasons, there was growing unease among electorates about the impact of globalisation. People feared the impact of external forces outside their control. Governments could not wholly allay these fears and sometimes felt obliged to give in to popular pressure. NGOs also appeared which regarded globalisation as a malign influence, combining old protectionist instincts with more recent fears. They began to mount violent demonstrations against meeting of international institutions and against summit meetings, which they regarded as symbols of globalisation.[9]

Managing Globalisation

As the darker features of globalisation were recognised, they called forth efforts to manage the process, with varying success. This section looks at these efforts, focusing in turn on the financial system; the trading system; the global environment; and the poorest countries.

The financial system

Severe though the financial crisis was in 1997-98, it did not shake the international system as such, nor the major developed economies.[10] Japan was the most vulnerable, as it had grown very slowly through most of the 1990s. But the United States remained remarkably buoyant and greatly helped the recovery of Asian countries by absorbing large amounts of their exports. European countries, though less dynamic than the US, continued to grow steadily; eleven EU members combined to launch the single European currency, the euro, from the start of 1999. In Asia too the countries stricken by the financial crisis, whether directly or indirectly, soon recovered and resumed their rapid growth.

The financial crisis stimulated a tremendous amount of activity to construct 'new financial architecture'. This was intended to deter future upheavals and to help those attacked if crises did come. The main features were:

- Stricter standards for the economic data that countries supplied to the IMF and for the conduct of their economic and monetary policies.
- New sources of IMF financing, especially for those at risk from a contagious crisis.
- Closer collaboration among financial regulators and supervisors.
- Efforts to involve the private sector in financial rescue operations.
- A continuing debate about the proper roles of the IMF and the World Bank in a world of plentiful private capital and floating exchange rates.

Much of this activity was more like plumbing than architecture and still depended on the existing institutions, the IMF and the World Bank.[11] But it gave new responsibilities to these institutions, which enabled them to go wider than simply making loans, on conditions, to developing countries. Calm returned to the financial scene - but no one was sure if this was a lasting stability or merely a period of remission before the next crisis.

The IMF tempted fate once again by offering a buoyant forecast for the world economy in 2000. But it was obliged to scale it back as the US economy slowed down sharply. There were fears for a time that the US recession of 2001 might unbalance the entire system, especially as its emergence coincided with the terrorist attacks. Both the stockmarket and the dollar exchange rate looked over-valued, with the risk of a destabilising correction. But the underlying strength of the American economy enabled growth to revive in spite of these difficulties. The financial system was not disturbed, even though serious crises broke out in Turkey and Argentina. Massive IMF support was able to rescue Turkey, but could not prevent the collapse of Argentina at the end 2001. Even so, Argentina's troubles did not prove as contagious for the system as the Asian crisis.

The trading system

After the Asian crisis, the financial system clearly needed attention. But the trading system, managed by the WTO, seemed robust. It helped the Asian countries to export their way out of trouble, while new WTO agreements were reached on IT products and financial services during 1997. But the Asian financial crisis had called in question the economic strategy based on opening up to competition and the private sector, by showing that in some conditions liberalisation could lead to disaster. It encouraged the critics of globalisation, both in developing and developed countries.[12]

After five years' experience, many developing countries were concluding that the Uruguay Round agreements were biased against them in favour of rich countries. For example, most developing countries had to act in 2000 to implement commitments on intellectual property, while rich countries still had another five years of protection for textiles. The developed countries were trying to get new issues on to the WTO agenda, like labour standards and the environment, which would raise extra barriers to the exports of developing countries. The functioning of the WTO itself was also a cause for complaint for developing countries. Negotiations often took place in restricted groups, where they were not present. Proceedings in the dispute settlement mechanism demanded costly legal fees.

In the developed countries, governments had not realised that the Uruguay Round agreements, by going deeper into the domestic economy, would generate new types of resistance. This resistance focused especially on concerns outside trade, such as labour standards, the environment and food safety. NGOs argued that the WTO was overriding these concerns in its mission to remove barriers to competition. The United States and the European Union became involved in intractable disputes on these subjects. They did not realise how this added to the discontent of the developing countries, who not only feared new trade barriers would be raised against them but were suspicious of the claims of NGOs mainly based in the rich countries.

That was the background to the WTO ministerial meeting in Seattle. It was intended to launch a new round of trade negotiations. Such a round was necessary, both to continue work left incomplete in the Uruguay Round and to address new sorts of trade, especially electronic commerce. But the G7 countries were not agreed among themselves on what the agenda should be. The EU, with Japan, proposed a 'comprehensive round', in which the difficult topic of agriculture could be buried among other issues. The US wanted a much shorter agenda, focusing on non-trade items like labour and the environment.

In the event, the Seattle meeting was a disaster and broke up on 3 December 1999 with nothing agreed. The hostile NGOs demonstrating in the streets claimed the credit for this failure. But the real reason was the rebellion of the developing countries against what they were being offered, both on substance and procedure.

The blame must largely go to the G7 and other rich country governments, for not having understood the demands which globalisation made upon them.[13]

After Seattle, there were low-key attempts in the WTO to keep alive the idea of a new round. But no decisive action could be taken till there was a new US President. George Bush the younger and his chief trade negotiator, Bob Zoellick, came to office with good free trade credentials. Zoellick cooperated well with the EU Trade Commissioner, Pascal Lamy, to neutralise bilateral disputes and agree a common approach to the round. This was endorsed by the G8 summit at Genoa in July 2001, in terms calculated to appeal to developing countries.

The WTO ministerial at Doha, in November 2001, held in the shadow of the terrorist attacks on the US, succeeded in launching a new trade round, where Seattle had failed. The preparations in Geneva were much more inclusive; the agenda included many items of interest to developing countries; and both the EU and US showed flexibility of a kind that had been lacking two years before. So the multilateral trading system was back in operation again. But this good result was soon clouded by evidence, especially from the United States, of the persistent strength of domestic protectionist measures. The US Administration, as it struggled to obtain trade negotiating authority from a divided Congress, felt obliged to raise tariffs on steel and increase the subsidies offered to its farmers. In the European Union, the Commission's proposals to reform the CAP, to reduce its impact on trade, met with strong opposition from Member States, while there were other signs of protective reflexes.[14]

The global environment

The 1992 Rio summit was a high tide of the environment movement. Thereafter, progress in turning general principles into firm national commitments, for example in climate change and biodiversity, was hampered by deep divisions between Europe and North America. This was partly for reasons of geography, but mainly because policy in Europe was driven largely by 'green' popular movements, while in the United States, and even in Canada, private industry was more influential. Meanwhile, developing countries were reluctant to take any commitments that might hold back their economic growth, holding the industrial world responsible for the problems.

So progress was spasmodic at best. The Kyoto Protocol of 1997, which set targets for reductions in greenhouse gas emissions, was always unpopular in the United States and Bush came out in open opposition to it. The Cartagena biosafety protocol, which implemented the biodiversity agreement, was agreed only with great difficulty in Montreal in early 2000 - but the US had not even signed the main agreement. Responsibility for different subjects was scattered around the United Nations in a confusing way. Developing countries sought financial support for any environmental commitments they made. So the preparations for the World Summit on Sustainable Development in 2002, which would mark ten years after the Rio Conference, focused more on development than environmental issues. Even so, there were a few signs of hope. The scientific basis for environmental threats was becoming more widely accepted. There were even some positive results from international action, notably from the Montreal Protocol to protect the ozone layer.

The poorest countries

One of the darkest aspects of globalisation is that it appears to be good for the rich but bad for the poor - unless active measures are taken to help those left behind. During the 1990s targets were set at UN conferences for reducing world poverty (defined as those living at under $1 a day), getting children into primary education and lowering child and maternity mortality rates by the year 2015. Reviews conducted in 2000 showed good progress in East Asia, especially China, but disappointment elsewhere, while parts of Africa had gone backwards.[15]

Poor countries needed more help, but did not always get it. Official aid transfers, measured as a proportion of rich countries' GNP, declined in the 1990s.[16] In correcting their budget deficits to become more competitive, many countries cut their aid spending together with everything else. Many countries also diverted money to Eastern Europe that would otherwise have gone to the developing world. There was much more foreign private finance available for investment. But very little of that went to poor countries, except for very large ones like China or Indonesia.

There were some measures taken for the benefit of the poorest, notably in debt relief. During the 1990s the IMF and World Bank, together with Western creditor governments, brought in several initiatives to reduce the debt of poor countries, encouraged by the worldwide campaign of NGOs called Jubilee 2000. The Cologne G8 summit in June 1999, promised deeper and faster relief than was available before. By July 2001, 23 of the 41 Heavily Indebted Poor Countries (HIPC) eligible for relief were in the programme. Political unrest and civil war were the main factors holding back most of the remaining debtor countries, chiefly in Africa.

Debt relief, in any case, addressed only one corner of the problem of world poverty. The rich countries still had more to do to enable the poorest nations to share in the benefits of globalisation. There was some recognition of this as the 2000s began. Successive G8 summits, from Okinawa in 2000 to Kananaskis in 2002, launched new initiatives of potential benefit to the poorest countries, working closely with the private business sector and with NGOs. They encouraged making information technology (IT) available to poor countries and enabling them to leap-frog several stages of development. To reduce the damage done to poor countries by infectious diseases, they launched the Global Fund to fight AIDS, malaria and tuberculosis. They agreed an Africa Action Plan to underpin the efforts being made by African leaders themselves, in the New Partnership for Africa's Development, to improve political and economic governance and stimulate development.

Many poor countries gained little from the international trading system. The G7 members had promised, at their Lyon summit back in 1996, to offer duty and quota free access to the products of the poorest countries, which amounted to only 0.5% of world trade. This commitment was slow to be implemented. But in the early 2000s the United States (through the Africa Growth and Opportunity Act), the European Union and Canada all moved to improve market access for the poorest countries.[17] There were also promises to reverse the decline in official aid flows. At the UN meeting on finance for development in Monterrey, Mexico, in March 2002, the United States undertook to increase its aid by $5 billion per year over five years. Parallel commitments by the European Union and Canada raised this total to $12 billion per year in additional aid, half of which could go to reforming African countries. But while this new concern for poor countries was encouraging, lasting results would depend on the promises being made at Monterrey and the G8 summits actually being honoured, so as to improve the progress towards the poverty targets set in the 1990s.

New Strategies in Economic Diplomacy

This review of recent developments has explained the challenges facing the new economic diplomacy. The final part of this chapter pulls together the demands made on governments by globalisation and examines the strategies adopted by states in conducting their economic diplomacy in the early 2000s, so as to meet these challenges.

The demands of globalisation

Globalisation, as Chapter 3 has already shown, expands the range of actors in economic diplomacy. But it also makes other heavy demands on governments:

- First of all, globalisation has greatly increased the *range and variety* of economic diplomacy. Many new subjects became active in the 1990s and 2000s: converting former communist countries to prosperous market economies; a much wider trade agenda; the global environment; new international financial architecture; debt relief and other programmes for the poorest countries; issues which arouse strong popular concern, like food safety, international crime and - since 11 September 2001 - terrorism and its financing.
- Second, the *domestic penetration* of economic diplomacy has intensified. Most of the issues covered by economic diplomacy up to the 1980s, for example in trade policy, concerned policies applied at the border. Now they extend to domestic policies, such as industrial subsidies, support for agriculture and rules of establishment for services firms. All of these have become subject to international discipline, while there is debate about how trade should be linked to labour and environment standards. This evolution emerges from the two case studies on international trade politics, in Chapters 6 and 9.
- Third, the range of *countries active* in economic diplomacy has expanded and now spans the entire globe. Till the Cold War ended, most of the communist states were outside the system. Many developing countries were also inactive. But developing countries participated fully in the Uruguay Round and now want to make the WTO work for them. They will not automatically endorse proposals advanced in the IMF by the G7 finance ministers.[18] The international

system and its institutions now have to operate for the benefit of the entire membership, not just the richer ones.

- Fourth, the *power of governments* to shape events is shrinking, in relation to other forces, and so are the resources available to them. More power is shifting to the private business sector and to other actors. This is not necessarily a bad thing. The Cold War showed that regimes that clung onto control over their economies eventually collapsed. But the decline in relative power and resources means that governments are often trying to do more with less.

These new challenges sharpened all three of the tensions underlying economic diplomacy: between economic and politics; between international and domestic pressures; and between governments and other forces. Governments looked for new ways to improve decision making and negotiation in economic diplomacy, which would compensate for their relative loss of power and address international economic issues which touched their domestic interests ever more closely.

In the course of the 1990s and early 2000s governments developed four strategies, all of which remain active today:

- Involving ministers;
- Bringing in non-state actors;
- Greater transparency;
- Using institutions.

These will be examined in turn.

Involving ministers

The first strategy is the greater involvement of ministers, thus raising the political profile. Up to the 1980s economic diplomacy, outside the European Community, was left largely in the hands of bureaucrats. In the old GATT, for example, ministerial meetings were rare. But the WTO has a regular cycle of ministerial meetings every two years or so, while smaller, informal ministerial groups helped to prepare for Doha. Ministerial committees at the IMF and World Bank used to be routine affairs. Now they are more purposeful and are surrounded by satellite ministerial meetings of smaller Groups of Seven or Ten or Twenty. The heads of the GATT and the OECD used to be former officials. Now they are former ministers - Renato Ruggiero and Mike Moore at the WTO, Donald Johnstone at the OECD.[19]

Ministers make their contribution not only at international meetings but by their impact on the domestic decision-making process. What do they contribute, when they launch their own initiatives, rather than relying on the work of their officials?

- *First,* as they are usually elected themselves or otherwise linked to the electoral process, ministers are closer to the people and have more domestic political authority. Their involvement enhances accountability and is a natural response to the greater penetration of international issues into national economic life that globalisation brings.

- *Second,* while bureaucrats prefer continuity - their instinct is to adapt an existing technique or institution - ministers are innovative. They put a premium on change and new ideas.
- *Third,* ministers tend to be impatient: they want quick, visible results.
- *Fourth,* ministers put a lot of weight on public presentation. They advocate greater transparency (see below) but may sometimes settle for show rather than substance.

Heads of government - prime ministers and presidents - have even more to contribute than their departmental ministers. As compared with other ministers, their authority is greater; their democratic legitimacy is often more direct; and they are better equipped to reconcile domestic and international pressures. This is fully documented in the case studies in Chapters 7 and 8 on the evolution of the G7/G8 process.

So there is a natural expansion of international summit meetings in economic diplomacy. When the G7 summit and European Council were founded in the 1970s, they were almost alone of their kind. Now international economic summit meetings happen all the time. The EU has regular summits with the US, with Canada and with Asian countries. Asia-Pacific Economic Cooperation (APEC) has summits and so do the participants in the future Free Trade Area of the Americas (FTAA). The UN has occasional summits on special issues, on the Rio environment model. And when heads of government meet bilaterally - Zhu Rongji in Washington or Tony Blair in Tokyo - economic issues make up most of their agenda.

Bringing in non-state actors

The second strategy is to involve players from outside central government in the decision-making process. The different actors have already been covered in Chapter 3, so that only a brief account is needed here to explain why and how this grew so fast in the 1990s and early 2000s.

As governments' own powers and resources shrink, they try to get the private sector to share their burdens. In development, for example, they encourage the use of private capital for investment; and they work with charities like Christian Aid and Médécins sans Frontières. In financial crises they do not want IMF money simply to bail out private banks - they want the banks themselves to contribute. Many governments of developed countries include representatives from business and NGOs in their delegations to international conferences, as the EU and UK did at the Seattle and Doha WTO meetings.

In all this, the challenge for the government is to spread the load while remaining in control of the agenda. This has so far been easier to manage with private business than with the NGO community. There are now established parallel business channels for economic diplomacy at several levels aimed at facilitating agreement between governments. In a regional context, the Trans-

Atlantic Business Dialogue encourages closer EU/US relations; the Pacific Business Council meets alongside APEC. Multilaterally, firms may subscribe to the Global Compact initiated by the UN Secretary-General.

As for the NGOs, their violent demonstrations, which started at the WTO meeting in Seattle and led to a death in Genoa at the 2001 G8 summit, make the headlines. But the street protests are only the visible part of the iceberg and do not reflect the positive influence of the NGOs. In fact, NGOs exert much more influence through their direct contacts with governments and with institutions, such as the UN on the environment and the World Bank on development issues.[20]

Greater transparency

The third strategy in economic diplomacy is the drive for greater transparency - for better information, greater clarity and more publicity. The pressure for this comes both from within government and from outside. It follows from the greater involvement of ministers and from the participation of NGOs, since both seek and use publicity to mobilise support for their objectives.

NGOs in their campaigns give high priority to transparency. They complain about the secrecy of negotiations and want more public scrutiny. Governments seek to respond to this, so as to counter popular anxieties about globalisation. Institutions like the IMF and the WTO are responding to pressure to become more accessible to the public and to explain their activities better.

Transparency means different things in different policy areas. In the new financial architecture, the IMF requires governments to observe codes of openness about their economic policies; governments in turn require banks to do the same about their operations. The argument is that with greater transparency financial operators would not make unwise investments and governments would be able to anticipate financial crises. Similarly, transparency is integral to many of the agreements in the WTO. In services, for example, the barriers to trade in practice consist of regulations. If these regulations are obscure or ill-defined, that amounts to an obstacle to competition.

Transparency is a useful strategy, but it raises some problems. Transparency can on occasion be the enemy of fruitful negotiation. In many ways, negotiation is like courtship: there is usually a period of private exploration and preparation before the parties are ready for public commitment. In negotiations governments make tentative proposals to see what responses they produce - and may later withdraw or modify them. All this is harder if conducted in public. Chinese Premier Zhu Rongji, when in Washington in April 1999, made proposals on trade policy going well beyond what had been authorised before he left Beijing. He was damaged back home not only because Clinton turned him down but because the Americans made his proposals public - via the internet.

Using institutions

The fourth strategy is the greater use of international institutions. Where governments' individual powers are shrinking, it makes sense to act collectively whenever possible. The years after World War II, up to the 1960s, were active in institution building, both globally and regionally. The next two decades were barren in comparison, with the G7 summits as virtually the only innovation. But the 1990s have seen a wave of new institutions and the transformation of old ones.

Among global institutions, the WTO was essentially new, far more than the successor to the GATT. The Rio process produced a network of new environmental bodies linked to the UN. These have not yet coalesced into a World Environment Organisation, though some argue for this. In finance, the 'new architecture' has left the IMF and World Bank largely unaltered in their basic structure. But there has been extensive innovation round their edges and the process of change may not be complete.

Among sub-global, plurilateral institutions, the EBRD, launched in 1991, was wholly new. During the 1990s the G7, since 1998 the G8, mutated from an annual summit meeting into an apparatus of distinct groups in finance, environment, employment, energy, crime and many other things. The OECD took on new members and the Commonwealth has found an economic vocation, centred on the problems of the poorest and the smallest countries.

But it is at regional level that the institutional growth has been most striking: NAFTA in North America, Mercosur in South America, the ASEAN Free Trade Area (AFTA) in South-East Asia and similar, if less ambitious, groups in South Asia, Southern Africa and the Caribbean. Some of the new regional groups have a very wide geographical scope: Asia-Pacific Economic Cooperation (APEC) goes all round the Pacific rim; the Free Trade Area of the Americas (FTAA) covers the whole Western Hemisphere. This growth continues in the 2000s, with new initiatives in Asia and the decision to convert the loose Organisation for African Unity (OAU) into the African Union.

In Europe, the EU deepened its economic integration during the 1990s in ways which had strong international impact, with the completion of the single market, the reform of the Common Agricultural policy (CAP) and the launch of economic and monetary union (EMU). As well as preparing for its own enlargement Eastwards in Europe, the EU reached out to its neighbours in the Mediterranean; and it went through two cycles of new relations with North America, with the Transatlantic Declarations of 1990 and the Action Plans of 1995-96.

The change is not just in the number and range of institutions. It is also in the way governments make use of them in support of their domestic objectives. They do not just use the institutions to extend their reach internationally, but also to endorse and justify their domestic actions and to share the burden of politically difficult decisions. As governments reduce their ability to intervene nationally, through privatisation and deregulation, they become keener on international rules, for example in telecommunications or financial regulation or even in agriculture. There is, however, an unsolved problem over resources. The institutions, like other players in economic diplomacy, are often asked to do more with less.

All this activity reinforces the multi-level nature of economic diplomacy. While countries may still conduct their economic diplomacy bilaterally, they may also mobilise a whole range of different institutions - regional, plurilateral and multilateral - and use them for a variety of functions. Multi-level economic diplomacy, which takes advantage of the different levels and the interaction between them, provides the main content of Part II of this book.

Conclusions

This chapter has examined the new challenges to economic diplomacy in the 1990s, stimulated by the end of the Cold War and the advance of globalisation. As the demands on governments increased, but their relative power shrank, they resorted to new strategies in their domestic decision-making and international negotiations. It remains to see how these strategies help to reconcile the different tensions in economic diplomacy: between international economics and politics; between international and domestic pressures for both efficiency and accountability; and between governments and other forces.

Involving ministers - and heads of government - is partly intended to reconcile politics and economics. The end of the Cold War, at the beginning of the 1990s, mounting concern about the poorest countries, as the decade ended, and the response to the terrorist attacks of 11 September 2001 all required a fresh balance between politics and economics. This, for example, has moved the G7/G8 summits in new directions. But ministers and heads of government also have greater capacity than their officials to reconcile conflicting domestic and international pressures by virtue of their political authority. They enhance accountability through their obligations to parliament and the electorate. They are likewise better equipped to deal with outside forces, because of their democratic legitimacy and their involvement with domestic politics and the public at large.

Bringing in non-state actors is a direct response to the tension between government and outside forces. Governments co-opt business, NGOs and others into their domestic decision-making in order to engage them and forestall potential opposition, though they need to take care against being 'captured' by them. The same process is beginning in international negotiation: environmental NGOs and epistemic communities are advising the UN; private banks and debt relief campaigners are engaged with the IMF. The involvement of non-state actors is also an essential part of the process of reconciling domestic and international pressures because it widens the scope of accountability.

Greater transparency is linked to the two previous strategies, as it responds to problems perceived both by ministers and by some outside actors. To that extent it contributes to reconciling governments and other forces. It can help in reconciling domestic and international pressures, when it improves accountability. But it can also hinder the process, when it makes negotiation harder by premature disclosures.

Using institutions is a natural response to the advance of globalisation. It is used to make economic diplomacy more efficient and responsive to the new demands generated by globalisation. It has become a favoured strategy for governments in reconciling domestic and external pressures, as will emerge from many of the chapters in Part II of this book. This accounts for the revival of institution building during the 1990s. But this strategy can have its political drawbacks, if the institutions are perceived to have a 'democratic deficit'. Then the improvements in efficiency are offset by a loss of accountability. This strategy can engage some outside actors effectively, but it can alienate others, like the obstructive demonstrators in Seattle and Genoa.

While Chapter 4 took ongoing economic diplomacy as its starting point, this chapter has focused on the causes and the main features of the new economic diplomacy. Taken together, they serve to introduce the case studies in the next four chapters. The first pair of these examine the historical development of decision-making and negotiation between the 1940s and the 1990s, concentrating on the multilateral trading system and the growth of the G7/G8 summits. The second pair of case studies introduce the first practitioner authors, one representing government and the other from a representative NGO. They look at the same subjects in reverse order, providing analyses of the summits and of international trade politics as perceived in the early 2000s. These case studies, like the others in this book, provide illustrations from real life of the analytical and theoretical concepts introduced in Chapters 1 and 2.

Notes

1   Stiglitz 2002 contains serious criticisms of IMF-sponsored policies in Russia during the 1990s. But he is better at saying what the IMF did wrong than at explaining how they could have done better.
2   On the New International Economic Order, see Spero and Hart 1997, Chapters 6 and 7.
3   For a fuller analysis of this process, see Bayne 1994.
4   The literature on globalisation is very extensive. This analysis draws chiefly on Cable 1999, Held and others 1999, Hirst and Thompson 1997, Gilpin 2001 and Woods 2001. Some scholars - especially those called 'sceptics' by Held and others - point out that globalisation dates back to the late 1800s and early 1900s. It was interrupted by the two world wars and, in some respects, such as movement of labour, has not regained its original intensity.
5   This is well illustrated in Cable 1999, Figure 1.1. The pattern in the early 2000s has been more erratic.
6   The official history of the Uruguay Round is in Croome 1995. Preeg 1995 gives a more reflective analysis. Ostry 1997 sets the results in a historical context and looks forward.
7   See IMF 1997.
8   See IMF 1997, p. 72f.
9   The first meeting to be the target of mass demonstrations was the WTO ministerial conference at Seattle in December 1999. The next targets were the meetings of the IMF and World Bank in 2000, first in Washington and then in Prague. Attention was then extended to summit meetings: the European Councils in Nice (December 2000) and Gothenburg (June 2001); the Summit of the Americas (Quebec City, April 2001); and the G8 summit (Genoa 2001). See Green and Griffith 2002.

10 The most dangerous moment came in October 1998, with the collapse of an American hedge fund with heavy exposure in Russia. But the Federal Reserve mounted a rapid rescue operation, while maintaining confidence by easing monetary policy.
11 For useful and compact analyses of the new architecture, see Eichengreen 1999, Evans 2000 and Kenen 2001.
12 The works of Dani Rodrik examine the political and social consequences of globalisation in both developed (Rodrik 1997) and developing countries (Rodrik 1999).
13 For analyses of Seattle and its consequences, see Bayne 2000b and Bhagwati 2001.
14 There were other examples of reluctance within the EU to opening up to wider competition in the early 2000s. Germany managed to frustrate new rules on take-overs, France continued to protect its public utilities and the liberalisation of financial markets met considerable resistance.
15 For an account of these and other international development targets, see DFID 2000, especially Figures 1.1 and 1.2.
16 Aid was often made dependent on poor countries following structural adjustment programmes agreed with the IMF and World Bank. But these programmes attracted criticism - see Killick 1995 and 1998.
17 The American actions benefited mainly African countries, with parallel benefits in the Caribbean, where, however, there are few of the poorest countries. The most radical action was taken by the European Union, which admitted all products (except arms) from least-developed countries free of duties and quotas from March 2001. There are transitional periods, however, for rice, sugar and bananas. Canada announced a similar programme in June 2002, excepting only eggs, poultry and dairy produce.
18 The G7 finance ministers proposed to the IMF in 1994 a new issue of Special Drawing Rights (SDRs) and expected this to be endorsed automatically. But the other members threw it out as not being generous enough.
19 These senior international posts are now filled not only by ex-ministers but by former heads of government: Supachai at the WTO, succeeding Moore; Gro Harlem Bruntland at the WHO; and Ruud Lubbers as the UN High Commissioner for Refugees.
20 A useful examination of the relations between NGOs and international economic institutions is in O'Brien and others 2000.

References

Bayne, N. (1994), 'International Economic Relations After the Cold War', *Government and Opposition*, vol. 30 no. 4, pp. 492-509.
Bayne, N. (2000b), 'Why Did Seattle Fail: Globalisation and the Politics of Trade', *Government and Opposition*, vol. 35, no. 2, pp. 131-151.
Bhagwati, J. (2001), 'After Seattle: Free Trade and the WTO', *International Affairs*, vol. 77, no. 1, pp. 15-30.
Cable, V. (1999), *Globalisation and Global Governance*, Royal Institute for International Affairs, London.
Croome, J. (1995), *Reshaping the World Trading System: A History of the Uruguay Round*, World Trade Organization, Geneva.
DFID (2000), *Eliminating World Poverty: Making Globalisation Work for the Poor*, White Paper on International Development Presented to Parliament by the Secretary of State for International Development, Stationery Office, London.
Eichengreen, B. (1999), *Towards a New International Financial Architecture*, Institute for International Economics, Washington.

Evans, H. (2000), *Plumbers and Architects,* FSA Occasional Papers, Financial Services Authority, London.

Gilpin, R. (2001), *Global Political Economy: Understanding the International Economic Order,* Princeton University Press, Princeton and Oxford.

Green, D. and Griffith, M. (2002), 'Globalisation and its Discontents', *International Affairs,* vol. 78, no. 1, pp. 49-68.

Held, D., McGrew, A., Goldblatt, D. and Perraton, J. (1999), *Global Transformations: Politics, Economics and Culture,* Polity Press, Cambridge.

Hirst, P. and Thompson, G. (1999), *Globalisation in Question,* 2nd edition, Polity Press, Cambridge.

IMF (1997), *World Economic Outlook, May 1997,* International Monetary Fund, Washington.

Kenen, P. (2001), *The International Financial Architecture: What's New? What's Missing?* Institute for International Economics, Washington.

Killick, T. (1995), *IMF Programmes in Developing Countries: Design and Impact,* Routledge, London and New York.

Killick, T. (1998), *Aid and the Political Economy of Policy Change,* Routledge, London and New York.

O'Brien, R., Goetz, A. M., Scholte, J. A. and Williams, M. (2000), *Contesting Global Governance: Multilateral Economic Institutions and Global Social Movements,* Cambridge University Press, Cambridge.

Ostry, S. (1997), *The Post-Cold War Trading System: Who's On First?* University of Chicago Press, Chicago and London.

Preeg, E. (1995), *Traders in a Brave New World,* Chicago University Press, Chicago.

Rodrik, D. (1997), *Has Globalization Gone Too Far?* Institute for International Economics, Washington.

Rodrik, D. (1999), *The New Global Economy and Developing Countries: Making Openness Work,* Overseas Development Council, Washington.

Spero, J. and Hart, M. (1997), *The Politics of International Economic Relations,* 5th edition, St Martin's Press, New York.

Stiglitz, J. (2002), *Globalisation and its Discontents,* Allen Lane, London.

Woods, N. (ed.) (2001), *The Political Economy of Globalisation,* St Martin's Press, New York.

Chapter 6

The ITO, the GATT and the WTO

Stephen Woolcock

The aim of this chapter is threefold. First and foremost it aims to provide an illustration of how the theoretical analysis discussed in Chapter 2 can be applied to a specific set of negotiations. Second, it gives a summarised history of the origins of the trading system and the factors that shaped the creation of the post-Second World War trading system, and as such provides something of an historical foundation for discussion of more current trade issues in the other chapters of the book. Third, the chapter compares the negotiations that led up to the failure of the ITO and the creation of the GATT with those that concluded the Uruguay Round and created the World Trade Organization.[1]

The chapter discusses the central questions that would need to be addressed in a comparison of trade diplomacy over time, and therefore provides a reference point for considering how economic diplomacy may also have changed (or not) over the past 50 years.

The chapter looks primarily at the period between 1941 and 1950. In 1941, for the first time, the nature of the post-war trade regime was discussed between the United States and Britain as one of the elements of the Atlantic Charter. October 1950 was when President Truman finally withdrew the legislation implementing the ITO from the US Congress and thus effectively killed the idea of a comprehensive global trade organisation for forty-five years. By way of comparison the chapter takes the trade negotiations during the Uruguay Round between 1986 and 1994. The comparison is not the failure of the ITO with the success in creating the WTO, because the actual creation of the WTO did little to change the trading system. What changed the trading system in the 1990s was the substance, in terms of enhanced market access, rule-making and institutional changes. These changed as a result of the Uruguay Round negotiations not simply through the formal establishment of the WTO.[2]

The chapter first goes over a few methodological questions, before recalling the factors identified in the theoretical analysis set out in Chapter 2, that one would expect to shape the outcomes of the relevant negotiations. The chapter then tells the story of the negotiations leading up to the failure of the ITO and discusses which factors appear to explain the course of the negotiations. A brief summary of the Uruguay Round negotiations is then provided.[3] The impact of the factors identified in the theoretical framework on the Uruguay Round are then discussed, before the chapter concludes with a comparison of the two sets of trade negotiations and some thoughts on what they tell us about the evolution of economic diplomacy.

Methodological Questions

Telling a story or developing theory?

As mentioned in Chapter 1, there are two approaches to seeking to understand economic diplomacy, as in other areas of international political economy (IPE) and international relations (IR): to explain what happened; or to develop theory inductively and then use empirical case studies to determine whether the theory is correct and how it might be refined. Economic historians focus on explaining why things happened the way they did. The danger of this approach is that historians may first of all get caught up in controversy over what actually happened and why. Second, a series of case studies, without any means of comparison, makes generalisation, such as on the nature of economic diplomacy and how it is changing, difficult or risky. Political scientists, at least many of those in the United States that have led in looking at the factors shaping foreign economic policy, tend to focus on developing theory in order to be able to say something about patterns of behaviour and possibly what might happen if a certain set of conditions exist. This second approach is based on inductive theory and hypotheses supported by empirical studies. The danger with this latter approach is of falling between two stools. On the one hand it may not be possible to develop a theory that is applicable without reducing the analysis to a limited number of key variables. At the same time using empirical studies to develop the 'science' or theory, may result in a less than complete coverage of the substance of negotiations.

Defining the case study

As in all historical case studies, the choice of period is important. By selecting a period one can skew the findings towards a particular result. For example, consider two different hypotheses on the nature of trade diplomacy:

- Trade diplomacy is influenced by precedent and by cooperation between governments in international institutions (an institutional or functionalist view);
- Trade diplomacy is shaped by the most powerful states, especially by hegemons (a realist view).

If one were to take a period from 1920 to 1950, one would find that technical work on trade undertaken in the League of Nations during the 1930s provided the models for future GATT and ITO negotiations.[4] Likewise, the Reciprocal Trade Agreements Act, adopted by the United States in 1933, influenced the nature of the post-war trade regime. The regime was thus based on reciprocity rather than on unilateral liberalisation, as was the case with the British-influenced regime prior to 1900. If, on the other hand, one looks at the period from 1945 to 1950, one might conclude that US leadership or hegemony was the only factor shaping the trade agenda.

A balanced approach

The purpose of this volume is not to develop a theory of economic diplomacy, nor to simply provide a list of case studies in economic diplomacy. The aim is to find a balance between the two approaches discussed above in which it is possible to say something about the factors that help form economic diplomacy and how they have changed, but also provide some useful substantive knowledge on trade policy and diplomacy.

The Potential Factors Shaping the Outcomes on the ITO and the GATT

As Chapter 2 set out, there are a number of factors that could shape trade negotiations. There are what we called the systemic factors in Chapter 2, such as *power relationships* between states. This goes for the influence of relative power relationships to shape outcomes, in the sense that the more powerful states could be expected to shape the agendas and results of trade negotiations. It may also be true in the sense that trade policy, like other policies, may serve the realist aims of states to enhance their power relative to other states. Realists would also argue that trade agreements will fail if they threaten national sovereignty.

Concern with relative power may have an impact in the sense that *strategic factors* may have a bearing on the trade policy chosen by a country. For example, it has been argued that agreement in trade negotiations is facilitated between allies or when a group of countries faces a threat from a potential superpower competitor.[5] The strategic explanation of trade policy outcomes would, for example, argue that agreements are more likely during the Cold War because of a desire for the western, liberal democracies to show solidarity in the face of competition from Soviet or Chinese communism. Another theory based on the power of states, namely hegemonic stability theory, argues that trade agreements are more likely to be concluded, or trade regimes established, when there is a *hegemonic power* (such as the United States) with the will and ability to shape outcomes. In theory dependency theory might also be applied to trade policy. During the early period of our comparison there were few developing countries involved in forming the GATT, so it might be argued that a group of core industrialised countries formed the system in their own interest. Finally, institutional approaches might help to illustrate the differences between 1947, when there were no functioning institutions governing international trade, and 1995, when there was fifty years of experience of cooperation within the GATT and other institutions.

Chapter 2 also discussed domestic factors, such as *societal and state centred* explanations in economic diplomacy. In trade policy these take the concrete form of national sectoral interests, such as the balance between sectors of the economy seeking protection and those interested in liberalisation. Alternatively societal approaches might compare the relative weight and influence of business (capital) and consumers or organised labour. The growing role of civil society NGOs also fits easily into a societal based approach which compares the positions of key interests. *National institutional factors* will also influence outcomes. For example, it has been argued that divisions within government (between the executive and legislative branches in the United States) was one reason the US adopted the GATT but not the ITO.[6] A less obvious domestic factor shaping trade outcomes might be the degree of scope or discretion given to negotiators by national political interests, whether these are embodied in legislatures or in other forms of interest representation.

It has been argued that the greater the 'negotiating slack' (ie discretion granted to negotiators), the less likely it is that trade agreements will be ratified and thus successfully concluded.[7] Alternatively, the dialogue between national ministries or departments with differing preferences will shape outcomes. A case in point would be the contrast between the US State Department interested in strategic goals such as reconstruction in Europe and containing Soviet influence in Europe, and the US Department of Commerce interested in export markets for national industries.

We also saw that *ideology* or shifts in the prevailing paradigm shaping national policies may have an impact. A comparison between 1947-51 and the Uruguay Round provides a comparison between a period when the Cold War was beginning to one when capitalism had been accepted by virtually all countries. Did the absence of ideological conflict between communism and capitalism facilitate the conclusion of the Uruguay Round or make it harder? Have other ideological divides, such as between free trade and sustainable development, reflected in the post Uruguay Round debate rather than the negotiations of the Uruguay Round itself, only become apparent because of the absence of the old ideological divide that influenced most of the 20th century?

Finally, what role did individuals play during the two periods? Personalities such as Cordell Hull, the committed free trader in the US State Department may have shaped the outcome in the late 1940s. Perhaps individual negotiators had an impact by judgements at key times in negotiations. Instinctively one would expect individuals to have less of a role in the 1980-90s because as Chapter 3 has shown there were far more actors around than in the rather select groups that negotiated the GATT and the ITO.

Linkage has also been identified as a potential factor in outcomes.[8] In trade policy this means, in practice, linking progress in one area with that in other policy areas or sectors. There are multilateral 'rounds' of negotiation, rather than continuous negotiations, in part because negotiators have found it helpful to negotiate packages. This permits all negotiators to come out of negotiations with successes and, in terms of negotiating process, enables negotiators to overcome zero-sum or value claiming negotiations and opt for outcomes that benefit all. There may, of course, be other linkages between trade policy and other policy areas, perhaps non-economic issues. In the case of the early debates on the post-war trade regime, for example, the US could have linked its aims in trade with aid for Britain during the whole of the 1940s.

If decision-makers in government are preoccupied with political crises or other pressing issues, this may also affect outcomes. For example, it has been argued that the US Congress was preoccupied with Marshall Aid and NATO when the ITO legislation was due for ratification.[9] Likewise, the end of the Cold War in

Europe in the late 1980s and its impact on European politics has been seen as a distraction for the European governments at a critical stage in the Uruguay Round negotiations.[10]

The ITO and the GATT

Background to the negotiations

The negotiations on the ITO must be understood against the background of the economic recession of the 1930s and the war. The recession taught policy-makers a clear lesson that beggar-thy-neighbour policies were damaging for all. Prior to 1914, trade and investment had been broadly liberal under British leadership. Diplomacy was almost exclusively political diplomacy. The 1914-18 war shook the foundations of economic liberalism. America overtook Britain in economic muscle and became the world's leading creditor, but it was not ready to assume leadership of the international economy.

The 1920s and 1930s saw efforts to check the growth of economic nationalism and establish a trading regime, but these failed. In 1922 the Genoa ministerial conference sought but failed to reduce barriers to trade. In 1927 the World Economic Conference reached agreement on a detailed programme based on non-discrimination, tariff reductions, the removal of quantitative barriers to trade and the ending of export subsidies. But this was negotiated by trade officials and was not supported by their political masters. A high level meeting in October 1927 did agree to a convention on tariff reductions balanced by an escape clause, but the requisite number of countries did not ratify this and it also failed.

The economic depression of the 1930s made things worse. In 1930 the League of Nations produced proposals for a one year truce in tariff wars followed by progressive reductions in tariffs. But in May 1930 the US Congress passed the Smoot-Hawley Tariff Act, which raised US tariffs to higher levels still and provoked Britain to finally break with free trade and support the introduction of imperial preferences in 1932. In 1934 the US began to reverse its policy of high tariffs with the passage of the Reciprocal Trade Agreements Act (RTAA). This was not unilateral free trade but trade liberalisation based on reciprocal reductions in tariffs. It took Congress out of trade policy and gave the officials in the Administration more control over the process.

By the end of World War II most economies were in ruins, except the United States, which accounted for more than 50% of world industrial output, had a balance of payments surplus of $11bn (in 1945 prices) and, with Canada, was the only creditor. Elsewhere countries introduced controls on trade and currency in order to preserve the limited resources they had and many countries moved towards large-scale nationalisation.

The positions of the major actors

In these circumstances the United States sought increased trade and reconstruction to provide export markets for its products and avoid surplus capacity. It wished to achieve this through sector-by-sector and country-by-country tariff reductions in line with the aims of the RTAA; these would then be applied on a non-discriminatory or 'most-favoured-nation' (MFN) basis to other countries. The US was committed to private enterprise and opposed much of the national planning in Europe. US exporters wanted an end to trade preferences, especially the British imperial preferences, which affected most of their export markets. Ideologically the US was deeply opposed to discrimination in trade, which it saw as the source of much of the political friction of the 1930s. Finally the US sought a rules-based trading regime in which there would be continuous negotiations to reduce tariffs and other barriers to trade.

Britain and France placed priority on national economic reconstruction, full employment and the introduction of social policies in health and education. Such domestic political goals took precedence over wider strategic aims. Economic planning was seen as a means to this end and short term restrictions on trade were considered necessary to achieve these aims.

Latin American countries, such as Brazil and Argentina, had been able to capture markets during the war and wished to use this as a springboard to promote industrialisation. The emerging countries, such as India, were determined to establish their independence and also sought protection for infant industries. The USSR was not to participate in any of the post-war trade negotiations and opposed any intrusion into its relations with its East European satellites. Germany and Japan played no part until the early 1950s.

The Atlantic Charter and Lend Lease

The first negotiations on the post-war trade regime began in 1941. The Americans wished to get the British to commit themselves to ending imperial preferences during the negotiations of the Atlantic Charter. This was resisted by Churchill, who was conscious that the right wing of his Conservative Party wished to retain the preferences at all costs and saw the US aim as an attempt to break up the empire. The Labour party members of the coalition government were also determined to put full employment before free trade. On the other hand, the British were in no position to deny the US what it wanted and so compromise wording was found in Article 4 of the Atlantic Charter. John Maynard Keynes held talks with Dean Acheson to persuade him not to pursue the ideological commitment to liberal multilateralism of Cordell Hull. The Article, as agreed, committed the parties to:

> endeavour, with due respect to existing obligations, to further the enjoyment of all states, great or small, victor or vanquished, of access on equal terms, to the trade and to the raw materials of the world which are needed for their economic prosperity.

'Respect to existing obligations' meant imperial preferences and 'equal terms' meant non-discrimination.

Similar issues arose in the negotiation of the Lend Lease agreements, in which there was an obligation in Article VII:

to promote open trade and reduce tariffs... which is the foundation of liberty and welfare... and to the elimination of all forms of discriminatory treatment...

The intention in the wartime planning was for the future trade regime to run in parallel with that for the monetary regime. But things did not go as smoothly. While negotiations continued on money, and finally led to the Bretton Woods agreements in July 1944, the talks on trade stalled, mainly due to differences between the US and British positions. Early in 1943 the British government initiated a proposal for the creation of a commercial union. This was proposed by James Meade, one of the leading British economists, and was developed and endorsed by an interdepartmental committee led by the Treasury.

The main element of this proposal was for sweeping horizontal reductions in tariffs. All tariffs would be reduced by a set percentage, in what has been called a formula approach. If the US tariff reductions were big enough, it was thought possible to get support, in Britain and in its main Commonwealth partners - Australia, Canada and South Africa - for phasing out imperial preferences. This was at odds with the majority view in the Democratic-controlled Congress, which was that tariff reductions were good provided they were not radical and took place on a sector-by-sector basis. The commercial union also included proposals to end agricultural export subsidies, which the US resisted because much of the New Deal support for farming took the form of price support. Without export subsidies US agricultural production could not be sold abroad. (Paradoxically this has been exactly the kind of support provided for European agriculture that the US has opposed, since the introduction of the CAP.) But the commercial union appealed to the officials in the Administration, especially the State Department, who favoured liberal trade and sought a means of breaking the deadlock.

An inter-departmental committee, chaired by the State Department, produced its own proposals in October 1943 - the Washington Report - which incorporated the idea of a commercial union. At this point the British cabinet checked any further progress. In the course of 1943 it had become more committed than before to planning rather than free trade as a means of post-war recovery. But this did not stop the Executive Committee on Foreign Economic Policy in Washington from producing concrete proposals for a multilateral convention on commercial policy. This envisaged tariff reductions based on horizontal or sectoral negotiations.

Preparing for an International Trade Organisation (ITO)

In 1945 the US produced further proposals for 'the Expansion of World Trade and Employment'. These proposals were essentially the first draft of the ITO Charter and comprised:

- Tariff reductions; the elimination of all preferences; non-discrimination in taxes and domestic regulation; common principles for customs valuation, anti-dumping duties and countervailing duties; transparency; subsidies to be subject to international consultation. (These are the principles of what later came to be the GATT.)
- No distortions to trade by public enterprises (limited coverage in the GATT).

- Provisions to prevent distortions to trade by international cartels (lost with the ITO).
- Provisions to limit market distortion by commodity agreements (favoured by raw material exporters such as Australia and Canada but opposed by the US).
- The creation of an international trade organisation as an integral part of the United Nations.

At the end of 1945 US and British officials found a compromise which would in effect mean that tariff preferences would continue, but be reduced progressively through product-by-product negotiations, rather than sweeping horizontal reductions.

The United States proposed a conference on international trade and development and produced the draft of the ITO. It invited 15 other countries to participate in the preparatory conference in London in 1946. These included Britain and its colonies and dominions - Australia, Canada, New Zealand, South Africa and India - France, Holland, Belgium and Luxembourg, Russia, Cuba, Brazil and China. Chile, Syria-Lebanon and Norway later joined. It is not clear why Syria-Lebanon were involved, but they did represent a customs union. It was their presence that was largely responsible for the inclusion, in Article 24 of the GATT, of the exemption from MFN for customs unions. The main opponents to the liberalisation elements in the negotiations appear to have been Australia, India and Syria-Lebanon.

By this point it seems clear that the executive branches of government on both sides of the Atlantic were working on proposals that were considerably more liberal than what the majority of interests wanted. It has indeed been argued that the US negotiators in the State Department focused on the international or level I negotiations and made a conscious effort to avoid much public debate of the draft ITO provisions until quite late.[11] But American farmers, much of industry and the Republican Party opposed liberalisation and the policy of the Roosevelt Administration. The domestic position in Washington became more difficult, as Congress toughened its stance. It insisted on inserting an escape clause into the US proposals (which later became Article 19 of the GATT) and restated its opposition to any agreement that did not result in the end of imperial preferences. It also made clear it would only accept moderate tariff reductions.

In Britain industry, in the shape of the Federation of British Industry (FBI), opposed liberalisation, the political left remained committed to economic planning as a basis for the post-war economy and the right was fearful that Britain would make concessions on imperial preferences and sell out the dominions. But this had also been the case with the negotiations on Bretton Woods. In contrast to the claims that the US negotiators had too much 'slack', it would appear that the British negotiators were only too aware of the political pressures from the various national party and economic interests.

Negotiating the GATT and the ITO

Negotiations took place in Geneva, from May to September of 1947. These involved tariff negotiations among 23 countries, with bilateral tariff negotiations conducted with the 'principal suppliers' of goods. These tariff agreements were then extended on an MFN basis to all others. By the end of the negotiations tariff reductions covering two-thirds of world trade had been negotiated by these countries and tariffs reduced by about 35%. These tariff reductions had the effect of reducing the imperial preferences.

The second aspect of these negotiations was the General Agreement on Tariffs and Trade (GATT). Agreement was reached on core principles, such as non-discrimination in the shape on most-favoured-nation and national treatment provisions. Common rules governing anti-dumping, customs valuation and other issues were also agreed. President Truman signed an Executive Order implementing the GATT before the trade negotiating authority under the Reciprocal Trade Agreements Act expired in 1948. In the end this negotiating authority was extended by the US Congress for another year, but in 1947 seeking an extension seemed a risky option.

In contrast to the Uruguay Round, in which there were over 130 delegations by the time the round was concluded and perhaps hundreds of people in the General Council chamber when key provisions were agreed, the GATT negotiations took place over a summer on Lake Geneva, with just 20 or so negotiators involved. Another important point to note is that by opting for the tariff agreement and the rules of the GATT in 1947 there was no comprehensive agreement on trade that also included the creation of the ITO, as was the case with the so-called single undertaking of the Uruguay Round and the creation of the WTO.

Negotiations also began in Geneva on the ITO. Britain and other countries, given their chronic balance of payments problems, sought the ability to use trade barriers to protect their balance of payments. It was agreed that balance of payments restrictions should be permitted but the IMF was to have a veto; this would allow the Americans to use their voting rights in the IMF to prevent abuse of this exception. India, which was about to gain its independence, also insisted upon a general development exemption.

The negotiations on the ITO were continued in Havana, Cuba, with the positive impetus from the Geneva talks. Here the US lost, if anything, more ground. On investment, which had come on to the agenda in Geneva, the US negotiators made concessions to developing countries. These represented in effect an acceptance for the first time that US investment in other countries could be expropriated, provided this was not done unfairly. This provision, as well as other compromises on the principle of liberal trade, was probably responsible for the loss of support for the ITO among US international business. The US negotiators also accepted voting rules for the ITO based on 'one country, one vote'. This reduced the prospects of ratification by Congress, because of deep-seated scepticism in the US Congress about international organisations, especially when the US could be outvoted. But Clayton, the chief American negotiator, believed that the main US objectives set out in its original draft had been achieved and along with 53 other countries signed the Havana Charter.[12]

Problems with ratification

During the negotiation and ratification of the other Bretton Woods institutions the Congress had been controlled by Democrats, with a Democratic President. In the election in 1947 the Republicans gained control, thus creating a divided government. The Republicans had been critical of the ITO proposals from the start and were not disposed to pass the requisite legislation. With Congress already tending to oppose the agreement, international business, one of the main lobbies in favour of liberal trade, shifted its position and came out against ratification of the ITO. As Diebold has argued, business believed that provisions calling for full employment and accepting expropriation provided too much scope for the state planning that was favoured in many other countries as a means of recovering from the devastation of the war.[13] Given that the GATT already existed, there was also an alternative for the business interests to fall back on. Such domestic political goals took precedence over wider strategic aims. To put it in terms of the BATNA defined by Odell (see Chapter 2), changes in the ITO negotiations resulted in no agreement being seen as favourable to a bad agreement by many US businesses. In Congressional hearings on the ITO the major US companies that had campaigned for a new trade regime distanced themselves from the ITO proposals. Protectionist interests, for example in agriculture, had opposed the ITO all along. As Diebold put it, the ITO failed because domestic support was undermined by the perfectionists and the protectionists.

In the face of this opposition, the Administration could have played the security card and argued that the ITO was essential if a liberal multilateral trading order was to be created as a foundation for western liberal democracy in the face of Soviet communism. By late 1947 it was clear that the East-West ideological conflict of the Cold War was on its way. At the time, however, there were arguably more pressing issues. In June 1947 General Marshall had proposed the policy which became the Marshall Plan, to help rescue Europe from economic weakness and potential social unrest, leading to gains for communist parties. The Truman Administration put its effort into pushing the Marshall Aid legislation through Congress and felt that the ITO was a lower priority. Without enthusiastic support from business or the Administration, there was little prospect of Congress accepting the ITO. Without US ratification the question of whether other countries would ratify was moot. There was clearly some doubt about the British House of Commons ratifying the agreement, but this was not longer the issue.

Application of the Theoretical Analysis

How can one explain the success of the GATT but failure of the ITO? Can it be explained in terms of *power relationships?* During the period under discussion the US was a hegemon. It accounted for more than 50% of world industrial output, it was almost the only creditor nation and other former economic powers, such as

Britain, depended on US credit. During the war, when the initial negotiations occurred on such issues as imperial preferences, Britain was highly dependent on US support. But despite being a hegemon the United States did not get what it wanted. US negotiators made concessions to their negotiating partners on a range of issues. Trade negotiations were held up because of difficulties in reaching agreement with the British and others and only finally concluded after the US made concessions that undermined domestic support for the ITO. Security issues were always present in the debates on the GATT and ITO but also do not appear to be very important. Agreement was reached in the GATT before the Cold War began in earnest, but the US Congress did not ratify the ITO in 1948 and 1949 when tensions between the West and the Soviet Union were intense.

National sovereignty appears initially as quite a convincing hypothesis. As Ruggie was later to put it, the post-war system was based on 'embedded liberalism' in which countries agreed to a liberal order based on non-discrimination, but one that ensured national policy autonomy.[14] This was the GATT with its commitment to national treatment and MFN. The ITO would have been more intrusive into national policy autonomy. But if this were the case, why did the countries sign up to the ITO? Even if in the United States there was a case of 'voluntary defection'[15] - in other words the US negotiators were sincere in their aims but misjudged the level of domestic support - are we to believe that all the other signatories were not aware of the implications for national sovereignty?

International institutions did not play a big role, as there were none. The League of Nations had, as noted above, provided some precedents and some of the technical expertise used in the GATT had been developed by the League. But in contrast to the Uruguay Round, where there was an established international regime in place, negotiators in the 1940s had to start from square one. In a sense the absence of institutions provided for flexibility.

Societal factors appear to provide a more convincing explanation for the success of the GATT and the failure of the ITO. The *balance of economic or sector interests* between free traders and protectionists was not favourable, with protectionists consistent in their opposition to the ITO and the GATT, but the free trade lobby getting cold feet about the ITO. *State centred* approaches focused on the inter-departmental debate within the executive were also important in explaining why the WTO was ratified but not the ITO. Indeed, who controlled the negotiators is also seen as critical. The US State Department negotiators had enough discretion to make compromises with their international partners (the Putnam level I game). But too much slack meant they were not properly engaged with domestic interests (the level II game). The British cabinet and parliament were united in seeking to retain imperial preferences, which, under the Putnam model, may explain why the British were able to get quite a lot of what they wanted, despite American strength. In the US *the institutional structure of domestic decision-making* played a major role. For example, the changes in the composition of the US Congress in 1947 made ratification much more difficult, with Republicans in control. So domestic institutions clearly played an important role.

Ideology played a part in the outcome. The US approach was in part driven by the liberal ideology of Cordell Hull in the State Department, but the overall US position was a much more qualified support for free trade. There were also important ideological differences between the countries negotiating. The US was opposed to state intervention while Britain and France and developing countries favoured economic planning in the pursuit of full employment and industrial reconstruction. But these differences did not prevent agreement being reached.

Individuals, as suggested above, played a role. For example, key decisions on compromises to be made by the United States during the ITO negotiations in order to get agreement were taken by the US chief negotiator, not by Congressional Committees.

Linkage played only a minor role in the negotiations. The US could have used the leverage it possessed as a result of its military power, but did not press this home, at least not with the British. They did not ensure that the British made binding commitments to end imperial preferences in return for Lend Lease aid. Such an approach would have been 'value claiming' and was generally at odds with the value creating preference of the US at that time. In contrast to later negotiations, the trade negotiations themselves were effectively split when, in the interests of US domestic factors, the GATT was agreed and adopted separately from the other provisions included in the ITO.

The Uruguay Round Negotiations and the World Trade Organization

Only a very summarised version of the Uruguay Round will be given here. The negotiations, which began formally in September 1986 and finished in December 1993, with ratification during 1994, consisted of four main elements:

- First, there were negotiations on market access issues, such as further tariff reductions, liberalisation of trade in agricultural products, textiles and clothing and some specific market access commitments in service sectors such as financial services and telecommunications.
- Second, there were a series of agreements strengthening and extending the multilateral rules. These included technical barriers to trade, sanitary and phyto-sanitary measures, government procurement, anti-dumping and subsidies and countervailing duties.
- Third, there were framework rules adopted for services, intellectual property and investment.
- Fourth, there were institutional innovations. These included: the strengthening of dispute settlement provisions, putting an end to the ability of governments to veto the findings of dispute settlement panels; a trade policy review mechanism to enhance transparency in the trade policies of countries; and finally the creation of a World Trade Organization (WTO), to provide a unified institutional framework for all these measures.[16]

How do the factors identified earlier help to explain why the Uruguay Round, including the adoption of the WTO, succeeded where the ITO failed? Systemic factors such as *power relationships* seem to have played less of a role in 1994. The US was no longer a hegemon.[17] Other actors, such as the European Union, were equal in influence in trade policy. There were also more than 130 countries in the final negotiations in 1994. If the existence of a hegemon was a requirement for agreement, then agreement was more likely in 1948 than 1994. *Strategic factors* appear to have played even less of a role in the results of the Uruguay Round. The Cold War had ended before the round was completed, so there was no security imperative for the agreement to be negotiated and ratified as there had been in 1948-50. The defence of national sovereignty should also have made agreement more difficult in 1994 than in 1948-50, because the trade rules were far more intrusive into national sovereignty, reducing as they did the scope for national industrial and regulatory policies and even obliging countries to adopt common international norms.[18]

International institutions played a much more important role than during the negotiations in the late 1940s. Over the period from 1947 there had been a steady growth and strengthening of international institutions of relevance to trade and investment negotiations. The GATT, although a provisional contractual agreement, had resulted in the evolution of a secretariat with extensive technical expertise to support negotiations and in some cases play a key role behind the scenes. The OECD also played an important and generally overlooked role in shaping the agenda of negotiations and providing a forum in which the developed countries could explore the potential for mutual gains and thus help to pave the way for wide ranging value creating agreements.

In contrast *domestic factors* appear to have had a significant impact on the outcome of the Uruguay Round. Interest group lobbying shaped the agenda, with its inclusion of services, intellectual property and sanitary and phyto-sanitary rules (ie food safety). Protectionist interests resisted liberalisation in agriculture and textiles and defended the lax rules on anti-dumping in order to have an effective de facto selective safeguard. It was the trade-off between these interests in the developed countries and the developing countries which shaped the final package that represented the results of the Uruguay Round.

Institutional features of the major protagonists had also changed radically over the years. The US negotiators no longer benefited from discretion in negotiations. Through a series of institutional changes, such as the creation of the USTR under close Congressional scrutiny and the Trade Advisory Committees, the considerable slack enjoyed by the US negotiators in the late 1940s has been removed. This made negotiations more difficult to conclude, because both level I and level II games had to be successfully completed, but once negotiated the ratification was feasible if not easy. The reduction of this 'slack' has been seen as one of the main reasons why the US Congress accepted the WTO but not the ITO.

The institutional structures had, of course, become somewhat more complicated elsewhere. If we are to explain why the Uruguay Round was a success, it is not sufficient to look only at the US. In Europe there were equally difficult level II negotiations, between the European Commission, the chief negotiator in the EU, and the 12 Member States. Sweden, Austria and Finland were also in the final stages of EU accession and were therefore de facto negotiating with the EU. The limited work that has been done on the EU decision-making processes suggests there was little negotiating flexibility for the European Commission, as the Member State governments maintained very close control during the negotiations. The European Parliament did not yet play a major role during the Uruguay Round.[19]

Linkage was of central importance in the Uruguay Round. As noted above, all major trade negotiations since the 1960s have taken the form of 'global rounds': in other words, nothing was agreed until everything was agreed. In the case of the Uruguay Round there was also a single undertaking. In other words countries could not pick and choose what they wanted to sign and what they did not wish to. In practice this was designed to ensure that developing countries could not opt out. This meant that the alternative to an agreement was the somewhat outdated GATT, as it stood after the Tokyo Round. For business interests this would have meant no multilateral rules on intellectual property or services; for agricultural exporters it would have meant continued exclusion of agriculture from GATT disciplines. Therefore there was no fall-back option as there had been in 1948 with the GATT.

Arguably US business might have settled for the use of aggressive unilateralism to open markets.[20] This approach had found considerable acceptance and support during the 1980s, but this trend was one of the major reasons the US's trading partners were keen to bind the US to strong multilateral commitments including the creation of the World Trade Organization. Acceptance of provisions on services and intellectual property rights by developing country members of the WTO was a quid pro quo for multilateral discipline over US unilateralism. Again linkage seems to have been a key factor.

Linkage to factors outside of trade was also important. This was not so much for the United States, although Presidential elections in 1988 and 1992 affected the timing of some negotiations. It was developments in Europe that were most disruptive, with the end of the Cold War leading to major political reform and change throughout Europe. Intergovernmental conferences on the future of the European Union held up progress in trade negotiations.

Ideology also cannot be overlooked as a factor in the outcome of the Uruguay Round. By 1994 there was no ideological competitor to market capitalism. Not only had the standard bearers of central planning either collapsed or moved towards market mechanisms; the vast majority of developing countries had, for better or worse, also opted for market capitalism and liberalisation as a development strategy. The liberal paradigm was therefore ascendant and the WTO the only show in town.[21]

Epistemic communities also played an important role in various aspects of the Uruguay Round negotiation. It is not possible to trace the role of these groups of experts, who share broad common values and are credible enough to shape policy outcomes, but they were clearly important in some of the negotiations. In agriculture, work carried out by a group of agricultural economists on the costs of national subsidies, which was integrated into OECD work to produce the so called Producer Subsidy Equivalent, a measure of the level of subsidisation inherent in any form of agricultural support programme, did much to pave the way to an eventual agreement on agriculture in the round. In services, including the sector in the trade regime meant that new ideas and approaches were needed. Groups of experts in different countries, from the government departments concerned, the private service sectors (especially financial services) and academia, contributed to the approach to services negotiations and the shape of the General Agreement on Trade in Services.

Finally, individuals probably played a smaller role than at the time of the GATT/ITO negotiations. There were a number of prominent individuals in the GATT Secretariat and in the national delegations. But these individuals were working within the constraints set by, first, well established national and sector interests and, second, much tighter control by their principals back home, whether this took the form of the US Congress or the European Council of Ministers.

Conclusions

This chapter has shown that the theoretical analysis introduced in Chapter 2 can be reasonably applied to real cases of economic diplomacy and can help to provide insights that may not always be immediately apparent. For example, as Odell and Eichengreen suggest, the reason why the ITO failed was in part because of US negotiators having too much negotiating discretion, while a divided government may help explain why the GATT succeeded but the ITO failed. The concept of BATNAs, or when it is better to have an agreement than no agreement, is also useful when considering the balance of sector interests for and against any agreement. For US business the GATT offered an alternative to what it saw as a flawed ITO agreement. Finally, the two level game approach proposed by Putnam is helpful in understanding the negotiating dynamics.

A comparison of negotiations at different periods in history can also help to illustrate how economic diplomacy has evolved. For example, the slack or scope for discretion provided to US negotiators was progressively reduced between the 1960s and 1980s. Thus when it came to the negotiation of the Uruguay Round, US negotiators were more attuned to the views of Congress and of US business and NGO interests. This reduced the risk that the Uruguay Round would not be ratified by the US Congress but it also made the negotiations much more difficult. Diplomats were less able to weigh commercial interests against wider political aims, so that domestic interests and ideas shaped US policy more than at the time of the GATT/ITO negotiations.

These lessons learned by looking at US experience might also be of value in assessing other countries. With the increased number of governments active in economic diplomacy it becomes more and more important to understand how decisions are made elsewhere. The discussion of EU decision-making suggests that the scope for discretion available to EU negotiators is also tightly constrained. In other words, the fact that trade negotiations have become more difficult to conclude may not be only due to the increased scope of coverage, but also because negotiators have less scope to make compromises and accommodations in level I negotiations.

It is also instructive to compare the use of linkage in the two periods. During the negotiation of the ITO there was no link made between it and the GATT, so opponents of the ITO could still fall back on the GATT. By the time the proposal for a World Trade Organization (WTO) was included in the Uruguay Round negotiations, it had been firmly established that there would be no agreement until everything had been agreed. This is the concept of the global multilateral round of negotiations. In the case of the WTO this linkage seems to have been an important factor. Given the opposition to the WTO in the US Congress, there would have been some doubt about Congressional ratification for the WTO had the rest of the Uruguay Round results not been linked to it. If the US got more or less what it wanted on trade in services, intellectual property and agriculture, it came at the price of the WTO that many saw as helping to rein in US unilateralism. The importance of this kind of linkage, which has became standard practice in international trade negotiations during the past 30 years, appears to have been somewhat overlooked in the existing studies of the adoption of the ITO and GATT in the US.

On the basis of the chapter it is possible to suggest a number of hypotheses on how economic diplomacy has evolved. First, domestic factors have come to play a more important role in decision-making, as the scope for negotiators has been reduced. This makes the process of negotiation more difficult but reduces the risks of non-ratification. This is likely to vary between countries. There may, however, be limits to how far one can go in tightening domestic control over negotiations. Already one might argue that trade negotiators have precious little scope to negotiate and find solutions to divergent national positions.

A second hypothesis is that linkages between issues are important as a means of breaking what would otherwise be insuperable obstacles to agreement. Indeed the more domestic interests control negotiations, the greater the need for trade-offs between issues, so that protectionist or otherwise difficult interests can be compensated by interests in favour of an agreement. This suggests that more flexible approaches that weaken the 'package deal' nature of international trade negotiations may result in much slower progress in negotiations.

Notes

1 Other studies have also made such comparisons. See for example, Odell, J. and Eichengreen, B, 'Changing Domestic Institutions and Ratifying Regime Agreements', in Odell 2000 and Milner, H. 'The Bretton Woods Monetary Agreement and the International Trade Organisation, 1943-1950' in Milner 1997.

2 The creation of the WTO brought the General Agreement on Tariffs and Trade, the General Agreement on Trade in Services (GATS) and the intellectual property provisions agreed in the Uruguay Round under a single institution and unified the dispute settlement procedures. This is important, but it was the decisions on a range of elements of the Uruguay Round package which counted, not simply the creation of the WTO.

3 For further reading on the substance on the Uruguay Round see, for example, Croome 1995 for a good factual account of the negotiations.

4 See Viner 1950 for some discussion of the role of the League of Nations.
5 Gowa 1994 argues, for example, that trade negotiations only really succeed between allies because of an aversion of states to 'helping' their potential enemies by trading with them.
6 See Milner 1997 for a description of this process at work.
7 See, for example, Odell and Eichengreen 2000.
8 Both Odell 2000 and Putnam 1988 argue that linkage is a factor in international negotiations.
9 See Odell and Eichengreen 2000.
10 At a critical point during the trade negotiations, the European Union was busy discussing the future of European political and monetary union at the two Inter-Governmental Conferences that led to the Maastricht Treaty on European Union. See Woolcock and Hodges 1997.
11 See Odell and Eichengreen 2000.
12 There was no consensus within the US negotiating team, however, and Clair Wilcox the deputy negotiator is believed to have advised that no agreement in Havana would have been better than a weak agreement.
13 See Diebold 1952.
14 See Ruggie 1982.
15 On voluntary defections, see Putnam 1988.
16 For more reading on the Uruguay Round, see Schott 1994, Croome 1995, and Preeg 1995.
17 Some would contest this. Even if the US state was less able to shape events in 1994 than 1948, US commercial interests may well have had the power. For example, a coalition of business interests, led by US companies, was able to get intellectual property right standards integrated into the WTO.
18 In the years since the ratification of the Uruguay Round results, there has been a backlash against the loss of national policy autonomy, which suggests that some interests were not fully aware of the implications of the agreement. See Chapter 17 below.
19 For a discussion on the institutional structure of decision-making in the EU on trade policy see Chapter 12 below, as well as Hodges and Woolcock 1997, Meunier and Nicholaidis 1999.
20 For a discussion of US unilateralism see Bhagwati and Patrick 1991.
21 See Desai 1996.

References

Bhagwati, J. and Patrick, H. (eds.) (1991), *Aggressive Unilateralism: America's Article 301 Trade Policy and the World Trading System,* University of Michigan Press, Ann Arbor.
Croome, J. (1995), *Reshaping the World Trading System; A History of the Uruguay Round,* World Trade Organization, Geneva.
Desai, M. (1996), 'Organising the Only Game in Town', *The World Today,* vol. 52, no. 12, pp. 310-312.
Diebold, W. (1952), *The End of the ITO, Essays in International Finance* No 16, Princeton University Press, Princeton.
Gowa, J. (1994), *Allies, Adversaries and International Trade,* Princeton University Press, Princeton.

Meunier, S. and Nicholaidis, K. (1999), 'Who Speaks for Europe? The Delegation of Trade Authority in the European Union', *Journal of Common Market Studies,* vol. 37, no. 3, pp. 477-501.

Milner, H. (1997), *Interests, Institutions and Information: Domestic Politics and International Relations,* Princeton University Press, Princeton.

Odell, J. (2000), *Negotiating the World Economy,* Cornell University Press, Ithaca and London.

Odell, J. and Eichengreen, B. (2000), 'Changing Domestic Institutions and Ratifying Regime Agreements' in Odell, J. *Negotiating the World Economy,* Cornell University Press, Ithaca and London.

Preeg, E. (1995), *Traders in a Brave New World: the Uruguay Round and the Future of the International Trading System,* University of Chicago Press, Chicago.

Putnam, R. D. (1988), 'Diplomacy and Domestic Politics: the Logic of Two-Level Games' *International Organization,* vol. 42, no. 3, pp. 427-460.

Ruggie, J.G. (1982), 'International Regimes, Transactions and Change: Embedded Liberalism in the Postwar Economic Order' *International Organization,* vol. 36, no. 2, pp. 379-415.

Schott, J. (1994), *The Uruguay Round: An Assessment,* Institute of International Economics, Washington.

Viner, J. (1950), *The Customs Union Issue,* Stevens and Sons, London.

Woolcock, S. and Hodges, M. (1997), 'The European Union in the Uruguay Round: the story behind the headlines' in Wallace, H. and Wallace, W. (eds.), *Policy-Making in the European Union,* 3rd edition, Oxford University Press, Oxford.

Chapter 7

Creating the Economic Summits

Nicholas Bayne

This chapter, the second of the historical case studies in this book, examines the foundation of the G7 summits in the mid-1970s and their subsequent development. This links into the first of the contemporary case studies in Chapter 8, where Colin Budd reflects on G8 summits and their preparation today, drawing on his experience as Economic Director at the Foreign and Commonwealth Office. These two chapters therefore compare summitry past and present.

Why does this book give so much attention to summitry? This is because the G7 summit - now the G8 - provides an excellent laboratory for research and experiment in the study of economic diplomacy. The summits cover the whole range of international economic relations. They deal with the issues of greatest concern of the day. The number of actors involved is limited and they can be observed directly, without the distorting lens of a formal organisation. Above all, summitry makes it possible to observe the efforts made (not always successfully) to reconcile the tensions between politics and economics and between external and domestic factors in decision-making - two central themes of this book. That is not surprising, as that is why the summits were invented.

This chapter is structured as follows:

- *First*, it looks at why the summits began in the early 1970s, their original objectives and the achievements of the early summits, up to 1978.
- *Second*, it analyses decision-making and negotiation in the context of the early summits, in terms of the sequences described in Chapter 4 and the questions formulated in Chapter 1.
- *Third*, the chapter examines why the summits since 1978 have never been as ambitious as the early ones.

The conclusions bring the record of summitry up to the present, looking at their recent contribution to resolving the tensions of economic diplomacy.

Why the Summits Began

From the late 1940s to the end of the 1960s, after the creation of the Bretton Woods institutions and the GATT, the world economy recovered steadily. Growth rates were strong, inflation and unemployment low. But all that was shattered on 15 August 1971, when the United States, unilaterally and without warning, ceased to defend the dollar against gold. This introduced a period of great turbulence and uncertainty, fed by three political trends and three economic crises.[1]

Political trends

One motive in creating the cooperative post-war economic system had been to avoid any risk of another world war. By 1970 this looked remote. The European Economic Community (EEC) was steadily making another war in Western Europe unthinkable. There was a parallel process in Asia with Japan.

A second motive for cooperation in the late 1940s and the 1950s had been the fear of Soviet communism, which inspired the Marshall Plan.[2]   By 1970 the security danger from the Soviet Union was still high, but the rival centrally planned system no longer looked like an economic threat. So that factor weakened too.

The third trend was the rise of the European Economic Community. With the admission of Britain, Denmark and Ireland, the EEC embraced all the leading powers of Western Europe. It was potentially a strong partner of the United States or a strong rival. Which would it be? In an attempt to create a partnership, Henry Kissinger, then US Secretary of State, launched what he called the 'Year of Europe' in 1973. But in the EEC there was a tendency, led by France under President Georges Pompidou, to define Europe in terms of its difference from the United States. So the 'Year of Europe' ended in discord and recrimination.[3]

Economic crises

The first crisis was in the monetary system. After the Americans broke the dollar's link with gold, the system clearly had to be reformed - but how? The United States wanted a system still centred on the dollar, but with greater freedom to adjust it up and down. But the Europeans and others had lost confidence in the dollar and wanted a more widely based system. The dollar remained unstable, so that by mid-1973 all the major currencies were floating against it. Despite intense discussion at the IMF, there was no agreement on reform.

The second crisis was in energy supplies, provoked by the decision of the Organisation of Petroleum Exporting Countries (OPEC) to raise oil prices from about $3 per barrel to $12 per barrel late in 1973. Again, there was transatlantic disagreement on the response. The United States, which produced enough energy to meet two-thirds of its needs, favoured firm resistance to OPEC and collective action to conserve energy. The Americans pioneered the creation of the International Energy Agency (IEA), attached to OECD. But the Europeans and Japan, who were more dependent on oil imports, favoured conciliation with OPEC and France refused to join the IEA.

The third was a macroeconomic crisis, provoked by the steep rise in oil prices. For oil-importing countries, the effect of this was to increase inflation, cut back growth and weaken their balance of payments. The balance of payments pressure made it even harder to get back to fixed exchange rates. But otherwise governments had a choice. Either they could act to keep inflation under control, at the cost of greater loss of growth. Germany advocated this. Or they could act to sustain growth, at the cost of higher inflation. Britain and Italy argued for this.

The matter was debated intensely at the OECD; which course was right? Most other leading economies inclined at first to check inflation. But they found that unemployment was rocketing up, from 9 million in the OECD area in 1973 to 15 million in 1975. So most of them changed course and adopted measures of fiscal and monetary stimulus.

Interdependence and the genesis of the summits

Under all these pressures, it looked as if the international system, that had worked so well for over two decades, was coming apart:

- The political stimuli to cooperation were weakening;
- There were many examples of unresolved disputes between the United States, the former dominant power, and the Europeans and Japan;
- The instruments created for economic cooperation, like the IMF and the OECD, were working flat out. But they seemed unable to reach durable agreements or generate a sense of common purpose.

Underlying all this was the advance of interdependence. During the 1950s and 1960s, trade had risen rapidly, growing on average 2% faster than output. Foreign direct investment had begun to flow. All the OECD economies were becoming more interdependent and thus more vulnerable to external disturbance. Policies could not just be determined domestically; they could be frustrated by what others did.[4]

With these turbulent conditions and persistent policy deadlock, many people began to fear a complete breakdown in cooperation and a relapse into the inward-looking policies that had proved so disastrous in the inter-war period.[5] Some new approach was urgently needed.

During this period Valéry Giscard d'Estaing became French finance minister and Helmut Schmidt became German finance minister. They went together to meetings of the IMF and got very frustrated by the formality of the proceedings. So in 1973 they created a smaller group of five members - themselves and their American, British and Japanese colleagues. They would meet for informal exchanges in the library of the White House and so were called the Library Group.

The following year Giscard became President of France and Schmidt became Federal German Chancellor. They decided to replicate, at head of government level, the informal encounters of the Library Group. So, after careful preparation, Giscard invited his friend Chancellor Helmut Schmidt, US President Gerald Ford, and Prime Ministers Harold Wilson of Britain and Takeo Miki of Japan to the first summit at Rambouillet, near Paris, in November 1975. The Italian Prime Minister, Aldo Moro, was added at the last minute. Canada was included from the 1976 summit onwards and the Commission and Presidency of the EEC from 1977. The composition remained at seven plus one till Russia joined 20 years later.

The Objectives of the Summits

The summits had three original objectives:

- First, to generate *political leadership* to resolve economic problems that were beyond the capacities of bureaucracies;
- Second, to *reconcile the tensions of interdependence* between external and domestic pressures on economic policy-making;
- Third, to develop a system of *collective management* of the international system, to spread the responsibilities hitherto exercised by the United States.

These three objectives remain as valid for the summits today as they were in 1975 - only substituting 'globalisation' for 'interdependence'.[6] This chapter will not say much about the third objective - collective management. The analysis will focus on the first and second.

The focus on *political leadership* arose because the problems of the early 1970s had clearly proved too much for government officials, or even ministers, meeting in the existing international institutions. They had got bogged down in sterile disputes or bureaucratic rivalries. The belief was that heads of government, speaking directly to each other in a small, select, informal gathering, could find the innovative and imaginative solutions that had eluded lower-level meetings. Giscard believed this passionately. To keep the group small, he resisted adding Italy, Canada and the EEC or allowing foreign and finance ministers to attend. He wanted only economic items to be discussed, fearing other issues would be a distraction. Giscard's purist approach was not fully accepted, even at the outset. But the summit has always had an anti-bureaucratic bias.

In the context of *reconciling the tensions of interdependence*, heads of government were perceived as having certain advantages, as Chapter 5 has already noted. They embodied the supreme authority of their countries. They could arbitrate between conflicting demands within their governments. They could respond to popular pressures by virtue of their democratic legitimacy. Instinctively, heads of government incline towards domestic interests. So a regular meeting with their fellow leaders could act as a useful corrective. It could make them aware of their international responsibilities and encourage them to build up domestic coalitions in favour of outward-looking policies.

The Achievements of the Early Summits

This section looks at what the early summits achieved in their three areas of greatest concern - monetary reform, international trade and economic policy coordination. Table 7.1 lists the summits from 1975 to 1978, with their main achievements in cooperation.

Table 7.1 Cooperation Achieved at the Early Summits

Year	Site	Topics of Cooperation
1975	Rambouillet	Monetary reform
1976	Puerto Rico	Nothing significant
1977	London I	Trade; growth; nuclear power
1978	Bonn I	Growth, energy and trade

Source: Putnam and Bayne, *Hanging Together,* 1987

Monetary reform

Giscard's main aim at Rambouillet was to have the summit end the long deadlock over reform of the monetary system. By this time the Americans had realised that they could not recreate a fixed-rate system with the dollar at the centre, as it had been before. But they had concluded that a system of generalised floating would still have the dollar at its centre, while giving them the flexibility they wanted. So they became strong advocates of amending the Articles of the IMF to legitimise floating, which up to now was only allowed in emergencies. By 1975 only France was resisting reform on these lines. Giscard could see that the oil crisis made floating inevitable for many countries. But he wanted to trade French consent to legitimising floating against measures that would facilitate a later return to fixed rates.

In the run-up to the summit, French and American finance ministry officials met and worked out a bilateral deal. Floating could be a permanent regime; but the central banks of the major powers should intervene to iron out 'erratic fluctuations' in exchange rates. This deal was revealed to the other leaders at Rambouillet and endorsed there. On this basis, the reform of the IMF Articles was rapidly agreed.

In monetary reform, Rambouillet did exactly what a summit was expected to do. The heads resolved a problem that had resisted settlement up till then. They produced a durable outcome, since this amendment of the IMF Articles has not been superseded. In retrospect, however, this result came at a price for Giscard's own objectives. The undertaking to iron out erratic fluctuations in exchange rates - the most important element for him - soon fell into disuse.

International trade

The enlargement of the EEC in 1973 had prompted another round of trade negotiations in the GATT. This was launched in Tokyo just one month before the oil crisis broke and is called the Tokyo Round.[7] But it made slow progress at first and the growing economic turbulence generated pressure for protectionist measures. In Europe, Germany under Schmidt was strong in the defence of open markets. But France and Italy were wavering, and so was Britain under the Wilson government.

At Rambouillet the heads made firm commitments to resist protectionism and to complete the Tokyo Round by the end of 1977, two years off. The value of these commitments was soon put to the test. Wilson believed the summit gave some loopholes for Britain to introduce trade restrictions. He proposed to do so, citing the Rambouillet results in justification. But his summit partners soon made it clear they did not share his interpretation and Wilson backed off.[8]

In the Tokyo Round, however, progress continued to be very slow. When the heads met in London in May 1977, the end-year deadline was clearly out of reach. The next summit was made the target for decisive progress. Robert Strauss, the energetic US trade negotiator, used that commitment to drive forward agreement on the final shape of the round. The approach of the Bonn summit in July 1978 concentrated minds at the GATT in Geneva. The G7's trade negotiators came to the summit with a major agreed document and continued their bargaining behind the scenes. As a result, the heads could set a final deadline of December 1978 for completing the round. This deadline was met in substance, though procedural delays prolonged the round for another six months.[9]

The heads of government did not get into the details of trade negotiations, as they did with monetary reform. The outcome of the Tokyo Round was mixed, being good on tariffs but less good in other areas. But the summit made a positive contribution. It kept protectionism at bay while the Tokyo Round lasted, showed that summit statements could not be used to justify trade restrictions and concentrated efforts to get the round concluded with only a year's slippage.

Economic policy coordination

The story is more complicated in economic policy coordination.[10]   At the time of the Rambouillet summit in November 1975, most G7 governments had recently stimulated their economies. Growth had begun again, after the recession generated by the first oil shock. The heads of government could confidently say in the Rambouillet declaration: "We will not allow recovery to falter" - without having to do anything more. Most of them were in fact more worried about rising prices and took anti-inflation measures in the next few months. However, growth remained buoyant up till the second summit, at Puerto Rico in June 1976, where the heads again confidently stated it would continue. But this time they were wrong. The G7 economies all slowed down later in 1976, as a result of the restrictive measures taken earlier. In the United States, this helped Jimmy Carter to get elected as US President on a programme to revive economic growth.

Carter stimulated the US economy and urged Germany and Japan to reflate also. This was the so-called 'locomotive' approach, where strong economies would act to pull the weaker ones along. But Germany and Japan resisted. The 1977 London summit endorsed the high growth targets set by the three countries, but did not agree on measures to ensure they would be met. In fact Germany and Japan did not hit their targets; the summit's forecasts proved wrong again. Meanwhile the US economy was growing at over 5% - much faster than the others - at the cost of rising inflation, a falling dollar and a huge increase in oil imports. In 1978 imports supplied nearly half of US oil consumption, as against only 18% in 1977.

So before the 1978 summit Carter pressed Germany and Japan for actual measures to increase their economic growth. In return Schmidt and the other leaders insisted on American action to cut back its oil imports, which were distorting the market. The Bonn summit produced an ambitious set of agreements across different issues. The US undertook to reduce oil imports and bring domestic oil prices up to world levels. Germany promised to stimulate its economy by measures equal to 1% of GNP. Japan had already taken measures of economic stimulus, which were working well, but it agreed to cut back its export surplus. In every case the head of government - Carter, Schmidt and Fukuda - supported these measures, but faced domestic resistance. The summit helped each of them to overcome this resistance and get the measures implemented.

But within six months the second oil crisis broke. All this economic strategy was thrown off course. The summits never attempted such an ambitious bargain again.

Decision-Making, Negotiation and the G7 Summit

The second half of this chapter looks at decision-making and negotiation in the summit context, in relation to the sequences outlined in Chapter 4 and the analytical framework formulated in Chapter 1.

Innovation and the summit

Summitry clearly does not follow the sequence of domestic decision-making given in Chapter 4. That sequence is driven by the officials of a lead department, consulting internally and externally to produce an agreed inter-departmental view. Only then is political authority sought from ministers, with the head of government intervening as arbiter, if at all. Summitry starts this process from the opposite end. It provides an early example of ministerial initiative, which has become such a feature of the new economic diplomacy.

One key element is *innovation*. At the early summits, heads of government acted as innovators, deploying their own ideas. They gave priority to economic issues because of the background of the early summiteers as former finance ministers: not only Giscard and Schmidt, but also Fukuda in Japan, Callaghan in the UK and Jenkins at the European Commission. They used their position as heads to overcome the frustration they had encountered at lower levels. Not only the ideas at the summit but the summits themselves were an innovation in the mid-1970s, created to rescue the international system from the deadlock prevailing in its existing institutions.

Giscard, as noted, believed passionately in the ability of small groups of heads of government to agree on new and imaginative solutions. He regarded bureaucrats and even other ministers as distracting from this process. He tried to construct the 1975 Rambouillet summit as the personal instrument of the heads of government.[11] At Rambouillet, a small chateau outside Paris, Giscard accommodated the other heads of government, plus two advisers only, in the chateau itself. (Ford was worried about security, so he was put in a medieval tower with walls twelve feet thick.) Giscard did not want other ministers at the summit at all. When the Americans insisted that foreign and finance ministers must support their leaders, being nervous about what Ford might agree to on his own, Giscard made these ministers stay at some distance away. A very small office was given to each delegation - the British office had earlier been Napoleon's bathroom. Only a very few passes to the chateau were issued, so overflow staff were in caravans in the grounds. Giscard even wanted the leaders to meet wholly alone, without advisers, but the others said they must at least have note-takers present.[12]

This stress on the personal contribution of the heads, to the exclusion of everyone else, clearly went too far. There was a danger of misunderstanding, as happened between Wilson and the rest over trade. The monetary agreement would never have been concluded without the meetings beforehand between American and French officials. There had to be a mechanism for preparation and follow-up.

The impact of summit preparations

The heads of government left their personal mark not only on the summit itself but on how it was prepared. Here the main influences came from Schmidt and Carter, rather than from Giscard.

Helmut Schmidt also had a low opinion of bureaucrats. Even before Giscard had decided to call a summit, Schmidt had created his own small international group to reflect on the state of the world economy and offer advice. Each member had to be personally selected by his head of government; and they had to be in the private sector, though they could have held public office before. The German member was Wilfried Guth, a banker. The Frenchman was Professor Raymond Barre, who had been in the European Commission (and would later become French Prime Minister). The American was George Shultz, President of the Bechtel Corporation, formerly US Treasury Secretary and another founder member of the Library Group.

Schmidt, like Giscard was looking for new ideas so as to escape the economic turbulence and deadlock. He turned to the private sector - to academics and business - as another source of innovative thinking in economic diplomacy. In this he anticipated, by several decades, the part played today by the business firms, NGOs and epistemic communities analysed in Chapter 3.

There would have been a case for having this private sector group prepare for the summit, thus stressing its detachment from the bureaucracy. But it did not work out that way. Barre and Shultz were given this responsibility by Giscard and Ford. But the other leaders chose people from government as their personal representatives for summit preparations - even Schmidt, who saw that the heads needed some link with their government machinery. In due course all the personal representatives came to hold government positions. When Carter became US President he named Henry Owen and gave him summit preparations as his principal task. Under pressure from Carter and Owen, summit preparations became much more institutionalised.[13]

The personal representatives became known as the 'Sherpas', after the Nepalese guides who lead Western climbers up the Himalayas. The practice varied between G7 countries on whether the Sherpa was closer to the head of government or to the bureaucracy.[14] But wherever the Sherpa sat, he or she came to be supported in the preparations by two 'Sous-Sherpas', one from the foreign and one from the finance ministry - see Chapter 8 below. This was a consequence of the foreign and finance ministers being present at the summit and of the institutionalisation advocated by Carter and his team. The Sous-Sherpas embedded the summit preparations even deeper into the bureaucracy.

The catalytic effect of the summit

Creating this mechanism enabled the summits not only to innovate but also to exercise a powerful catalytic effect on the whole decision-making process, by increasing the pressure to reach agreement. The heads could leave their officials to get as close to agreement as they could and only intervene to close the remaining gap at the summit itself. But often the leaders did not have to discuss the topic at all. The knowledge that the topic was on the summit agenda could be enough to stimulate agreement at lower levels, as happened at the end of the Tokyo Round. The summits thus provided an additional spur to agreement. They were like Shakespeare's Sir John Falstaff, who said: "I am not only witty in myself, but the cause that wit is in other men".[15]

As a result, the Sherpa could intervene on behalf of the head of government throughout the domestic decision-making sequence, to make things happen. Decision-making, as noted in Chapter 4, does not follow a simple linear pattern, but is an iterative or cyclical process. In summitry the cycles were usually marked by the three or four meetings the Sherpas held to prepare for each summit, each one providing an opportunity for the Sherpa to intervene. Even so, the Sherpas were people, not institutions. They could act as a stimulus to innovation or to reaching agreement, but they could not be a substitute for the lead department or the whole bureaucratic process.

At the same time, Giscard's concept of the summit as a personal encounter had abiding appeal with the leaders themselves. In consequence the summit never developed a written charter, a fixed base or a permanent staff - nor was there ever pressure from the heads to create such things. The numbers were always kept small - both the number of countries taking part and the people in the meeting room. A surprising amount of the personal, informal and spontaneous character survived, as Colin Budd's chapter will testify. The summit became an institution, but not an organisation.

Summitry and the Eight Questions of Economic Diplomacy

Chapter 1 identified eight questions in economic diplomacy, summarised in Table 1.1. Economic diplomacy seeks to reconcile the tensions which underlie each of those questions. This section looks at each question to see how the early summits contributed to them.

1. How to reconcile economic and political objectives?

The founders of the summit recognised that the political pressures for cooperation had weakened since the post-war period. They tried to generate new incentives to cooperate. Although Giscard - a former finance minister - insisted that the summit was a wholly economic instrument - in fact he was seeking to restore political unity in the face of the threat from OPEC. The concept that heads of government could succeed in solving economic problems that had baffled their bureaucrats depended on their greater political authority, rather than their economic expertise.

2. How to reconcile economic and political methods?

The early summits were strongly influenced by 'Keynesian' ideas of how fiscal policy could be used to stimulate economic growth and employment. This fitted in well with the interventionist political instincts of leaders like Schmidt and Wilson - and even Giscard and Carter. But there was an abrupt change in economic strategy after 1978, with priority given to 'monetarist' ideas for controlling inflation - this will be explored further later in this chapter. This change in economic strategy matched the political shift marked by the arrival of Reagan, Thatcher and Kohl.

3. How do governments reach common positions internally?

As already explained, the G7 heads of government intervene systematically in the domestic decision-making process to introduce new ideas and to resolve differences.   The Sherpa system stimulates the search for inter-departmental agreement, while the approach of the summit itself concentrates people's minds on resolving differences.   The summit has a catalytic effect on the bureaucratic process. But it cannot substitute for this process, as Giscard wanted.

4. How can domestically agreed positions be deployed internationally?

Getting better international agreement and overcoming widespread deadlock was the fundamental reason for creating the summits. The record outlined in the first part of this chapter shows that the early summits had some clear achievements, by reaching agreement in monetary reform, trade liberalisation and economic policy coordination. Putnam's work uses the summits' achievements, especially the Bonn summit of 1978, to illustrate how the interaction between domestic and international pressures works. This is the foundation of his model of 'two-level games'.[16] But of course the summits did not always succeed in meeting their objectives.

5. Which is better - voluntary cooperation or binding rules?

This requires some more detailed analysis. The institution building at the end of World War II was intended to create new rules for trade and money. The full trade rules of the International Trade Organisation (ITO) were still-born, as explained in Chapter 6. The GATT was much weaker and full of loopholes, but it was still a rule-based regime. The rules for money were agreed in the IMF and were applied progressively. But they collapsed in 1971 and for a time no one could agree on their replacement.

The summits relied not on rules but on voluntary cooperation. Such a small group could not make rules for the rest of the world and never intended to do so. The whole idea behind the summit was that the heads of government, by agreeing voluntarily to cooperate among themselves, would lead the international system out of deadlock.

Putnam and Henning, in their study of the 1978 Bonn summit, stress the contrast between voluntary cooperation and rule-making.[17] They commend the Bonn summit as an example of how voluntary cooperation can lead to ambitious and fully implemented agreements. But a full examination of the record of the early summits does not support such a favourable conclusion. For example:

- In *monetary reform*, that part of the Rambouillet agreement concerned with the legitimisation of floating was endorsed by the IMF and became a durable part of the rules. But the understanding on voluntary cooperation to counter 'erratic fluctuations' in exchange rates did not endure.
- In *trade*, the voluntary cooperation to resist protectionism worked well while it was linked to the Tokyo Round negotiations in the rule-based GATT. But once the round was over, these promises ceased to be kept.
- In *economic policy coordination*, the voluntary commitments made at Bonn were indeed implemented. But the earlier promises made at the summits of 1976 and 1977 were not.

The summit record leads to the conclusion that voluntary cooperation, unrelated to rule-based systems or institutions, does not survive under pressure. This issue will be taken up again in the final chapter.

6. How to ensure democratic legitimacy and accountability?

The early summit leaders were mainly concerned to improve the efficiency of economic diplomacy and did not perceive accountability as a serious problem. There was not the same degree of popular alienation from government as prevails in the early 2000s. Even so, the heads of government, as indicated earlier, were in a good position to respond to popular anxieties, since they all had direct or indirect mandates from their electorates. This gave them strong democratic legitimacy to take international decisions, to defend them nationally and to seek ratification when needed. They were well placed to be active in the latter stages of the domestic decision-making sequence - legitimisation and ratification.

7. How do governments deal with private business and markets?

Schmidt's initiative in creating a group of senior private sector figures was an early example of using business and academic circles as a source of new ideas. But this was not in fact integrated into the early summit process, which remained limited to governments. Business interests had no visible impact.

8. How should governments respond to NGOs?

NGOs were not yet active in the early 1970s. But the question of transparency, which NGOs demand today, was already a subject of controversy and deserves comment. Giscard was against transparency: for him, summits were private conversations between heads of government. He wanted the media kept at a respectful distance and only agreed under pressure that the summits should issue a public declaration. But from the outset the Americans, led by Kissinger, maintained that this approach was not only impracticable but misguided. The summits were an opportunity to educate the public about the merits of cooperation at the highest level and the ways in which it could be achieved. In the early years the press took a positive view of the summits and treated their conclusions seriously. But as the media presence at the summit expanded, they became critical, even cynical, about the events.[18]

Why Were the Later Summits Less Ambitious?

The agreements concluded at the 1978 Bonn summit, which led to mutual policy adjustments across different areas, were the most ambitious achievements of any G7 summit. Bonn scores the highest grade for cooperation in the Putnam and Bayne comparative table of summits.[19] Why did the summits never try to do so much again?

The simplest answer is that G7 governments concluded that the locomotive approach, where strong economies boosted growth to pull along weak ones, was the wrong policy. It led directly to the second oil crisis, which struck in early 1979. Oil prices stayed around $12-13 per barrel from 1974 to 1978, but in real terms they had fallen. Inflation had risen, the dollar had dropped and Western oil consumption still remained high. The OPEC members were discontented, as their earnings from oil sales and oil-related investments were being eroded. They saw that the West was still vulnerable to another steep rise in oil prices - and they drove them up to $36 per barrel.

Some argue that the G7 members, and especially the United States, had a range of legitimate government interventions available, to influence growth and inflation. In retrospect, it appeared that they chose the wrong combination. That would be the conventional wisdom of the 1970s.[20] Others argue that governments should always intervene to check inflation; but they should never intervene to stimulate growth, which is the task of the private sector. That became the conventional wisdom of the 1980s. Having made the wrong policy choice would be enough on its own to make the summit leaders more cautious about economic policy coordination. But in fact the change from a growth strategy to an anti-inflation strategy had a more profound effect upon the summits.

Strong growth in a country with a large open economy also promotes growth in that country's trading partners, even when they may be unable to promote growth themselves. Strong growth in the United States in the late 1990s, for example, was the main factor behind the rapid recovery of countries hit by the Asian financial crisis. They could export themselves out of trouble, by selling into the US market. So growth strategies naturally lend themselves to cooperation, to spread the benefit. Stronger growth also brings immediate political benefits to governments that can deliver it. So growth strategies had an obvious appeal to G7 leaders.

With anti-inflation strategies, however, every country has to act on its own. Governments can give each other mutual encouragement, but they have to introduce their own policies - others cannot reduce their inflation for them. Furthermore, anti-inflation policies usually involve a period of hardship before the rewards appear. So they carry political drawbacks.

From 1979 onwards the summits shifted sharply from supporting growth to checking inflation, as British Prime Minister Margaret Thatcher found to her surprise when she arrived at the Tokyo summit after only a month in office. There was no scope for mutual adjustments; the heads of government did no more than encourage each other to keep up the pressure on inflation.[21] Quite soon they delegated economic policy coordination to their finance ministers, where it has remained ever since.

All this goes to explain why the summits never again tried ambitious mutual adjustment of macroeconomic policies. It does not explain why the summits did not in future attempt cross-issue linkage of any kind, balancing commitments by one country in one policy area against commitments by another country in a different area.

The summits clearly have the capacity to do this if they wish. But they very seldom do. After Bonn 1978, the next clear example comes from the 1982 Versailles summit. There the Americans again agreed to intervene in exchange markets to 'counter disorderly conditions' in return for European restraint on export credit to the Soviet Union. But this deal collapsed in mutual misunderstanding within hours of being announced. After these unhappy experiences with cross-issue linkage, it was perhaps not surprising that it was seldom attempted. But there were other reasons, linked to the decision-making process. Cross-issue deals required both innovative ideas and meticulous preparation and in both respects the later summits lost their comparative advantage.

As regards innovation, the ability of the heads to generate original economic ideas declined after 1978 as the initial generation of former finance ministers went out of office - and by 1983 there were none left. But the summits of the late 1990s and early 2000s regained the capacity to innovate in other areas, as Chapter 8 will show. Cross-issue deals surfaced at the early summits because the traditional bureaucratic system, centred on a single lead department for each policy area, found it difficult to accommodate deals where several departments shared responsibility. But, as Chapter 6 showed, policy linkage became much more common in complex negotiations and no longer required the intervention of the summits. Yet the most recent summits provide their own examples of such agreements, as when the Genoa 2001 and Kananaskis 2002 summits produced action plans on Africa which combined economic and political elements.[22]

Conclusions: Summitry Today

Reconciling the tensions of the 2000s

What happened next to summitry, in the 1980s and 1990s? After Rambouillet the summits did not need to return to monetary reform for a long time. After Bonn the leaders soon delegated economic policy to their finance ministers. Energy policy occupied the heads after the second oil shock, but interest in that too faded as oil prices fell back in the mid-1980s. By then the summit leaders were paying as much attention to political issues like nuclear missiles and terrorism as to economic issues.[23]

The end of the Cold War, from 1989 onwards, gave the G7 summits a new lease of life.[24] The heads of government recognised a new responsibility to help countries emerging from communism - and to help Russia above all. But they also felt responsible, once again, for ensuring that the open international economic system worked efficiently and fairly. These responsibilities led them during the 1990s to focus more and more on the implications of globalisation, both good and bad; to change their attitude to established international institutions; and to admit Russia to membership. In the process, their decision-making methods changed pretty radically, so that some of the earliest ideas became topical again.[25]

The implications of these new moves are examined by Colin Budd in Chapter 8. His chapter shows that the contribution of today's summits to reconciling the tensions of economic diplomacy, as set out in Table 1.1, has changed in the following ways:

Tension between economics and politics

1. *Economic and political objectives.* In the 1990s, the political aim of inducing Russia to behave responsibly led to its admission to the G8, though the economic justification was weak. In the 2000s, the summits gave priority to development issues, because of their concern that poor countries were being marginalised by globalisation.
2. *Economic and political methods.* The arrival of more interventionist leaders like Clinton, Blair and Schroeder from the mid-1990s led to a profound change in the summit format. The heads decided to meet on their own, without supporting ministers.

Tension between domestic and international pressures

3. *Reaching common positions internally.* The summits still exercised a catalytic and innovative effect on their bureaucracies, helping to open up discussion of new issues in economic diplomacy like international crime, the digital divide and infectious diseases.
4. *Deploying domestically agreed positions internationally.* The summit apparatus expanded greatly, with many more G7 and G8 ministerial groups to which issues could be delegated. But the Sherpas remained at the fulcrum of the process.

5. *Voluntary cooperation or binding rules.* The G8 members no longer relied on voluntary cooperation among themselves. The G8 increasingly acted as a ginger group in multilateral rule-making institutions, though working by persuasion rather than presenting faits accomplis.
6. *Securing accountability and legitimacy.* The heads of government still had strong legitimacy nationally and could rely on their domestic political authority, though this weakened as they approached elections.[26] (They became more concerned with their international legitimacy, as an exclusive group in a globalising world, and began developing their links with non-G8 leaders.)

Tension between government and other forces

7. *Dealing with private business.* The G8 moved to involve private business in both summit preparation and follow-up, for example in IT and renewable energy, as Colin Budd records.
8. *Responding to NGOs.* In the late 1990s, the summits reacted positively to peaceful lobbying on debt relief. As with business, the G8 increasingly involved responsible NGOs in preparation and follow-up. But the summit had to denounce the destructive protests at Genoa in 2001.

The operation of the summit and its supporting apparatus will be compared with other plurilateral and multilateral institutions in Chapter 14.

Notes

1 The circumstances which led to the creation of the summits are analysed in Putnam and Bayne 1987, Chapter 2, and de Menil and Solomon 1983. These are the two essential sources for the early development of summitry.
2 For the creation of the Marshall Plan, see Marjolin 1989.
3 For the course of the 'Year of Europe', see Kissinger 1982, Chapters 5 and 19.
4 A prescient analysis of the consequences of interdependence is in Cooper 1972.
5 These fears were clearly articulated by German Chancellor Schmidt - see Putnam and Bayne 1987, pp. 33-34.
6 On this, compare Putnam and Bayne 1987, Chapter 1, with Bayne 2000, Chapter 1. In both books, the summit objectives are given in the reverse order to what is used here.
7 For an assessment of the Tokyo Round, see Winham 1986, Preeg 1995.
8 The details of this episode are in Putnam and Bayne 1987, p. 38.
9 On trade at the 1978 Bonn summit, see de Menil and Solomon, pp. 25-6.
10 Putnam's detailed analysis of the summit record, especially the Bonn summit of 1978, forms the foundation for his theory of two-level games. See Putnam 1988 and Putnam and Henning 1989.
11 The following account is based on the author's personal recollections of Rambouillet, still vivid after more than 25 years.
12 Many of the original features of Rambouillet were recreated at the G8 summit of 2002. Largely for security reasons, the Canadians hosted it at Kananaskis, a small and secluded resort in the Rockies, where limits on accommodation obliged G8 members to cut back the size of their delegations.

13 The key analysis of the early institutionalisation of the summits is in Putnam and Bayne 1987, Chapter 3.

14 In Britain always, in France under Mitterrand and Chirac and in America under Carter, Clinton and Bush the younger, the Sherpa has been part of the leader's own staff, sitting in No 10 Downing Street, in the Elysée Palace or in the White House. But the Japanese Sherpa has always been an official of the foreign ministry. That is also the current arrangement in Canada and was the American practice under Reagan and Bush the elder. In Germany the Sherpa was always from the finance ministry, until Schroeder moved it away on taking office, first to his own Chancellery, then to the economics ministry.

15 *Henry IV, Part 2* (1600), Act I, Scene ii.

16 See Putnam 1988 and Evans, Jacobson and Putnam 1993.

17 See Putnam and Henning 1989.

18 For this the leaders themselves were largely to blame. In the first few years the leaders always appeared together for the press briefing when the summit finished. This, symbolically at least, stressed the solidarity between them. But then it became the custom for each leader to brief separately, drawing attention to what he or she had achieved at the summit for Britain or France or the United States. This was inevitably divisive.

19 This table first appears in Putnam and Bayne 1987, p. 270, Table 11.1, and is updated in Bayne 2000, p. 195, Table 12.1.

20 It is also broadly the conclusion of Putnam and Henning 1989.

21 This, however, had its value for governments seeking encouragement to maintain unpopular polices, as Prime Minister Thatcher found. See Thatcher 1993, pp. 290 and 586-87.

22 There was a similar cross-issue deal at the G8 summit of 2002, though it was not explicit. The American endorsement to the $1 billion replenishment of the World Bank trust fund to finance debt relief unlocked the European and Japanese contributions to the $20 billion programme to clean up nuclear weapons and other materials in Russia.

23 For an analysis of the summits' performance in the Reagan years, see Putnam and Bayne 1987, especially Chapter 10, or Bayne 2000, Chapter 3.

24 For the post-Cold War summits and their achievements, see Bayne 2000. An excellent source of documentation and analysis on the recent summits is the web site of the University of Toronto G8 Research Group, www.g8.utoronto.ca.

25 A brief treatment of this, focusing on the 2001 Genoa summit, is in Bayne 2001. A more detailed analysis, centred on the role of the Sherpas, should appear as a chapter in a volume edited by Bob Reinalda and Bertjan Verbeek of the University of Nijmegen (Bayne forthcoming).

26 The durability in office of the G8 leaders varies greatly between countries. US Presidents can be sure of four years in office, but never more than eight. Some European leaders, however, stay much longer: Kohl took part in 16 summits, Mitterrand in 14, Thatcher in 12. In Japan and Italy, however, the rotation of leaders has been much faster, which reduces their impact on summit decisions. This emerges from the tables in Sherifis and Astraldi 2001, pp. 217-253.

References

Bayne, N. (2000a), *Hanging In There: the G7 and G8 Summit in Maturity and Renewal*, Ashgate, Aldershot.

Bayne, N. (2001), 'G-8 Decision-Making and the Genoa Summit', *The International Spectator*, vol. XXXVI, no. 3, pp. 69-75.

Bayne, N. (forthcoming), 'Are World Leaders Puppets or Puppeteers? The Sherpas of the G7/G8 System', in Reinalda, B. and Verbeek, B. (eds.), *Decision-Making within International Organisations*, Routledge, London.

Cooper, R. N. (1972), 'Economic Interdependence and Foreign Policy in the Seventies', *World Politics*, vol. 24, no. 2, pp. 159-181.

De Menil, G. and Solomon, A. M. (1983), *Economic Summitry*, Council on Foreign Relations, New York.

Evans, P. B., Jacobson, H. K. and Putnam, R. D. (eds.) (1993), *Double-Edged Diplomacy: International Bargaining and Domestic Politics*, University of California Press, Berkeley.

Kissinger, H. (1982), *Years of Upheaval*, Weidenfeld and Nicholson, London.

Marjolin, R. (1989), *Architect of European Unity: Memoirs 1911-1986*, Weidenfeld and Nicholson, London, translated by William Hall from *Le Travail d'une Vie*, Robert Laffont, Paris 1986.

Preeg, E. (1995), *Traders in a Brave New World*, Chicago University Press, Chicago.

Putnam, R. D. (1988), 'Diplomacy and Domestic Politics: the Logic of Two-Level Games', *International Organisation*, vol. 42, no. 3, pp. 427-460.

Putnam, R. D. and Bayne, N. (1987), *Hanging Together: Cooperation and Conflict in the Seven-Power Summits*, SAGE, London.

Putnam, R. D. and Henning, C. R. (1989), 'The Bonn Summit of 1978: A Case Study in Coordination', in Cooper, R. N. and others (eds.), *Can Nations Agree? Issues in International Economic Cooperation*, The Brookings Institution, Washington.

Sherifis, R. F. and Astraldi, V. (2001), *The G7/G8 from Rambouillet to Genoa*, FrancoAngeli, Milan.

Thatcher, M. (1993), *The Downing Street Years*, HarperCollins, London.

Winham, G. (1986), *International Trade and the Tokyo Round Negotiations*, Princeton University Press, Princeton.

Chapter 8

G8 Summits and Their Preparation

Colin Budd

What follows sets out to describe the G8 process as it seemed to one British participant in the calendar years 1998-2000. This provides a contemporary assessment to set against the historical account of the earlier summits, from 1975 onwards, in Chapter 7 above.[1] For those who are more familiar with the concept of G7, it should be observed that the Birmingham Summit of 1998 was the first at which Russia was present as a full member, since when the correct appellation has been G8.

This chapter aims to cover three aspects of this subject:

- The mechanics of summitry.
- The process of trying to distil all the rhetoric about globalisation down to outcomes which make a difference in the real world.
- The objectives which one member of G8 - the United Kingdom - sought to achieve in the period in question.

The Mechanics of Summitry

The mechanics of the system are relatively simple, the number of countries involved being relatively small. As the name suggests, there are only eight, plus the European Union (EU).[2] This makes organisation relatively easy, and tends to promote lively brainstorming. Whatever its other shortcomings, discussion round a G8 table is at least closer to the cut and thrust of real debate than the ponderous, heavily multilateral gatherings characteristic of so much of international affairs today. At its best, the G8 is refreshing, intimate, and - like small boats as opposed to oil tankers - manoeuvrable. Also like small boats, it can, at its best, move fast.

The preparations for the annual summit, usually held in June or July, follow what is now a fairly well trodden route. Each country uses a team of Sherpas, following the mountaineering image, both to coordinate its own preparations and to represent it in the sequence of meetings leading to the summit. The head of each team is known as the Sherpa, and is usually (but not always) one of the key personal staff of the President or Prime Minister in question. Each Sherpa has two deputies, or Sous-Sherpas (a French term, now used by all G8 countries) - one from the foreign and the other from the finance ministry. For discussions of traditional 'political' foreign policy, each country fields its foreign ministry's Political Director.

The G8 countries take it in turns to chair the process, for a calendar year at a time, and the country in charge at any one time is known as the Presidency.[3] The rhythm of the summit preparatory process begins in January or February, often with meetings of the two Sous-Sherpa groups, sometimes interspersed with meetings of experts in various fields. The process is nowadays much facilitated, and enriched, by the use of e-mail; in theory it would also lend itself rather well to video-conferencing, but that has so far proved a bridge too far (though conference telephone calls have occasionally been introduced). Usually the Sous-Sherpas will meet up to half a dozen times, and the Sherpas four or five, in the approach to the summit, with the final way-station being a plenary meeting of the three Sherpa groups and the Political Directors, all meeting together. Finally, immediately preceding the summit there are usually separate meetings of the foreign and the finance ministers.

So much for the internal dynamics of the process. But there are also, of course, important external elements: the contacts with other governments, with non-governmental organisations (NGOs), and with the media. Each G8 Presidency takes good care to maintain a dialogue with the rest of the world, with civil society, and with journalists, some six thousand of whom normally attend each Summit. The scale of the world's interest in the G8 can be overpowering, and each Presidency has the challenge of having simultaneously to satisfy the intense interest of the global community and respect the wish of the G8 heads of government to keep their own meetings as close as possible to the cosy, relaxed intimacy associated with the original summits of the late 1970s. While the G8 countries have an evident interest in maintaining their own freedom of manoeuvre, their conclusions will also command more respect insofar as they reflect dialogue with others in the course of the preparatory process.

Practical Responses to Globalisation

As well as getting the mechanics right, each Presidency also has to rise to the challenge of both identifying the right agenda and ensuring that the G8 tackle it in the most effective way. These are no easy tasks. The sheer quantity of discussion now going on in the world has become almost immeasurable. To sort out the wheat from the chaff is already very difficult - and the question then has to be asked: where can G8 really do most to make a difference?

The first aim has to be to identify and discard all the windy, overblown rhetoric: much of the globalisation debate is conducted in terms of airy generalisations, with very little, if any, real substance. Then one has to examine what is really going on in the world: what are the interesting or worrying trends, the problems or opportunities coming round the corner, to which solutions need to be found or strategies shaped to make sure that advantage is taken of the best moment for action.

At its best, the G8 succeeds in being ahead of the curve, in being more perceptive and moving faster than anyone else. The world is of course now amply provided with large scale global institutions, often with highly qualified staff and a comprehensive global membership. Such bodies have their uses, but they tend undeniably to be cumbersome, condemned often to move at the pace of their slowest members - whereas G8, as already noted, is small enough sometimes to be able to move quickly, and can have a crucial catalytic effect. If a really good idea surfaces, there is a chance that support for it can get critical mass inside G8 much faster than in larger gatherings. This does not always happen, by any means, because G8 operates on the basis of consensus, so any idea can always be vetoed by just one country. But the opportunity at least exists to get there first, with a new solution for an incipient problem, or to provide a new spark capable of reanimating a long dead bureaucratic process. The aim is to try to catch and identify the Zeitgeist, before anyone else does - or, even more difficult, to work out what the Zeitgeist is going to be in five or ten years time, and pre-empt it.

In the category of reanimation, the achievement which pleased me personally the most in the course of the British G8 Presidency of 1998 related to the campaign of the World Health Organisation (WHO) to eradicate malaria. This campaign was already in existence and doing much very good work, but it needed a bit of extra momentum to allow it to shift into a higher, still more effective gear. The G8, by identifying and highlighting the issue in front of the 6,000-odd journalists present at the May 1998 Birmingham Summit, provided an extra push which was certainly much appreciated by the WHO - the more so since the UK, the country holding the G8 Presidency at the time, marked the occasion by donating for the same purpose an extra £20 million. (Malaria came back to future summits, associated with other infectious diseases, as will appear later.)

Another classic task for G8, when a new world trade negotiation is in the offing, is to find the right formula for a G8 statement which will help to get a new round moving, on a basis likely to work well. The art is always - while taking care to avoid an approach likely to be perceived by the developing world as patronising behaviour on the part of the rich - to seek to detect what is intelligent and timely, where value can be added to an existing process, or a new one helped to get off the ground.[4]

Increasingly the process is part of an exercise in open government - not just governments going through their own secretive, internal processes, but governments listening to their Parliaments, to civil society more widely, and to their most expert NGOs in the field in question. Here are two examples of how, in the British case, such exercises can take shape. Both featured quite prominently in the Okinawa Summit of July 2000.

Renewable energy

The first concerns renewable energy - a subject of perennial interest for the world community. This story began with a seminar held at No 10 Downing Street in the autumn of 1999, under the chairmanship of Jeremy Heywood, Principal Private Secretary to the British Prime Minister, Tony Blair (and the UK Sherpa in the G8 process). The topic for the seminar was simply 'Energy', and the aim to consider whether any worthwhile initiative in that general field could be identified, for pursuit in the G8 campaign of the following year. The invitation list was made up of some 20 leading experts from NGOs and half a dozen key officials from relevant ministries.

A lot of ideas were floated. In the end, the one which received most support was not a new idea, as such, but an elegant and forceful restatement of a very familiar problem. Something like one in six of the world's population have inadequate access to energy. Action cannot be taken to give them energy by conventional means without highly undesirable side-effects. Hence the need is to find responsible ways of meeting this requirement, at a price moreover which those concerned (who are mostly very poor) can afford. The obvious, though far from easy, solution is some form of renewable energy.

Following the seminar, further meetings were held inside government to take the idea further. Eventually Prime Minister Blair put his authority behind it, and it was put forward as a British proposal to other G8 partners. After a long process of debate, at the Okinawa summit agreement was eventually reached on the establishment of a G8 Task Force to consider the problem further, and report back to the Genoa summit of July 2001. This body was deliberately set up on a mixed private/public basis, and co-chaired by Sir Mark Moody-Stuart, the Chairman of the Committee of Managing Directors of Shell, and Corrado Clini, a senior Italian civil servant. It included some of the key players from all the relevant disciplines - liable, on any rational analysis, of having as good a chance as anyone in the world of coming up with an imaginative and constructive solution to what has for a long time been seen as an intractable problem.

As an experiment in cooperation at the highest level between the public and private sectors the task force broke a certain amount of new ground and proved far from easy to run, but those involved found it nonetheless highly stimulating.

The Task Force Report submitted to the Genoa summit contained a set of well-argued conclusions with impressively wide support - from governments, industry and NGOs. But though these findings were backed by the American private sector, the new US Administration was concerned that they might conflict with its national energy programme. Because of this resistance by one G8 member, the Task Force itself was wound up. But the work was not lost for this reason - G8 energy ministers were charged to take matters further.

Health and development

The second example of British G8 policy formation concerns health. This too started with a seminar at No. 10 Downing Street in the autumn of 1999, on much the same scale as the other: again a mixture of NGO representatives, players from industry (such as Glaxo[5]), and senior civil servants. The original spark for this exercise had been struck by an article in *The Economist* some six months before, by Professor Jeffrey Sachs of Harvard University, who had argued with much force that vaccines were in many cases too expensive for those people in the world who needed them most, and had urged the need for radical, imaginative solutions to that problem.[6] But that was only one set of the questions addressed by the No 10 seminar, which ranged widely over the full scope of the global health improvement agenda.

The eventual conclusion reached, which again can be traced all the way through to the communiqué of the Okinawa Summit, was that it would be highly desirable for G8 to preach to the rest of the world the crucial message that health is absolutely fundamental to development. At the same time the summit should list key targets in a number of health fields which the world community, in the view of G8, should aim to achieve within specified periods of time: measurable benchmarks against which progress could in future be assessed, and appropriate conclusions then drawn. The Okinawa summit focused attention on three infectious diseases which hold back the development of poor countries: AIDS, malaria and tuberculosis. The Genoa summit of 2001 went further in launching, together with the UN Secretary General, a new Global AIDS and Health Fund to fight these diseases.

In both cases - renewable energy and health - the British government gained a good deal of credit with a number of constituencies: with the NGOs in question, of course, for being seen to take both them and the problems under debate seriously, but also with Parliament, the press and the developing world. No categorically new solutions were identified, but modest progress was made, and agreement was reached on the basis of pragmatic, feet-on-the-ground common sense, rather than the mindless verbosity which can all too easily characterize international debate on issues of this kind.

The Achievement of British Objectives in the G8

The third part of this chapter considers the extent to which the United Kingdom, in the G8 Summit campaigns of 1998, 1999 and 2000, actually achieved its objectives.

Birmingham 1998

I joined the process in September 1997, as the British Foreign Office Sous-Sherpa. By that stage it had already been agreed, at the Denver Summit of 1997, that the principal focus at the 1998 Birmingham Summit would be on employability and crime - to which eventually was added, in the light of the implications of the financial crisis in Asia in the second half of 1997, a general discussion on the global economy, looking at how best to resuscitate and further promote growth.

The British Presidency was also determined, from an early stage in its planning, to contribute at Birmingham to a fundamental renewal of the summit process, helping to return it to the model originally envisaged in 1975. The Birmingham Summit reintroduced the 'heads of government only' approach. Foreign and finance ministers held separate meetings well in advance, thus enabling some reduction in the size of the delegations at the summit itself, and a return to a more intimate style. This was promoted also by the fact that part of the summit was held in 'retreat', at a country house well outside Birmingham.

As regards employability, the main event in the 1998 UK Presidency was a joint conference in February, chaired by British Finance Minister Gordon Brown, of G8 finance and employment ministers, whose conclusions were later endorsed by the Birmingham Summit, as the UK had planned. Crime, an important subject for G8 ever since the Halifax Summit in 1995, also featured prominently at Birmingham - with discussion of everything from high tech crime and money laundering to asset confiscation, the smuggling of illegal immigrants, joint law enforcement projects, firearms and drugs trafficking. On the global economy, the heads of government in the end discussed not only the implications of the Asian crisis, but also the need to make further progress with the liberalisation of international trade and investment, the importance of helping poorer developing countries to achieve faster sustainable growth and reduce poverty, and the international energy situation.

Finally, the spotlight also fell, as the British government had long been intent that it should, on the importance of taking action to reduce the burden of debt of the IMF/World Bank list of Heavily Indebted Poor Countries (HIPC). On this front the commitments made in the G8 communiqué were widely viewed as disappointing, but the G8 agreement was on any analysis a step forward, and was defended as such by the British Prime Minister.[7] Overall, the UK emerged from the Birmingham Summit well pleased with what it had achieved. In addition to the points made above, the communiqué itself was signally shorter and crisper than its recent predecessors, and there was a general recognition that some useful reforms had been introduced.

Cologne 1999

The Cologne Summit of 1999 set out to focus quite consciously on how to make the best sense of globalisation, and was also - under the pressure of events in the Balkans - heavily preoccupied by the situation in Kosovo. For the UK, the most important step forward was the further progress achieved in the field of HIPC debt reduction. The Cologne Debt Initiative was a major advance, building in a number of areas on what had been agreed at Birmingham, as regards both the speed and depth of debt relief and its total value. It was duly endorsed at the annual meeting of the IMF and World Bank in September 1999.[8]

Other major UK objectives at Cologne were:

- Agreement, in the wake of the Asia crisis, to strengthen international financial architecture; this was duly achieved.
- The launch of an education charter, committing G8 leaders to a set of principles and targets for education and life long learning in the new millennium; this was successful.
- Agreement on a new political and practical framework for engaging Russia in G8 and successfully integrating Russia into the global economy. The first of these aims succeeded, but not the second. That is nothing if not a long haul, since it involves preparing Russia to clear the hurdles en route to membership of the WTO and the OECD.

The UK finished the Cologne Summit with satisfactory progress in all areas, including debt, save for the Russian economy.

All in all, the Birmingham and Cologne Summits can both be seen as having been modestly but significantly successful: no mean achievement, given that in the view of at least one historian, only one other Summit in the 1990s - Halifax in 1995 - reached even that level.[9]

Okinawa 2000

The Okinawa Summit of July 2000 is not associated with any dominant single success, but did make modest progress in a considerable number of areas. The UK for its part failed to get agreement on the establishment of the new independent scientific panel it wanted set up to cover biotechnology and food safety - largely because the French and US positions were different both from each other and from that of the UK.

On the other hand there was a long list of UK successes in achieving its objectives. There was agreement, subsequently ratified by the OECD, to a deadline of 1 January 2002 for untying aid to least developed countries. There were a number of new commitments on health, as noted above. The UK led the drive to get G8 support for the thrust of the Dakar framework for action on education[10] - like malaria in 1998, this was an example of G8 using its weight to help get an existing bandwagon moving a bit faster. Britain pressed hard for a further signal of commitment to the HIPC debt reduction scheme and led the call for greater support for enhanced market access for least developed countries. There was satisfactory language on drugs, including the British proposal for a conference to examine the global economy of illegal drugs. The summit met UK objectives on active ageing, conflict diamonds (an attempt to reduce the extent to which profits from trading diamonds have fuelled in certain areas of the world the growth of conflict) and illegal logging, and also reached useful agreements on plutonium disposition and the destruction of chemical weapons.

Conclusion

One thing above all is clear: no one at work in the G8 process can complain about the lack of variety! But just how important is the work that G8 do? Clearly the process is by no means always successful, as is eloquently brought out by the gradings given to different summits in Table 12.1 in Nicholas Bayne's *Hanging In There*.[11] But even on his fairly stringent marking system the summits of the 1990s emerge as more successful, on average, than those of the 1980s, which is perhaps reason for a modest optimism in looking towards the future.

As noted at the start of this chapter, in a world in which organisations with global membership are frequently very constipated in style and slow to get moving, a quite lightly manned small commando group like G8 can, if well led, move quite quickly in the right direction. Every now and again it can light on a really important idea before the rest of the world does, and then move at a seriously useful pace to nudge debate along.

There is certainly no shortage of problems to tackle. To name but two, the questions thrown up by the interface between biotechnology and food safety are still staring us all in the face, and the implications for all our societies of the increasingly complex patterns of migration and immigration are also plain to see. If the G8 in the years ahead can confront, rather than sidestep and evade, these and other problems of this magnitude, then it will continue to be performing a real service not just for its own citizens but for the world as a whole. And as electronic communication and methods of governance are further improved, it should steadily become easier both to gather and sift world opinion and proactively to build constituencies for imaginative and constructive solutions. That, at any rate, will remain G8's aspiration, and as honourable a way as any for practitioners of economic diplomacy to seek to make their mark.

Notes

1   The key documentary sources are Putnam and Bayne 1987, which covers the period up to the Venice summit of 1987, and Bayne 2000a, which brings the story up to date.
2   The EU is represented by the Commission and the Presidency. When the Presidency is held by a Member State not already in the G8, this adds a ninth country to the participants.
3   The established order is France, United States, United Kingdom, Germany, Japan, Italy, Canada. Russia has not yet hosted a summit.
4   The statement on a new WTO round agreed at the 2001 Genoa summit was a good example of this.
5   Glaxo has since merged with SmithKline Beecham and is known as GlaxoSmithKline or GSK.
6   The article in question was 'Helping the World's Poorest', *The Economist*, 14 August 1999 (Sachs 1999).
7   For more details on debt relief at Birmingham, see Bayne 1998.
8   The Cologne Debt Initiative is analysed in Bayne 2000a, pp. 180-186.
9   Bayne 2000a, p. 195, Table 12.1, awards a grade of B+ only to Halifax 1995, Birmingham 1998 and Cologne 1999 of the summits of the 1990s. No summit has scored an A or A- grade since the Bonn summit in 1978.
10 The World Education Forum in Dakar, Senegal, in May 2000, brought together 181 governments with NGOs and international institutions, especially UNESCO and UNICEF. The participants adopted six broad educational targets to be achieved by 2015.
11 Bayne 2000a, p. 195 - see note 9 above.

References

Bayne, N. (1998), 'Britain, the G8 and the Commonwealth: Lessons of the Birmingham Summit', *The Round Table*, no. 348, pp.445-457.
Bayne, N. (2000a), *Hanging In There: the G7 and G8 Summit in Maturity and Renewal*, Ashgate, Aldershot.
Putnam, R. D. and Bayne, N. (1987), *Hanging Together: Cooperation and Conflict in the Seven-Power Summits*, SAGE, London.
Sachs, J. (1999), 'Helping the World's Poorest', *The Economist*, 14 August 1999.

Chapter 9

Is Trade Policy Democratic?
And Should It Be?

Phil Evans

One of the great clarion cries of the non-governmental world since the signing of the multilateral trade agreements of the Uruguay Round, at Marrakesh in 1994, has been that the WTO is not democratic. Allied to this is the argument that greater involvement of the NGO community in trade policy-making will enhance the democratic accountability of the WTO and will rebalance the agenda of the organisation away from a perceived bias towards corporate interests.

This statement of the world as seen from many parts of the NGO world has become both an accepted fact among most NGOs and part of the new orthodoxy of the global trade community. Indeed, the involvement of NGOs in the trade policy system in most developed countries has been increased quite markedly in the last few years. However, the manner of this involvement has tended to leave government officials and NGOs frustrated and disillusioned. The reasons for this frustration and disillusionment are not immediately apparent to the participants and indeed the root causes of the problem are not directly capable of identification. To understand the relationship between trade policy and democracy one has to first ask a number of basic questions. One has to identify the sort of politics that trade politics is; one has to find out whether trade politics is national, regional or global politics; and one has to see how the answers to these questions have changed over time.

What Sort of Politics is Trade Politics?

The notion of democratic accountability is very much like the fable of the six blind men and the elephant - everyone feels a small part of the beast and thinks it to be a different creature; one feels the trunk and thinks it to be a snake; one the leg and thinks it to be a tree. Democratic accountability is similar in that some will see it only in the representation of people through the ballot box; some will grasp it and see it only when their interest group manages to persuade a government of a particular policy; yet more will see it when a government minister bows to 'popular pressure'.

Of course for the purists democracy is 'a system of government by the whole population, usually through elected representatives.'[1] This is hardly an earthshaking definition. However, it is probably the most widely accepted definition and one that places the locus of democracy and accountability in the elected representatives of the populace voting under universal suffrage. However, such a basic, and rather rose-tinted-spectacle view of democratic accountability fails to take into account that rather important element of the process; politics.

Democracy and Politics

The manner in which politics evolves from the democratic will of a people is far from straightforward. What is clear from the study of the real world operation of politics is that it does not play by some form of model set of rules. Real world politics is a far cry from the 'Mr Smith Goes to Washington' view of the world. Again, this is not a particularly new view of politics. However, it is important to identify exactly what we are dealing with in trade policy if we are to trace its links to democratic accountability. It is also important because of the vision of democratic accountability that is espoused (consciously or unconsciously) by commentators in this debate.

What has clearly emerged in the last thirty years of the study of regulation and politics is that it is a terribly messy affair. Interestingly, and appropriately for this issue, most of the best work on the complications of modern politics has occurred in the United States. Two of the most interesting issues in this modern literature of regulation and politics are the role of the interest group and the different 'types' of politics that are found in modern democratic discourse. In relation to trade policy a dual approach is needed. One has to first heed the literature on interest groups and then apply it to the type of politics that is found in the realm of trade policy.

The accumulated scholarship on the relationship of interest groups and politics is best summed up in the US Annual Report of the Council of Economic Advisers of 1994:

> As recognised by both the framers of the Constitution and modern scholars of public choice, all political systems provide interest groups with an incentive for 'rent seeking' that is, manipulation of collective action for private benefit...[rent seeking] can lead government agencies to make decisions that benefit a particular interest group even though they are costly to society as a whole.[2]

This model of the interest group as a rent seeking body is common in the literature and indeed is common in most political systems. In trade policy the great Jagdish Bhagwati has taken this approach further and coined the term 'Directly Unproductive Profit Seeking' activity in relation to the seeking of trade protection by industry.[3]

It has to be pointed out that the rent seeking interest group is broadly defined. When one hears of civil society and interest groups today one tends to only hear of them in a 'public interest' sense. It has to be noted that there are enormous difficulties with the term 'public interest'; who defines it, who classifies the means of promoting the 'public good' and how is such a definition influenced? What is clear from the literature on regulation is that the definition of interest group is sufficiently broad to include the business community. Indeed, one can argue that the definition requires the inclusion of the business community; for without the business world the creation of trade policy is a little like Hamlet without the Prince.

Perhaps the most insightful (and useful) application of the interest group model of politics is found in the work of James Q. Wilson.[4] Wilson's model of political activity fits neatly into a four part box reproduced below.

	COSTS	
	Concentrated	**Diffuse**
BENEFITS		
Concentrated	Interest Group politics	Client politics
	Controversy/Uncertain Govt Action	*Govt Action*
Diffuse	Entrepreneurial politics	Majoritarian politics
	Govt Action	*Uncertain Govt Action*

Figure 9.1   Models of Politics

The enormous benefit of the Wilsonian approach is that politics is divided along two axes; the benefits and costs. It is clear that in political activity one always seeks to derive a benefit (be it a specific one or societal one) and for this to occur another group must suffer some form of loss. The beauty of the Wilson model is that one can divide up the types of political activity that one sees in day to day life.

Concentrated benefits and concentrated costs

When one sees set piece battles between interest groups over a policy, one can observe this model clearly in play. The battle becomes controversial as the benefits and costs are both concentrated on specific groups of interest. Such a type of politics leads to heated debates and genuine battles for the ear of the government. Here government action is not certain and will hinge on the success of one party over another. Such battles can occur in areas such as laws governing agriculture, where farmers and retailers fight it out over regulatory issues. More recently such fights have occurred in the United States between producers of steel and their consumers (like car makers). These sorts of battles are classic examples of 'interest group' politics.

Concentrated benefits and diffuse costs

This sort of political activity centres around a small group that derives enormous benefit from a policy, but can pass on the cost to a very large number of other citizens in small increments. This model of politics tends to lead to 'client politics' where the governmental actor is 'captured' by the interest group that seizes the benefit of regulation. All agricultural policies in the developed world are clear examples of client politics - the very, very few (farmers) capture huge gains at the expense of the great majority (the consumer).

Diffuse benefits and diffuse costs

This model of politics is closer to the Frank Capra view of life than any of the others. Here, operating under 'majoritarian politics' the benefits and costs are so evenly spread and small that society and politicians can debate the greater good of society and engage in discussion across political lines. The sorts of issues amenable to such activities tend to be almost entirely social and moral in nature. Of course, in a zero sum game world of political activity (where only so many parliamentary hours exist), such policy debates can be squeezed out by client and interest group political issues.

Concentrated costs and diffuse benefits

The 'entrepreneurial' model of politics is perhaps the most interesting one for interest groups to run. Here a cost is borne by a very small segment of the society and the benefits that accrue from this policy are small and evenly spread. The manner in which such a campaign is run is a challenge to any interest group. The clearest examples of such policies are those in the environmental field. The Climate Change Levy introduced in Britain, for example, imposes a large cost on a very small number of players (heavy industrial firms) and produces a small benefit to almost everyone (cleaner air). Wilson argues that the only effective means of running and winning such a battle is for the interest group proposing the policy to appeal to broad societal mores and ethical principles.

So Where Does Trade Policy Fit in?

The importance of history

One of the core problems of the current debate about trade policy and democracy is its ahistorical nature. Most participants in the debate are both new to trade policy and profoundly ignorant of where trade policy has come from. I would argue that to fully understand the relationship of trade policy to politics one has to take a broad historical view. As so often, the current debate about trade policy starts in 1930 with the passing of the 1930 Tariff Act, better known as the Smoot-Hawley Act. Smoot-Hawley is important for two main reasons. Firstly, it became associated with the deepening of the US depression (already underway by 1930, but exacerbated by the collapse in trade following the Tariff Act) and thence with World War II. Secondly, it was the last general tariff-raising act of its kind. The raising of tariff levels collectively to 60% of the value of imports triggered retaliatory action on the part of US trading partners and a collapse in world trade.

The link between the Smoot-Hawley Act and the onset of World War II is a controversial one. However, this is not actually very important for the purposes of this argument. What is important is that the legislators of the day, and their descendants to this day, saw a link between radically increased protectionism, economic conflict and military conflict. For those legislators emerging from World War II the desire to avoid any repeat of Smoot-Hawley was a significant one.

In many ways Smoot-Hawley was a high watermark for a certain style of US trade policy. Indeed, Smoot-Hawley was the last in a series of very specific tariff raising laws that had set the tone of trade law and policy for a little over a century. The level of specific tariffs had been one of the key battleground political issues in that preceding century and reflected the Congressional centrality in the making of trade policy. However, while the tale of the century to 1930 had been one of Congressional centrality and high tariffs, the tale begun just four years later led in completely the opposite direction.

By 1934 the United States had begun negotiating reciprocal trade agreements with other countries aimed at reducing tariffs and stimulating trade. The Reciprocal Trade Agreements Act of 1934 was important for two key reasons. Firstly, it indicated a desire of the US to undo the damage of the Smoot-Hawley Act of 1930 and secondly, it was the first statement by Congress that it wished to withdraw from specific trade policy formation.

The 1934 Act authorised the executive to reduce tariffs on items of interest to trading partners by up to 50% without recourse to Congress. This authority was repeatedly reaffirmed right up to the 1970s. The US Congress had effectively withdrawn itself from the setting of tariffs. It has to be remembered that constitutionally Congress has the sole authority over trade policy; what the 1934 Act clearly indicated was that Congress could not trust itself to do the job. The self-awareness in Congress, that they could not trust themselves to do the job properly, lasted for little over fifty years. During that time the US trade policy community established a network of institutions and mechanisms designed to place a buffer between the politicians and the making and implementing of trade policy.

This process reached its apogee in the first granting of 'fast-track' trade authorisation in 1974. Under fast-track, when the Administration submitted a trade agreement for ratification, Congress could accept it or reject it, but could not amend it. The granting of fast-track grew from the general tariff authorisation of the 1934 Act and extended it to new negotiating areas to reflect the increased importance of non-tariff barriers. Fast-track allowed the President and his executive to negotiate trade agreements within parameters without fear that Congress would pick apart each element of the deal and add pet projects or scupper particular bits. What has happened of late is that the idea of fast-track has come under attack for not reflecting the 'will of the people' and, following the furore over NAFTA, has become a hot political issue.

Trade Politics Today

The current state of US trade politics has come about for a number of reasons. Firstly, the early 1990s saw a removal of a large number of 'old-style' free traders from US politics. These politicians were steeped in the post-war consensus that equated protectionism with conflict. This group of politicians had constructed the edifice of US trade policy that buffered the policy from undue political influence, for the good of the world. Secondly, these politicians were increasingly likely to be replaced by a more populist model of politician, in many ways harking back to the turn of the century populism of such figures as William Jennings Bryant. This cohort did not share the same world-view as their predecessors; the consensus for freer trade was starting to break down.

This breakdown of the consensus that viewed freer trade as a public good came about at the same time as trade policy itself started to focus on matters of domestic regulation. What is also important about this shift is that the political consensus in favour of trade allowed politicians to champion freer trade and extol its virtues in a public interest manner. With the withdrawal of the political elite from support of freer trade it was left largely to corporate bodies to argue in favour of the benefits of trade. One of the key problems with this is that they tend to do so only when it favours their particular interest; some argue against freer trade when it suits them (textiles and steel spring to mind) and their involvement signals to opposing forces that they were right all along to think of trade policy as a creature of industry.

The importance of the United States as a driver in world trade cannot be overemphasised. There is no way on earth that the GATT could have been conceived and nurtured without the support of the US. The strategic interests of the United States allowed the GATT to grow and prosper, at some cost to the US in traditional tariff terms. The evolution of US trade policy also occurred directly alongside the evolution of the GATT. So what, one may ask, of other democratic regimes? In the US democratic politics and trade politics were buffered from each other for the good of the world. Democratic politicians recognised that they would damage the greater good if they sought to influence trade policy too directly. In Europe, a similar situation occurred. The great compact of the European Community, and later the European Union, established a complex web of internal negotiations and debates around the Article 113 (now 133) Committee. This web of negotiations acted as a typically European buffer between politicians and trade policy. The regular committee of officials kept the wheels of trade policy oiled and spinning and sought to resolve the core problems of EU trade policy in a totally non-transparent and opaque manner. However, this, again, was done for the best of reasons.

Unlike in the United States, European trade policy has been as much a creature of professional administrators as it has been of politicians. Many of the major trade policy questions were 'settled' a century before the US reached its freer trade consensus. The political consensus on trade thus became embedded in the culture of the administration system. In the UK, the general tendency towards freer trade is built into the collective culture of the civil service. In France, the desire to protect the farm community (and, it has to be said, almost any industry!) is deeply embedded in the French view of the State and the role of 'la belle France'. The longevity and stability of the trade policy community left the European administration of trade policy to evolve as a meeting of officialdom, rather than as a matter of major political controversy. Bodies like the Article 113 Committee became the embodiment of the awkward consensus of administrators and the implicit statement that politicians did not, and should not, be too heavily involved in trade policy for fear that they would unravel all of the good work of the previous century or so.

The Evolution of Trade Policy

The idea that trade policy in the United States and Europe was explicitly (in the US) and implicitly (in Europe) removed from politicians for the general good places the current debate in context. Freer trade was seen as the public good that the trading system was there to advance. The administrations of the United States and Europe needed to protect this public good against the viler intentions of the interest groups that would seek to capture the rents from dismantling that public good.

The view of the trading system as the public good in need of protecting fits rather neatly into the Wilsonian box. The century of trade policy prior to Smoot-Hawley in the US was a century of client politics. US politicians recognised that unchecked, the trading systems' benefits would be captured by small interest groups (specific industries like tobacco, textiles, steel etc) to the disbenefit of the US public and other less well organised industries. Trade policy as client politics was clearly seen as a thing to be avoided. However, the creation of the policy buffer also required the installation of some pressure valves. These pressure valves allowed those seeking protection (and there are always industries seeking protection!) to be channelled through policies like anti-dumping and anti-subsidy laws and later on through trade adjustment assistance for communities. What started to happen during the 1960s and beyond was the emergence of countervailing forces that contested the use of pressure valves. These forces were mainly those of the consuming industries. For example, the seeking of protection by the steel industry (a regular occurrence) started to be met with opposition from industries that imported steel. Trade policy thus evolved from being primarily a client politics system, filtered through buffers and pressure valves, into an interest group system that made outcomes less clear. It has to be noted that in some policy areas, such as agricultural trade, policy has barely moved from its client politics status!

One of the other key developments in trade policy occurred from the 1970s onwards. The Kennedy and Tokyo Rounds of trade negotiations started to deal with non-tariff issues. One of the results of this was to require broader trade negotiating authorisation from Congress (fast-track). But a longer-term implication involved the type of politics that trade politics would now become. Non-tariff barriers (NTBs) involve a huge range of issues from the simple to spot protectionist wheeze (France directing unwelcome imports to the single customs post at Poitiers) to more troublesome regulatory issues such as labelling of foodstuffs. The ticking off of the simple NTBs during the 1980s and 1990s cut away the obvious problem areas. However, it also started to involve trade policy more directly with national regulatory systems. The response of the trade community was, quite naturally, to apply the clinical methodology of the previous decades to the issues in hand. However, the clinical technocratic world-view fitted very poorly with the more complex manner in which domestic policy was formed.

The technocratic approach is fine if you are dealing with client politics regulation - where an industry has gained benefit at the expense of consumers and where this can be dismantled in return for the dismantling of a reciprocal rule abroad. However, as trade negotiations at a global level clung to the diplomatically based reciprocal mercantilism of the past, its agenda was being plunged into the murky world of entrepreneurial and majoritarian politics. While the system could handle interest group politics reasonably well through its vestigial mercantilism, it found itself completely non-plussed by a model of regulation based on majoritarian or entrepreneurial politics. If you look at some of the key problems raised by NGOs in relation to the WTO and its remit and the role of trade policy, one finds a huge number of issues that are majoritarian in nature (where costs and benefits are diffuse) or entrepreneurial (where costs are concentrated and benefits diffuse). The cornerstone issues of the environment, health, welfare and consumer protection are all areas where interest groups have either fought and won battles to impose costs on business to the general good (such as climate change levies and product safety laws), or where complex societal debates have been resolved in compromise positions (many of the developed world health systems in operation).

Where Do We Go From Here?

If one looks at the relationship between trade policy and mechanisms for democratic accountability from a historical perspective one is struck by the fact that the link was strongest when protectionism was at its most damaging. This has to be borne in mind when calls for greater 'democratic' control of trade policy are voiced. Trade policy is a considerably more complex beast than it was prior to the formation of the GATT. Indeed, there is no longer one simple model of politics that trade policy fits within. In some areas, most notably agriculture, steel and textiles the old-fashioned client politics is still strong. In other areas the rise of the countervailing force has created a much greater area of political contestability. In others still the more complex realms of entrepreneurial and majoritarian politics butt up against a system of trade negotiation still structured around dealing with client politics at least and interest group politics at most.

One of the great ironies of this new engagement of the trading community with issues of complex domestic regulation is that, at the very time when an appeal to the public good is required to advance an agenda of freer trade, the political consensus in support of that public good has evaporated or is in retreat. The legitimacy of the trading system is under greater scrutiny than at any other time in its history. Prior to the injection of the trading system into the area of domestic regulation, the legitimacy of the GATT sprang from the diplomatic nature of negotiations. The signing of treaties on behalf of a citizenry based on a reciprocal exchange of trade concessions suited a tariff-based model very well. However, with the signing of the Uruguay Round this diplomatic process, with significant leeway built in for states, was replaced with a highly juridical process based on binding interpretation of often vague laws.

The system of regulation at the WTO thus became much more akin to a nation state; citizens (members) signed up to all laws in return for protection against transgressors and acceptance that punishment could be meted out if they themselves transgressed. However, unlike a nation state the WTO did not develop a governing administration that reflected the job in hand, nor did it establish (nor could it) legislative arms that were able to reflect the will of its citizens. The WTO was left lopsided, with a binding constitution negotiated primarily by a very small number of members, a theoretically strong judicial arm, but no legislative or administrative heart. The unwillingness of members to change the WTO into anything other than the GATT writ large has left the legitimacy of the GATT stretched to breaking point and beyond in trying to accommodate the broadened agenda and judicial structure of new treaties.

The position we are left with is little more than a mess. The trade community has avoided democratic control for good reasons. This consensus was based on democratically elected politicians accepting that the real world of politics meant that they would succumb to the basest of instincts and damage the greater good for their citizens. This worked well for as long as the realm of trade policy was that of the tariff level and the blatantly protectionist rule or regulation. As long as trade policy focused on this it was safe from an unravelling of legitimacy. However, the agenda of trade politics has moved increasingly toward domestic and regional regulation. Here the consensus on the greater good of freer trade runs up against the consensus on the greater good of social protection, cultural values and protective, rather than protectionist, regulation. As trade policy appears to have run into the sands of domestic regulation a new orthodoxy has emerged. Central to that orthodoxy, alongside the need to overload the trading system with all manner of social democratic objectives held dear only in Europe, is that civil society has a rightful place at the heart of trade policy-making. While this orthodoxy has some important truth to it, it has three major drawbacks.

Civil Society and Trade Politics

The greatest opponents of the WTO tend to come from civil society groups in developed countries. This is not to say that those in developing countries are supportive. This is more a statement about resources and profile. Part of the argument of these groups is that trade policy and the WTO are undemocratic. As a result there is demand for greater access and openness in the trade system to allow civil society to have more influence on talks.

There are a number of core problems with this argument. Firstly, the WTO is an organisation of states. As argued above, the WTO was established without effective legislative mechanisms and without a powerful executive. The power in the WTO thus rests entirely with its membership. Prior to the Seattle WTO meeting of late 1999, this effectively meant the Quad members (United States, European Union, Japan and Canada), a couple of middle ranking developed countries and a few large developing ones. Most other countries were observers only. The lack of representation on the part of developing countries can be viewed as either a profound structural problem in the WTO or as a failure of those countries to take advantage of the powers that they had. It would appear, first from Seattle and then from the Doha WTO meeting of 2001, that the developing countries are increasingly using the powers that they do have. From a blocking stance at Seattle they have already moved to a more proactive stance in demanding policies. This would tend to suggest that the problem is more attitudinal than structural. This is not to suggest that there are not real resourcing issues at stake, particularly in Geneva, but it does indicate that the solution to the 'democratic deficit' at the WTO is more in the hands of members than previously argued.

A second problem with the demands of some vocal elements of civil society for greater involvement in trade policy is the issue of democratic accountability itself. It has to be noted that some of the NGOs most critical of the 'undemocratic' nature of trade policy are hardly models of democratic accountability themselves. NGOs range in their accountability mechanisms enormously. Some are market driven with their accountability coming from their ability to extract money from subscribers. Some are relatively safely funded by large (usually corporate funded) foundations and have relatively few active supporters. Many of the foundation-funded groups tend to operate on a principle close to the old democratic centralism manner of organisation - the centre controls and directs and the members follow. Others still are little more than one person bands.

It has to be said that this is not meant to be an attack on the provenance of NGOs per se, nor is it meant to be an attack on the structure of those organisations. Very often the manner of organisation best suits the function of that body. A purely single issue campaigning organisation with a clear target does not need to engage in a good deal of internal debate to know what to do. The observation is more meant to indicate two things. Firstly, anyone raising the issue of democratic accountability or democratic deficits does so at their peril. The old adage about people in glass houses not throwing stones comes to mind. If you raise the issue of someone else's accountability then you have to accept that someone will eventually ask you about your own. Secondly, there is a significant problem of groups acting on 'behalf' of others. This is particularly true for those that seek to 'represent' the voices of developing country peoples. Assuming democratic governance, then the most obvious representative of those people is the government negotiating on their behalf at trade rounds. If one looks at the policy stances of some NGOs that seek to 'represent' the views of the developing world, then one often finds that policies are advanced that act against the interests of those countries. For example, a number of groups seek, on the one hand, to claim that the developing world is not listened to enough while, on the other, promoting policies like a social clause that those very countries oppose wholeheartedly.

The third reason why one needs to be at least sceptical about all demands for greater access relates to the very reason why democratically elected politicians sought to distance trade policy from themselves. Client and interest group politics dictates that those that seek protection will have the greatest incentive to advance their interests and probably the best resources to do so. The buffers and pressure valves have at least managed to channel that demand for protection down certain administrative alleys. Opening up the entire process and handing control back to elected politicians displays a worrying naivety on the part of those seeking to protect the public good. Ironically the best way of advancing the public good is to control the process of access and accountability to insulate the system from the forces of protectionism. In the same manner that one would not want the economic regulation of the telecommunications, water or gas markets voted on by members of parliament on a regular basis, so one should not have the economic regulation of trade controlled on a day to day basis by those in whose private interests it would be to undermine that system.

Resolving Trade Politics

Given that the evolving orthodoxy about the 'democratic deficit' in the trading system appears to be both naïve and ahistorical, one has to ask how one resolves the issue satisfactorily. The question must be answered at both the national and international level.

At the national level it has to be recognised that the system for making trade policy has to be reformed, rather than totally restructured. The buffer and pressure valve mechanisms have to be slowly reformed to make the former stronger and the latter weaker. However, the job of defining the public interest has to be, in the main part, the job of the political class. The elected political class has the ability, through election and through parliamentary scrutiny, to decide if the consensus on trade policy is the right one or not. The direction and scope of trade policy is best influenced through this process. Artificially created 'consultation' processes are rarely productive and tend to promise more than they can deliver. The established governmental mechanisms of policy consultation and parliamentary scrutiny should certainly form the core of future deliberations. The problem here lies in those countries without any formal process of consultation at all. Here national mechanisms must be a priority and their establishment should be a key objective for the post-Doha world.

At the international level the solution for the WTO is actually pretty straightforward. First, one has to accept that there is a realm of transnational decision-making that requires greater legitimacy and interaction with representative organisations of civil society. Secondly, one has to accept that civil society, in the enlightenment meaning of the term, includes the business community. Thirdly, one has to accept that for transnational accountability very strict rules will have to be adopted about those seeking enhanced consultative status. Here there are lessons from other international organisations. The WTO could easily develop the rules used by the UN for Category 1 status before them. Here, firstly, organisations have to have proper internal mechanisms of democratic accountability and financing. Secondly, they have to have true representative status in a number of different regions of the world. Third, they have to have an interest in and be supportive of the organisations that they seek to influence. At present there are only around forty or so organisations with Category 1 status. Not all of these will have sufficient interest in trade to wish to apply for an equivalent status at the WTO.

Conclusion

The relationship between trade policy and democratic accountability has rarely been a straightforward one. When it was, it was disastrous for the world economy and the stability of global politics. Democratically elected politicians the world over have tended to place buffers and pressure valves between themselves and trade policy. This has been done with the best intentions, so as to avoid returning to petty protectionism and losses in world welfare. Demanding that these mechanisms are dismantled to allow greater 'democratic' control are dangerous. When these demands mean that trade policy will be handed back to those who wanted it as far away from them as possible, then the recipe is for disaster or instability. When the demand is really for unelected non-governmental organisations to be given greater control, then demands must be made of those groups to explain their own democratic legitimacy.

The WTO has seen the legitimacy of the GATT stretched beyond breaking point. The first solution to this problem is for the developing world to be given, and to take, the power that they have always had on paper. This is starting to happen, as the events of Seattle and Doha indicate. This has to be helped through real funding of offices for developing countries in Geneva and by developing countries themselves prioritising trade policy within their administrative budgets. However, it can also be aided by establishing very tight criteria for non-governmental groups to seek greater access at the WTO itself. Such groups should be given special access and rights to be heard before panels, but not the right to engage in negotiations. In a contract-based organisation only those that will be bound by rules should be able to write those rules.

In the longer term the real legitimacy of the WTO will need to come under scrutiny. The 'democratic deficit' in trade policy is there for a good reason; the trick is to ensure that the forces of protectionism are not unleashed in the quest for a democratic nirvana; the good must not be sacrificed on the altar of the perfect. Reform must be made to bring the system into line with the new demands of the trade agenda; however that reform must be done progressively and slowly to ensure that it is not misused.

In the longer run the real problems of the WTO system will have to be addressed. One has to ask whether a judicial system is appropriate for a diplomatically structured Round of negotiations. The proper realm of decision-making in trade policy and economic regulation has not been settled by the creation of the WTO; if anything it has been confused further. Here, the experience of the European Union holds out some hope. The experience of European integration has been one of increasing harmonisation accompanied by greater devolution and the establishment of opt-outs, carve-outs and pressure valves. If such a system can operate in the region with the greatest economic integration, why can't it be applied globally?

Notes

1   Oxford English Dictionary Online edition.
2   See Zajac 1995.
3   See Bhagwati and Srinvasan 1982.
4   See Wilson 1980.

References

Bhagwati, J. and Srinvasan T. (1982), 'The Welfare Consequences of Directly Unproductive Profit-seeking (DUP) Lobbying Activities: Price *Versus* Quality Distortions', *Journal of International Economics,* vol. 13, no. 1, pp. 33-44.
Wilson, J. Q., (ed.) (1980), *The Politics of Regulation,* Basic Books, London.
Zajac, E. E. (1995), *Political Economy of Fairness,* MIT Press, Cambridge, Massachusetts.

PART II
MULTI-LEVEL ECONOMIC DIPLOMACY

Chapter 10

Bilateral Economic Diplomacy: the United States

Nicholas Bayne

Introduction to Part II

This chapter is mainly about bilateral economic diplomacy and especially the United States. But it also serves to introduce the second half of this book, beginning with a reminder about its structure. The next eight chapters look at the multi-level nature of economic diplomacy. They examine how it is practised in four distinct levels: the bilateral; the regional; the plurilateral; and the multilateral. They also consider how the different levels interact with one another.

The chapters are divided as follows:

- Chapters 10 and 11 deal with bilateralism. The current chapter first defines the bilateral level; it then looks at the United States and its attachment to bilateral economic diplomacy, which is contrasted with Canada. It is followed by Matthew Goodman's case study on US-Japanese economic relations.
- Chapters 12 and 13 are concerned with regionalism. One chapter analysing the European Union in general is supported by the case study by Patrick Rabe on how the EU makes its international environmental policy.
- Chapter 14 examines how governments work through international economic institutions, covering both plurilateralism and multilateralism. This is illustrated by three case studies:
  - The first is by Ivan Mbirimi, who examines the constraints on developing countries practising economic diplomacy in Chapter 15. He draws on the experience of the Commonwealth, which is a large and active plurilateral institution.
  - The second and third focus on the leading multilateral bodies in economic diplomacy. Chapter 16, by Nigel Wicks, looks at the IMF and World Bank. Chapter 17, by Richard Carden, examines the world trading system and the WTO.

These case studies are not meant to be about the institutions as such, but more about how member governments and others make use of the institutions in their economic diplomacy.

Levels of Economic Diplomacy

But what does it mean to speak of the different levels of economic diplomacy? What do these levels consist of? What do they have in common and how do they differ? And what is special about bilateral economic diplomacy? The main part of this chapter aims to do five things:

- To establish a basic taxonomy of the four levels, set out in a simple matrix.
- To isolate the bilateral level more precisely, with some words about *unilateral* economic diplomacy.
- To identify the main features of bilateralism.
- To demonstrate how far the features of bilateral economic diplomacy satisfy the needs of the United States.
- To compare the US with Canada, as a country for which bilateralism is much less suited.

The conclusions look more widely at the use made by the United States of the other levels, especially under Presidents Clinton and Bush the younger, relating these to the tensions of economic diplomacy.

Taxonomy of the Levels

The first task is to differentiate between the four levels, so as to create a simple taxonomy. **Bilateral** economic diplomacy is the simplest level, practised between just two parties, usually single states. The most complex is **multilateral** economic diplomacy as practised in institutions of global membership, like the IMF, the WTO or the UN. Though these two levels are at the extremes, they have one thing in common. They are open to all countries. Any state can conduct bilateral economic diplomacy. All states can belong to multilateral economic organisations and most of them do. There are still a few exceptions to this - Russia is not yet in the WTO, for example - but essentially the multilateral system is now fully global, for reasons explained in Chapter 5.

The two intermediate levels are the **regional** and the **plurilateral**. Here there are distinct criteria for taking part - not every country can play. In regional economic diplomacy the criteria are based on geography. At the plurilateral level the criteria may be wholly objective - only oil-exporters can be members of OPEC. Or they may be more subjective - only industrial democracies can be members of the OECD, but this term allows quite a flexible definition. These intermediate levels can accommodate groups of varying size, from NAFTA with three members to the Commonwealth with over 50; but they are all exclusive in a sense that the IMF or UN can never be.

Two more propositions can be advanced about what differentiates the four levels. Neither proposition is an absolute rule and there are certainly exceptions, but they are true more often than not. The first proposition is that all the levels except the bilateral require a degree of organisation and shared responsibility. This can range from elaborate institutions with independent secretariats, like the World Bank or OECD, to arrangements for rotating chairmanship in an informal group with few members, like the 'Quad' of trade ministers; but it cannot be escaped altogether. Of course, bilateral relations can be organised too and must be if one party is a complex entity like the European Union. But if they only concern two national governments they can be very fluid and informal.

The second proposition is that the intermediate levels - the regional and the plurilateral - especially appeal to medium-sized countries. The solidarity and common purpose provided by these levels enables medium powers to combine either to resist their more powerful neighbours or to emulate them. In contrast, very large and powerful countries see less need to combine with others and less advantage in doing so. Small ones, on the other hand, may not want to be tied to stronger neighbours. They may also feel that their limited resources are better deployed in a multilateral context, where they will go further. As a result, every country, however small, seeks to be in the United Nations and other multilateral institutions. (They cannot always ensure a physical presence there, but that is for other reasons.)

It is now possible to establish the basic taxonomy of the four levels in a simple matrix, as set out in Figure 10.1 below.

	Bilateral	Regional	Plurilateral	Multilateral
Open to all countries:	x			x
Selected countries only:		x	x	
Requires organisation:		x	x	x
Large countries favour:	x			
Medium countries favour:		x	x	
Small countries favour:				x

Figure 10.1   Basic Taxonomy of the Levels of Economic Diplomacy

Isolating Bilateral Economic Diplomacy

Having differentiated the four levels, the next task is to look more closely at the bilateralism. This immediately leads to a problem: bilateral economic diplomacy is so common and mundane that diplomats tend to practice it without really thinking about it.[1] They are like the character in Moliere's play *Le Bourgeois Gentilhomme*, who was amazed to find he had been speaking prose all his life without realising it. Some more precise limits are needed in order to pin down the bilateral level.

First of all, it is clear that all four levels interact and the simpler ones, especially bilateralism, contribute to the more complex. The operations of the European Union illustrate this well. For example:

- In the *multilateral* WTO, the countries of the *regional* EU combine so as to negotiate as one.
- When the EU negotiates a free trade agreement, say with Mexico, the European Member States operate at the *regional* level, while Mexico follows the *bilateral* level.
- Within the *regional* EU there is an active network of diplomacy at the *bilateral* level. This may be systematic, as in the regular contacts between France and Germany; or occasional, as when the French Presidency of the EU summoned each Member State in turn to a 'confessional' during the Nice European Council of December 2000.

More generally, during any multilateral gathering there will be an immense number of bilateral contacts, and often these will provide the foundation for any wider agreement reached. Some scholars tend to argue that all negotiations are in fact bilateral; multilateral deals only result from adding up a series of bilateral ones.[2] There is, however, a different dynamic to bilateral economic diplomacy conducted within a wider regional or multilateral context, as compared with bilateral diplomacy conducted on its own account and for its own sake. At this stage the aim is to screen out bilateral diplomacy in wider contexts and to focus on diplomacy involving just two partners. One way into this is by considering an even simpler method of conducting economic diplomacy by unilateral action.

Unilateralism

Unilateral economic diplomacy may sound like a contradiction in terms, since diplomacy implies at least two parties. But as Chapter 1 indicated, there are many examples of countries taking unilateral actions, without agreeing with, consulting or even informing others in advance, which have evident effects on the international system and require others to react. One notorious example is President Nixon's decision to break the dollar's link with gold in August 1971; Nixon deliberately decided to act unilaterally instead of with consultation and negotiation.[3]

Unilateral actions, as part of economic diplomacy, usually fall into two distinct types: they are either signs of weakness; or they are signs of strength. Weak actions are taken when countries do not feel able to enter into commitments with others, or where they know that others would take no notice. Ecuador's dollarisation of its currency is an example of this; the Ecuadorians have no illusions that the US will change its monetary policy because they have adopted its currency. In a similar way, in the late 1980s, the UK did not feel able to accept the full obligations of the European exchange rate mechanism, but tried to keep the pound in line with it unilaterally.[4]

By contrast, strong unilateral actions are taken in economic diplomacy by countries that are convinced they have chosen the right course, however others may react, and believe they can make an impact, whatever others may do. Many countries over the last two decades have undertaken programmes of unilateral trade liberalisation, independent of GATT negotiations. They believed this would bring them benefit, even if others did not open their markets too. Where economic sanctions are imposed, not as part of a UN operation but by national decision, that too is a sign of strength.[5] It is conspicuous that almost the only country to impose national sanctions is the United States, because of its great weight in the world economy. For other individual countries to do so would seldom make sense. In other contexts too, the strength of the United States enables it to act unilaterally where other countries cannot - this theme will recur later in the chapter.

The same unilateral actions may betoken either strength or weakness, depending on the circumstances. Threats by Russia, early in 2001, not to service its debts were a sign of strength. But Argentina's debt defaults at the end of the year indicated weakness, as it was unable to pay.

The Main Features of Bilateralism

In order to isolate bilateral economic diplomacy, as practised for its own sake, it is necessary to identify the main features of the bilateralism. Eight such features can be distinguished.

First, bilateralism is the traditional level for diplomacy of all kinds and the most ancient. There is evidence of bilateral economic diplomacy going back to 2500 BC, with a trade treaty between the Pharaoh of Egypt and the king of Babylon.[6] The bilateral level was developed at a time when countries were less exposed to international competition than they are now. It is the natural level for inward-looking countries with low international dependence. Outwardly oriented countries are likely to favour more complex forms.

Second, bilateral diplomacy is simple. With only two parties involved, as noted earlier, no elaborate organisation is required. It is easy to fix agendas and to find out about the other party's position. This provides scope for 'two-level games', where one party tries to influence domestic opinion in the other.

Third, bilateral diplomacy is easy to explain to others. Where agreement is reached, the provisions are likely to be clear and free from ambiguity. In countries where the demands of domestic accountability are high, this is a considerable advantage. Members of the legislature, for example, are likely to respond well to accounts of bilateral economic dealings but to be either bored by or suspicious of complex multilateral agreements.

Fourth, bilateral diplomacy is easy to control. It is easier to determine the pace and scope of any negotiation, if it only depends on one other party. Where a country is concerned to preserve its independence or worried about potential loss of sovereignty, it will tend to prefer bilateralism, as it can more readily draw back from undue commitment.

Fifth, bilateral diplomacy will tend to favour the stronger party. There is no scope for smaller parties to offset their weakness by combining with others.

Usually the stronger party will stand to lose less by the failure of the negotiations and can thus drive a harder bargain. Bilateral economic diplomacy is therefore the easiest level to analyse according to realist theories, which give most weight to power relationships.

Sixth, bilateral diplomacy tends to be confrontational. As the balance of advantage will tend to be clearly perceived, there is a strong pressure to get a better deal than the other party. It is easy to think of diplomacy in the terms or the imagery of competitive sport, or even of war, when it is between only two parties. Bilateral economic diplomacy therefore encourages value claiming negotiating strategies. In contrast, when three or more parties are involved, it becomes easier to find a balance where everyone looks like a winner. This favours value creating or mixed strategies.

Seventh, the bilateral level readily allows for differentiation. When several deals are negotiated on the same issue with different partners, it is possible for a country to favour its allies and penalise its rivals. But there is also the risk of alienating those who are offered worse terms than other parties. It is an effort to ensure that a network of bilateral agreements or relationships is kept in consistent balance.

Eighth, bilateral diplomacy is labour-intensive and time-consuming, especially in a world with many active participants. It is difficult to operate an international system based on a network of bilateral relationships. It was done in the 19th century, with fewer players; it is hard to imagine now. Where separate bilateral deals have to be struck with each partner, this requires a lot of time and resources. Only very well endowed countries can afford an active economic diplomacy based mainly on bilateral dealings.

These features of bilateral economic diplomacy are summarised in Table 10.1 below.

Table 10.1   The Features of Bilateral Economic Diplomacy

1.	The **traditional** level, natural for inward-looking countries.
2.	**Simple,** needs no organisation.
3.	**Easy to explain,** especially to domestic interests and legislature.
4.	**Easy to control,** to protect independence.
5.	**Favours stronger party,** as weaker ones cannot combine.
6.	Often **confrontational,** as each party seeks the better deal.
7.	Allows **differentiation,** though also risks inconsistency.
8.	**Laborious** in a system with many active players.

Why Bilateralism Suits the United States

The next section of this chapter examines the proposition that the bilateral level of economic diplomacy is particularly attractive to the United States. This is, of course, not a complete explanation of US economic diplomacy, nor is the United States unique. Bilateralism is attractive, for different reasons, to many other countries, such as Brazil, France, India and Switzerland. The United States, like all other countries, makes widespread use of the regional, plurilateral and multilateral levels as will appear later in this chapter.

Indeed, the United States has been the creator and promoter of many of the existing multilateral and plurilateral regimes, both the Bretton Woods institutions of the 1940s and others since. So it may seem odd to argue that the US is an instinctive bilateralist. But there is evidence to show that, even within multilateral institutions, the United States prefers to act bilaterally; and that it is always a struggle for internationalist impulses to overcome these bilateral instincts.

An examination of the features of the bilateral level identified earlier reveals how well they fit with the United States.

The traditional level

Bilateral economic diplomacy is likely to be the preferred level for a country whose size and natural resources provide almost all its needs and which does not depend much on the outside world. These factors fit the United States precisely. Though its dependence on the outside world has greatly increased over the last 50 years, it is still much less than most of its other partners.

Simple and easy to explain

The political structure of the United States strongly favours a level of diplomacy that is simple to conduct, without much organisation, and easy to explain and justify, to domestic interests or the legislature. In the US, domestic interests are able to impose unusual constraints on the conduct of its economic diplomacy. The US Congress maintains very close control over many areas of economic decision-making, especially in trade policy, and often reflects quite narrow local interests. While monetary policy is rather more independent, it is still at the mercy of Congress for the voting of funds, for example for IMF quotas. The need to engage Congress means policy-making is very transparent and gives openings to other domestic forces, such as private business - Matthew Goodman expands on this in Chapter 12. So in the US the domestic board in the two-level game is so complex that there is a clear preference for keeping the game simple on the international board.[7]

Easy to control

Bilateralism appeals to countries that want to preserve their freedom of action and are concerned about any loss of sovereignty. This too applies very powerfully to the United States, which shows a strong reluctance to being subject to any rules imposed from outside. This is based both on a long historical tradition of independence and defence of civil liberties and on a deep conviction that the way the United States does things is the best way. The United States, for example, is the only major country to apply its laws extra-territorially, not accepting the jurisdiction of others.

These arguments suggest that it is difficult for the United States to accept any international rules at all. This can often be achieved only where the international rules are in fact the same rules as the US practises itself; and because the US is so strong, this is often what happens. Clearly, if the rest of the world will adopt American rules, that will help to make the US overcome its scepticism about international regimes. But in circumstances where the rest of the world can agree on something that is different from what the United States does, for example in accounting standards or measures against global warming, the Americans do not feel the same pressure to join the consensus as other countries would.

Favours the stronger party

Since the United States is, by virtually every measure, economically the strongest single state in the world, this gives bilateralism an obvious attraction. By the same argument, the United States would have little incentive to take part in the more complex levels of economic diplomacy, which would allow other countries to combine against it. This, however, seems to go against the observed facts. The US manifestly is very active in various international institutions. Indeed, as noted in Chapter 2, hegemonic stability theory argues that multilateral regimes can only work properly if there is a dominant power, as the United States was at the end of World War II. This issue clearly requires more analysis.

The US and multilateralism. The historical evidence suggests that the conditions at the end of World War II had an exceptional effect on US policy-making - Chapter 6 bears this out. Both the devastation caused by the struggle against Nazism and the impending threat from Soviet communism generated strong internationalist impulses within the United States, which overcame its normal bilateral instincts. These impulses were political more than economic, coming from leaders like Cordell Hull and George Marshall, but they used economic instruments like the Bretton Woods institutions and the Marshall Plan. The Americans thus became subject to two influences which continued to counter their bilateral instincts. First, as the creators of these multilateral and plurilateral instruments and the great advocates of the non-discriminatory economic system, the Americans long felt an obligation to defend and observe them, setting an example to the rest of the world. Second, both the multilateral trade and monetary system and the Marshall Plan proved very successful and satisfied American objectives better than earlier bilateral arrangements had done.

That accounted for the initial impulse towards multilateral and plurilateral institution-building. But as American post-war dominance declined, the balance of perceived advantage shifted. The US was still the strongest single power, but now other states could sometimes combine against it and oblige it to accept decisions in wider institutions which it judged to be less favourable than what it could have got bilaterally. The Americans began to fear getting trapped or surrounded in international institutions. They also convinced themselves that they gave more than they got, for example in multilateral negotiations on trade liberalisation. The consequence was that the United States, as far as it could, favoured those economic institutions where it could operate closest to the bilateral level. That meant ensuring that American views could prevail, if necessary, against the combined weight of all the other members.

This has led to a differentiated attitude to international institutions:

- The IMF and the World Bank are the preferred institutions, because the weighted voting system means the US very seldom finds its views do not prevail, as Nigel Wicks explains in Chapter 16. On the rare occasions where that does happen, the US may act unilaterally, as Nixon did in 1971.
- Institutions like the WTO and the OECD, which operate by consensus, are the next favoured. Consensus means that the US can never be obliged to accept anything it does not want. Since the US is so large an economic power, few agreements that it does not accept can come into effective operation. So far the United States has always respected the judgements of WTO panels. But in case they should be unsatisfactory, the US retains trade legislation which can be applied bilaterally. For example, in 1995 the US pursued its dispute with Japan over sales of luxury cars bilaterally, rather than through the WTO.[8]
- Finally, the institutions of the United Nations family, which can adopt majority votes that can go against the United States, are the least favoured. Except in the Security Council, it is very difficult for the United States to feel in control of UN activities. Though votes are rarely used in the UN's environmental discussions, the US emerges as a reluctant participant. It has held back from subscribing to the Biodiversity Agreement and come out in opposition to the Kyoto Protocol on Climate Change.[9]

The US and regionalism. This analysis may explain how the US operates at multilateral and plurilateral levels. What about the regional level? Why should the United States want to combine with its neighbours, rather than dealing with them bilaterally? For very many years the United States indeed showed no interest in regional integration, either on a close or a wider scale. This changed quite suddenly in the early 1990s, with the creation of NAFTA in North America and APEC round the Pacific - followed by the initiative for a Free Trade Area of the Americas. This change was due to a realisation by the Americans that, as their relative power declined, even they could gain by joining forces with others. But at first they took precautions against being encircled even in regional groupings.

NAFTA was seen as a regional counterweight to the EU, at a time when it looked as though the Uruguay Round might fail. The Americans regarded it mainly as a framework for their bilateral relations with the other parties. The intention had been that NAFTA would steadily add new members - but this was not possible because of Congressional reluctance to grant negotiating authority. APEC was not originally intended by the Australians, who invented it, to include the Americans. But the US could not tolerate being left out of a pan-Pacific grouping. In practice APEC, with its large and varied membership and reliance on voluntary cooperation, operates more like a plurilateral body than a regional one. Most recently, President George Bush the younger, on taking office early in 2001, has given new priority to US links with Latin America, focusing on the completion of the Free Trade Area of the Americas (FTAA).

In short, the US prefers those regional, plurilateral and multilateral contexts where it can simulate bilateral dealings, though it has come to favour regional integration more as its relative economic power declines.

Often confrontational

Returning to the features of bilateral economic diplomacy, after that long digression, there is a strong tendency for American economic diplomacy to be confrontational and 'tough'. This is often in contrast to the 'softer' approach of the Europeans or the Japanese. American diplomats regularly reproach their European colleagues for leaving them unsupported in economic negotiations to drive a hard bargain and incur a lot of odium, though the Europeans would come in afterwards to take advantage of the new arrangements. Since European Member States have usually had to devise value creating strategies or package deals so as to achieve a common position, they always try at least to appear value creating to their other negotiating partners. In contrast, the Americans do not shrink from value claiming strategies. Americans also worry about 'free-riders' taking advantage of the economic system - but there are no free riders at the bilateral level.

There are two possible reasons underlying this rather confrontational approach. The first concerns attitudes to the law. Many Europeans are legalistic in that they want everything tied down in precise legal formulae; this again reflects their experience of decision-making in the EU. Americans, on the other hand, draw on their native tradition of litigiousness in taking a forensic attitude to their economic diplomacy. They expect economic diplomacy to deliver the sort of judgements *for* them and *against* the other party that they would expect in a court of law. That is inevitably confrontational.

The second reason is linked to the basic motives for countries to engage in economic diplomacy at all. Many countries negotiate about the removal of barriers to their economies because of the improved efficiency such opening can bring them. But the Americans - rightly or wrongly - believe that their economy is the most open in the world already and that they are providing much better standards of market access and transparency than Japan or the EU or their other negotiating partners. This means that their main motive in economic diplomacy is usually to get other countries to lower their barriers to access for US trade or investment or capital flows. This attitude also adds a confrontational tone to American economic diplomacy and leads them to favour the bilateral approach.

Allows differentiation but laborious

The last two features of the bilateral level can also be traced very clearly in US economic diplomacy. The post-war multilateral economic system, which is based on *non-discrimination*, was created largely on US initiative. But there has been a gradual American retreat from this ideal. Already in the Uruguay Round, the Americans became reluctant to endorse non-discrimination for trade in services. In the late 1990s it was the European Union, not the United States that was pressing for another ambitious multilateral round of trade negotiations. The US under Clinton became more interested in using trade measures to enforce labour and environment standards. This has been reversed under Bush, so that the US Trade Representative, Bob Zoellick, has combined with EU Trade Commissioner Pascal Lamy to promote a new WTO trade round. But on specific issues, such as anti-dumping, the United States resists any tightening of the multilateral rules which reduce its ability to act bilaterally.

Even for the United States, however, the bilateral level is laborious and it cannot give the same attention to every country in the world, great or small. The Americans seem to be most at ease and to get the most satisfaction in pursuing bilateral economic diplomacy with their major partners. This avoids the entanglements of multilateral diplomacy and the risk of others 'ganging up on them'. It provides them with some worthy negotiating partners, who are large enough to have something serious to offer, but are still not as powerful as the United States itself. This explains the high priority given to bilateral economic dealings with China; with Japan, as analysed in the next chapter by Matthew Goodman; and with the European Union.

The dynamics of relations between the United States and the European Union are very curious. In principle, and on general grounds, it suits both sides very well for the US to deal with the EU as a single entity. For the Europeans, it enables them to mobilise their combined strength. For the Americans, it avoids the tedium of having to negotiate with each Member State separately and gives them a serious partner to deal with. But in practice, and on detailed issues, EU-US relations often run into serious difficulties. Both the domestic policy process in the United States and the collective decision-making process among EU Member States - to be explained in Chapter 12 - place severe constraints on American and European negotiators. These constraints operate in such different ways that it is hard to find the balance between the two sides and misunderstandings easily creep in. So the two largest economic powers, who have every incentive to agree with each other, often fail to do so.[10]

Why Bilateralism Does Not Suit Canada

Bilateralism suits the United States, for the reasons given above. But it does not suit other countries so well. The final part of this chapter applies the features of bilateralism to Canada and shows that they do not fit Canada well at all. Canada is included here, so that Chapters 10 to 13 of this book can reflect the economic diplomacy of all the members of the G7.

The traditional level

Bilateralism does not suit countries with high dependence on the outside world. Because it is so large in relation to its population and communications are so difficult, Canada has always had to look outwards for markets and economic links.

Simple and easy to explain

The second and third features of bilateralism - simplicity and ease of explanation - are not necessary for Canada. The federal government's powers over most parts of international economic policy are beyond dispute.   While there may be disagreements between Ottawa and the provinces over aspects of policy, Ottawa usually holds most of the cards.   So the Canadian government has not been constrained by the domestic context of decision-making from pursuing the more elaborate forms of economic diplomacy.   This may change, as economic diplomacy reaches more issues in provincial jurisdiction.

Easy to control and favours stronger party

The fourth and fifth features of bilateralism come to the heart of the difference between Canada and the United States and require fuller explanation.
    Canada has been nervous of bilateralism - and even of regionalism - precisely because the US is both so strong and Canada's only close neighbour. This meant that in bilateral dealings with the US, Canada was likely to come out worst, as being so much the weaker party. But Canada could not easily combine with its regional neighbours against the United States, because any such combination must include the US itself.

Canada and multilateralism. In consequence, Canada's traditional preference has always been to pursue its international economic relations through multilateral or plurilateral institutions. Multilaterally, Canada's attachment to the UN is well known. It has also always been active in the IMF, the World Bank, the GATT and the WTO. Plurilaterally, Canada attaches a lot of importance to its membership of the OECD, the Commonwealth and especially the G7/G8.   These institutions provide opportunities for Canada to form alliances with like-minded countries and steer their decisions in favourable directions. The advantages of this outweigh any sense of loss of sovereignty. This approach makes Canada always inclined to favour value creating over value claiming strategies.

Canada and regionalism. However, much as America's policy shifted so did Canada's. By the mid-1980s plurilateral and multilateral institutions were no longer adequate to satisfy Canada's interests. While politically Canada could perform on a wider stage, economically it was becoming ever closely tied to the United States. This determined Prime Minister Brian Mulroney to reverse all previous trends and conclude a bilateral Free Trade Agreement with the United States.

This was a tremendous risk to take, but Mulroney judged the balance of advantage correctly. Economically, the Canadian economy was just competitive enough to survive alongside the American giant and profit from access to this much larger market. The dispute settlement arrangements, where both countries sat as equals, helped to protect Canada as the weaker party.[11] Politically, Canada soon got the chance to convert this risky bilateral arrangement into a series of regional links of a kind not available before. The emergence of NAFTA and the FTAA in the Western Hemisphere and APEC in the Pacific have both been highly beneficial to Canada, in enabling it to offset undue dependence on the United States.[12]

Often confrontational

After another long digression, it is time to return to the sixth feature of bilateralism. It may suit the US to be confrontational, but it does not suit Canada. Canadians are natural conciliators - it is part of the national character that is emphasised so as to be different from the United States. In the context of their multilateralist tradition and the pursuit of value creating strategies, Canadians have cultivated many gifts that make them valued members of wider institutions and enable them to derive advantage from them.

Allows differentiation but laborious

The prospect of discrimination in economic diplomacy has few attractions for a country like Canada. It has no need to reward or penalise different partners; non-discrimination suits Canada well. It has every advantage in conducting its international economic relations collectively and on equal terms with groups of partners, organised regionally or in wider institutions.

Conclusions: Multiple Approaches in US Economic Diplomacy

More than in any other country, American economic diplomacy is dominated by the Administration's obligation to be accountable to Congress - ie by Question 6 from Table 1.1. This not only inclines the United States to bilateralism, as argued earlier, but also affects its use of the other available levels. It casts a particular shadow over US decision-making at electoral periods, so that new Presidents, like Clinton and Bush the younger, usually start their term in office by stating that they will give priority to domestic issues over international ones.[13] Clinton was further constrained by a loss of Congressional support in mid-term, while Bush has to handle a Senate exactly divided between Republicans and Democrats. These conclusions examine the implications of this for the United States' use of all the levels in reconciling the tensions of economic diplomacy.

Tension between economics and politics

It is often easiest for the Administration to win Congressional support for measures of international economic cooperation when these serve clear political objectives. In the period after World War II, as noted in Chapter 6, the aim of avoiding future wars brought support for the IMF, World Bank and GATT (though not the ITO), while the need to contain the Soviet threat ensured backing for the Marshall Plan, which led to the OECD. Today, Bush's pursuit of the FTAA is justified as a means of reinforcing democracy in Latin America, as agreed at the Quebec summit of April 2001. His need for international support in the fight against terrorism after 11 September 2001 facilitated agreement on a new trade round in the WTO.

In all these examples, the United States pursued its aims at regional, plurilateral or multilateral levels. Even so, the Americans often subordinate these wider levels to their bilateral strategy for reconciling economics and politics. After the end of the Cold War, the US did not give consistent support to new collective economic measures to help Central and Eastern Europe. While it pushed action by the IMF and World Bank, initially it opposed the EBRD, which was an EC initiative. It was most concerned to develop a privileged bilateral relationship with Russia - first Clinton with Yeltsin, now Bush with Putin. Likewise, recent US measures in favour of Africa are closely targeted on Bush's planned visit there and only loosely tied to the joint Africa Action Plan agreed at the G8 summit of 2002.[14]

Tensions between domestic and international pressures

Members of the US Congress often reflect narrow local interests, which can lead them to press for unilateral economic measures. The powers given to the states, who are insulated from international pressures, incline them in the same direction. The Administration has to find ways of channelling or diverting these unilateralist pressures in its economic diplomacy.

One method is to show the United States as always in charge of the international process. This not only favours bilateralism (as argued above) but encourages the practice of building up plurilateral and multilateral agreements from a series of bilateral deals between the US and its main partners. In trade policy, this goes back to the pre-war Reciprocal Trade Agreements Act, which was the foundation for the early tariff-cutting rounds in the GATT. During the Uruguay Round, the US struck bilateral deals with the EU on agriculture (the Blair House accord) and on services, which formed the basis for the multilateral agreements embodied in the WTO. The same practice has been followed between the US and Europe in public procurement, leading to a plurilateral agreement, and in mutual recognition agreements on a range of goods and services.

Congressional opinion, being domestically motivated, regards US practice as the best in the world and therefore expects international rules to conform to American standards. This too affects the choice of approaches to economic diplomacy. The United States has a network of bilateral investment treaties, which embody strict rules. In promoting international rules for investment during the Clinton Administration in the late 1990s, the US avoided the WTO, fearing that the multilateral approach would dilute its bilateral standards, and opted instead for the plurilateral OECD, even though it did not have a strong tradition of negotiating binding instruments.[15]

Despite this, the US is a frequent user of the dispute settlement mechanism of the WTO as a useful means of obliging other countries to accept the same standards of openness and transparency as its own. So as to preserve the integrity of the WTO mechanism, the United States has respected all panel judgements, even those that went against it. Although domestic pressures have obliged the US Administration in 2002 to introduce new tariffs on steel and Canadian timber and to adopt a law expanding subsidies for agriculture, it has defended these moves as being in line with its WTO obligations.

Finally, the Administration has developed methods to deter Congress from adding unwelcome conditions to international economic agreements and measures. When 'fast-track' trade negotiating authority is given to the Administration, that means that Congress undertakes either to accept or reject an agreement, but not to amend it. Clinton was unable to persuade Congress to grant such authority after 1994; Bush has been more successful in winning 'trade promotion authority' to cover WTO and FTAA negotiations, but this has involved a long, hard struggle and major concessions to domestic interests. The increased $5 billion per year in aid announced by Bush at Monterrey in March 2002 will be drawn from 'Millennium Challenge Accounts' opened for countries that meet the Administration's standards of good governance. But the US was reluctant to say that half of this could go to Africa, as part of the G8's Africa Action Plan, for fear that this would stimulate Congress to attach conditions to the new aid spending.

Tension between government and other forces

In its dealings with Congress, the Administration looks for allies who will advocate outward-looking, cooperative policies to offset the Congressional preference for domestically motivated unilateralism. Its most frequent ally is international business, which has thus become increasingly integrated into decision-making. Throughout most of the period since the 1940s the Administration relied on manufacturing industry to press for multilateral trade liberalisation. When their support flagged in the 1980s, the Administration turned to the food and financial services sectors and to knowledge-based industries like pharmaceuticals and electronics. This brought agriculture, services and intellectual property onto the agenda for the Uruguay Round. There is concern in the United States now at the lack of business interest in the new round launched at Doha.

But reliance on the support of business interests can have a distorting impact on US approaches to economic diplomacy. American advocacy of capital market liberalisation through the IMF and their approach to financial rescues of countries like Mexico in 1995 and Korea in 1997 have been attacked for favouring the interests of large US banks more than those of the countries concerned. Pressure from large energy firms influenced Bush in his outright rejection of the Kyoto Protocol on climate change, though it was already unpopular in Congress.

US firms often want the Administration to press for the removal of practices in other countries which they consider put them at a competitive disadvantage. Thus, because the US has strict anti-corruption laws, it argued strongly for an agreement with matching provisions to be introduced in the OECD. Several of the cases brought by the United States in the WTO, for example against the EU on bananas and Japan on photographic film, were brought at the behest of American firms.

NGOs can have a comparable influence on US decision-making, especially in electoral periods. Pressure from trade unions and 'green' NGOs, traditional Democrat supporters, induced Clinton to speak out in favour of trade sanctions to enforce labour and environmental standards at the WTO meeting in Seattle late in 1999, as the Presidential campaign was beginning. The US has also sought GATT and WTO panels on behalf of environmental interests, on fishing practices endangering dolphins and turtles. However, NGOs are less integrated into decision-making than they are in Europe. Obstructive protests at economic meetings, organised via the internet, began in the United States, at Seattle and Washington, before they spread to Europe and reached their lowest point at the Genoa G8 summit.

In short, the United States employs all the available approaches to economic diplomacy, in addition to bilateralism, though each of them is coloured by the need for Congressional endorsement. The remaining chapters of this book will contain more examples of how both the United States and other countries make choices between the different levels and seek advantage from the interaction between them.

Notes

1   Recent studies of diplomacy, like Barston 1997 and Marshall 1999, explain why multilateral diplomacy has grown, but content themselves with explaining how bilateral diplomacy is conducted.
2   This view emerges from Odell 2000. Most of his case studies are of bilateral negotiations involving the United States.
3   On Nixon's action and its consequences, see Kenen 1994, Chapter 1 and Odell 2000, Chapter 4.
4   In some circumstances groups of countries may even take coordinated unilateral actions, where none of them wants to feel bound by what any of the others do. But this was more common in earlier decades; it is rare in the new economic diplomacy.
5   The classic study of economic sanctions in Baldwin 1985 has been updated by Pape 1997 and Haass 1998.
6   This is quoted in Winham 1992.
7   Paarlberg 1995 gives and interesting analysis of the domestic origins of US economic diplomacy, which has become especially topical again since Bush the younger succeeded Clinton.
8   On this, see Chapter 11 below.
9   The decision of the Bush Administration, early in 2001, to come out in open opposition to the Kyoto Protocol was much criticised. But even though the Clinton Administration had accepted the Protocol, the prospects for getting it ratified by the Senate were very low. Bush has also taken the US out of other UN activities on the political side, for example in biological weapons and the international criminal court.
10 A useful recent summary of US-EU economic relations is in Woolcock 1999. See also Featherstone and Ginsberg 1996, Peterson 1996 and Smith and Woolcock 1993.

11 This did not prevent persistent trade disputes with the US, for example over softwood lumber. But Canada was even worse off without the agreement.

12 Canada also took the initiative in the late 1990s in proposing a Trans-Atlantic Free Trade Area with the United States and European Union. But neither the EU nor the US was interested.

13 Clinton's attitude emerges from the memoirs of his first Secretary of State, in Christopher 1998.

14 In the same way, Clinton proposed that Africa should be a leading subject of the 1997 G8 summit at Denver in advance of his own African visit. His aim was also to encourage the passage of the Africa Growth and Opportunity Act through Congress (which in fact took till early 2000).

15 For the fate of the OECD negotiations on a Multilateral Agreement on Investment, see Henderson 1999.

References

Baldwin, D. A. (1985), *Economic Statecraft*, Princeton University Press, Princeton.

Barston, R. P. (1997), *Modern Diplomacy*, 2nd edition, Longmans, London and New York.

Christopher, W. (1998), *In the Stream of History*, Stanford University Press, Stanford.

Featherstone, K. and Ginsburg, R. (1996), *The United States and the European Union in the 1990s: Partners in Transition*, 2nd edition, Macmillan, London.

Haass, R. N. (ed.) (1998), *Economic Sanctions and American Diplomacy*, Council on Foreign Relations, New York.

Henderson, P. D. (1999), *The MAI Affair: A Story and its Lessons*, Royal Institute of International Affairs, London.

Kenen, P. B. (ed.) (1994), *Managing the World Economy: Fifty Years After Bretton Woods*, Institute for International Economics, Washington.

Marshall, P. (1999), *Positive Diplomacy*, Palgrave, Basingstoke.

Odell, J. (2000), *Negotiating the World Economy*, Cornell University Press, Ithaca and London.

Paarlberg, R. (1995), *Leadership Begins at Home: US Foreign Economic Policy after the Cold War*, The Brookings Institution, Washington.

Pape, R. A. (1997), 'Why Economic Sanctions Do Not Work', *International Security*, vol. 22, no. 2, pp. 90-136.

Peterson, J. (1996), *Europe and America in the 1990s: Prospects for Partnership*, Routledge, London.

Smith, M. and Woolcock, S. (1993), *The United States and the European Community in a Transformed World*, Pinter for Royal Institute of International Affairs, London.

Spero, J. and Hart, M. (1997), *The Politics of International Economic Relations*, 5th edition, Routledge, London and New York.

Winham, G. L. (1992), *The Evolution of International Trade Agreements*, University of Toronto Press, Toronto and London.

Woolcock, S. (1999), 'The United States and Europe in the Global Economy' in Burwell F. G. and Daalder, I. H. (eds.), *The United States and Europe in the Global Arena*, Macmillan, London, and St Martin's Press, New York, pp. 177-207.

Chapter 11

When the Twain Meet: An Overview of US-Japanese Economic Relations

Matthew Goodman

Introduction: the Breadth of the Relationship

When former American Ambassador to Tokyo Mike Mansfield called US ties with Japan "the most important relationship in the world - bar none,"[1] he may have had a particularly vivid image in mind. There is an unusual map in the Pentagon portraying the former Soviet Union as if from a helicopter hovering in mid-Pacific; looming in the foreground, like a pair of wings embracing the southeast coast of Siberia and all of the Korean Peninsula, lies the Japanese archipelago. This explains why the US-Japanese security alliance remains a cornerstone of both nations' defence and foreign policies.

But Mansfield may well have had another image in mind - a bar chart showing the individual gross domestic products of the economies of Asia. Here, one bar towers above the others. Japan, with a GDP of nearly $5 trillion, accounts for some two-thirds of total Asian GDP; in other words, its economy is roughly double the size of the rest of Asia's put together. The ambassador from the world's largest economy could be excused for considering bilateral relations with the world's second largest to be pre-eminent above all others.

Indeed, the US and Japanese economies are not only large but deeply intertwined. Over $200 billion of total trade flows between them each year, carrying everything from soybeans to advanced machine tools, from semiconductors to luxury cars. Japanese and American firms work together as buyers, suppliers, and business partners - and they compete fiercely on their home turfs and in third markets. They also invest heavily in each other: direct investment worth tens of billions of dollars crosses the Pacific each year, as manufacturers set up shop in each other's territory or acquire land and other fixed assets. And FDI transactions are dwarfed by capital flows, with trillions of dollars of portfolio investments coursing back and forth across the Pacific, in the form of Japanese purchases of US Treasury bonds, American purchases of Japanese shares, and so on.

All of these flows create a neat symmetry between the two economies: Japan is a large net exporter of goods and capital - to the United States first and foremost - while America imports goods and capital - much of it from Japan - to feed its voracious appetite for consumption and debt. This mutual dependence has helped to bind the two countries inextricably to each other over the past quarter century; it has also, paradoxically, been a primary source of tension between them.

With so much at stake, US-Japanese relations naturally require careful management by governments. Washington and Tokyo engage with each other on economic issues to a degree unparalleled in any other bilateral relationship. Media attention in both countries tends to focus on areas of disagreement, so it is easy to forget that much of this engagement is cooperative and constructive. The two countries coordinate their macroeconomic policies as leading members of the G7. Through an array of multilateral institutions such as the IMF and World Bank, the BIS and APEC, they work together to promote common objectives, whether emerging-market development, financial-system stability, or regional economic integration. On a bilateral basis, too, the United States and Japan engage in a wide range of cooperative initiatives, from fighting financial crime and industrial collusion to exchanging medical and scientific know-how.

But like all close long term relationships, trans-pacific ties occasionally descend into disagreement and conflict. It was a trade dispute that launched bilateral relations a century and a half ago, when a fleet of 'Black Ships' led by US Commodore Matthew Perry sailed into Tokyo Bay in 1853 to demand that Japan open its ports to foreign commerce. In more recent times, and especially over the past quarter century, trade tensions have bedevilled US-Japan relations. A chronic Japanese trade surplus has been the backdrop to an endless series of sectoral trade disputes, which have occasionally flared up into serious confrontations. Over this period, Washington has sung an almost constant refrain about the need for Tokyo to promote 'strong, domestic-demand-led growth', through stimulative fiscal and monetary policies, and to deregulate its domestic economy. In addition, the two countries have had periodic spats on third-country issues such as tied aid and Asian regional integration.

It is impossible to do justice in a few pages to the full depth and texture of US-Japanese economic relations. Instead, this brief case study will focus on just three enduring features of diplomacy between the two countries: first, the almost cyclical pattern with which Washington and Tokyo engage with each other on economic issues; second, the imbalance of initiative between the two governments; and third, the domestic factors in each country that lie behind its diplomatic positions and style. The chapter will end with some thoughts about whether and how these features may be changing.

Cycles of Engagement

Economic diplomacy between the United States and Japan does not follow a steady course but rather ebbs and flows like the tide, with occasional turbulent waves crashing on shore. It is characterised by periods of intense engagement, followed by stretches of relatively little activity, at times bordering on neglect. These cycles roughly track the US political calendar on the one hand, macroeconomic conditions in the two countries on the other.

Recent US Administrations - Democratic and Republican - have tended to come to office with their own prescriptions for solving the 'Japan problem'. This consists of some combination of policies to address the chronic trade imbalance between the two countries, to open and liberalise Japanese markets, and to promote strong, domestic-demand-led growth in Japan. There is generally sufficient recognition of the importance and uniqueness of Japan to warrant a special policy approach, although often the Administration can be forced to act by external political pressure, notably from Congress.

Thus one typically finds in the first 12 to 18 months of a new Administration a flurry of activity on matters Japanese. Within weeks of the presidential inauguration,[2] position papers begin circulating around Washington, ultimately leading to inter-agency agreement on a new 'initiative' for managing bilateral economic relations. Senior officials then travel to Tokyo to vet and refine the new approach with their Japanese counterparts. Around the time of the mid-year G7 summit, the US president and Japanese prime minister announce the new initiative to the world with great fanfare. Negotiations begin in the autumn, and the first deals - trade concessions or agreement on structural reform measures - begin to emerge within six to nine months thereafter.

Throughout this process, press coverage of the outstanding issues may be intense, with every contentious statement by one side or the other, every setback in the negotiations, the subject of close media scrutiny. Meetings between the two heads of government, typically held two-three times a year, become focal points for diplomatic activity and benchmarks for progress. No Japanese prime minister is comfortable meeting his US counterpart without bringing some kind of *omiyage* ('souvenir'), whether a package of fiscal stimulus measures or new trade concessions. For its part, the White House sees these summits as important pressure points for resolution of outstanding disputes.

But after the first 12-18 months of intense activity, there is typically a change in the dynamics of bilateral economic diplomacy. Fatigue sets in, especially on the American side, as the Administration comes to realise that it is unlikely to be able to squeeze further concessions out of Tokyo without a significant additional commitment of time, resources, and political capital. As one former US official colourfully put it, "There's only so much banging your head against the wall a person can take."[3] Meanwhile, other international concerns create distractions that absorb increasing amounts of senior policy-makers' time and energy.

As a result, the level of activity in US-Japanese economic diplomacy drops off, sometimes precipitously, only to be revived if the force of events - such as the banking crisis in Japan in the late 1990s - intervenes. Without such action-forcing events, negotiators from the two sides may go through the motions of continuing to meet and talk. But without the active involvement of senior policy-makers, these talks rarely accomplish much. Thus for the final two-three years of an Administration, US-Japanese economic relations settle into a kind of 'auto pilot' mode. Commentators in both countries, but particularly in Japan, may begin to grumble that bilateral relations are being dangerously neglected. As the next election approaches, this may lead in turn to a last-minute burst of activity on the trans-pacific policy front, as the Administration tries to head off partisan criticism that it has not been vigorous in pursuing US economic interests.

Of course, these cycles of engagement are also influenced by macroeconomic conditions in the two countries. In general, the level of tension in the relationship is correlated with relative growth rates in the two countries, and with the size of the trade imbalance between them. Periods of cyclical economic slowdown - and even more, periods of significant structural adjustment - in the United States have often been associated with heightened tension with Japan. At these times, politicians find it easy to point to import competition as a major contributor to rising unemployment in the US manufacturing sector (whether there is evidence of this or not). Many of the most visible imports bought by American consumers are of Japanese origin, and for most of the past quarter century Japan has been the trading partner with which the United States has had its largest bilateral trade deficit, so it is an easy target for Americans seeking a scapegoat in bad economic times.

Macroeconomic conditions in Japan exert more ambiguous pressures on the bilateral relationship. On the one hand, a weaker Japanese economy may reduce tension, by making Japanese companies appear less of a competitive threat to their American counterparts. On the other hand, less growth in Japan denies US firms export opportunities and may highlight problems of market access there. As in the recent past, slower growth in the world's second largest economy may even heighten US concerns about global growth and stability, putting another strain on the bilateral relationship.

US-Japanese economic diplomacy in the 1980s and 1990s

A brief review of US-Japanese economic diplomacy in the 1980s and 1990s demonstrates these cyclical forces at work.[4] Ronald Reagan entered the White House in 1981 as a President philosophically predisposed to free trade and little inclined to engage in intense economic diplomacy with Japan. However, Congressional pressure to address the 'Japan problem', against the backdrop of US economic dislocation and growing trade deficits, had grown to the point when Reagan entered office that he had little choice but to adopt an assertive policy stance toward Japan. Within its first year, the Reagan Administration negotiated what were arguably the most restrictive controls on bilateral trade in the post-war period: 'voluntary' restraints on Japanese automobile exports to the United States. The remainder of the first Reagan Administration generally saw a return to form and relatively little drama on the economic front with Japan (although this period did see negotiation by the US Treasury Department and Japanese Finance Ministry of a landmark accord on financial services).[5]

With the start of Reagan's second term in 1985, however, Japan was once again at the forefront of US international economic policy concerns. Though America's overall economic prospects had improved, this had come at the cost of significant labour-market adjustment and a sharply rising dollar, fuelling Congressional pressure for action on the trade front. In the spring of that year, the Reagan Administration launched the so-called 'market-oriented, sector-selective' (MOSS) talks with Japan to improve market access in four key US export sectors.[6] In September, the Administration negotiated the Plaza Accord with its G7 partners to bring down the 'Super Dollar', which had appreciated to levels that seriously threatened US export competitiveness, notably vis-à-vis Japan. Over the next two years, the Reagan Administration also initiated a number of anti-dumping and market access cases against Japan, and in 1987 imposed the only retaliatory duties against Japanese imports in the post-war period, for violations of a bilateral semiconductor accord.

Although the activism toward Japan waned in the final 18 months of the Reagan Administration, Congressional passage of omnibus trade legislation in 1988 ensured that it would remain a front burner issue into the 1990s. The 1988 act required the Administration to initiate so-called 'Super 301' negotiations with trading partners deemed to be 'priorities' - Japan being clearly first among these in Congressional minds. George H.W. Bush therefore entered the Presidency in January 1989 with his economic policy toward Japan already largely defined. In the spring of that year, the Bush Administration launched Super 301 negotiations with Japan in three sectors.[7] At the same time, the Administration announced an innovation in bilateral economic diplomacy: a broad-based, high-level dialogue aimed at addressing entrenched obstacles to structural adjustment in both countries (but principally Japan), known as the 'Structural Impediments Initiative' (SII). Intensive negotiations over the next year involving a substantial commitment of government resources on both sides yielded a 'final report'[8] under SII in June 1990 that contained a range of commitments by Japan to reform its economic structure.

As early as mid-1990, however, the first signs of fatigue in Bush Administration policy toward Japan had already become apparent. Super 301 accords were ultimately reached in all three targeted sectors, and although the SII talks continued for a second year, they did so at a much lower level of intensity and produced few new commitments. In fact, it was largely criticism from business leaders that he had neglected the relationship that persuaded President Bush to lead an ill-timed and poorly executed trade mission to Japan in January 1992 (made memorable by the President's illness at a State Dinner). In fact, that trip has been cited by some political analysts as the beginning of the end of the Bush Presidency, as the once-revered victor of the Gulf War belatedly tried to establish his economic policy credentials in the face of attack from a determined political rival.

Thus Bill Clinton came into office in early 1993 promising a more activist, 'results-oriented' trade policy toward Japan. The Administration spent its first six months designing and negotiating with the Japanese government the 'US-Japan Framework for a New Economic Relationship', which was designed to produce a 'highly significant reduction' in the Japanese current account surplus over the medium term, as well as wide-ranging market opening and structural reform. At US insistence - and over fierce Japanese objections - the so-called 'Framework' talks introduced the concept of 'objective criteria' to measure progress in implementing commitments reached in the negotiations. A complex process involving negotiations in over 20 sectors as well as on cross-cutting issues, the Framework reached its high-water mark in June 1995 when the two sides barely averted a trade war (the US government had already announced sanctions on Japanese luxury imports) by reaching a last-minute accord on automobile trade.

Thereafter, the air largely went out of the Clinton trade policy toward Japan and, although the two sides maintained a low-intensity dialogue on structural

186 The New Economic Diplomacy

reform and deregulation, the rest of Clinton's first term was relatively quiet on the economic front. Most of the second term, by contrast, was dominated by concerns over the Japanese macroeconomy and financial sector. Slow Japanese growth and a banking sector saddled with a huge amount of non-performing loans, against the backdrop of a financial crisis in Asia, caused the US Administration to step up its pressure on Japan to stimulate domestic demand and stabilise its financial sector. Currencies were another source of tension over this period, as the yen-dollar exchange rate fell precipitously from a peak of 80 yen per dollar in early 1995 to nearly 150 yen in mid-1998, while the two sides squabbled over the efficacy of central bank intervention to address this volatility.

Despite this engagement on macroeconomic and financial issues, there was significant anxiety expressed in Japan during this period over the Clinton Administration's perceived neglect of Japanese relations overall. A new term 'Japan passing' (a play on the familiar 'Japan bashing'), was coined to reflect Japanese dissatisfaction over the Administration's perceived tilt in the region toward Chinese affairs.

As this brief history has confirmed, relations between the United States and Japan on economic issues have tended to follow an almost predictable pattern of intensive engagement toward the beginning of a new Administration, followed by a lull, sometimes bordering on neglect, toward the end of the four-year cycle. Macroeconomic conditions, especially in the United States, tend to reinforce these political patterns.

It is no accident that the focus of the discussion so far has been almost exclusively on conditions and attitudes in the United States. As the next section will show, Washington has invariably been the source of initiative for most significant developments in bilateral economic relations with Japan.

Imbalance of Initiative

As it happens, most grand initiatives in economic diplomacy between the United States and Japan over the past quarter century have been presented to the world as a 'two-way street'. That is, the stated purpose is to give each side an equal chance to press the other for commitments to open markets, address macroeconomic imbalances, or promote domestic structural reform. (This is generally not the case for sectoral trade negotiations, which are specifically designed to address barriers in one country.) The SII process, for example, was aimed at 'addressing structural obstacles *in both countries* that stand as impediments to trade and current account adjustment'. The two-way street allows the Japanese government to persuade its domestic audience that it is an equal partner with the United States.

American action

In reality, virtually all of the major initiatives in US-Japanese economic relations in the past quarter century - whether voluntary export restraints, the MOSS talks, SII, or the Framework process - have been designed, proposed and driven by the US government. Despite its stated objectives and an ostensibly balanced agenda, SII was in fact dominated by US requests of Japan, measured by both the relative weight of the issues discussed and the time spent on each 'half' of the agenda. During a typical round of two days of meetings, for example, US concerns would be discussed well into the afternoon of the second day, with Japanese issues taken up only half-heartedly in the final few hours of talks.

Moreover, the actual dynamics of these negotiations are such that the US government is almost always on the offensive, probing and pressing for commitments, while the Japanese side is more passive, reacting, responding, and rebutting. The Japanese have a term to describe these dynamics: *gaiatsu*.[9] Literally meaning 'outside pressure', *gaiatsu* is a codeword for US government efforts to prod Tokyo into making a policy shift where the Japanese political system is unable on its own to deliver change. *Gaiatsu* is much maligned outside Japan, especially among Europeans and those Americans who would prefer a softer approach to bilateral relations. Within Japan, the verdict on *gaiatsu* is more mixed, with many people, even in the Japanese government itself, admitting that it plays a useful and necessary role in effecting domestic policy change.[10]

It is worth noting that *gaiatsu's* bark has typically been much worse than its bite. While Washington may cajole and occasionally threaten retaliation to achieve its economic objectives vis-à-vis Japan, it has followed through with trade sanctions only once in the post-war period (in the semiconductor case of 1987). But this is not the point: *gaiatsu* works because the perception of overwhelming US pressure arms Tokyo with the domestic leverage it needs to implement difficult policy decisions.

Japanese reaction

The emphasis here on US initiative should not obscure the fact that Japan has formidable advantages of its own in bilateral diplomacy. Put simply, where the United States is strong on 'offence', Japan excels at 'defence'. To begin with, Japan has a significant advantage in terms of resources devoted to bilateral ties. In a typical round of trade talks, it is not uncommon to find some 20-30 Japanese officials on one side of the table - often three rows deep - facing no more than six or seven officials on the American side. The Japanese officials naturally tend to be more specialised on a particular aspect of the negotiation, and to have done far more 'homework' than their US counterparts in preparing their part. Moreover, most of the Japanese officials are likely to speak at least some English, and many will have studied in the United States. (Although less so than it once was, it is still rare to find similar linguistic and educational credentials on the American side.) The few seconds to ponder a response while the interpreter is speaking gives Japanese officials a significant advantage in face-to-face negotiations with their linguistically challenged American counterparts.

Moreover, the Japanese government is much better organised than the American to develop unified, consistent positions in international negotiations, especially on trade issues. Most trade-policy functions in Japan are concentrated in just two ministries - the Ministry of Foreign Affairs and the Ministry of Economy, Trade and Industry (METI) - making policy coordination relatively straightforward. The key decision-makers are all part of the same educational and professional elite, typically having graduated from the Law Department of Tokyo University and spent many years together in the government. By contrast, trade policy is highly decentralised in the US government, with a multitude of agencies vying for leadership, including the US Trade Representative's office, the departments of Commerce, Treasury, and State, and the White House itself. Most top officials are short term political appointees who may have never met each other at the start of a round of negotiations.

Finally, the Japanese government has an advantage in the public relations dimension of bilateral diplomacy. The Japanese media devote far more coverage to US affairs than the reverse, and ties between the government and media are far closer in Japan, giving Tokyo a significant edge in its ability to shape domestic thinking on bilateral issues. Moreover, once actual negotiations are underway, US officials tend to focus on content first and to look at public relations 'spin' as something that flows from the outcome of the talks. The Japanese, on the other hand, consider control of the message an integral part of the negotiating process and will pay considerable attention to media strategy from beginning to end - holding pre-briefings of the press to set expectations for the talks, insisting that time be allotted on the formal agenda to agree with US negotiators on the precise language of press briefings to follow, and nevertheless taking the liberty afterwards of 'spinning' the results with their own press as they see fit.

But despite Japan's defensive advantages, the United States remains in the driving seat when it comes to bilateral economic diplomacy. It decides when to engage, sets the agenda, and makes most of the demands. On the whole, Japan merely reacts, responds, and resists.

This imbalance is not healthy for either side: it causes resentment in Japan, frustration in the United States, and friction in the overall relationship. Of course, a certain amount of tension between two such large and intertwined economies is inevitable. Yet the persistence and intensity of conflict in the US-Japanese economic relationship is due in large part to the fact that their styles of engagement are so unevenly matched. Thus it is worthwhile exploring the features of each country's domestic economic objectives, political systems, and even cultures that contribute to these idiosyncratic styles of diplomacy.

The Domestic Roots of Diplomacy

Why Japan reacts

Ask any football manager how to preserve an advantage in the tough closing minutes of a game, and he will tell you to play defence. For Japan, there is arguably much to preserve: an economic system that it took great pains to construct after World War II and that arguably served it well for at least four decades. There is an extensive literature on Japan's post-war economic strategy.[11] Suffice it to say here that the main features of that strategy were government-sponsored inducements for households to restrain consumption in favour of savings, and to channel those savings through public and private banks to productive industry;

restraints on industrial competition in the domestic market through import protectionism and relaxed antitrust enforcement; and incentives to export the domestic production surpluses that inevitably resulted (with most of those exports going to the United States). Consumers qua consumers were the big losers in this system, forced to pay high prices in the domestic market, but they were rewarded in their role as employees through steadily rising incomes and the guarantee of lifetime employment.

The United States was willing to tolerate this system as long as its own domestic economy was growing and Japanese economic recovery was seen as critical to America's Cold War strategy. Eventually, however, the competitive threat of Japanese products in the United States and in third markets, the lack of openness to American exports to Japan, and the downshift in US growth potential following the oil shocks in the 1970s, all coincided to upset the previous balance of interests. As Washington began to demand market-opening measures and policies to stimulate domestic demand, Tokyo fought to preserve a system that, in its eyes, was continuing to deliver economic success. But where other governments might have made tactical concessions to assuage an important critic, or even made demands of their own to deflect inbound pressure, Tokyo merely stalled, made excuses, and refused to budge. In other words, rather than simply playing *defence*, Japan tended to play *defensively*.

The reason for this defensiveness is that the Japanese government is constrained by its own politics and culture. Both constitutionally and in practice, the organised Japanese political system is generally unable to deliver the kind of timely, decisive policies that are essential tools of economic diplomacy.[12] The prime minister and cabinet are designed as relatively weak institutions in the Japanese Constitution, certainly in their role as policy-makers. Although the Diet has more formal power in this regard, in practice it has not had the resources or inclination to exert policy leadership, particularly on international issues. Political parties, for their part, are organised more as special-interest coalitions or personality cliques than as ideologically coherent groupings of like-minded politicians pursuing a well-articulated platform of policy positions.

As important as the formal political system in this regard is the relative lack of robust policy debate more broadly in Japanese society. Japan has virtually no independent think tanks or consulting firms able to develop policy ideas in support of, or constructive opposition to, those of the government. There are relatively few journalists or academics of any clout willing to challenge the establishment consensus. Nor are there NGOs or consumer groups that demand rights for those they nominally represent or that routinely question government policies. In sum, the government in Japan faces little opposition, either formal or informal.

In the absence of policy leadership from the political world, or articulation of opposing views in society at large, the bureaucracy has generally been given free rein to set the nation's policy course. Though Japanese civil servants are among the brightest and most technically competent in the world, they are, like any bureaucracy, far better at tactics and execution than at defining and articulating a bold 'vision' for the country. Benefiting, as they effectively do, from lifetime employment with a guaranteed promotion track, they also tend to be highly risk averse.

It is not surprising that this bureaucratic form of governance creates tension in relations with the United States. Instead of taking the policy initiative, the Japanese government merely responds to US initiatives, and does so slowly, cautiously, and incrementally. American officials are further frustrated by their inability to identify who in this system is in charge.[13]

Before turning to the domestic idiosyncrasies of the United States, it is useful to consider the role of culture in shaping Japan's reactive approach to economic diplomacy.[14]   Rudyard Kipling surely overstated the role of culture in international affairs when he famously wrote, "East is East, and West is West, and never the twain shall meet".[15] 'Culture' can be difficult to define, is prone to generalisation, and often serves to obscure more objective explanations of behaviour. For example, the failure of the Japanese government to respond effectively to a decade of economic dislocation in the 1990s owes more to the nation's tremendous cushion of wealth - which tends to temper the sense of crisis in Japan - than to an alleged cultural disposition to self-denial or stoicism. Nevertheless, even the most ardent proponent of realpolitik would find it difficult to argue that culture plays no part in Japan's diplomatic style.

In a landmark work published in the early 1970s, Japanese sociologist Takeo Doi argued that interpersonal relations in Japan are governed by a concept known as *amae*. Derived from the word 'sweet', *amae* has no direct translation in English but loosely describes the kind of mutual dependence that exists between parent and child, older and younger sibling, or boss and subordinate. The junior partner naturally has obligations toward his or her senior, but the latter has obligations as well: to protect and defend the junior, to bestow certain favours on him, to attend to his psychological needs. Though Doi did not apply these ideas to Japan's foreign relations, *amae* is a useful concept in explaining the Japanese tendency, as the self-acknowledged junior partner in the relationship, to look to the United States to take the initiative and to ensure that Japanese sensitivities are respected. When Washington fails to honour its side of the bargain and makes 'unreasonable' demands of Japan (or worse, is perceived to ignore its partner), a psychologically wounded Tokyo tends to dig in its heels. The inevitable result is friction in the bilateral relationship.

Another cultural characteristic often attributed to the Japanese by scholars is a preference for social stability over social change, or for equality of economic *outcomes* over equality of *opportunity*. Whether in baseball - where draws are possible in Japan - or in economic competition, it is argued, the Japanese prefer that there be no winners or losers. Everyone should benefit from national progress, or share in the pain of economic dislocation. One measure of this reputed preference for equality is the number of Japanese - some 75-80% - who identify themselves as 'middle class' in regular surveys of public opinion.

There is plenty of evidence to refute this hypothesis. Income disparities in Japan are in reality large, competition in the domestic marketplace can be cutthroat - and there are numerous Japanese sports in which the winner takes all. However, the *myth* of social stability may be more important than the reality when it comes to determining national policy. It certainly seems to explain why the government feels the need to consult extensively with key affected social parties before embarking on any major policy decisions. This slows down the process of decision-making and tends to support the status quo. Again, it also reinforces the tendency for Japan to be the passive, reactive partner in economic relations with the United States.

Politics and culture in the United States

Some would argue that culture - again, whether as myth or reality - plays an important part in American diplomacy as well. The generally pro-market orientation of US economic policy arguably owes as much to the nation's frontier experience and faith in the American dream as it does to economic theory. Similarly, belief in the country's 'manifest destiny' as a 'shining city on the hill' has been said to create a kind of missionary bent in Americans, a desire to change the world in its image. In the context of relations with Japan, all of this may help to explain persistent US efforts to open and deregulate the Japanese economy, or more broadly to make Japan, as one observer put it, "more like us".[16]

Those not satisfied with cultural explanations can look to American politics to understand what drives US policy toward Japan. To begin with, the US system creates a variety of outlets for expression of opinion on policy. The Constitution somewhat awkwardly divides power over foreign economic policy between the legislative and executive branches: while the President has the prerogative to 'make treaties'. Congress has the power to 'regulate commerce with foreign nations'. Decision-making on these issues is further diffused within each branch. The House of Representatives and Senate each have several committees with some jurisdiction over international economic policy, including Ways & Means, Financial Services, Commerce, and Agriculture in the House; and Finance, Banking, Commerce, and Agriculture in the Senate. A similar division of labour exists within the executive branch, with the Treasury Department having the lead on foreign exchange and macroeconomic policy issues, the US Trade Representative on trade negotiations, Commerce on enforcement of anti-dumping laws, State on overall relations with foreign nations, and so on.

Thus there is no clear centre of authority in Washington on foreign economic policy-making. Against the backdrop of an open and transparent political system, this means that interest groups, think tanks, and NGOs with a point of view on policy have a multitude of channels through which to get their voices heard. This in turn puts the US government under near-constant pressure to deliver new policy initiatives, in order to demonstrate its responsiveness to this cacophony of opinion. It also explains why US policy can be somewhat incoherent at times, and inconsistent *over* time.

Given that Japan is the second-largest economy in the world and a fierce economic competitor of the United States, it is not surprising that many of the interest groups that descend on Congress and the Administration are interested either in opening the Japanese market to US exports or in closing down the American market to Japanese competition (though of course the latter is rarely admitted publicly). As a result, the US Trade Representative's office has at any given time a long laundry list of trade issues to raise with Japan. This is the kindling for the periodic fires that erupt in the bilateral economic relationship, sparked by either the political calendar or by macroeconomic conditions, as described earlier in this chapter.

A number of Japan-specific factors in US policy-making make this situation even more combustible. One is the scarcity of Japanese expertise in the US government. There are relatively few officials in the American government, certainly at a senior level, with Japanese-language ability and either private-sector or government experience working on Japanese affairs. This situation has improved somewhat with the deepening of cultural, business, and governmental ties with Japan over the 1980s and 1990s; however, the level of Japanese expertise in the US government falls well short of what is required for a relationship as deep and broad as that between America and Japan.

In addition, there is an unusually sharp contrast between the perspectives of those few in Washington who *are* engaged in Japanese affairs and those who are not. The experts often have an intense fascination with the country, viewing the 'Japan problem' as an equal challenge to the 'German problem' or 'Soviet enigma' of old. This fascination is especially strong among some academic economists entering government who find Japan a challenge to economic orthodoxy. Former Treasury Secretary Larry Summers was a prominent example of this kind of official, visiting Japan an unprecedented six times in his first year in the Clinton Administration and retaining a peculiar fascination with the country throughout his eight years in Washington.

By contrast, non-experts inside (and outside) the US government reveal little interest in Japan unless forced by events to do so. Many of them appear to view the country as 'inscrutable' or too remote geographically or culturally to be worthy of attention. Of course, ignorance and disinterest in foreign affairs can be a badge of honour for Americans, but Europe, and even China, seems to hold far more interest for non-experts in the US government than does Japan.

This expertise gap presents two problems. First, it can leave the experts with too much control over the agenda with Japan, without the checks and balances that normally constrain policy-making, often to positive effect. Second, when certain conditions come together - say, the flaring up of a sensitive trade dispute during a political election cycle - apathy and ignorance can quickly turn to anger and distrust, making it difficult even for the experts to develop sensible policy responses. An improvement in the general level of understanding of Japan in the US government would not resolve all issues between the two countries, but it would likely help to smooth out the cycles of crisis and neglect, and to produce greater balance in the relationship as a whole.

Conclusions

In a number of respects, the US-Japanese economic relationship has become more balanced with the passage of time. For one thing, Tokyo is now more assertive in its dealings with Washington. A quarter century of economic friction has inevitably hardened Japanese attitudes toward US demands, especially among younger officials who have no memory of the more benign era in bilateral economic relations following World War II. Moreover, the Japanese government has made real strides toward opening and deregulating the domestic economy, arming it with more positive achievements to point to in response to American pressure.

The Japanese government has also become more skilful at exploiting weaknesses or inconsistencies in US positions. This was clearly witnessed at the start of the Framework talks in the early 1990s, when Tokyo not only resisted American pressure for quantitative targets in the negotiations but accused the US government - with considerable public relations success - of pursuing 'managed trade'. The Japanese government has also shown a growing willingness to take the United States to the dispute resolution mechanism under the World Trade Organization, for example over the US anti-dumping regime. In short, Tokyo appears to have discovered the wisdom of the old military maxim, "the best defence is a good offence".

Furthermore, the Japanese government has increasingly tried to exert its leadership vis-à-vis the United States in Asian regional affairs. An often-cited example is Japan's proposal in the early stages of the 1997 financial crisis for an 'Asian Monetary Fund'. Though the idea was eventually shot down by the US Treasury (which saw it as a threat to the IMF's leadership in global financial crises), the incident was significant in that the Japanese government, for the first time, did not feel the need to vet with Washington in advance a proposal of such importance to the region. Despite the 1997 setback, Tokyo has continued more quietly to advance its leadership credentials in Asia, by promoting other forms of regional cooperation such as currency-swap arrangements among the area's central banks.

Even as Japan has asserted itself more on trade and regional affairs, the United States has found it harder to flex its muscles on economic issues with Japan. The disciplines established under the Uruguay Round multilateral trade agreements put new constraints on the US government's ability to use domestic trade legislation as leverage in seeking market-opening concessions from Japan. In more subtle ways, too, Washington appears to have become less assertive in bilateral trade affairs. A quarter century of contentious negotiations with Japan has created a perception in Washington that such negotiations reap relatively little return for the time, energy, and resources invested in them. In fact, it may well be that the very success of those talks, and unilateral moves by Japan to reform its own economy, has taken the edge off Washington's traditional market access complaints. The inroads made by the US automobile industry in Japan, for example, including substantial investments in Japanese domestic manufacturing capacity, have fundamentally changed the dynamics of bilateral trade - and therefore of governmental negotiations over market access - in what was once the most contentious of all issues in bilateral relations.

For all of the reasons cited above, greater balance does appear to have been established in economic relations, and in the conduct of bilateral economic diplomacy, between the United States and Japan. This augurs well for a reduction in the frequency and intensity of friction in the relationship. Indeed there were signs at the turn of the Millennium that the old cycles of conflict and neglect have smoothed out to some extent, and that both sides have found new, more constructive ways of managing differences of interest.

However, it could be premature to predict a fundamental shift in the patterns of bilateral economic diplomacy. For one thing, cyclical factors, notably relatively benign economic conditions in the United States, may have masked some of the underlying differences and tensions that remain. Moreover, the relationship between the United States and Japan remains (with apologies to Ambassador Mansfield) "the most *complex* in the world, bar none". The world's two largest economies are deeply intertwined, fiercely competitive, and shaped by distinct national experiences, political systems, and cultures. It is inevitable that the sparks will fly occasionally - indeed, probably more often than in any other bilateral relationship - and that this will continue to severely test the diplomatic skills of both governments.

Notes

1   In numerous speeches during his tenure in Tokyo (1977-88).
2   And even before - see, for example, Stokes 2000.
3   Former US trade negotiator who prefers to remain anonymous.
4   For a more detailed account of bilateral economic relations over this period, see Lincoln 1999 and Schoppa 1997.
5   The so-called 'Yen-Dollar Agreement' of 1984.
6   Medical equipment and pharmaceuticals; forest products; telecommunications equipment and services; and electronics.
7   Satellites, supercomputers, and forest products.
8   The Japanese generally resist labelling bilateral understandings 'agreements,' fearing that this will make their commitments binding under Japanese and international law.
9   For a thorough discussion of *gaiatsu*, see Schoppa 1997.
10 When serving at the US Embassy in Tokyo, the author had several personal experiences of being lobbied by Japanese government officials and private-sector representatives to bring US pressure to bear on a particular policy matter.
11 The classic work on Japan's post-war economic system is Patrick and Rosovsky 1976.
12 For a description of the Japanese political system, see Curtis 1988.
13 This lack of a focal point for political decision-making is the central thesis of von Wolferen 1989.
14 For the seminal Western analysis of Japanese culture, see Benedict 1954.
15 Rudyard Kipling, *"The Ballad of East and West"* (1892).
16 See Fallows 1989.

References

Benedict, R. (1954), *The Chrysanthemum and the Sword*, Charles E. Tuttle & Company, Inc., Tokyo.
Curtis, G. (1988), *The Japanese Way of Politics*, Columbia University Press, New York.

Doi, T. (1981), *The Anatomy of Dependence*. Kodansha, Tokyo.

Fallows, J. (1989), *More Like Us: Making America Great Again*, Houghton Mifflin Company, Boston.

Lincoln, E. J. (1999), *Troubled Times: US-Japan Trade Relations in the 1990s*, The Brookings Institution, Washington.

Murphy, R. T. (1996), *The Weight of the Yen: How Denial Imperils America's Future and Ruins an Alliance*, W.W. Norton & Company, Inc., New York.

Patrick, H. and Rosovsky, H. (1976), *Asia's New Giant: How the Japanese Economy Works*, The Brookings Institution, Washington.

Schoppa, L. J. (1997), *Bargaining with Japan: What American Pressure Can and Cannot Do*, Columbia University Press, New York.

Stokes, B. (2000), *A New Beginning: Recasting the US-Japan Economic Relationship*, Council on Foreign Relations, Washington.

Van Wolferen, K. (1989), *The Enigma of Japanese Power*, Alfred A. Knopf, New York.

Chapter 12

The Regional Dimension: European Economic Diplomacy

Stephen Woolcock

This chapter considers the regional dimension to economic diplomacy. It does so on the premise that economic diplomacy - as explained in Chapter 10 - is a multi-level process that includes unilateral measures, bilateral negotiations, regional negotiations and actions, plurilateral measures (such as in the G7/G8 or the OECD), and multilateral measures in the WTO or IMF or other bodies. The multi-level nature of economic diplomacy appears in a variety of ways:

- Countries may handle specific policies at different levels: market integration regionally in the EU, tax policy plurilaterally in the OECD, climate change multilaterally in the UN.
- Governments may shop between different levels in the same subject. For example, investment in services could be treated bilaterally; regionally in NAFTA; plurilaterally in OECD (though the MAI failed); and multilaterally in the GATS of the WTO.
- The different levels may be used to do different things within the same policy issue. For example, multilateral agreements may provide broad principles, which are then applied at the regional level.

This chapter looks first at the growth and importance of the regional level in international economic diplomacy. It then focuses on the European Union as the most advanced and complex regional agreement. This provides an opportunity to look in some depth at EU decision-making in its external economic policies. In this book we do not look at the 'domestic' European issues, but treat the EU as an actor in economic diplomacy. The 'domestic' factors in EU economic diplomacy then become the institutional and other elements that shape EU decision-making in foreign economic policy. Trade policy is the most developed aspect of EU economic diplomacy and will therefore be the main issue covered in this chapter. This can be compared with the case study in the following chapter, which covers the EU's international environment policy.

The chapter considers how the EU case relates to the theoretical analysis discussed in Chapter 2. Drawing on this analysis, it will concentrate on *institutional features*. The key questions are:

- What institutions are involved in the decision-making process and how do these influence the nature of EU economic diplomacy?
- What is the role of non-state actors, whether business or civil society, compared to government actors, and what channels exist for the representation of such groups?
- Who are the chief negotiators in the EU and how much discretion or 'slack' do they have in international negotiations?
- What are the means of ensuring democratic accountability and do these make decision-making in a union of 15 Member States (soon to become 20 or more) slow and unpredictable?

More broadly, the chapter considers how well the models developed to help with our understanding of economic diplomacy (and examined in Chapter 2) fit with the European scene, bearing in mind that the models were almost all developed by American political scientists?

The Importance of the Regional Level

Regional agreements appear to have become a permanent feature of the world economy. It is possible to identify three phases in the growth of regional trade agreements (RTAs).[1] The first phase occurred in the 1960s and resulted from the widespread emulation of the European common market. The common market was in fact a customs union, completed ahead of time in 1968. The fact that the EU created a customs union meant there had to be a common external tariff and thus a common external trade policy. The African and Latin American countries that emulated Europe negotiated only free trade agreements (FTAs). Most of these were more efforts at sharing markets rather than liberalising markets. As a result none of the non-European FTAs were much of a success. During this first phase the United States remained committed to multilateral liberalisation.

The second phase of regional agreements occurred during the 1980s. This was again initiated by a rejuvenation of European integration, following the moves in the European Community to create a single European market.[2] This single market was effectively extended to cover Scandinavia and Austria (and de facto Switzerland) through the creation of the European Economic Area. ASEAN moved to establish an Asian Free Trade Area, and renewed efforts were undertaken in Africa and Latin America to create effective free trade areas, or, in the case of Mercosur, a customs union. Australia and New Zealand created a free trade area more through a kind of organic growth than through a treaty, but the approach adopted was similar to many of the EU measures. Most importantly of all, however, the United States moved to conclude free trade agreements with Canada, later joined by Mexico to form NAFTA, and thus added the regional dimension to its economic diplomacy. The United States also supported the efforts in APEC to create free trade in the Pacific region by 2020 and redoubled the efforts to negotiate a FTAA (Free Trade Area of the Americas) Agreement covering the whole of the western hemisphere. There were even some discussions about a US -

EU free trade agreement. These came to nothing, but there has been considerable cooperation between the EU and US on a wide range of commercial policy issues.[3]

A third phase of regional trade and integration agreements could be said to have started after the Uruguay Round and in particular after the failure of the WTO Ministerial in Seattle in December 1999. This phase has seen the expansion of some existing regional approaches, such as the European Union's negotiations with its Mediterranean neighbours, the Balkan states and potentially with Russia. There have also been negotiations on cross-regional agreements, such as EU-Mexico (concluded in 2000), EU-Mercosur/Chile and EU-South Africa (concluded in 2001). The EU is also in the process of converting its Lomé Agreement with a range of African, Caribbean and Pacific (ACP) developing countries into WTO-compatible free trade agreements.[4] The United States negotiated a cross-regional agreement with Jordan and is negotiating another with Singapore. Perhaps most remarkable of all, Japan, which had hitherto held high the banner of multilateralism, also began negotiating with some of its South-East Asian neighbours, such as Singapore, Korea and possibly some other countries in the region.

The WTO Secretariat recently identified 170 RTAs in July 2000 with no less than 68 further RTAs under negotiation.[5] Many of these agreements are of relatively minor importance, but some, such as those undertaken by the major trading entities like the EU, US and Japan, will have a profound impact on economic diplomacy. In addition to the dangers of trade diversion that were identified by Viner in the 1950s,[6] there is concern that regional agreements in newer fields of trade policy could result in the development of regulatory regionalism.[7] Regulatory regionalism is when countries concluding RTAs with a large country or region (such as the US or the EU) are more or less obliged to adopt the approach to market regulation employed in its larger partner. For example, the EU's neighbours, whether they are seeking accession to the EU or not, are under considerable pressure to adopt the *acquis communautaire* (the EU approach to standards and regulation) if they want to have guaranteed market access to the single European market. Much the same exists in NAFTA and the FTAA, where the dominant approach to regulation is that of the United States. If such dominant players shape approaches to regulation of integrating markets, there is a risk that divergent approaches to regulation develop. Such divergent approaches then jeopardise the future of multilateral agreements.

On the other hand regional economic diplomacy can help to break down protectionist barriers and pave the way to multilateral liberalisation. The major RTAs are not inconsistent with the WTO in that they defer to rights under the WTO, but seek to deepen economic integration by making WTO-plus commitments. For example, some of the more advanced RTAs include mutual recognition agreements, to help facilitate market access in instances when there are regulatory barriers to trade. The WTO provides for and indeed encourages mutual recognition agreements, provided these are open to all countries that meet the technical requirements. RTAs can also be 'WTO-plus' in the sense that they promote regulatory best practice and thus greater transparency and non-discrimination in regulatory policies that might otherwise be liable to the exercise of discretion by national regulators to favour local suppliers. There is, however, concern about the systemic impact of so many RTAs on the nature of the multilateral system.[8]

Why so many regional agreements?

The growth of regional agreements raises the question of what motivates them. This is the subject of a considerable literature and can only be touched upon here.[9] Broadly speaking the motivations fall into four categories:

* Political or strategic factors;
* Commercial benefits;
* Response to globalisation;
* Trade or regulatory policy factors.

Political or strategic factors have played an important role in motivating governments to negotiate regional agreements. The origins of the European Union were, of course, in efforts to promote Franco-German reconciliation and avert future European wars. The enlargement of the EU has also been significantly shaped by political and strategic considerations. Membership for Greece, Portugal and Spain was in each case the means of anchoring liberal democratic regimes in these countries and thus contributing to European security. Accession negotiations for the Central and East European countries is seen as a means of tying them into the region of prosperity and security that the EU has come to represent. For the existing EU Member States, accession for their Eastern neighbours provides a means of cementing European security after the Cold War and of bringing the two halves of Europe together in a peaceful fashion. RTAs with the Southern and South-Eastern (Balkan) neighbours of the EU also offer a means of promoting economic and political stability in the countries concerned and thus enhance European security. In the case of NAFTA, the United States and the political elite in Mexico were keen to lock in the reforms Mexico had undertaken in the second half of the 1980s. Similar arguments can be made for other regional initiatives. For example ASEAN was essentially a security agreement to start with and economic dimensions were only secondary or added later.

Commercial benefits are clearly an important motivation. A regional approach can offer access to a larger market more rapidly than more complex and lengthy multilateral negotiations. When trade and investment patterns are regional, then regional policy initiatives support traditional trade patterns. As noted above, countries neighbouring large markets will be motivated by a desire to ensure access to such markets. In terms of industrial or sector interests, there will clearly be a difference between those sectors that stand to gain from regional markets, such as companies benefiting from increasing returns, and those who will face stiffer competition. Regional agreements may also be seen as a means of strengthening the competitiveness of the regional industries in order to compete more effectively in international markets. Protectionist forces may see this as a means of gaining from the regional market, but insulating themselves from competition from outside the region by retaining protection at the regional frontier.

Regional agreements can be seen as a *response to globalisation.* If the internationalisation of trade and investment undermines national policy autonomy, it may still be possible to retain some control of policy preferences at the regional level. Forming regional groupings may also strengthen the negotiating position of the participating countries. This was one of the explicit motivations for Mercosur, when Brazil and Argentina saw themselves as losing influence in an international economy increasingly shaped by groups like NAFTA and the EU.

Finally, there may be *trade policy or regulatory motivations* behind regional agreements. Some of the recent cross-regional agreements cannot be completely explained by politico/strategic or commercial motivations - for example, the EU agreements with South Africa or with Mexico. In the case of Mexico there may have been some trade or investment diversion involved as a result of NAFTA. The Hispanic influences in the EU have also seen agreements with Mexico and Mercosur as a means of retaining European influence in the region in the face of US-led trade initiatives. The conclusion of such cross-regional or bilateral agreements may serve as a means of seeking to 'export' the approach to market regulation favoured by the initiating country. For example, the US-Jordanian agreement focused on intellectual property rights and labour standards. These are issues that the Clinton Administration wanted to see included in all agreements, so that the precedent of covering them in an agreement between the US and a developing country may be important from a trade policy point of view. One motivation may therefore have been the desire to establish precedents or models for future trade agreements that include these elements.

The European Union

The chapter looks at the European Union because it provides something of an illustration of the regional level of economic diplomacy. But the EU is in many respects the exception to most other agreements in that it involves deeper integration and has a common external economic policy, with complex decision-making procedures - see Figure 12.1. The main contribution of this part of the chapter is therefore to an understanding of how decisions are made in one of the major actors in economic diplomacy.

The Essentials of EU Decision-Making

Competence

The first question to ask concerning EU economic diplomacy is who is competent. Is it the European Community and thus the Member States acting through the Council, albeit with the involvement of the full supranational institutional framework of the Commission, European Parliament and European Court? Or is it

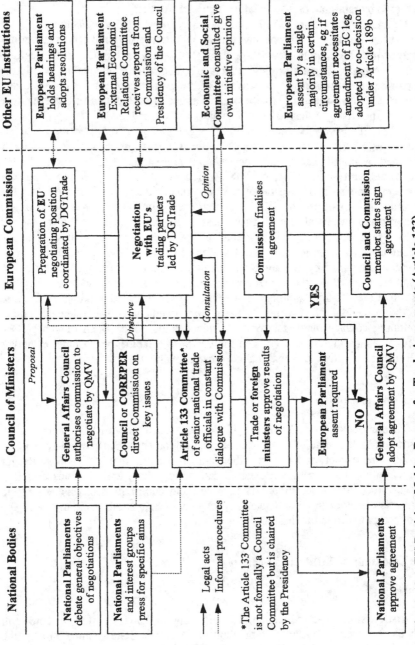

Figure 12.1 EU Decision-Making Process for Trade Agreements (Article 133)

the national governments? The Treaty of Rome gave exclusive competence to the European Communities for Common Commercial Policy, but did not define what common commercial policy was.[10] This clearly meant tariffs, because a customs union requires common external tariffs, and the treaty also referred to subsidies and anti-dumping measures. But trade policy has increased in scope since the Treaty of Rome was signed. Whenever new issues come onto the trade agenda, therefore, there is a debate as to whether the issue concerned is covered by EC or national competence or, as is sometimes the case, by mixed competence. For example, trade in services is part EC competence (for services provided across borders) and part national competence (when services are provided through establishment). Of the current new issues in the WTO, competition is probably EC or mixed competence but investment is still largely national competence.

Competence is important because it determines who negotiates. If the national governments were competent there would be 15 negotiators. In practice this issue has been resolved by the Member States delegating the job of negotiating to the European Commission, even on issues where there is national or mixed competence. But this is done without prejudice to the formal legal question of competence. The issue of legal competence has however had to be resolved before agreements could be signed. The rationale for this was that in international trade negotiations there are always linkages between issues on which the EC is competent and issues of national competence. In such circumstances it would be counter-productive to have had both Commission and Member States negotiating.[11]

This pragmatic approach has worked as long as the Commission has kept the Member States adequately informed. Differences in policy have been more of a problem in practice than competence issues. In the Uruguay Round for example, the biggest difficulties in developing and retaining a common position were in agriculture, where the EC is competent, not in services or intellectual property, where there was mixed or national competence. The European Court of Justice (ECJ) interprets the Treaties and thus ultimately rules on who is competent.[12] In judgements up to 1994 the ECJ tended to support the European Commission's expansive interpretation of EC competence, but in its decision 1/94, on who was competent to adopt the results of the Uruguay Round, the ECJ leaned towards the Member States' position.[13] This has therefore put something of a check on the growth of EC competence in the field of trade. In response to the ECJ's decision on services the European Commission and Council had to reach agreement on a Code of Conduct for negotiations on services in 1995, so as to avoid multiple negotiators and sending mixed signals to the EU's trading partners.[14]

In the 1996 Inter-Governmental Conference (IGC), the Commission argued that services and intellectual property should come under EC exclusive competence, as indeed it had in the 1991 IGC.[15] This was rejected by the Member States. The compromise solution proposed and adopted was the introduction of an enabling clause in the Treaty of Amsterdam, in paragraph 5 of Article 133. This measure, which is sometimes designated by the German *Kompetenzkompetenz*, (or competence over competence issues) enables the Member States, acting unanimously, to extend EC exclusive competence to include services, without having to change the treaty. This provision may help to overcome some of the problems mentioned above. Further efforts were made to shift competence for services and intellectual property to the EC at the 2001 IGC, but without success.

Setting objectives

In the EU it is the Council of Ministers (General Affairs) that formally determines the EU's negotiating 'mandate' for trade negotiations. The Council, acting on the basis of a Commission proposal, drawn up by Directorate General (DG) Trade, in cooperation with other Commission DGs, and on a qualified majority vote if necessary, authorises the Commission to negotiate on the basis of a 'mandate'. In the pre-negotiation phase of a multilateral round, as at any time in a negotiation, the Council may also give directives to the Commission modifying the mandate.

A good deal of work is done before the formal adoption of the mandate. For example, in preparation for the EU's negotiating position in the run-up to WTO ministerial meetings, including that in Doha that resulted in the launch of a new round, the Commission will produce informal papers on a range of potential agenda items. These will be discussed in the Article 133 Committee and its various specialist sub-committees. The Article 133 Committee is named after the treaty article that sets out its role and consists of senior trade officials from the EU Member States. The EU's position will also be influenced by discussions in specialist Councils, such as, in particular, agriculture and industry and these days also environment and consumer affairs.

The involvement of the European Parliament (EP) and the various national parliaments in this agenda-setting phase is at best indirect. The EP is not closely involved in developing detailed positions and only discusses a summary of the negotiating mandate after it has been adopted by the Council. At this point there is little prospect of the EP shaping the EU's objectives. The difficulty here is that any public debate of a detailed negotiating mandate would inform the EU's negotiating partners of the EU's 'bottom line', and thus undermine the Commission's ability to trade concessions with other WTO members. For these reasons the formal mandate is not a public document. Alternatively the published version of the mandate remains of a general nature, with the Member States having a more detailed understanding on how elements of it should be interpreted.

The EP can, however, shape the atmosphere in which EU objectives are determined and thus have an indirect influence by holding hearings and producing reports on topics relevant to the WTO agenda. This indirect role of the EP contrasts with the role of the US Congress, which can shape the US objectives in negotiations by granting or withholding negotiating authority. Consultation with national parliaments in the EU is the business of national governments. But in most cases national legislatures appear to play no direct part in setting negotiating objectives, and as with the EP, they do not have an opportunity of debating the official EU 'mandate'.

The EU's negotiating objectives may also be influenced by links between the Commission and national officials on the one hand and non-governmental organisations (NGOs) on the other hand. The Commission actively encourages input from important constituencies in order to help it shape specific negotiating objectives. In some cases detailed negotiating positions cannot be established without NGO input, such as private sector priorities on market access to third country markets. Information on impediments to third country market access has been improved with systematic efforts by the Commission to collect information centrally on impediments to market entry for EU exporters or investors.[16] Unlike the position in the United States, which has a set of formal Trade Advisory Committees, there is no formal structure of advisory committees at an EU level. Contacts, though informal, are reasonably well structured with bodies such as UNICE (the Union of European Industry and Employers Confederations) and EU level sector associations. In late 1998 the Commission also initiated a new series of consultations on the WTO agenda with 'civil society', ie environmental, developmental and other NGOs. This reflected the heightened awareness of the influence of such groups following the collapse of negotiations on a Multilateral Agreement on Investment (MAI), which was, in part, due to the NGO campaign opposed to the agreement.[17] The meetings with NGOs take two forms: larger consultations with anything up to 100 or more NGOs present, that are open to all but as a result tend to serve as a means of exchanging information; and a smaller group of some 12 NGOs that meets more frequently.

Negotiation

A key issue in the negotiating phase is the degree of flexibility for the Commission to interpret EU objectives. Too much flexibility for the Commission would mean little control for national governments over the course of negotiations and too much discretion or 'slack' for the EU chief negotiator. Too little flexibility would make it impossible for the Commission to negotiate. Critics of EU decision-making in trade policy have accused the European Commission of being unwilling to negotiate without a mandate from the Council and unable to negotiate once it has a mandate, because the mandate is so tightly drafted. In reality the mandate is only tight on sensitive issues, such as agriculture. In response to this - mainly American - criticism it has been suggested that the EU adopt a procedure equivalent to the 'fast-track' procedure used in the United States.

Under the Treaty of Rome, as amended in the Maastricht Treaty on European Union, it is the foreign ministers of the Member States, meeting in the General Affairs Council, who grant negotiating authority to the European Commission (Articles 133 and 300). The treaty provisions are similar to the US arrangement and could be interpreted as providing a kind of 'fast-track' procedure. A European 'fast-track' would operate with the European Commission negotiating as it wished, subject only to the critical condition that whatever it negotiated would have to be approved by the Council. One might argue that such an approach would provide flexibility, whilst at the same time guarantee that EU policy was accountable to the Council and thus the European electorate. The need for the European Commission to get the Council's approval for what it negotiates would ensure it maintained constant contact with the Council. But the Member States are not ready to grant the Commission discretion to choose how and when it consults with the Council. They fear, for example, that the Commission will strike deals between issues which impinge upon national interests that the Member State governments would then find difficult to reverse.

The EU Member States favour constant dialogue with the European Commission during any negotiation. The main forum for this dialogue is the Article 133 Committee, which discusses the EU's negotiating position on individual topics and the links between them. Before all sessions in international negotiations there will also be preliminary meetings with national officials to go over any last minute modifications to the EU's position. At important stages of a negotiation, the ministers responsible for trade are generally in attendance. This was the case, for example, at the final meetings of the Uruguay Round in Geneva in December 1993 and Marrakesh in April 1994. It was the case in Seattle in 1999 when the WTO Ministerial failed and in Doha in 2001 when the WTO Ministerial succeeded in launching a new round of trade negotiations.

Constant 'consultation' is needed because of the dynamic nature of international negotiations. Even when the negotiating mandate is tightly drawn, which is not generally the case outside such sectors as agriculture, there is always a need to reinterpret it in the course of constantly shifting negotiations. This provides infinite scope for differences of opinion between the Commission and the Council and within the Council and Commission. The EU, like other WTO members, needs to respond to negotiations as they proceed. On the less politically sensitive and technical issues, this response is decided by the Commission after consulting the Article 133 Committee. In this mode, as in virtually all its work, the Article 133 Committee hardly ever takes formal votes, but the sense of the meeting is taken informally or in some cases formally through the conclusions of the Presidency. If the Commission decides to proceed with a policy approach or proposal which does not have the full backing of the Article 133 Committee it can expect difficulties in the Council, as trade officials reflect the preferences of their ministers.[18]   On more important interpretations of the mandate or shifts in negotiating position the Council may decide to issue formal directives to the Commission as provided for in Article 133. Whether the system works or not is as much a practical as a legal question. Effective communication is needed for the Member States to have confidence that the Commission is reflecting their interests. Efforts to develop a formal code of general application (ie not just for services) to govern the consultation process have failed.

For the EU to have negotiating flexibility the Commission must, on occasions, venture onto the 'tight-rope' of exploratory talks without the 'safety net' in the shape of support from the Article 133 Committee or Council. This is, for example, the case when the international negotiations are at an impasse and compromises must be made on both sides. This can lead to problems in the EU decision-making process, when Member State ministers get to hear about what the Commission has been doing. This was the case in agriculture at the December 1990 Ministerial meeting of the GATT that was to conclude the Uruguay Round; and at the 1999 Seattle Ministerial over the establishment of a biotechnology working group of the WTO, which was to try and resolve the question of trade in Genetically Modified Organisms (GMOs).

It is worth noting that neither the Commission nor the Council are homogeneous actors in trade policy. Proposals from the Commission are coordinated by DG Trade, the Directorate General responsible for international trade. But many other areas of policy have an external trade dimension, whether this is agriculture, the environment or industry. To reach a coherent position within the Commission it is therefore necessary to coordinate a range of Directorates General, which can pose considerable problems of 'horizontal' coordination. The positions of the Member States may also be less than homogeneous. The national governments are not only represented in the Article 133 Committee (not a formal Council committee but chaired by the Presidency), COREPER (permanent representatives of the Member States in Brussels) and the General Affairs Council (foreign ministers with the ultimate responsibility for EU international trade policy). They are also present in other specialist councils (agriculture, industry, finance, environment etc) and each of these councils has its relevant committees of officials. Trade ministers may feel they have a broader overview than ministers for agriculture, but the latter may still be able to hold wider EU interests hostage to their own sector aims. Foreign ministers have ultimate responsibility, but tend to be preoccupied with issues of 'high politics' concerning the wider EU agenda or Common Foreign and Security Policy (CFSP) issues. Foreign ministers may also wish to temper decisions on trade with wider foreign policy interests. In order to understand EU decisions on international trade policy it is clearly important to understand not only the positions of the various Member States, but also how these are represented in the various Councils and their supporting committees.[19]

Control over the EU negotiating position is therefore primarily exercised by the Member State governments either through the Article 133 Committee or the Council in its various forms. As in the agenda-setting stage, other bodies have little influence. The European Parliament is consulted on negotiations as they proceed and in recent years the Commission has gone out of its way to keep the relevant EP Committees informed. The European Parliament is also included as an observer in the EU's delegation to major negotiations, but with no speaking rights.[20] The European Parliament is also excluded from the key consultations (between the Commission and the Council) that determine the EU's negotiating position.

The issue of control over negotiations has created more tensions in EU trade policy than that of competence. A number of proposals have been made to help remedy these tensions. It has been suggested that the Council, in the shape of the Presidency, should be present in all negotiations 'alongside' the Commission. But this has been opposed on the grounds that it would upset the established balance between the institutions and risk undermining the principle of a single (Commission) voice for the EU. As noted above there has also been an attempt to draft a code, but this has failed because legal certainty would have robbed the EU negotiators of the flexibility they need. The efficacy of the EU therefore continues to depend on effective communication between the Commission and Member State governments.

The adoption of results

The Council of Ministers (General Affairs) is the body responsible for adopting international trade agreements. When the EC has exclusive competence under Article 133 of the Treaty, decisions are taken by qualified majority vote (QMV). Even where the Treaty provides for QMV, however, there has been a practice of seeking consensus on important trade agreements, such as for the conclusion of the GATT/WTO. The desire to avoid QMV on issues of vital national interest, combined with the virtual absence of voting in the Article 133 Committee, means there is no practice of resolving differences over trade policy by a vote. This contrasts with the decision-making on the Single European Market (SEM) where the threat of a vote provides an incentive for Member States likely to be outvoted to work for compromise positions. In trade policy the threat of a vote is less potent and does not have the same effect. Indeed, in bilateral association agreements unanimity is written into the Treaty. As discussed above, the contagion of exclusive competence with mixed competence issues may further reduce the credibility of the threat of a vote.

The absence of voting on the adoption of international trade policy has spill-back effects on the negotiating process. If consensus rather than QMV is the norm, the Commission has less flexibility in negotiations because it cannot rely on a qualified majority of Member States outvoting minority interests. Member States opposing elements of a negotiation, such as further liberalisation of agriculture, can then exercise an effective veto over EU decision-making.

The European Parliament (EP) has no power under the main provisions of the Treaty concerning commercial policy. Indeed, in redrafting the Treaty in the 1991 IGC member governments went out of their way to exclude the EP from any role in adopting trade agreements. This contrasts with the position for association agreements in which the EP must give its assent by a simple majority vote. The Treaty also requires the assent of the EP for any agreement which has institutional or budgetary implications or when the trade agreement requires changes to EU legislation adopted by co-decision. In the Uruguay Round this, together with powers under other articles of the Treaty, was enough to require the EP's assent. The more intrusive nature of international trade diplomacy means that future WTO rounds are likely to touch on more and more policy areas in which EC legislation has been adopted by co-decision, especially since the extension of co-decision with the implementation of the Amsterdam Treaty in May 1999. The adoption of the results of a major new round of the WTO covering, for example, further liberalisation of trade in services and provisions on trade and the environment will almost certainly require the assent of the EP.

Even if it were not legally necessary, it is difficult to see how it would be possible to deny the EP the right to give its assent to the results of a major trade negotiation such as the new WTO round agreed at Doha. The EP could, therefore, have more leverage than it currently exercises. But as with the EP in general, there is the question of whether this political leverage is credible. The Parliament would only be able to reject the end result of a negotiation after it had been concluded and accepted (although not formally adopted) by the Member States. The rejection of the results of a round that had been accepted by the Member States and the 120-odd other WTO members would create a major political crisis in the EU and the international trading system.[21] Despite the EP's show of strength in forcing the Commission to resign in March 1999, the threat of the EP voting to unravel the results of a round negotiated over a number of years among so many countries is not credible, at least not for the moment. Only when there is a credible threat of a negative vote will the Commission and Council be obliged to include the EP as an equal partner in decision-making. Until this is the case the EP's ability to shape EU international trade policy will remain at best indirect and its ability to provide effective scrutiny limited.

National parliaments could help to fill this democratic deficit in EU trade policy, but scrutiny at the national level is at best non-systematic and usually superficial. National parliaments exercise a scrutiny role over EU trade policy via national governments, but the remoteness of international trade negotiations limits the possibility and inclination of national parliamentarians to follow the events and thus exercise any effective control. The negotiations are remote because concessions are made on national positions within the EU and then in negotiations with the EU's WTO negotiating partners. Most national elected representatives therefore feel they have no effective control over the process, and the ratification of the results of international negotiations in national parliaments becomes a rubber-stamping exercise.

If there is a broad populist interest in a trade related topic, national parliamentarians will become more interested. For example, the case of the European ban on fur imported from countries permitting the use of metal leg-hold traps comes to mind. In that case national parliamentarians voted for a policy that was in direct conflict with the EU's international obligations under the GATT. Animal rights groups will argue with some justification that international trade rules should not limit policy preferences on animal rights, but the difficulty is that national parliaments, because of their lack of any systemic scrutiny of European or international trade policy are not generally in a position to balance animal rights against the wider interest in maintaining a rules-based international trading system. This need to balance special against wider public interest in trade policy is not, of course, new. What has changed, however, is that the special interests are no longer specific industries such as textiles or footwear seeking protection, but wider constituencies who are now affected by the more intrusive nature of international trade diplomacy.

Conclusions

What conclusions can we draw from the summary of EU decision-making on international trade policy?

Institutional structure. The chapter shows that the institutional structure of decision-making within the EU is important. This determines whether the agenda-setting, conduct and adoption of negotiations will be decided by a qualified majority, or by the higher hurdle of unanimity. It shows that the EU tends, in practice, to operate by consensus. This is true in the Article 133 Committee as well as at the ultimate level of the General Affairs Council. This suggests that Member States have close effective control over the process of negotiations. The European Commission negotiator, the Commissioner for Trade, has only limited scope for discretion in how he conducts negotiations and even less when it comes to accepting compromises in international negotiations (level I in Putnam's two-level game model).

One must not exaggerate this point about de facto consensus, however. The fact that there are few formal votes does not mean that Member States that find themselves in a minority do not come under pressure to make concessions and fall into line with the majority. The EU may also use side payments in order to help ensure that all Member States accept the deal that has been negotiated at the international table (ie they ratify it at Putnam's level II). This was the case in textiles in the Uruguay Round, when Portugal was given funding to help adjustment in its textile industry. It was also the case in agriculture, where income support schemes were introduced to help buy off those who supported small farmers in France, Germany and Ireland.

Negotiating slack. In terms of negotiating discretion or 'slack', there does not appear to be too much in the EU, thanks to the tight scrutiny exercised by the Council. This would suggest that the EU is unlikely to 'defect involuntarily' - in Putnam's terminology - from an agreement it has negotiated. This is indeed the case. The EU has never failed to ratify an agreement that the Council has adopted. The Council has, however, quite often rejected agreements the Commission has negotiated. The so-called Blair House agreement on agriculture, negotiated between the Commission and the United States Administration in November 1992, is a case in point. France refused to accept this agreement until late 1993, when there had been some further minor concessions from the United States.

If one considers the degree of 'slack' in terms of the scrutiny provided by parliaments, the picture is somewhat different. Due to the limited role granted to the European Parliament for trade policy under the EU Treaty provisions, the EP has always struggled to have much of an impact on trade policy. In reality the EP will probably have to give its assent to the outcomes of major trade agreements in the future, because of the increased scope of international negotiations means that policy areas in which the EP has 'domestic' competence will be affected. But the EP can only veto an agreement after it has been accepted by all 15 Member State governments and the EU's negotiating partners. This is not a credible power. Even the US fast-track approach is not intended to result in the legislature actually having to veto an agreement reached in international negotiations. Active involvement in decision-making during the negotiations, to ensure that the final agreement will be ratified, is the preferable option. The lack of credibility of an EP veto means, however, that it has limited real power to shape negotiations as they happen. Very much the same argument can be made with regard to national parliaments, which are divorced from the course of negotiations on international trade and investment issues, but have the power to veto agreements reached that are of mixed or national competence.

In short there is a danger that if national governments fail to bring public opinion with them in supporting international trade and investment agreements negotiated by the EU, a backlash could result in either the European Parliament or national parliaments vetoing the agreements adopted. This would be involuntary defection, in Putnam's terminology. At present the means deployed to prevent such an outcome involve active consultation and communication with a range of NGOs, but the role of the elected EP and national parliaments remains limited.

Democratic accountability. The third, related question is whether the balance between efficiency and democratic accountability within the EU is in need of some adjustment. In the past the EU decision-making process has been shaped by what has been a predominantly bureaucratic process, in which national and Commission officials (perhaps with the involvement of experts from NGOs and the EP and national parliaments) have shaped outcomes. This has been relatively efficient at developing the EU interest and promoting EU positions in international negotiations. But the process has been criticised as lacking in transparency and democratic accountability. With the general backlash against globalisation, which has also resulted in criticism of the EU processes, there is the question of whether EU decision-making should not become more democratic in the sense of becoming more open to influence by national and European Parliaments. Traditionally this has been opposed by European practitioners on the grounds that it is a recipe for inertia. A move to more actively engage the European Parliament and national parliaments in order to avoid or reduce the risk of 'involuntary defection' could therefore result in less efficient EU decision-making or even paralysis.

Democratic accountability seems likely to continue to be provided mainly through the Council of Ministers. There may nevertheless be a case for strengthening the consultation between national ministers responsible for trade policy and national parliaments. This could mean for example, a more systematic scrutiny of the EU position in specialist committees in national parliaments. An alternative would be for more intensive EU-level scrutiny through the European Parliament. This would be more efficient because it would avoid parallel scrutiny in 15 national committees. But at present links between the EP and national parliaments are weak in many Member States.

This chapter has provided evidence that the regional level in economic diplomacy is assuming a greater importance. In most cases this involves one-off regional free trade agreements, but in the case of the EU we can see the evolution of a regional actor in its own right. Broadly speaking the theoretical analysis developed with single countries in mind and summarised in Chapter 2 can be applied to the institutional structure of the EU. The chapter discusses the decision-making process in the EU and points to the options for the future. There are serious drawbacks to muddling through with the existing procedures. But there is also resistance to a fundamental reform of the institutional framework. The most likely option is for continued small modifications in EU decision-making in trade policy, as pressures build up. But these may not be adequate to reflect changes in the nature of trade policy and economic diplomacy in general over the past decade.

Notes

1   See Bhagwati 1992.
2   See Pelkmans and Winters 1988.
3   See Frost 1999.
4   At the Doha WTO Ministerial meeting the EU, together with its ACP partners, won a waiver from the GATT provisions (in Article 24 of the GATT 1994) which require preferential agreements to cover substantially all trade, for its so-called Cotonou agreement with the ACP.
5   See WTO 2000.
6   See Viner 1952.
7   See Van Scherpenberg 1999.
8   See Bhagwatti and Kreuger 1995.
9   See Mansfield and Milner 1997 and Lawrence 1996.
10 European Communities is formally correct, although the current usage is becoming more and more the European Union. Note that this does not mean the European Commission is competent; the main legislative body in the European Communities is the Council of Ministers (the Member State governments).
11 See Bourgeois 1987 and Macleod, Hendy and Hyatt 1997.
12 The European Commission had initialled the agreement struck in December 1993, but this was subject to ratification by the Council of Ministers.
13 Opinion 1/94, *European Court Reports* I - 5267, 1994.
14 This was necessary despite the fact that the Uruguay Round had been completed, because the sector negotiations in financial services, telecommunications and transport implementing the GATS framework agreement continued throughout the 1995-97 period.
15 For a debate on the 1991 IGC as it relates to commercial policy see Maresceau 1993.
16 See the European Union Market Access Database, http://mkaccdb.eu.in.
17 The failure of the MAI was in fact probably due to other factors such as the EU and Canada seeking the exclusion of 'cultural' industries (ie film and audio visual) from the obligation to provide right of establishment and the US seeking a broad 'national security' exemption. The intensity of non-business NGO lobbying on the MAI issue nevertheless illustrated the growing influence of such interests and led the Commission to seek a closer dialogue with them.
18 See Johnson 1997.
19 See Hayes 1993.
20 This would normally be the Chair of the REX Committee of the European Parliament.
21 The European Parliament would prefer to have a positive power to shape EU trade policy, see De Clercq 1995.

References

Bhagwati, J. (1992), 'The Threats to the World Trading System', *The World Economy*, vol. 15, no. 4.
Bhagwati, J. and Kreuger, A. (1995), *The Dangerous Drift to Preferential Trade*, American Enterprise Institute, Washington.
Bourgeois, J. (1987), 'The Common Commercial Policy: Scope and Nature of the Powers', in E. L. M. Völker (ed.), *Protectionism and the European Community*, Kluwer Law and

Taxation Publishers, Deventer, pp. 1-16.

De Clercq, W. (1995), 'Introduction' in Bourgeois J., Berrod, F. and Gippini Fourier, E. (eds.), *The Uruguay Round Results: a European Lawyer's Perspective*, European Interuniversity Press, Brussels.

Frost, E. (1999), *Transatlantic Trade: A Strategic Agenda*, International Institute for Economics, Washington.

Hayes, J. P. (1993), *Making Trade Policy in the European Community*, Macmillan, Basingstoke.

Johnson, M. (1997), *European Community Trade Policy and the Article 113 Committee*, Royal Institute of International Affairs, London.

Lawrence, R. (1993), *Regionalism, Multilateralism, and Deeper Integration*, Brookings Papers on Economic Activities, The Brookings Institution, Washington.

Macleod, I., Hendy, I. D. and Hyatt, S. (1997), *The External Relations of the European Communities: a Manual of Law and Practice*, Clarendon Press, Oxford.

Mansfield, E. and Milner, H. (eds.) (1997), *The Political Economy of Regionalism*, Columbia University Press, New York.

Maresceau, M. (1994), *The EC's Commercial Policy after 1992: the Legal Dimension*, Nijoff, Dordrecht.

Pelkmans, J. and Winters, L. with Wallace, H. (1988), *Europe's Domestic Market*, Routledge for Royal Institute for International Affairs, London.

Van Scherpenberg, J. and Thiel, E. (eds.) (1998), *Towards Rival Regionalism? US and EU Economic Integration and the Risk of a Transatlantic Rift*, Stiftung Wissenschaft und Politik, Eberhausen.

Viner, J. (1952), *The Customs Union Issue*, Stevens and Sons Ltd, London.

WTO (2000), *Inventory of Non-Tariff Provisions in Regional Trade Agreements*, Background Note by the Secretariat, WT/REG/26 5 May 1998, World Trade Organization, Geneva.

Chapter 13

Making EU International Environment Policy

Patrick Rabe

This chapter tries to give a personal but hopefully informative outlook on the way international environmental issues are being prepared in the European Union and negotiated with other partners, notably in the UN system.[1] It assumes a general knowledge of the EU institutions and of the UN system. But by way of introduction the next section briefly describes the institutions of the European Union concerned with the environment.

The EU Institutions and Environment Policy

The Council of Ministers

The Council is the law making body of the Union, deciding according to weighted votes or unanimity and led by a Presidency rotating every 6 months. The Council consists of a number of sector Councils, a General Affairs Council and a top-level European Council of heads of state or government and is serviced by the Council Secretariat. Below the ministerial level there is the Committee of Permanent Representatives (COREPER) and a series of working groups of officials. The Council of Environment Ministers meets formally (adopting decisions, which have the form of law, and recommendations) four times per year and informally twice. Like other Councils it has a set of working groups to prepare each question.

The European Commission

The Commission is the 'Guardian of the Treaties' with the sole right of initiative (for legislation) in the Union, the executor of most Community business, and the enforcer of Community legislation. Since 1973 the Commission has had an Environment Commissioner, supported first by a service and now by a Directorate-General for the Environment with a staff of some 500. There is also the European Environment Agency, located in Copenhagen, which focuses on information gathering, analysis and reporting, and whose 'State of the Environment' publications are widely influential.

The European Parliament

The Parliament has gradually extended its powers and now participates in the law making through the 'co-decision procedure', exercises political control over the Commission and has a veto over the Community budget.   Since 1973 the Parliament has an Environment Committee (currently 59 members) which prepares the Parliament's votes and views on environmental issues.   Increasingly, the Parliament is also taking an interest in international affairs, and is sometimes represented (as part of the European Community delegation) at international negotiations.

The Committee of the Regions and the Economic and Social Committee also have sub-committees dealing with environmental issues in an advisory capacity.

European treaties and programmes

The work of the EU is based on the Treaty of Rome[2] (1957), as amended by the Single European Act (1987), the Maastricht Treaty on the European Union (1992) and the Amsterdam Treaty (1997).   The environment is addressed in Articles 174-176 (of the Treaty establishing the European Community, TEC) and international cooperation is covered by Article 174, paragraph 4.   Other important bases are Article 6 (of the TEC) requiring the integration of environmental concerns into all other policies, and Article 2 (of the Treaty establishing the European Union, TEU) setting out sustainable development as an overarching objective of the EU.

The EU, or the European Community (EC) to be correct (since only the Community not the Union is a legal entity), has adopted more than 200 pieces of environmental legislation that are transposed into national legislation in the Member States.   This is what is termed the 'acquis' in the enlargement negotiations: the existing body of legislation.

This legislation is developing and so is the 'soft law' of the EU - recommendations, programmes and strategies.   *Action Programmes on the Environment*[3] have been in place since 1973.   It is worth mentioning the Fifth Action Programme[4] (1992-2000), because it addressed economic sectors for the first time and the need for them to **integrate** environmental concerns into their decision-making based on the principles of Agenda 21 (on which see below).   It launched a process, that was endorsed by the Cardiff European Council during the UK Presidency in 1998, of integrating environmental concerns into all sectors of Community policy.   Since then various sector Councils have been developing strategies for integration.   The General Affairs Council adopted a strategy for the integration of environment into external policies at the end of 2001.

The Sixth Environmental Action Programme,[5] 'Environment 2010 - Our Future, Our Choice', was presented by the Commission to the Council and Parliament in mid-2001 and was adopted in the spring of 2002.   At its meeting in Gothenburg, Sweden, in June 2001, the European heads of government adopted an EU Sustainable Development Strategy, which addresses a few key long term policy issues, and indicates how environmental, social and economic objectives could be met in an integrated way.

EU Coordination on International Environmental Issues

The positions of the EU in environment, as in other issues, are prepared in Council groups. Having had a single Environment Working Group, the Council has now expanded to create an international environmental group, with several formations on different international issues. This reflects the increasing number of international negotiations as well as their increasingly technical nature. The working group experts are mandated by their governments to negotiate and agree EU positions. Often these positions are then adopted at Council/Ministerial level to reinforce their weight, or negotiated by ministers should issues not have been solved at working level.

For agreements where Community legislation is concerned, or in areas of exclusive Community competence (trade, agriculture, fisheries and Community aid), the Commission presents and is accorded a negotiating mandate from the Council, and subsequently negotiates on behalf of the Union. For all other issues and for political negotiations that are not legally binding, the rotating Presidency of the EU negotiates.

The practice for the EU to *speak with one voice in international contexts* is now firmly established. Based on the 'loyalty clause' in Article 10 of the Treaty on European Union, Member States have a duty to preserve unity in external fora, or, in the words of the Court of Justice: "l'unité de la représentation internationale de la Communauté".

The Council preparations bring a certain *transparency* to the EU negotiating position. The Council decisions or conclusions are automatically made public, and Ministers often debate these EU positions at home. There is plenty of room therefore for the EU position (and internal differences of view!) to be known by other negotiating partners. Together with the practice of most EU Member States and the Commission to include representatives of NGOs in their delegations, this makes the EU a very open partner. Its advantages are that it improves the understanding of European positions, it can generate public support which sometimes proves crucial in making progress, and it corresponds with European ideals of democracy and accountability. On the other hand, it may sometimes give the opportunity for opponents to divide the EU common line. And it certainly makes it more difficult for the EU to agree on negotiating tactics and fallback positions in good time and in advance.

Positions are rarely finalised in Brussels, but rather through *EU coordination on the spot* at negotiations. Sundays before international meetings start are regularly devoted to EU coordination, which continues in early mornings as negotiations progress. This takes place either in Council Secretariat offices (in New York and Geneva) or in specially designated conference rooms, but late at night it may well take place in corridors or in a corner at the back of the negotiating room.

The direct influence of Member States is generally large in international areas, due to a number of factors linked to the role of foreign policy in EU cooperation. In the field of environment, however, views are relatively uniform among members and there is often strong coherence in the EU line. Based on this, and the trust that develops between colleagues who are used to working together, *internal job sharing* has developed where different countries may take on the preparation of different sub-items under each negotiation. This system has proved indispensable in many of the processes, which have included just too many technical issues for any one EU Presidency or the Commission to handle alone.

A Member State's influence depends on knowledge and capacity, which of course partly depends on the size of the country and its administration. But certainly several smaller capitals have a disproportionate influence thanks to national priorities and experience. On international environmental issues there is a group of countries that always has influence, others less so. The Commission is conscious of this imbalance and is deliberately trying to engage a broader group of countries through targeted initiatives and regional programmes.

Finally, the EU (its Member States and/or the European Community) is currently Party to more than 200 international agreements and treaties, and has signed an even larger number of soft law instruments, such as UN resolutions, declarations, sets of principles or codes of conduct, etc. In turn, international environmental cooperation and in particular the over 50 international treaties signed by the European Community, has a significant impact on internal EU affairs. It is estimated that around 35% of EU legislation is in fact the implementation of international commitments.[6]

The Evolution of International Environmental Law and Cooperation

So, where did it all start? Although some of the first environmental treaties between nations, relating for example to shared rivers, date back to the 1800s, it was not until much later that international environmental protection became a public issue. When it happened varies between countries. Rachel Carson's *Silent Spring*,[7] the book about chemical pollution, was the wake-up-call for many in the United States. In Sweden it was perhaps the discovery of tons of toxic waste in rusting barrels buried in land later sold for family housing. This was accidentally unearthed by someone who shoved his shovel deep enough into his lawn, explaining suspiciously high rates of abnormal births, allergies and cancers.

Throughout the 1960s environmental awareness had risen, and ranged from local waste problems to habitat loss and air pollution. The United Nations decided to hold the *Stockholm Conference on the Human Environment* in 1972,[8] the first global recognition of environment as an international, diplomatic issue. In essence, it concluded that everybody ought to protect their own environment and help protect the global environment. But many still considered that environmental protection was a potential brake on developing countries' progress, and should not get in the way of tackling poverty. Basically, the environment was seen as a luxury.

Nevertheless, many countries set up environment ministries and/or agencies in the following years, and within those or within foreign offices a small cadre of international environment officials started to form. The Stockholm Conference also established the *United Nations Environment Programme (UNEP)*[9] as the main

UN institution for environmental issues. It was located in Nairobi, which gave Africa a rightly deserved major UN institution.

The 1980s saw an economic surge in many industrialised countries and some developing countries, while there was an apparent lack of economic progress in many other developing countries, leading to a questioning of the efficiency of aid and international cooperation. The challenge for global development appeared more complicated than what many had thought. At the same time increased economic activity led to an increased pressure on natural resources and saw increasing environmental pollution. Environmental issues were also becoming more and more international or at least internationally known. The loss of tropical forests in Brazil, for example, became a domestic political issue in such far-away countries as Germany.

The UN decided to put the question of reconciling development and environmental protection to a World Commission headed by Norwegian Prime Minister Gro Harlem Brundtland. The Brundtland Commission in 1987 reinforced the Stockholm Declaration and took it a step further: Care for the environment was **not** a luxury, but was a **necessary condition** to combating poverty.[10] Environmental protection and social and economic development were mutually supportive and needed to be integrated. The Commission termed it *Sustainable Development*. International environmental policy-makers now went into a higher gear, and most importantly, started working with development colleagues in foreign offices and aid ministries.

This led to the *UN Conference on Environment and Development (UNCED)* in Rio in 1992. Still today Rio remains a high-point of the multilateral expression of solidarity and vision. Few remember Stockholm in 1972, but many probably remember the Earth Summit in the summer of 1992. Everyone asked: "Would US President Bush (senior) come?" He finally did, and joined 174 other leaders in signing on to the Rio Declaration and the Agenda 21.[11]

The *Rio Declaration* contains 27 principles, including the important notion of **common** but **differentiated** responsibilities. *Agenda 21* embodies 40 chapters of actions and targets to achieve sustainable development. If all countries followed what is in the Rio Declaration and Agenda 21, we would live in a perfect world. As such they are far-reaching documents and, not surprisingly, they are not implemented in full. They were both intended as 21st century visionary documents.

The Rio Conference also adopted the *Framework Convention on Climate Change*, the *Convention on Biodiversity*, agreed a set of *Forest Principles* and agreed to launch negotiations on a *Convention to Combat Desertification* which was adopted in 1994.

Finally, the 'institutional' outcome of Rio was the establishment of the *UN Commission on Sustainable Development*,[12] known to everybody in the game as the CSD. The CSD is a functional commission of the UN Economic and Social Committee (ECOSOC), and has met yearly since 1993. The CSD has its own rules of procedure and has introduced new practices in the UN, where 'stakeholders' - environment and development NGOs, business and trade unions, academia, women's groups, youth and indigenous peoples - are involved in the government-to-government deliberations. This has had a profound impact on the debates, and also helped implementation on the ground.

It is clear from the above that international environmental issues are inextricably linked to issues of international development and that no international negotiation on environment can ignore issues of development or the concept of sustainable development. This has forced the global environmental agenda to take a wide range of issues into account, which sometimes has made progress more difficult and slow, but which has also given it credibility and wide participation - more so, perhaps, than other areas of international cooperation.

What the Guided Tour of the UN Headquarters Might Not Tell You

Most international environment negotiations are conducted in a UN forum and UN rules and practices apply. This means for example, that there are five official politico-regional groupings when selecting chairpersons, members of bureaux and other formalities. Negotiating positions, however, are normally coordinated between the three developing country regions - Asia, Africa and Latin America - as the Group of 77 (G77), which now comprises 133 members and has an annually rotating Presidency, speaking on its behalf. The Western Europe and Others Group (WEOG) is split between the EU countries, which coordinate their positions, and the rest of the group calling themselves 'JUSCANZ' (Japan, US, Canada, Australia, New Zealand, Switzerland, Norway and Turkey), which normally do not. Finally, there is the Eastern Europe Group, reflecting a cold-war world, now consisting mostly of countries associated with the EU, which normally align themselves with EU positions, and a few others, heavily dominated by Russia. The basis for decisions or resolutions is practically always a text drafted by the G77, reflecting the fact that this is the biggest group in the UN system.

The Plenary meeting of a negotiation is mostly where nothing happens. All documents must be in the six UN languages, there is interpretation, records are kept - the lot. In Informal meetings some things do happen, and there is only interpretation. In Informal-informals even more happens; there is no interpretation, but there must be a decision on which language to use (regularly English). Informal-informal-informals are instead where it really happens and where there are no rules. This might also be physically reflected by moving into small rooms at the back of the building, without air-conditioning, and with only enough seats to seat the key players. This is often what is needed to get the deal done.

Food and drink are other essentials to get the deal done, and the UN is sure to close its cafés at some unreasonable time (already at seven in the evening), to ensure starvation makes negotiators more amenable.

The Role of the EU and the Main Partners

Before describing some examples of the international environmental negotiations that have preceded and followed Rio, I would just like to mention some general issues on the role of the EU vis-à-vis its partners.

The EU often acts as a key bridge between developing countries and the US. Why is this? It is partly thanks to remaining ties from a colonial past, partly to the EU incorporating three of the four 'G 0.7 countries', ie those that actually live up to the agreed development aid target of 0.7% of GNP: Denmark, the Netherlands and Sweden (Norway being the fourth club member). In addition, of course, some Member States contribute large absolute figures of aid, notably France, Germany and the UK. Finally, in environment as in other foreign relations, Europe has a different diplomatic doctrine from the US: one of long term engagement, prevention and government-to-government cooperation.

However, the roles and interests vary on different issues. Alliance building is constantly changing, depending on the issue and the environmental or economic interests at stake. This is perhaps different from other fields of foreign relations where alliances are more stable. The 'issue-based' structure of international environmental negotiations may also be the reason for the relative decentralisation and dispersion of international environmental agreements and institutions.

In the *Montreal Protocol* negotiations, for example, the Nordics (before Sweden's and Finland's accession to the EU in 1995) and the US were allies, pulling a reluctant EU along. They had regional agreements in place but realised that, to mend the ozone hole, developing countries also had to curb their production. This was not at all a priority of the developing countries. Jointly the US and the EU had to convince the developing world that this was a global problem which needed a global regime, and together they realised that they had to foot the bill. The Montreal Fund was created and India and China signed the Protocol.

Biosafety started out as a developing country concern about the sale of genetically modified organisms (GMOs) on their markets, and the patenting of plant genetics 'belonging' to developing countries. The EU development ministries shared this concern and environment ministries saw environmental problems from GMOs. It turned into a strong European case in support of the precautionary principle. The main exporters of GMOs were of course the US, but also some developing countries, like Argentina. The developing world split and the rift between the EU and what was to become the 'Miami Group' in the biosafety negotiations was huge.[13]

On all issues relating to *finance and development assistance*, the EU and the developing countries have a special love-hate relationship. As mentioned above, the EU is the main global donor, and is recognised for it. But the Europeans are also very active players on the environment, and so are perceived as 'demandeurs'. A lot of difficulties stem from the 'broken promises of Rio' where the agreed UN target of 0.7 % was reiterated, but to which only a small group of countries live up. In fact, until 1998, levels of financial assistance went down, and this caused a serious confidence rift between developed and developing countries. An increasing awareness that private financial flows, such as in foreign direct investment and trade, are supplying much larger shares of developing countries' income, and some positive signals from donors, including the UK, on increasing levels of development assistance, will hopefully go some way to undo this knot.

The US simply refuses to entertain any requests for international, governmental commitments on finance.

A Practitioner's Reflections on International Negotiations

The contribution of this chapter to the publication is one of practical experience, focused on the process of international decision-making rather than its environmental or developmental significance. I would like to return therefore to some of the major Rio negotiations, through some examples of typical traits in these negotiations. I would not be surprised if they share these traits with other areas of international economic diplomacy.

The 'New York Network'

The UN in New York is a main negotiating place, and the EU Council of Ministers has a well-serviced centre for EU coordination. EU Member States and other countries of the North are often represented from capitals. But many developing countries are represented by their embassy staff, who are often posted there for many years. Due to lack of resources they cannot have the rotation schemes that most European foreign offices have. So they follow many or most of the UN processes in New York and few elsewhere.

This is sometimes very frustrating, as when the negotiation of a text on finance for sustainable development in the CSD brought up the hot topic of good governance (ie issues of anti-corruption etc). The EU had just signed the Cotonou Agreement, a major agreement with all the ACP countries (former colonies in Africa, the Caribbean and the Pacific) who are the main focus of Community aid and represent 71 of the 133 members of the G77. The Cotonou Agreement includes commitments on good governance. When the EU tried to replicate the language in New York, it was like a red rag to a bull. No, no, no! In one free and frank exchange the G77 chairman told a key EU negotiator: "I don't care what an ACP country is, we are in New York!" As it happened, her country was an ACP country.

But coherence in international representation is definitely not only a problem of developing countries but applies to all countries. This is partly due to lack of coordinating resources, partly to short-sighted pursuit of what are seen as national interests according to where they are best pursued. Regularly countries trade off between different fora, and in this way, such seemingly disparate issues as oceans and desertification may become entangled.

"If in doubt, take it out"

This is an often-cited suggestion, when you have run out of arguments. The failed, much-publicised Sixth Conference of the Parties to the Climate Convention, meeting in The Hague in November 2000, provides an example. British Deputy Prime Minister John Prescott, during the last night, tried to broker a deal between the main protagonists, the US and the EU. But when he brought it back to his EU ministerial colleagues, some of them just dragged out of their beds, they found it too complicated and were too uncertain whether it would fly with domestic public opinion. It was rejected. Prescott's disappointed reaction was rapidly well known.

"If in doubt, take both"

This is another compromise trick, and perhaps worse. At the Kyoto climate negotiations in 1997, some 'simply' wanted commitments to reducing emissions of greenhouse gases, but others not only resisted that, but added Clean Development Mechanisms, Emissions Trading, Joint Implementation, 'Hot Air' and Sinks. Good or bad, the details of this Christmas tree took another three years to negotiate and hardly any projects got under way.[14]

The compromises of 4.30 in the morning or the pressure of impending sunrise

Both of these climate change cases are examples of what results from 'stopping the clock' as if it never passed 18.00 on the last official day, which seems to be unavoidable in any negotiation. Being completely exhausted might be a way to get an agreement, but it might not be the best one. The succession of anodyne acronyms for the very important global issue of forests reflects the fact that the international community cannot agree on whether to have a legally binding convention instrument or not. Talks continue, but under new names. What was the IPF (Intergovernmental Panel on Forests), became the IFF (Intergovernmental Forum on Forests), which in turn became UNFF (the United Nations Forum on Forests)!

'The apocalyptic prophecies' and 'The diplomacy of the streets'

This deals with the very important issue of the increased role of civil society in international negotiations. Some time ago now, negotiations on the Montreal Protocol on protecting the ozone layer started as a controversial issue pushed by NGOs, which producing countries did not support. The hole in the ozone layer was exaggerated and not proven that it was because of CFC in refrigerators, it was said. The scenarios of skin cancer levels etc were said to be wildly overstated. But as evidence grew, and perhaps most importantly, as new technology was found, countries turned around. And yet afterwards one could hear "What did we tell you? The hole didn't grow!" No, but maybe that was because we got the Protocol thanks to those prophecies. And, incidentally, the ozone hole does still grow.

An international regime on investments is another thorny issue, where the EU and others were seeking a Multilateral Agreement on Investment within the OECD. It met with stiff political opposition when environmental NGOs denounced the negotiations, which had been held behind closed doors in Paris, as limiting the rights of a country to regulate its own environment. Negotiations fell into a coma in 1998, from which they have yet to come out.

When trade negotiators, together with some environment colleagues, went to Seattle for the WTO ministerial meeting late in 1999, they could not have imagined what they would live through. Seattle dealt a serious blow, not just to the WTO, but much wider.   It has changed the positions of many countries on the involvement of civil society in international negotiations and the need to make the process of economic globalisation palatable perhaps not to the demonstrators, but to consumers who increasingly vote with their wallets.   Since then, the Gothenburg European Council and the Genoa G8 summit, in June and July 2001, have further put the spotlight on the need to maintain credibility and accountability in international negotiations.

The Seattle debacle had an immediate impact on the biosafety negotiations on trade in GMOs, which were suspended in disagreement in Cartagena in February 1999 and were due to resume in January 2000.   With the shock of Seattle still affecting many governments, the pressure to show that the international community could act, that consumer and developing country concerns were being taken into account, and that free trade was not perhaps the solution to everything, ensured that the deal went through in an ice-cold Montreal, where the demonstrators were less violent, but nonetheless there.

The interface between trade and environment is indeed one of the most difficult issues on the international environmental agenda.   Since the WTO's inception in 1994 its Committee on Trade and Environment, which has had the same ten agenda points ever since, has not agreed on much.   Trade is an exceptionally difficult area to deal with from an environmental point of view.   On the one hand, trade clearly brings many negative environmental impacts, but economic benefits and resource efficiency are positive impacts directly or indirectly benefiting environmental protection.   The parallel with the Single Market of the EU is clear - while the EU has had to couple the free movement of goods with raising and harmonising levels of environmental protection, this is not yet the case in the global market place which is increasingly becoming one big free trade area.   This is not to say that the EU does not have a lot left to do, for example in dealing with the implications of increased freight transport and other issues.

The weight of strong personalities

The biosafety deal clearly would not have been struck had it not been for Colombian Environment Minister Juan Mayr's strong personal commitment and personality.   It sounds easy, but in fact he made a major breakthrough just by rearranging the way countries sat in the room, reflecting interests in the Protocol, rather than the normal UN groupings.   At the negotiations of the Malmö Ministerial Declaration of UNEP, the Swedish host Minister Kjell Larsson sat through the night himself and negotiated paragraph by paragraph, asking a diplomat who had just stated his country's standard line objection to one or the other issue "but what is **actually** the problem for anyone in your country of this formulation? Please explain to us!" And as a politician he would not take "it's a political problem" for an answer.

'The travelling circus on environment and development'

This phenomenon meets up for negotiations at the CSD, at UNEP, in a Multilateral Environmental Agreement or at the OECD, and gradually gels as a group.   This might be bad in that it makes these negotiations 'happen in a box' of pre-determined people and departments, which do not manage to integrate the results throughout their administrations and thereby make implementation slower. Negotiations might go off at a tangent and then only later realise the obstacles to actual implementation. But it is also extremely helpful. It creates a working environment where there is give and take over time, where you get to know the players, develop friendships and can have those 'free and frank' exchanges and build alliances in formal and informal ways. You develop a common terminology to communicate.

Most importantly, however, governments from all over the world are engaged. Maybe not everyone in everything, but certainly everybody in something, and this is a major achievement. The results on the ground are there, even if they are not enough. The work is part of a bigger picture. I am certain that international cooperation on environment and development has brought positive spill-over effects to general development cooperation and has been a stabilising factor in global security.

Ways Forward

I would like to end by hinting to some cross-cutting issues which are currently debated in the international environment and development field.

Integration. There needs to be better knowledge of how different elements of good quality of life interact, both within Europe and globally, through the integration of economic, social and environmental objectives. There should also be stronger links between the UN system and the Bretton Woods institutions and the WTO. Negotiators must concentrate on their specific tasks, but in so doing they need to be able to see the wider picture and take a multitude of concerns into account. Open government, or 'multi-stakeholder participation' in UN jargon, helps to do that.

Coherence. Governments must pay particular attention to integration of objectives in their international policies, so that what they say and do in different international contexts is coherent. For example, countries must not knock down with trade restrictions what they have built with development assistance money. The international system will never be stronger than the coherence of its main players.

Governance. The need for multilateral cooperation and its supporting global institutions must be restated again and again. The deal on UN financing reached with the US Administration, where the scales were changed to give the US a rebate, was an all-time low-point in international solidarity. It increases the need for the EU and perhaps most of all the UK to be a transatlantic bridge-builder, defending the integrity of the international community's supporting institutions.

Science and technology is at the heart of environmental policy: knowing what is going wrong, and knowing how to solve it. There must be quicker and clearer ways, however, of bringing the knowledge of scientists to policy-makers and bridging the communication gap.

Transparency. International processes and negotiations need to be understood and supported by the public to succeed. The sustainable development process since Rio may serve as an example in bringing in stakeholders into the process; perhaps not all the way to the back room where the final deals are done, but at least very close to where the discussion takes place. The Earth Negotiations Bulletin, for example, is an NGO that reports directly from all international meetings on sustainable development direct on the web, thereby enabling immediate reactions. At the national and European levels, the Aarhus Convention on Access to Information, Participation and Decision-making will provide for much more solid civil society involvement in environmental decision-making, and these principles need to be brought also to the global level.

Governments are now gearing up for the *World Summit on Sustainable Development*[15] in Johannesburg in 2002, ten years after Rio and 30 years after Stockholm. British Prime Minister Tony Blair has said he will come, and, as ten years ago, we will see if another US President Bush heeds the invitation. The EU has already started its preparations with a series of positions agreed by environment ministers, and a Sustainable Development Strategy agreed by heads of government in Gothenburg. But more is necessary in terms of consensus building and negotiations, formal and informal, to arrive in Johannesburg with a fair chance of making a leap forward in international environment and development policy.

Notes

1   The views expressed are purely those of the writer and may not in any circumstances be regarded as stating an official position of the European Commission. The author would like to acknowledge the contributions to this article from current and former colleagues, notably Jill Hanna and Margaret Brusasco-Mackenzie.
2   Treaty on European Union, available on the Europa web-site: www.europa.eu.int.
3   First four action programmes: 1973, 1977, 1983, 1987.
4   Fifth Action Programme COM(92)33 and its review COM(95)647 final.
5   COM(2001)31.
6   Global Assessment of the European Community Programme of Policy and Action in relation to the Environment and Sustainable Development, COM(99)543.
7   Carson 1962.
8   The conference produced the Action Plan for Human Environment and the Declaration of United Nations Conference on the Human Environment (www.unep.org).
9   www.unep.org.
10 For the Commission's report, see Brundtland 1987.
11 www.unep.org/esa/sustdev/agenda21.htm.
12 www.un.org/esa/sustdev/csd.htm.

13 The leading members of the Miami Group include Japan, Canada and Argentina. The United States dominates the group and participates actively in the biosafety negotiations as an observer, as it has not signed the Biodiversity Convention.
14 The details of the Kyoto Protocol are analysed in Grubb and others 1999.
15 www.johannesburgsummit.org.

References

Brundtland, G. H. (Chairman) (1987), *Our Common Future*, Report of the World Commission on Environment and Development, Oxford University Press, Oxford.
Brusasco-Mackenzie, M. (1997), 'The Earth Summit + 5: The United Nations General Assembly Special Session, June 13-27 1997; the Role of the European Union', *European Foreign Affairs Review*, vol. 3, no. 2, pp. 197ff.
Carson, R. (1962), *The Silent Spring*, Penguin Books Ltd, London.
Grubb, M. with Vrolijk, C. and Brack, D. (1999), *The Kyoto Protocol: A Guide and Assessment*, Royal Institute of International Affairs/Earthscan, London.

Chapter 14

International Institutions: Plurilateralism and Multilateralism

Nicholas Bayne

This chapter is about how governments use international institutions in economic diplomacy. It elaborates on one of the principal strategies in the new economic diplomacy identified in Chapter 5. It covers the ground often described by the term 'global governance'. But the study of global governance usually puts the **institutions** at the centre of the enquiry. In contrast, this chapter is mainly about what **governments** do, as members of international institutions, and how they try to make the institutions serve their national purposes, domestic as well as external.

The chapter begins with a general analysis of how governments approach the institutions: what governments want from international economic institutions; and how they get what they want, in conditions of advancing globalisation. These arguments apply mainly to industrial democracies, like the G7 members, but it is also relevant, for other countries, including developing and ex-communist countries.[1] This general analysis embraces the use made of both plurilateral and multilateral institutions.

The main body of the chapter contains separate assessments of plurilateral institutions, focusing on the OECD, the G7/G8 and the Commonwealth, and of multilateral ones, concentrating on the WTO, the IMF and World Bank and the environmental work of the UN. These are all examined and compared in relation to their contribution to economic diplomacy, using a method based on the analytical framework set out in Chapter 1. Two of the practitioner case studies in this book - Chapter 8 on the G8 and Chapter 13 on the environment - have already looked at individual institutions from this selection. The three remaining case studies, by Ivan Mbirimi in Chapter 15, Nigel Wicks in Chapter 16 and Richard Carden in Chapter 17, expand on this examination with reference to the Commonwealth, the IMF and World Bank and the WTO.

What Governments Want from the Institutions

The argument of this chapter is that governments want international economic institutions to do four things for them:

- *First,* to reinforce their current economic policies. That is their most desired objective.

- *Second*, to share their burdens.
- *Third*, to extend their reach.
- *Fourth*, to give good value.

Each objective will be examined in turn.

Reinforcing current policies

With a few exceptions, such as Malaysia under Prime Minister Mahathir, governments value the endorsement of international institutions like the IMF, the WTO and the OECD. These are the institutions that set the standards in the international economy. Their endorsement impresses financial markets, foreign investors and trading partners and may be necessary to release flows of funds, from both public and private sources. Governments do not like to go against them.

On the other hand, sovereign governments want to be making their own decisions. They do not want to be taking orders from outside. That looks weak and exposes them to popular and parliamentary criticism, especially with the rise of the anti-globalisation movement. So the ideal is if the policies already chosen by the government are endorsed without change by the institutions. Governments thus get the best of both worlds.

Governments therefore have an incentive to anticipate what the institutions will recommend and do it before they are asked. With the possible exception of the United States, even G7 governments are not able to tell the institutions what line to take. So what happens is that those departments within governments that are closest to the institutions will invoke them in policy arguments. Thus finance ministries will argue the need for IMF endorsement when promoting policies of economic and monetary rigour and opposing the extravagant spending plans of other ministries, which would enlarge the budget deficit. Departments responsible for international trade will invoke the WTO when arguing for competition and open markets against those who want more protection. As noted in Chapter 4, members of these departments can come to feel greater solidarity with their foreign colleagues, whom they see at IMF or WTO meetings and regard as their allies, than they do with people from other ministries at home, whom they regard as their rivals.

So the institutions act as the *conscience* of governments, in helping to make them internationally minded. At the same time, the institutions realise that their public intervention may not be helpful to the government. They often therefore supply the government with ideas they can pretend they thought of themselves.

Sharing their burdens

Reinforcing current policies, though desirable, may not be sufficient or sustainable. Governments realise that economic policy changes may be necessary and that these changes will be unpopular. In these conditions, it can be helpful to a government if it can share its burdens with the institutions and their other members. For example, it may be able to demonstrate to its people that it is not suffering alone. Other countries are also having to introduce painful or unpopular measures; there is a sort of 'equality of misery'. G7/G8 members have often used their annual summits for burden-sharing of this kind.[2]

This burden-sharing is especially valuable in GATT or WTO trade negotiations, which operate on the basis of reciprocity. It may be economically advantageous for a country to open its market unilaterally, as many have done in recent years. But, as noted in Chapter 1, it is politically helpful if this market opening is matched by similar actions by other countries, so that no one gets something for nothing.

In some cases, when painful change is inevitable, governments may seek to make the institutions the *scapegoat* for unpopular measures. This often happens with IMF programmes. If a government is obliged to introduce unpopular measures to get access to IMF and related funds, it will be happy if popular discontent is directed against the IMF rather than against itself. But if the IMF programme restores prosperity, then the government will take the credit.

Of course, this strategy depends on the IMF medicine working and this does not always happen. During the Asian crisis of 1997-98 the IMF was blamed for prescribing the wrong policies. The IMF largely defended itself, but did admit some mistakes, eg in Thailand. This put the Thai government in an embarrassing position, since the IMF's admission of error suggested that Thailand had been wrong to put so much trust in IMF advice.[3] The IMF was blamed again for the collapse of Argentina late in 2001; but that was more because the Fund went on supporting the government's risky policies for too long. More generally, countries often do not identify themselves with policies agreed with the Fund. They follow IMF guidance for long enough to get the finance required and then relapse until they need a new fix from the Fund. It is important that countries take 'ownership' of their economic strategy and do not become dependent on the IMF. This has become a key component of the Poverty Reduction Strategies agreed in the context of the Heavily Indebted Poor Countries (HIPC) programme of debt relief.[4]

Extending their reach

The first two objectives show governments making use of international institutions to advance their domestic policies. This third objective, in some respects, relates more to their external interests. Governments try to use the institutions in order to gain access to markets or to get their debts paid. Rather than exerting direct pressure, governments shelter behind the institutions, which have the advantage of being highly reputable and relatively anonymous. In particular, smaller governments can sometimes use the institutions as a check on the abuse of power by major powers like the United States and the European Union. For example, several countries have brought cases against the US in the WTO and have won them. But this depends on the institutions being regarded as sufficiently independent of its larger members and able to stand up to them. This is, in practice, not always the case, as the analysis later in this chapter will show.

Governments also use the institutions to extend their reach in a different, more domestic way. This is done so as to compensate for loss of power at home. Many states have conducted programmes of privatisation and deregulation, which move responsibility away from national government towards the private sector. As long as activities remain under their own control, governments tend to resist international rules. This is why international negotiations on agriculture are so difficult - governments will not let go. But privatisation and deregulation at home make governments seek better rules internationally. Thus the WTO has moved ahead with agreements on trade in services, like telecommunications; and the IMF, in developing new financial architecture, is paying attention to improved international supervision of financial markets.

Getting good value

These activities - serving as conscience or scapegoat for governments, sharing their burdens and extending their reach - create lots of extra work for the institutions, for which they seek extra resources. But here governments make clear their desire to get good value. Domestically, many governments have reduced their spending to balance their budgets. They have shifted tasks to the private sector. Governments that are spending less on themselves are reluctant to spend more on international institutions. Those institutions, like the IMF and World Bank, that can generate their own income, are sheltered to some degree. But those that rely on contributions from their members, like the OECD, the WTO and the UN, are becoming severely squeezed. There must be doubt if they can continue to do all the extra things that governments want; and if the quality of their work falls, their authority declines too.

How Governments Get What They Want

So far this chapter has tried to identify what governments want the institutions to do for them. But how do they get what they want? How do governments manage the decision-making process in these institutions, which are often very large and cumbersome, so as to get the right results?

This section picks up some of the analysis from Chapter 4 and expands on it. It looks at five techniques - one negative and four positive. These techniques are:

- Use of the veto;
- Singleness of purpose;
- Coalition building;
- Manoeuvring for the middle ground;
- Exploiting the machinery.

For many of these techniques the WTO meetings at Seattle and Doha provide good examples of how they work - or do not work.

Use of the veto

International economic institutions usually reach decisions by consensus. Some, like the WTO or OECD, are obliged to do so and have little provision for votes. The IMF and World Bank have a voting system and so does the UN, but even these bodies prefer to proceed by consensus, since that ensures that all the members are committed. Consensus means that everyone has a veto, in principle; any member can use this veto to make sure that it does *not* get what it does *not* want. It can therefore be called a negative technique.

But governments that want to use the institutions for positive objectives will use their veto sparingly. If a government uses it too often, it will be accused of frustrating the institution's purposes; and other members will be quick to use their own vetoes to frustrate that government's favoured initiatives. The EU prevented the discussion of agricultural export subsidies for over four years in the Uruguay Round, but eventually gave way so as to make progress on its other objectives. Even the United States, for all its strength, is vulnerable to this. At Seattle the Americans sought an agenda limited to the items they wanted and excluding those that others wanted. But the rest of the WTO members rejected this.

Singleness of purpose

The first positive technique, called singleness of purpose, has already been discussed in Chapter 4 above. It means that a government should complete all its internal decision-making so that it has a clear objective and a clear strategy to which all departments are committed. At the same time it should be alert to signs of divisions in the position of other governments, which it can exploit to its own advantage. It sounds elementary; but governments often fall short and some, like the Americans, find this sort of internal discipline very difficult. The Americans showed this conspicuously at Seattle. Charlene Barshefsky and the US delegation had a strategy for getting labour standards treated by the WTO, which had some chance of international acceptance. But President Clinton himself had a different strategy, driven by domestic factors, and this undermined his own team.[5]

Coalition building

This is a very important technique. A member of an institution will aim to build up a group in support of its own position that is sufficiently large and varied to carry the day, with a band-wagon effect that sweeps everyone into an eventual consensus in its favour. But coalition building is hard work, especially for a single member. If it approaches other countries for their support, they will usually seek to trade this against something they want in return, so that the original member may end up having to pay too much for what it wants. So it is useful to have a circle of natural allies, who will work together in coalition building without having to be 'paid' for it. Bilateral agreements, especially between major players like the US and EU, can be used for this purpose; so can regional groupings, as when the APEC members agreed on an approach to multilateral tariff cuts. In particular, plurilateral bodies like the G7 and OECD are increasingly being used in outreach activities, to work for particular results on behalf of their members within multilateral institutions - more on this below.

Some of the most effective alliances in multilateral institutions are those that are broadly based and reflect all interests within the membership. That is why the Cairns Group of agricultural exporters, with members from all five continents, developed and developing, made such an impact in the GATT and WTO; and why the Commonwealth could exert a strong influence in debt relief for low-income countries.[6]   Of course, the more varied the alliance, the harder it is to keep it together, but likewise the greater the prospects of success in getting the institution to move in the desired direction.

Manoeuvring for the middle ground

This is an advanced and rather risky technique. Most decisions in international institutions are compromises, which find the middle ground between extremes. The art is to ensure that the point chosen for the middle ground satisfies a member's national objectives - ie it falls within the government's win-set. The risk is that if this technique is pursued without singleness of purpose, national objectives are abandoned in the interests of compromise. That exposes a member to the risk of failing to satisfy the interests at the domestic board in its two-level game.

This technique works best when there is a wide range of positions being taken. For a member whose national position is close to the middle there is no problem. But if it has an extreme position, it will need a very strong coalition and lots of natural allies to carry the day. Failing that, there are two possible tactical approaches. One tactic is for the member to advance an even more extreme position, beyond what it really needs, in the hope of pulling others in its direction. The member can then settle for what appears to be the middle ground, but is in fact what it wanted all along. A different tactic is to build up a large linked package deal, so that the extreme demand of one member is buried among the range of objectives of others.

In the discussions at Seattle on the scope of the new WTO round, the European Union was adopting the second tactic and the Americans the first. The Europeans were trying to bury their vulnerability on agriculture in a large agenda for the new round, with something for everyone. The Americans struck an extreme position on a limited agenda, in the hope that everyone else would move towards them. The European strategy did not work at Seattle, but had better success at Doha two years later. The Americans miscalculated at Seattle and their strategy collapsed, because other countries would not move. At Doha they showed more flexibility and agreed to a broader agenda. But this included the controversial issue of anti-dumping, which caused problems at the domestic level for the American negotiator, Bob Zoellick.

Exploiting the machinery

This last technique is less precise than the others. It requires a government to be expert in the work of the institution and to be well regarded and trusted by the staff and the other member governments. There are various ways of doing this. One is to pay subscriptions on time. Canada, for example, always does this, but the US often falls down. Another is for a member to have its own nationals well placed in the staff. France has some striking achievements here. In the early 1990s the Managing Director of the IMF, the Secretary General of the OECD, the President of the European Commission and the President of the EBRD were all Frenchmen. As most international institutions now use English as their main working language, those delegations fluent in English are in demand to chair committees or be rapporteurs, and that is also a source of influence.

This technique does require some investment and is difficult for poorer countries. That is why technical assistance programmes are being developed to enable poor countries to take more advantage of the WTO and this helped to win their support for the Doha agenda. But for some countries - such as Canada, as Chapter 10 explained - this activity is an established part of their economic diplomacy and their international reputation.

Classifying and Comparing Institutions

This analysis has so far looked at the general objectives and techniques of governments in making use of international institutions. The remainder of this chapter looks more closely at how specific institutions are used. The approach adopted is as follows:

- First, to differentiate between plurilateral and multilateral bodies and to select some examples of each;
- Second, to develop a method of assessing and comparing institutions for their contribution to economic diplomacy;
- Third, to apply this method to the chosen plurilateral institutions;
- Fourth, to do the same for the multilateral institutions.

Plurilateralism and multilateralism

The multiple levels available for economic diplomacy were defined at the beginning of Chapter 10. Bilateralism is the simplest level, which is open to all countries. Regionalism and plurilateralism are both exclusive to some extent. With regional bodies, the decisive factor is geography. Regional groupings are associations of neighbours and non-neighbours cannot join. The European Union, for example, cannot be a member of Asia-Pacific Economic Cooperation (APEC). In plurilateral institutions, however, geography does not come into it. They are associations of like-minded countries, from different parts of the world, which have chosen to pursue economic objectives together. They have non-geographic criteria for membership, which may be economic, political, historical or linguistic. They may associate entirely for economic purposes, or their economic activities may only be part of what the institution does.[7] This chapter concentrates on three examples of plurilateral institutions: the Organisation for Economic Cooperation and Development (OECD); the G7/8 summit and its associated bodies; and the Commonwealth.

While plurilateral institutions are exclusive, multilateral ones are not. They cover the whole world and, by definition, are open to all countries. They differ from one another not in membership, but in the subjects they handle - finance, trade or the environment. This chapter will also look at selected examples of multilateral institutions: the World Trade Organization (WTO); the International Monetary Fund (IMF) and World Bank; and those parts of the United Nations (UN) family concerned with the global environment. All these institutions have a common root - the great wave of institution-building 50 years ago at the end of World War II. But all are quite different now from what was imagined then; and the WTO, the successor to the GATT, is in many ways a new, post-Cold War institution.

Grading and comparing institutions

This section sets out a method of classifying international institutions in the light of their contribution to economic diplomacy. The method is derived from the eight questions in economic diplomacy, set out in Table 1.1 in Chapter 1 above. The performance of economic institutions - both plurilateral and multilateral - will be judged against a range of indices based on these eight questions, with marks allocated on a scale of 1 to 5, as set out in Table 14.1 below.

Table 14.1   International Institutions: Indices of Impact on Economic Diplomacy

Index	
1. Political/Economic	*[1 = low politics, 5 = high politics]*
2. Departmental Intensity	*[1 = few departments, 5 = many]*
3. Domestic/External	*[1 = high external, 5 = high domestic]*
4. Rules/Voluntary	*[1 = all voluntary, 5 = all rules]*
5. Accountability	
6. Business Friendly	
7. Transparency	
8. Staff/Member Driven	*[1 = member-driven, 5 = staff-driven]*
9. Outreach	*[1 = self-contained, 5 = reaching out]*

There are nine indices in all:

- First comes the *political/economic* index, which relates to questions 1 and 2 from Table 1.1, run together. It measures how far the institution reconciles economic and politics, with higher marks for greater political content.
- The second index, matching question 3 from Table 1.1, is of *departmental intensity*. The more parts of government involved in the institution's work, the higher the score.
- Third comes the *domestic/external* index, from question 4. If the institution covers only international issues, it scores low. The more domestic policy is involved, the higher the score.
- Fourth is the *rules or voluntary cooperation* index, from question 5. An institution based on voluntary cooperation scores low, whereas one devoted to rule-making and enforcement scores high.
- The fifth index matches question 6 and is an *accountability and democracy* index. It assesses how far the institution serves all its members and how far its decisions are accountable to its members' governments and citizens.
- The sixth index measures whether an institution is *business friendly,* matching question 7.
- Seventh is a *transparency* index, matching question 8. It measures whether the institution is open to the outside world, including NGOs.

Two more indices have been added:

- Index no. 8 measures whether an institution is *staff-driven or member-driven.* Institutions vary very widely in their staff resources. The IMF, the World Bank and the OECD are all very well-endowed with staff in relation to their membership, so that their staffs can take on ambitious tasks. In contrast the WTO and the Commonwealth have slender staff resources and have to rely much more on their members. In this index, member-driven institutions score low and staff-driven ones score high.

- Finally index no. 9, called the *outreach* index, applies only to plurilateral institutions, not to multilateral ones. It measures whether the members' benefits are limited to the institution itself, or whether it also helps them to pursue their objectives in wider multilateral organisations. Self-contained institutions score low, those with outreach into other bodies score high.

This completes the list of indices. The only point to add is that institutions change over time and may look different today against many of the indices than they did ten or even five years ago.

Assessing Plurilateral Institutions

These nine indices provide a basis for analysing the chosen plurilateral institutions. The passages that follow will go through the indices for each of the institutions - not in any fixed order - so as to construct a set of gradings for them.   These gradings are summarised in Table 14.2 below.

Table 14.2   Plurilateral Institutions: Economic Diplomacy Indices

Index	OECD	G7	Commonwealth
1. Political/Economic	3	4	5
2. Departmental Intensity	5	5	2
3. Domestic/External	5	5	2
4. Rules/Voluntary	2	1	1
5. Accountability	4	4	5
6. Business Friendly	4	3	3
7. Transparency	4	2	5
8. Staff/Member Driven	4	1	2
9. Outreach	3	4	4

The OECD

The OECD looks like a supremely *economic* institution.   It covers all the subjects of interest to governments, from agriculture to transport and including education and employment, but none of the political ones - no defence, law and order, culture or sport.   Even so, the OECD's underlying motivation is *political*, to support the open democratic system.   It developed out of the regional OEEC, which applied the Marshall Plan, with the political aim of checking the spread of communism. This role was continued by the plurilateral OECD, which settled at 24 members over a long period: the 15 current EU Member States, plus Switzerland, Norway, Iceland, Turkey and five non-Europeans - US, Canada, Japan, Australia, New Zealand.   For them the OECD was the standard-bearer of the West in the contest of economic systems in the Cold War.   When the Cold War ended, the OECD shifted again to helping bring ex-communist countries and others into the open economic order.   In the process it has added six new members - Poland, Hungary, Czech Republic, Slovakia, Mexico and South Korea.

The OECD is of interest to *all economic departments* and so scores highly in departmental intensity; that is part of its value.   It also goes deep into *domestic policy-making*. It can assess the impact of one policy, such as environment policy, on a range of others. Its method of work is based on a network of expert committees - trade, industry, economic policy, etc. These are attended by officials, and occasionally ministers, coming from capitals, not, as in other bodies, by representatives of the resident delegation. The presence of these officials means that, although the staff are numerous and highly intelligent, the OECD is not as highly *staff-driven* as one might expect.

The OECD pursues mainly *voluntary cooperation*. Countries are persuaded - never forced - to adjust their policies by the supply of better information or by peer pressure. It operates very tactfully, having the gift of supplying governments with good ideas they can then pretend they thought of themselves. This voluntary cooperation is what the OECD does best. It is still the favoured institution in many economic areas where its members seek higher standards or closer cooperation than are attainable in multilateral contexts, for example in employment and social policies, export credit, official aid policy, tax cooperation and money laundering.[8]

The OECD does less in rule-making, and does it less well, because it has no powers of enforcement. The great recent setback for the OECD was the collapse of the Multilateral Agreement on Investment (MAI) in 1998. Governments started to negotiate a MAI and then got cold feet, leaving hostile NGOs to claim victory - an obvious rehearsal for Seattle.[9] Other rule-making ventures, such as a treaty to counter corrupt practices or new guidelines for multinational companies, seem to have limited impact.

The OECD seems very *accountable*, as it is consensus-based and its member governments must answer to their electorates; very *business friendly* in that private firms usually welcome its policies; and very *transparent*, as it publishes a huge amount. But all this needs some qualification. The OECD is accountable and business friendly and transparent in output rather than input. It has its Business and Industry Advisory Council (BIAC) and Trade Union Advisory Council (TUAC), but they are kept at arms length. Since the OECD produces voluntary cooperation rather than formal agreements, very little of its work actually has to go to parliaments. Hardly anyone gets into the meetings where deals are struck except government officials (or sometimes ministers) and OECD staff. This is not unusual, of course, but it did make the OECD vulnerable to NGO attack over the MAI.

The OECD is *mainly self-contained*, working for its members. But while it rarely makes rules itself, its well-researched work is often used as the basis for rule-making in bilateral, regional and multilateral contexts. Principles on investment worked out by the OECD (before the failed MAI) have been used both in bilateral investment treaties and in NAFTA. It has had a special impact in trade negotiations, where the OECD can compensate for the weakness in resources of both the old GATT and the new WTO. The concepts which underlie the agreements on agriculture and on services in the Uruguay Round were originally worked out at the OECD.[10] The main constraint in multilateral contexts is that the OECD has to work indirectly or by stealth. Developing countries resent having measures openly imposed upon them by the OECD; this has emerged clearly from the OECD's attempts to discipline tax havens.[11]   This factor limits the OECD's *outreach* to wider institutions.

In short, the OECD is a wide-ranging, unobtrusive institution relying wholly on its powers of persuasion.[12]

The G7/G8 Summit

As an institution, the *G7/G8 summit*, with its apparatus, looks like the inner circle of the OECD - same subjects, fewer people. In fact it is quite different. President Giscard of France, who invented it, insisted it was a wholly *economic* instrument. Both he and President Mitterrand who followed him tried to prevent non-economic subjects being discussed at the summits. But both the method and the motivation were again *political*. Giscard realised that in 1975 the greatest threat to the West came not from the Soviet Union but from the confused response to the economic crisis provoked by the first oil shock.   His answer was to invoke political leadership instead of bureaucracy: leadership by the most important countries and the most important people in them. In due course the G7 added a parallel agenda of foreign policy topics, like terrorism and the Middle East, and admitted Russia, to make G8, for political reasons.

Originally the G7 heads of government were supported only by their foreign and finance ministers.   They have now been joined by so many other G8 ministerial groups that this apparatus has floated free, leaving the heads of government able to meet on their own, for the first time ever. But some things have not changed. The G7/G8 still has no written rules, no headquarters and no staff. *Everything is driven by the members*, led by the host country for the year - Canada in 2002, France in 2003.

The G7/G8 can potentially involve *as many parts of government* as the OECD - even more - but in practice it does not. It cannot do everything at once and has to be selective. Only the most intractable problems find their way up to summit level. The G7/G8 members have become accustomed to treating them on an iterative process; if they fail once, they try again.[13]   The G7/G8 does have great capacity to treat *domestic and external* issues together, especially at summit level. That was the second reason - political leadership being the first - for involving heads of government. As explained in earlier chapters, heads of government can reconcile the domestic and external pressures better than ministers with more limited authority. They also tend to have more *democratic* legitimacy and to be more *accountable* to the concerns of their people. The G7/G8 therefore scores highly on all these indices.

The G7/G8 only conducts *voluntary cooperation*.   Rule-making would not make sense in such a small group. At first the focus was largely on economic coordination among themselves. With international institutions the G7 leaders would throw stones into the pool but then stand back themselves. In some areas they set up their own parallel channels, which weakened established organisations. But this gradually changed as the G7 lost both its dominance in the world economic system and became more active below summit level. From the mid-

1990s the G7/G8 took a conscious decision to engage more directly and more persuasively in steering multilateral institutions, including rule-based organisations. This greater attention to *outreach* is seen in the G7/G8's proposals for reform of the IMF, the World Bank and a range of United Nations bodies.

The G7/G8 has been slow to adapt to the shift from state to non-state actors. For most of its life it has been *business friendly* in substance, but not in procedure, like the OECD. From 2000 onwards, however, the G8 has moved a long way, by involving business leaders in both preparation and follow-up. The G8 has also become more accessible to NGOs, after the summits of the late 1990s were the target of some massive NGO lobbying, over debt relief, of a gentle, benign variety. The violent demonstrations at the Genoa summit of 2001, however, were a shock to the G8 and drove the 2002 summit into seclusion in the Canadian Rockies. Despite these changes, however, the G8 remains almost totally *non-transparent*. Nothing gets out, except agreed statements and other documents interpreted at national press briefings.

In short, the G7/G8 summit is a highly select, member-driven institution, aiming to provide political leadership and to reconcile external and domestic pressures in economic policy-making.

The Commonwealth

The Commonwealth is very different from the other two institutions. It is much larger - it has 54 members - and more varied. G7 and OECD members are all 'high-income' countries. Commonwealth members range from the richest to the very poorest. G7/G8 members are large countries. The Commonwealth includes some of the smallest countries on earth. The factors which keep Commonwealth members together and determine new admissions are *political*, not *economic*: the use of English; similarities in legal and political systems; most recently, standards of democracy and human rights. The Commonwealth economic preferences which prevailed from the 1930s to the 1960s are long gone and have left hardly any legacy.

Yet the Commonwealth has a distinctive impact on the international economic system. It is largely *member-driven*, as the Commonwealth Secretariat is small and has limited resources. It engages *only a few departments* so far - education, finance, environment, trade. Apart from work on education, especially distance education, this economic work is focused on *external issues more than domestic ones* and it involves *voluntary cooperation* only. While the Commonwealth seeks to develop activities for its own members, like encouraging intra-Commonwealth trade, these are less influential than the Commonwealth's *outreach* activities focused on multilateral institutions.

The clearest example is in debt relief for low-income countries. Every year the Commonwealth finance ministers meet together in the week before the IMF/World Bank annual meeting. On three occasions in the last decade - 1991, 1994, 1997 - Britain, with Canada in support, launched a debt relief initiative in the Commonwealth as the springboard for getting agreement in the G7 and the IMF. Having support from Commonwealth members, who were so numerous and so varied in size, development and geographical spread, greatly strengthened their negotiating hand. It took two to three years to move from Commonwealth initiative to IMF endorsement and required help from other quarters too, but it worked every time.

There was similar evidence from the international environment. The Commonwealth contributed greatly to assessing the consequences of global warming in causing higher sea-levels, because this would endanger so many Commonwealth members, such as Bangladesh, the Maldives and small Pacific states. Commonwealth cooperation enabled members to launch joint initiatives in the UN on forests: Britain with Malaysia, Canada with India.

Trade has so far been more difficult. Commonwealth trade ministers do not meet regularly. Britain's trade policy is tied up with the EU. Commonwealth markets show great variations in their degree of openness, from Singapore to India. Yet Commonwealth members have realised that, if they could agree among themselves, they could exert a powerful influence both on the agenda for a new trade round and the course of such a round. In Durban in 1999, Commonwealth heads of government listened to the Commonwealth Business Council when they presented the report cited in Chapter 4 as prepared by their LSE academic advisers. Many Commonwealth trade ministers were active both at Seattle and Doha.[14]

The Commonwealth Business Council is a move to make the Commonwealth more *business friendly* - but it is a new body, only launched in 1997. In *accountability* and *transparency* the Commonwealth looks quite different from the OECD or the G7/G8. In addition to democratic standards for each state, the members are linked by the Commonwealth Parliamentary Association. The Commonwealth also has an easy and confident relationship with NGOs and does not fear upsets like those of the OECD or WTO. It clearly helps that the economic activities of the Commonwealth are part of a much wider whole with political content. Yet for all this apparent transparency, the real business at a Commonwealth head of government meeting is done in an exclusive 'retreat'.

In short, the Commonwealth is a very broad-based and varied institution, with strong potential to influence global organisations.

Interim Conclusions on Plurilateral Institutions

That concludes the assessment of these three plurilateral institutions. The main conclusions about international institutions will come at the end of this chapter, but three initial points can be made about these plurilateral bodies:

- All the institutions considered have a stronger political content than appears at first sight;
- All are better adapted for voluntary cooperation than rule-making;
- All are giving increasing attention to outreach activities, to help their members in wider multilateral activities.

Assessing Multilateral Institutions

The same method of analysis will now be applied to the selected multilateral institutions. The multilateral gradings are summarised in Table 14.3 below - the outreach index does not apply to multilateral institutions.

Table 14.3   Multilateral Institutions: Economic Diplomacy Indices

Index	WTO	IMF & World Bank		UN Environment
1. Political/Economic	3	3		4
2. Departmental Intensity	5	1		3
3. Domestic/External	5	5		4
4. Rules/Voluntary	5	3	2	4
5. Accountability	4	2		5
6. Business Friendly	4	4		3
7. Transparency	2	2	4	5
8. Staff/Member Driven	2	5		3

The WTO

The WTO again looks like a wholly *economic* institution, using economic instruments for an economic purpose, that is, the expansion of international trade. In some respects politics are separated out; for example, where security interests predominate, WTO rules do not apply. Yet *political* elements are at work in the WTO in various ways. The methods it uses to promote trade liberalisation, such as non-discrimination and reciprocity, are political methods. The deeper the WTO gets into rule-making affecting domestic policy, the more it impinges on politics. This is especially evident where members want the WTO to go beyond the scope of trade, into labour standards or intellectual property rights. The protests and the hostile criticisms of NGOs at Seattle were largely politically motivated, though some attacked the WTO for failing to deliver on its economic promises as well.

The old GATT, without agriculture or services, was largely the concern of specialised trade negotiators, based in trade ministries or elsewhere. But as a result of the Uruguay Round negotiations (as Chapter 3 recorded) the WTO involves *many more departments* - agriculture, finance, environment, transport, development - almost as many as the OECD. It is penetrating *deeper and deeper into domestic policy*, such as the regulation of services, industrial subsidies and agricultural support programmes.

The WTO is, almost entirely, a *rule-based institution*, devoted to drawing up, implementing and enforcing trade rules. Its principal activity consists of negotiating the removal of trade barriers; the results of these negotiations are formal obligations on members, subject to binding dispute settlement. There is some *voluntary cooperation*. There are a few plurilateral agreements to which not all members subscribe, the most important being on government procurement. The Trade Policy Review System, which examines the trade policies of individual members, does not lead to binding recommendations. But this is only a small part of the WTO's work.

In conventional terms, the WTO appears to be firmly *accountable* and *democratic*. It is a consensus-based institution; decisions require the assent or acquiescence of all participating members. Each formal agreement has to be ratified by all the members, who normally have to submit it to their legislatures, and the agreement does not enter into force until this process is complete. So to say that the WTO is non-democratic, as some NGOs claim, is misguided. Likewise, to say that the WTO is a creature of the multinationals is also wholly misleading. It is true that the WTO is *business friendly* in that the removal of trade barriers favours efficient, well-resourced and internationally oriented firms. But the WTO can also be a defence against aggressive multinational companies. When the US, pressed by Kodak, brought a case against Japan over the marketing of photographic film, the WTO found in favour of Japan.

The trouble is that conventional accountability in the WTO is not proving enough to reassure people worried about the advance of globalisation and about predatory multinationals. This has been compounded by an instinctive lack of *transparency* in the WTO. The WTO is a negotiating body, and, as was said in Seattle, 'negotiators are not good communicators'. That is because, as explained in Chapter 5, negotiation is like courtship, not easy to conduct in public. The WTO must continue to negotiate in private, as its members insist.

Since Seattle there have been efforts to open up the rest of the WTO's activities, both by taking in outside advice and making the results of its work more widely known. These have been slow to take off because of a shortage of resources for the WTO, as for the GATT before it. The WTO has to be a *member-driven institution*, because its staff is so small. That can sometimes be a source of strength, if it gets national delegations more deeply involved and committed. But it means the WTO is poorly equipped to conduct its own advocacy or to help its poorer members. It relies on its member governments to provide support for this, which they had largely failed to do up to the Doha meeting in 2001. But since then more resources have been committed to increasing the capacity of small or poor countries to benefit from their WTO membership.

In short, the WTO is devoted to rule-making, democratic but not instinctively transparent and increasingly intrusive into domestic policy.

The IMF and the World Bank

The IMF and the World Bank will be assessed together, though sometimes their marks will differ. They are again fundamentally *economic* institutions, using economic instruments for economic purposes, ie financial stability and economic development. But there are definite *political* influences at work as well. Sometimes the grant or the refusal of Fund or Bank lending is used as a political weapon for or against countries: eg to encourage reform in Russia, or to punish China, after the Tiananmen Square shootings. This is strictly against the rules, but it happens. The World Bank and even the Fund have gone beyond the strictly economic sphere into institution building, standards of governance and discouraging excessive defence spending. Finally, the policy adjustment associated with major Fund or Bank loans has inevitable political consequences.

The activities of both Fund and Bank go *deeply into domestic policies:* the Fund into monetary and fiscal policy and increasingly financial regulation; the Bank into every aspect of development from agriculture through education and health to transport systems. But their *departmental intensity* is very low. In general finance ministries have a near monopoly hold on the Fund and Bank, which they share with central banks and occasionally with development ministries, but not wider.

It is not easy to strike the balance between *rule-making* and *voluntary cooperation*, as regards the Fund and the Bank. The IMF used to define and enforce the rules for exchange rates, but that function is almost wholly eroded. As part of the new financial architecture developed since the Asian crisis, the Fund has developed codes of good practice in supplying economic data and in the openness of monetary and fiscal policy; there is a parallel code on social policy for the Bank. The Fund is also stimulating international disciplines in financial regulation. But not all of this is binding and none of it is enforceable.[15] For countries borrowing from the Fund and the Bank there are often conditions requiring policy adjustment. These conditions had become especially complex in the Fund and both institutions are trying to simplify them. This conditionality is certainly more than the wholly voluntary cooperation seen in the OECD, though well short of the rule-making practised in the WTO.

The Fund and the Bank are accountable to their members but are less *democratic* than the other institutions examined so far, because they have a system of weighted voting which favours the rich members. Rich countries that lend have more power than poor countries that borrow; the poor countries tolerate this because they need the funds on offer. Over the years this division has increased between the rich countries, who treat the Fund and Bank as if they were shareholders, and the poor countries, who are more like consumers of the services they offer. In earlier times the IMF lent funds and required policy adjustment for rich countries as well as poorer ones. But for over 20 years now no developed country has applied to the Fund nor, of course, to the Bank.

The Fund and the Bank have developed very close links with private suppliers of finance and are *business friendly* in this sense. Their annual meetings every autumn gather an immense crowd of bankers and investors, keen to meet the finance ministers coming from all over the world. Private financiers often wait for the approval of a country's policies by the Fund or Bank before releasing funds or agreeing to reschedule debt. They tend, however, to resist the idea that they should take part in the financial rescue operations of the Fund and Bank.[16] As regards *transparency*, the Bank has been ready to engage in dialogue with development NGOs and has at times adapted its policy strategy to their views. This openness of the Bank is in contrast to the Fund. The IMF is the guardian of financial stability, which is all too easily upset by rumour and speculation. So the Fund is traditionally sparing in its public statements and gained a reputation for being tight-lipped and sometimes arrogant. But this is now changing, so that the IMF too publishes more and explains itself more.

As indicated earlier in this chapter, the Fund and Bank finance themselves from their lending operations and that gives them a huge advantage over those institutions that rely on subscriptions from their members. This enables both to have large and active staffs, especially the Bank. Since only a small number of delegations actually sit on the Executive Boards, that gives more power to the staff. So the Fund and the Bank are strongly *staff-driven*; though the staffs do try to work for the entire membership, to offset the dominance of the rich countries on the Boards.

In short, the IMF and World Bank, driven by their staffs and dominated by finance ministries, are moving tentatively back into rule-making, with rich countries as shareholders and poor ones as consumers.

Environment Work at the United Nations

The United Nations is the last multilateral institution to be considered. This will be only a limited sampling of the UN's contribution to economic diplomacy, concentrating on the UN's environmental activities. It leaves aside all that the UN does in humanitarian or technical assistance activities, as well as the work of UNCTAD and agencies like the FAO and WHO.

The United Nations is both a *political* and an *economic* institution. It employs more staff on economic activities than political ones and spends more funds on them, except at the height of peace-keeping operations. But in the founding Charter the UN's political role is clearly defined, including its mandatory powers, while its economic role is left vague and ill-focused. Some features are common to all UN work: universality, equitable geographic distribution of staff and decisions by 'one member, one vote'. Much of the UN's economic activity over the years has been *voluntary cooperation* based on non-binding resolutions or technical assistance financed by unreliable national contributions. The results of this have tended to be disappointing.

However, the UN has developed a method of getting round these drawbacks. That is by the negotiation of binding international conventions that the members ratify formally and bring into force collectively. This has been done, for example, with the law of the sea and with narcotic drugs and psychotropic substances. In the 1990s this method was widely adopted for global environment issues. UN treaty instruments in this area include: the Montreal Protocol on the ozone layer; the climate change convention and the biodiversity convention launched at the Rio Conference of 1992; and later conventions on deserts and oceans. There has been much discussion of a convention on forests, though no agreement on one yet.

These conventions and their associated protocols take the United Nations clearly into *rule-making*. It is not as advanced as the WTO: in the climate change convention, for example, developed countries have made commitments to reduce greenhouse gas emissions, but developing countries have not. Even where developed countries have agreed on the action they will take, they often have trouble over implementation. There is no dispute settlement mechanism, which explains why some environmental disputes have gravitated to the WTO instead. Even so, this is a great advance on earlier voluntary measures.

Global environment work goes *deeply into domestic policy*, as countries have to take measures, for example, to cut back on their national use of CFCs or greenhouse gases. It engages a *growing range of government departments*, going well beyond environment ministries.

Much of the impetus for work on the global environment came originally from NGOs. As one might expect, this UN work leaves plenty of openings for NGO activity and is widely *transparent*; there are lessons here that the WTO and IMF could learn. The work is also *democratically accountable* in the conventional sense, in that it is agreed by consensus and endorsed by national parliaments.

The *attitude to business* is nicely balanced. Some firms, especially in conventional energy sectors, have regarded international environmental discipline as a threat and have tried to undermine it. For example, they have cast doubt on the scientific work that underpins it, since the environment is an area where epistemic communities of meteorologists and other scientists are highly influential. But other firms have recognised that conservation and lowering pollution make economic sense and seek to take advantage of the trend. The system of tradeable permits in greenhouse gas emissions was developed to make environmental discipline market-friendly and so encourage business to take part.

Much of the UN's other economic work is *staff-driven*, for example in UNCTAD. This is less true of the environment work. Scarcity of resources, as well as the choice of Nairobi as the site of the United Nations Environment Programme (UNEP), puts the staff at a disadvantage. So environment work depends a lot on the *initiative of the member governments*.

In short, the United Nations has developed a method for rule-making in the global environment that is transparent and democratic, though there are problems about getting commitments to stick.

Conclusions

The system of indices used in this chapter enables comparisons to be made between these institutions, from which conclusions can be drawn about their contribution to economic diplomacy. These conclusions, which incorporate the interim conclusions from earlier in the chapter, are as follows:

- First, though all these are economic institutions, the political content, both in objectives and methods, is higher than appears at first sight.

- Second, nearly all these institutions are going deeper into domestic policy-making and involving an increasing range of government departments. These are some of the consequences of the advance of globalisation.
- Third, plurilateral institutions concentrate on voluntary cooperation and do much less rule-making than multilateral ones. They are increasingly involved in outreach to wider multilateral contexts.
- Fourth, there is plenty of evidence of a general move from voluntary cooperation towards greater rule-making during the 1990s, though much of this has proved controversial.
- Fifth, there is not a close correlation between high staff levels and extensive rule-making, as one might expect - rather the contrary. Both the WTO and the UN are starved of resources as compared with the Fund and Bank. It is as if governments are reluctant to entrust rule-making to independent staffs.
- Sixth, the IMF and World Bank stand out in their low marks for democracy and departmental intensity, as well as transparency for the IMF. Their attitude to rule-making is also difficult to pin down - in some respects transparency is being introduced as a substitute for rules.
- Seventh, while all these institutions emerge as moderately business-friendly, hardly any of them have gone far in involving the private sector in their work. The exception is the environment, where initial business hostility has influenced the shape of agreements.
- Eighth, all the institutions are trying to become more transparent to the outside world, though with varying success. Those institutions have done best which are not just economic institutions but rather institutions with both political and economic responsibilities, like the UN and the Commonwealth.

From these conclusions the final question arises: are international economic institutions becoming more powerful?[17] This is the basic assumption of the anti-globalisation protesters, demonstrating against the WTO in Seattle, the IMF in Prague or the G8 in Genoa. The idea may be encouraged by the growing study of 'global governance', which concentrates on what the institutions do to manage the international economic system. But this analysis in this chapter does not support the conclusion that institutions, whether plurilateral or multilateral, are expanding their power to act on their own. It rather suggests that, while member governments are making much greater use of the institutions, for domestic as well as external purposes, they want the institutions to advance their national objectives, rather than operate autonomously.

Notes

1   The thesis set out here was originally formulated in Bayne 1997, though it has since been adjusted in the light of the Asian financial crisis and the disaster in Seattle.

2   This emerges clearly from the reasons given by British Prime Minister Margaret Thatcher for her regular summit attendance, even during election campaigns; see Thatcher 1993, pp. 290 and 586-87.

3   When the IMF was attacked by Martin Feldstein in *Foreign Affairs,* (Feldstein 1998), Stanley Fischer, IMF Deputy Managing Director, responded with a vigorous defence two issues later (Fischer 1998). A more radical condemnation of IMF policies has since been published by Joseph Stiglitz, at the time the chief economist of the World Bank, in Stiglitz 2002.

4   An account of the HIPC programme is in Bayne 2000a, Chapter 11.

5   For details of the different strategies adopted at Seattle by the American delegation to the meeting and by President Clinton and his advisers, see Bayne 2000b.

6   For the Cairns Group, see Croome 1995 and Preeg 1995. For the Commonwealth and debt relief, see Bayne 1998.

7   By and large, plurilateral economic institutions have been neglected by researchers. They do not attract as much academic interest as regional ones, like the EU, or multilateral ones, like the IMF or the UN. This study of economic diplomacy seeks to remedy this neglect, to some degree.

8   For an analysis of OECD discussions on export credit, see Ray 1995.

9   An important account of the MAI negotiations is in Henderson 1998.

10 The OECD's contribution to trade policy is covered in Blair 1993 and Cohn 2002. Ted Cohn's book also deals with the G7's involvement in trade policy and contains a very valuable analysis of the 'Quad' of trade ministers.

11 For contrasting views on this issue, see Persaud 2001 and Wechsler 2001.

12 I have in the past called it the Cinderella of economic institutions, as compared with its ugly sisters the IMF and World Bank - see Bayne 1987. For more recent studies of the OECD, see Henderson 1993 and notes 8 and 10 above.

13 This practice of iteration is explored further in Bayne 2000a, Chapter 12.

14 Sadly, however, they were not united. India took a much more reserved line than the others and held up the final agreement at Doha.

15 Professor Harold James, in the final chapter of his history of the IMF (James 1996), argues that the Fund has moved away from rule-making to voluntary cooperation and the provision of information - see Chapter 18 below.

16 They tend, however, to resist the idea that they should take part in the financial rescue operations of the Fund and Bank. See Eichengreen 1999, Chapter 5.

17 This question is examined, with examples, in Reinalda and Verbeek 1998.

References

Bayne, N. (1987), 'Making Sense of Western Economic Policies: the Role of the OECD', *The World Today*, vol. 43, no.1, pp. 4-11.

Bayne, N. (1997), 'What Governments Want From International Institutions and How They Get It', *Government and Opposition*, vol. 32, no. 2, pp. 361-379.

Bayne, N. (1998), 'Britain, the G8 and the Commonwealth', *The Round Table*, no. 348, pp. 445-457.

Bayne, N. (2000a), *Hanging In There: The G7 and G8 Summit in Maturity and Renewal*, Ashgate, Aldershot.

Bayne, N. (2000b), 'Why Did Seattle Fail? Globalisation and the Politics of Trade', *Government and Opposition*, vol. 35, no. 2, pp. 131-151.

Blair, D. (1993), *Trade Negotiations in the OECD: Structures, Institutions and States*,

Kegan Paul International, London and New York.

Cohn, T. (2002), *Governing Global Trade: International Institutions in Conflict and Convergence*, Ashgate, Aldershot.

Croome, J. (1995), *Reshaping the World Trading System: A History of the Uruguay Round*, World Trade Organization, Geneva.

Eichengreen, B. (1999), *Toward a New International Financial Architecture: A Practical Post-Asia Agenda*, Institute for International Economics, Washington.

Feldstein, M. (1998), 'Refocusing the IMF', *Foreign Affairs*, vol. 77, no. 2, pp. 20-33.

Fischer, S. (1998), In Defence of the IMF', *Foreign Affairs*, vol. 77, no. 4, pp. 103-106.

Henderson, D. (1993), 'International Economic Cooperation Revisited', *Government and Opposition*, vol. 28, no. 1.

Henderson, D. (1999), *The MAI Affair: A Story and Its Lessons*, Royal Institute for International Affairs, London.

James, H. (1996), *International Monetary Cooperation Since Bretton Woods*, International Monetary Fund, Washington.

Kenen, P. (2001), *The International Financial Architecture: What's New? What's Missing?*, Institute for International Economics, Washington.

Persaud, B. (2001), 'OECD Curbs on Offshore Financial Centres: A Major Issue for Small States', *The Round Table*, no. 359, pp. 199-212.

Preeg, E. (1995), *Traders in a Brave New World*, University of Chicago Press, Chicago.

Ray, J. E. (1995), *Managing Official Export Credit: the Quest for a Global Regime*, Institute for International Economics, Washington.

Reinalda, B. and Verbeek, B. (eds.) (1998), *Autonomous Policy Making by International Organisations*, Routledge, London and New York.

Stiglitz, J. (2002), *Globalisation and its Discontents*, Allen Lane, London.

Thatcher, M. (1993), *The Downing Street Years*, HarperCollins, London.

Wechsler, W. (2001), 'Follow the Money', *Foreign Affairs*, vol. 80, no. 4, pp. 40-57.

Chapter 15

Economic Diplomacy for Developing Countries

Ivan Mbirimi[1]

Economic diplomacy in developing countries is at a relatively undeveloped stage. Small countries in particular perceive themselves to be at the mercy of the rich and powerful, especially at the multilateral level. Often their only negotiating strategy is to stonewall, delay or plead for special treatment.

There is however, a growing realisation that more effective strategies are required if marginalisation is to be avoided. A striking example of a change of tack was the active participation of developing countries in preparations for the Seattle ministerial meeting of the WTO in late 1999 and their determination not to sign up to agreements they did not like. But the majority of developing countries are still a long way from being effective participants in the multilateral trading system.

This chapter examines the experience of developing countries in international economic negotiations; in particular, the way they conduct their trade policy. It focuses on three aspects of their approach to economic diplomacy: first, the basic assumptions on which economic diplomacy in developing countries is based; second, the implications of these assumptions; and third, it suggests components for an enhanced economic diplomacy by developing countries.

Basic Assumptions

Negotiations, particularly at the multilateral level, are a zero-sum game. The dominant approach to multilateral trade diplomacy is distributive (competitive or 'value claiming') rather than integrative (cooperative or 'value creating'). In other words, trade diplomacy is viewed as the art of extracting maximum concessions from the other side, while conceding very little in return. Thus, in spite of what economists say about the virtues of trade liberalisation, even when others keep their markets closed, developing countries have traditionally pursued a distributive strategy. In this they are not alone, because the traditional GATT approach to trade liberalisation is based on this mercantilist strategy. An unfortunate by-product of this approach, however, is that the hard bargaining involved does not promote trust among negotiators. It is hardly surprising that the failure of the Seattle ministerial conference was partly ascribed to the breakdown in trust between developing and industrialised countries.

251

On the Importance of Basic Assumptions

In 1984, Zambia had its first structural adjustment programme. A key element of the IMF-inspired programme was the removal of subsidies on maize meal - the staple diet in the country. In preparing the programme, IMF officials had assumed that, given what they regarded as President Kaunda's populist politics, he would reject this condition. Little did they know that President Kaunda was ready to accept the programme presented to him without questioning its premises and content. It turned out that President Kaunda neither had set targets nor what modern negotiating theorists call the BATNA (the best alternative to a negotiated agreement). So, their strategy, which was to revise their targets downwards in negotiations with the Zambian government, could not be put into play. While they knew that their programme was likely to provoke disturbances, they could not reveal their strategy to the government.

Figure 15.1   The Importance of Basic Assumptions

Economic diplomacy is about set-piece negotiations such as the Uruguay Round. In consequence, trade policy is rarely viewed from a long term perspective and few developing countries appreciate the ongoing nature of economic diplomacy. This is why many of them do not consciously train their officials in the processes of negotiations and hardly any of them have in place the requisite organisational structures and institutional set-up. Not surprisingly, it is countries like Brazil, India, Singapore and Jamaica - countries that have got in place at least the basics, and in the case of Brazil, a highly sophisticated negotiating machinery - which have the greatest influence in multilateral trade negotiations. Few people for example, would be aware that the phrase 'net-food importing countries' was introduced into the Uruguay Round discussions on agriculture by the Jamaican Ambassador. It is this handful of developing countries that have the most influence in shaping developing countries' positions in the WTO, UNCTAD and regional bodies to which they belong.

Marginalisation is the inevitable consequence of participating in negotiations in which the rules of the game are determined by the rich countries. The fear of marginalisation, particularly among African countries, is heightened by the perception that the world economy is dividing into regional trade blocs. The pursuit of regionalism has therefore become an important plank of developing countries' economic diplomacy. In a world in which 'economic security' is partly defined in terms of one's competitive position vis-à-vis that of others, many developing countries believe this to be the only way they can strengthen their autonomy. Their approach to these regional agreements is somewhat different from that taken in multilateral negotiations. They tend to follow a cooperative strategy, which means they are more inclined to probe issues and identify underlying concerns and interests of each country, rather than starting from fixed positions.

While generally speaking, industrialised countries view economic diplomacy and its results in a positive light, developing countries tend to be pessimistic about the ensuing outcomes. To a large extent, these attitudes are a product of experience. But there may be a cultural/historical aspect to these attitudes. Industrialised countries are arguably more accustomed to achieving success through adaptation to external influences. Developing countries on the other hand, have had relatively limited successes in their interactions with the outside world. This has bred caution and a 'victim' culture, which has no doubt precluded them from staking out their position in areas where they could gain and from taking full advantage of new technologies and other market developments. In many cases, developing countries do not even bother to define their bottom line.

Implications and Problems

Several implications flow from these basic assumptions and the problems they cause can be highlighted by reference to a few examples from the past.

First, developing countries have often embarked upon major economic discussions without observing some of the most basic rules of the game. These include setting targets, consulting stakeholders, exploring the boundaries of difficult issues so as to define the bottom line, researching the agendas of those they are negotiating with, and identifying possible scenarios of a future world economic system and how their own economy might fit into it. When multilateral trade liberalisation was mainly about tariff reductions, the disadvantages of not observing the basic rules were perhaps not significant. After all, multilateral trade liberalisation was essentially a redistributive issue, a zero-sum game, in which the more advanced countries exchanged concessions and developing countries benefited from them as a result of the multilateralisation of the concessions exchanged. But when negotiations moved on to address non-tariff barriers and to incorporate issues of a systemic nature, most notably the new issues, the disadvantages of non-participation and non-observance of the basic rules became more apparent.

The current controversies surrounding the Agreement on Trade-Related Intellectual Property Rights (TRIPS) in the WTO illustrate the point. In contrast to previous GATT agreements, the TRIPS accord is not about freeing trade, but about more protection, because it obliges governments to take positive action to protect intellectual property rights (IPR). By requiring governments to establish minimum standards of IPR protection, it also introduced into the GATT/WTO system the idea of harmonisation of domestic policies. It is therefore a major departure from the traditional GATT model of bringing down barriers to trade. So developing countries cannot afford to stand on the sidelines while the rules of the new system are being decided.

A review of the events leading to the conclusion of the TRIPS agreement shows the limitations of an approach that is not firmly grounded in some of the basics. The subject was first brought up by the United States in 1982. Under pressure from the pharmaceutical, entertainment and informatics industries, the US sought a comprehensive agreement on standards for protection of intellectual property rights. Developing countries, led by Brazil, India, Egypt, Argentina and Yugoslavia opposed comprehensive discussions and sought to distinguish between trade in counterfeit goods and TRIPS more generally. Their stance was largely defensive in that they were concerned to ensure that any agreed measures would not: (a) result in barriers to legitimate trade; (b) strengthen the monopoly power of multinational companies; and (c) preclude transitional periods for developing countries. In the agreement that was eventually signed, they won concessions on transitional periods, but arguably very little on their other key demands. And when one compares the adjustment costs of introducing minimum standards of IPR protection to the concessions on transition periods, it seems clear that the negotiating strategy of developing countries brought them what is now judged to be a lopsided agreement.

The contrast with events leading to the General Agreement on Trade in Services (GATS) is illuminating. Led again by Brazil and India, developing countries opposed discussions on trade in services. While they could not block negotiations on the subject, they managed to put services on a separate track, which they felt was crucial in order to prevent cross-issue linkages between traditional GATT issues and services. The striking feature about the services negotiations was the creation of an exploratory phase, in which the parties probed the boundaries of the field within which negotiations could go forward. Had the TRIPS negotiations gone through a similar exploratory phase, perhaps the current controversies would have been avoided.

Second, looking at the norms, conventions and practices of the GATT/WTO system, based as they are on reciprocal mercantilism, some people have wondered whether it has much to offer to the poorest countries of the world, especially those without the capacity to flourish in global competition. Doubtless, the GATT/WTO system offers the weak protection from the strong and acts as a guarantor of domestic trade policy reform undertaken by these governments. But it is self-evident that some of its basic norms mean that the poorest countries have a minor part to play and therefore can expect few immediate benefits - which is how the system is usually judged. The sense of alienation is sometimes palpable as when African countries attending the Seattle ministerial meeting issued a statement condemning the 'Green Room' process. This denunciation of the Green Room process could be seen as a turning point in the way diplomacy is conducted at the WTO. Developing countries finally recognised they had some power, which they could use to influence decisions in the organisation. Industrialised countries on the other hand, realised that they could not continue with the same negotiating methods, characterised by decision-making in small groups dominated by them, and then expecting others to fall behind the agreements reached.

Third, a by-product of the alienation of developing countries at the WTO is the much stronger commitment to special trading arrangements exhibited by these countries. Some of these agreements, especially the Lomé Conventions, do not only provide preferential tariff treatment, but also allow duty-free entry of specified quantities of important agricultural products traditionally exported by developing countries, which would otherwise be subject to duty or quota restrictions under the EU's Common Agricultural Policy (CAP). Unfortunately, being client relationships, they have never offered the security of market access available under the GATT/WTO system. Another deficiency of these arrangements is that they reinforced a culture of pleading for special status, which arguably prevented these countries from getting to grips with the complexities and range of opportunities open to them elsewhere.

Some of these opportunities might have presented themselves closer to home, at the regional level as in the case of the Southern Africa Development Community (SADC). In that region, the independence of South Africa was widely seen as ushering in a new era both politically and economically. Countries in the region (even outsiders too) felt they had a good opportunity to form a free trade area. This was considered the best way SADC could attract foreign investment and enhance its competitiveness vis-à-vis the rest of the world. However, there were a few obstacles in the way: some SADC Member States belonged to the Common Market for Eastern and Southern Africa (COMESA), which South Africa had (some would say unfortunately) declined to join; South Africa itself belonged to a customs union which included a few of the SADC Member States; Zimbabwe and Malawi had for a long while, had preferential trade agreements with South Africa; and Zambia had just gone through a comprehensive structural adjustment programme that brought its tariffs to levels much lower than most countries in the region.

The goal that SADC set itself was clear, a free trade area in eight years. Bringing this project to fruition has however proved difficult and a major factor in this is the negotiating strategies used. Instead of a cooperative approach, they adopted a distributive approach. The weakest member countries sought special and differential treatment; those with whom South Africa had preferential bilateral trade agreements wanted them extended; while South Africa itself sought to protect sensitive sectors of its economy. Given current political developments in the region, it is perhaps the case that an opportunity for improving the prospects of the region's economies has been delayed or lost.

Fourth, the limitations of approaching economic diplomacy as set-piece negotiations have never been fully appreciated by developing countries. This is somewhat surprising, given that set piece negotiations are characterised by power politics. Their focus on outcomes places developing countries at a relative disadvantage. If there was less emphasis on outcomes and bargaining, then the other aspects of economic diplomacy, most notably information exchange and learning, from which developing countries stand to gain the most, could come to the fore.

Fifth, there are issues related to how developing countries organise and manage their conduct of economic diplomacy. Most of them tend to view economic diplomacy as separate from political diplomacy. Many of the diplomats involved in trade negotiations are in fact from the ministries of Foreign Affairs, with little background in trade or economic matters generally. Few developing countries have an institutional framework for dealing with trade relations. Trade policy, unlike macroeconomic policy, which is usually determined by the IMF, also tends to be treated as separate from other aspects of economic policy.

One consequence of this is that countries have sometimes undertaken commitments on trade under an IMF programme, which contradicted commitments they have made at the WTO. But there is perhaps a deeper point to all this, related to how development is generally perceived. As a process or practice, development is to a large extent now viewed in terms of what development agencies and multilateral institutions do to improve the economic prospects of developing countries. In other words, it is arguable whether many developing countries, especially in Africa, still have a vision of their economic future. They will implement an IMF programme because they do not have an alternative. Similarly, they will accept the EU's proposals on regional partnership agreements because they have no alternative. However, these arrangements are unlikely to take them far if there is no local foundation on which to build. At the very least, developing countries must develop some vision of the future.

Components of Enhanced Economic Diplomacy

The rules of engagement in international economic diplomacy are basically the same as those followed in other types of negotiations, with perhaps one major difference. International economic negotiations generally involve hundreds of people from hundreds of countries as in the WTO. The negotiators must take on board the views of different interest groups and politicians at home and abroad. This means that the negotiators have to demonstrate competencies in a variety of contexts. Many of their competencies are accumulated over a long period of time involving exposure to the interests of those on whose behalf they negotiate and those they confront across the negotiating table. This is why capacity building must be seen as a long term process and one which cannot be adequately addressed through the provision of technical assistance alone.

Thorough preparations are essential to effectiveness in negotiations. This involves undertaking assessments of one's own position, the positions of other parties and the environment in which the negotiations are being conducted. Information is the crucial ingredient in such assessments. This is a major shortcoming in developing countries' current approach to economic diplomacy. While major differences exist between developing and developed countries on several economic issues, instances of ambiguity regarding what developing countries really want could be reduced by gathering relevant facts and figures about the issues under negotiation, so that politicians and the public in developed countries are not left with the impression that what developing countries want is what developed countries cannot give them.

Those win-win outcomes that politicians want to talk about cannot be realised in the absence of relevant information. This suggests that developing countries should be prepared to engage politicians and interest groups in their main markets so that differences in trading interests are approached constructively. This kind of engagement might help in discussions on controversial issues such as harmonisation of labour standards. One way in which developing countries could bring greater clarity to their negotiating positions is by articulating a coherent view of where they see their country in 15-20 years' time. This is only possible if they engage in some form of scenario planning. The sense of drift that is sometimes apparent among negotiators from developing countries partly reflects a lack of direction or aspirations and targets to aim for.

Some negotiations represent a major shift in thinking, in which case the historical context must be understood so that, if a break with the past is contemplated, this is done with the full facts to hand and a good appreciation of the likely future course of events. For instance, it has been argued that the Uruguay Round represented such a shift in that it brought into the multilateral trading system issues that lay outside the GATT's traditional remit. The point at issue is not whether this should have been allowed to happen; rather it is the fact that when it happened few developing countries grasped the implications of the change on their economies and their ability to participate in it effectively. It is now clear that the problem of implementation of the Uruguay Round commitments and the consequent challenges these problems pose for developing countries did not receive adequate attention during the negotiations. But many in industrialised countries have yet to grasp the fact that such problems cannot be resolved by technical assistance alone.

Commitment and consistency of beliefs and behaviour are essential components of effective diplomacy. One of the more striking features of trade diplomacy by developing countries is the almost haphazard way in which it is conducted, particularly in Africa, where the current proliferation of overlapping regional trade arrangements is causing great confusion and may be hampering efforts to build strong regional economies. There is no clearly discernible thread linking these various arrangements with the trading arrangements concluded with important trading partners like the European Union. An inconsistent approach opens the way for others, especially if they are more powerful, to determine your policies in a way that may be detrimental to your interests. In the upcoming negotiations between the African, Caribbean and Pacific (ACP) and the EU, in which the EU is proposing regional partnership agreements, there is a strong possibility that African countries will take what is offered by the EU, rather than negotiate on terms favourable to them. More worrying is the fact that the EU may choose the regional organisations as partners, thereby determining regional integration policy in Africa.

A noticeable feature of the conduct of economic diplomacy by developing countries is the leading role played by the ministries of foreign affairs (this is less so in financial matters). Ambassadors to what are key economic posts in Brussels and Geneva are often chosen from the Ministry of Foreign Affairs or worse, political appointees with no track record in economic matters. This means almost all their negotiating authority derives from their rank. Unfortunately a different kind of authority is also required - that which is bestowed on the negotiator by their peers on account of their knowledge of the issues and their negotiating skills. At the WTO, as in other international organisations, this kind of authority opens doors to key informal meetings where important discussions and exchanges of views take place. It is also likely to mean that when the powerful countries feel the need to approach politicians in capitals, this is not done over the heads of the representatives/ambassadors involved in day-to-day negotiations.

Developing countries have to learn and adopt some of the networking skills that NGOs have mustered. As well as taking measures to strengthen their capacity to negotiate, developing countries must also consider ways of influencing public opinion and influential groups in those industrial and developing countries which engage in protectionist trade policies. Stakeholder meetings to explore selected multilateral trade issues should become a regular feature of their economic diplomacy. Only this way, will they begin to shift to a posture that treats negotiations as an ongoing process.

Conclusion

It is important for developing countries to have a **strong vision** of the future supported by a **set of clear objectives** defined in the light of global developments and **a sense of the threats and opportunities** created by technological and market developments. This should be further supported by a readiness to engage positively in economic diplomacy, and when possible, seeking to influence decisions in accordance with stated national objectives and vision. This process of thinking through problems is likely to lead to an exploration of alternative ways of conducting economic diplomacy. Current efforts to promote public/private sector dialogues have not made much headway because they lack a firm foundation of analysis. Similarly, relying on multilateral institutions to provide the vision can be dangerous as the example of Zambia shows. These institutions do change their policy prescriptions from time to time, and when they make mistakes there is no mechanism for making them accountable. This means some opportunities for learning from mistakes are lost.

Looking at the outcome of the fourth Ministerial meeting of the WTO, held in Doha, Qatar, in November 2001, and the decision to launch a comprehensive new round of multilateral trade negotiations, it becomes clear that a great deal remains to be done to enhance the effectiveness of developing countries in trade negotiations. As indicated earlier, most of what needs to be done relates to the basics of negotiations. Obviously, the approach adopted by developing countries was heavily influenced by their experience in the Uruguay Round. However, it could be argued now that their desire to see positive action on the implementation of Uruguay Round Agreements and to resist a further expansion of the WTO agenda to include new issues left many of them with only one strategy in these important areas of negotiations. Thus, although developing countries were not alone in believing that they might be able to keep new issues off the agenda of a new round, that was before the external economic environment had changed. Once it did, as a result of the terrorist events in America, the dynamics of negotiations changed.

The US became convinced that a new round was vital to restoring confidence in the global economy. Under these circumstances, the EU was able to achieve virtually all its objectives on new issues. Had developing countries considered alternatives to the EU proposal, perhaps they might have been able to keep out one of the new issues. Ultimately, the fall back position India came up with was to obtain a clarification, which states that negotiations on competition and investment can only go ahead if there is consensus from all members. Whatever the merits and demerits of including new issues in the next round of negotiations, developing countries weakened their position by apparently following a single strategy on these issues. Arguably, the most important lesson that developing countries should pick out from the fourth WTO Ministerial meeting is that unexpected events can change the negotiating environment in a fundamental way. This is why it is important not to rely on one strategy.

During the ministerial meeting, a number of developing countries' negotiators complained about being undermined by direct approaches made to their capitals by industrialised countries. This points to shortcomings in how these countries' organise and coordinate their negotiating strategies. As long as key negotiators operate at a distance from other key decision-makers in capitals, this problem will continue to undermine the effectiveness of developing countries in negotiations. Similarly, allegations of 'bullying' made by some developing countries' representatives and non-governmental organisations will continue to be a feature of these negotiations until developing countries achieve better organisation and coordination, so as to ensure that the negotiating objectives are understood by all stakeholders and the lines of communication are clear.

Note

1   The views expressed in this note are personal and do not represent the official position of the Commonwealth Secretariat.

Chapter 16

Governments, the International Financial Institutions and International Cooperation

Nigel Wicks

The World of the International Financial Institutions

The men who established the international financial institutions shared a fundamental belief. Put simply, it was that mankind has the capacity through his own actions to be master of his economic fate. He need not be subject to the dictates of either random or deterministic economic forces. Economic policy, properly formulated and implemented, so goes the belief, can improve the economic lot of mankind.

This belief contrasts with the belief that iron laws of economics predetermine human progress. Marxism is one form of this belief and Marxist thought was dominant in a large part of the world when the Bretton Woods institutions, the International Monetary Fund (IMF) and the World Bank, were establishing themselves in the late 1940s. Paradoxically, the fall of the Marxist states East of the Iron Curtain has provided the Bretton Woods institutions, from 1989 onwards, with a substantial increase in its membership. Another form of 'the iron laws of economics' belief is the belief in the reliance on laissez faire market capitalism. This belief leads to a denial of the need for the international financial institutions. Indeed, the institutions could frustrate market forces. Modern day proponents of this belief provide the ideological capital for an influential school of opponents in the United States of the Bretton Woods institutions.

If mankind is to be master of his economic fate, governments, acting on behalf of their peoples, need instruments. Those instruments in the field of international finance are the International Monetary Fund (IMF) and the World Bank. Since the IMF and the World Bank are instruments of government, it follows that they are not autonomous self-ruling bodies. Of course, staffs working in the Fund and Bank have their own views on economic and development policies. Nor, naturally enough, are they motivated to minimise the role of their own institutions. Even so, it would be unfair to Fund and Bank staffs, as well as a misunderstanding of the essential power relationships, to deny that responsibility for the policy of the institutions rests with the governments that own the institutions. Since different governments have different levels of shareholding in the Bank and Fund, different governments bear different burdens of responsibility.

261

Yet governments have never found it easy to assume this mantle of responsibility. Governments, in the form of ministers and central bankers, find the Fund and the Bank to be convenient scapegoats when unpopular decisions have to be taken. Indeed, one of the reasons for establishing the two institutions was to provide a buffer between politics and economics. Individual governments working on a bilateral basis could not do this. The sensitivities of bilateral international diplomacy would blunt the thoroughness of policy appraisal, mute the frankness of policy advice and soften the terms of lending conditions for bilateral loans.

Institution building after World War II

The fundamental belief - the Bank and the Fund are instruments which permit man to be master of his economic fate - was evident from the earliest years of their foundation at the end of the Second World War. Indeed, the belief in the value of international organisations, economic, political and military, was characteristic of the spirit of the time. Those years saw creative acts of statesmanship in world politics, in international economic policy and in regional military and economic cooperation. In politics, there was the establishment of the United Nations. In international economic policy, there was the creation of the IMF; the World Bank; the General Agreement on Tariffs and Trade (GATT), forerunner of the World Trade Organization (WTO); and the Organisation for European Economic Cooperation (OEEC), the administrator of the Marshall Plan and forerunner of the Organisation for Economic Cooperation and Development (OECD). In regional economic integration in Europe, there was the Treaty of Paris, which established the European Coal and Steel Community (ECSC), the earliest component of what became the European Union. In regional military and political cooperation, there was the founding of the North Atlantic Treaty Organisation (NATO) and the Council of Europe respectively.

So the five years or so after the end of the Second World War saw a golden age of creative statesmanship, the like of which the 20th century had not seen before and was not to see again. Their establishment laid the basis for fifty years of cooperation between governments among the major countries. Fifty years on, these institutions are still the pillars of the international polity. The reason for these initiatives is clear. The post-war leaders believed that lessons could be learned from the study of history. They wanted to do everything possible to prevent the recurrence of the economic and political horrors of the interwar years. When the global financial system began to be rocked by the oil price crises in the 1970s, the leading governments again acted. They established the G5 and then the G7 process, with the United States effectively in the chair, as a sort of directorate to manage the process. The system produced half a century of unprecedented global prosperity, though some countries, especially in Africa, never benefited. One important reason for this success was the active stewardship and cooperation of governments. This was in stark contrast to the experience of the first half of the 20th century.

This model of international stewardship is now under challenge. For the forty-five years between 1945 and 1990, there had been a clear division of the world -

into Soviet bloc governments and their sympathisers, the NATO alliance and its sympathisers and the truly non-aligned. The collapse of the Soviet Union dissolved the certainties of these old super-power client relationships. There is now a more multilateral world with many more players on the scene, a world without much order and diplomatically a bit of a mess. The political predominance of the United States in the Fund and the Bank, once founded on their Cold War military leadership, is not so obvious. This is the new political environment in which the Bank and the Fund have to operate.

The IMF, the World Bank and globalisation

The Bank and the Fund need to operate too in the so-called 'globalised world' of fast moving ideas and capital. This has had four particular consequences for their work. First, the communication revolution, in the shape of e-mail, fax, cheap telephone calls and air journeys, enables activists, lobbyists and campaigners to seek to influence, criticise and assail, sometimes physically, the institutions. Second, the new forms of communication make it easier too for ministers and officials in national capitals to have deeper and more regular contact with their counterparts, either bilaterally or in groups (G7, G24, G20 etc), in a way which tends to bypass the Fund and the Bank.

The third consequence of globalisation is the profound effect on the work of the institutions of the power of the financial markets and the mobility of capital flows. This is well captured by the shift of the institutions' attention from the current account to the capital account and the national financial balance sheet. The fourth consequence of globalisation for the Fund also lies in the development of the international capital markets. This has brought about a sharp division between Fund members. It was over twenty years ago that the Fund last lent to a developed country. Developed countries now resort to the international capital markets when they run short of foreign exchange reserves. Developing countries cannot expect such support from the international capital markets, at least not without the support of the Bank and the Fund.

So Fund borrowers nowadays are always developing and emerging market countries. This has undoubtedly altered the relationship between the Fund and its members. The Fund's relationship with many developing countries is now centred on the provision of resources and the associated lending conditionalities. For the developing countries not immediately in receipt of Fund loans, the prospect of such a relationship dominates their perception of the Fund. The Fund's main interest in the developed countries lies in the surveillance of their economies. This dichotomy of interest would disappear if developed countries borrow again from the Fund. This is not likely for the foreseeable future. It might disappear too if developing countries find themselves in the same position as developed countries and can rely on the capital market in times of economic stress. That is a very long time away!

Much has been written about the effectiveness of Fund surveillance of (ie examination of and comment on the prospects of) its members' economies and of the world economy generally.[1] Inevitably surveillance can, and if it is to be effective must, occasionally be a cause of tension with its member governments, whatever the size of the country concerned. But the effectiveness of Fund surveillance relies heavily on the continued ability of Fund management and staff to make independent and unbiased judgements of the economic prospects of its members and of the world economy. Increasingly, and rightly, these judgements are being published. The Fund's Managing Director has a big responsibility here in resisting pressures from Member States for the Fund to blunt the edge of the message in its surveillance judgements.

The Governance of the IMF and the World Bank

There are five actors on the IMF's stage: the management, the staff, the Board of Executive Directors, the Board of Governors and the International Monetary and Finance Committee, formerly the Interim Committee. Besides these five, there is another set of actors lurking in the wings, but more of them later.[2]

The IMF management

The Fund's management comprises the Managing Director and three Deputy Managing Directors, one of whom, as First Deputy, is primus inter pares. Until a few years ago, the Fund had only one Deputy Managing Director and his main responsibility was the Fund's internal administrative management. Managing Director Michel Camdessus appointed three Deputy Managing Directors. One of the new arrivals took over the functions formerly held by the single Deputy Managing Director, leaving the senior Deputy, called the First Deputy, free to act, to all intents and purposes, as the Fund's Chief Operations Officer. This proved to be a significant move. Hitherto power below the Managing Director had been dispersed among the Fund's many staff departmental heads and their senior subordinates. Under Camdessus it became centred, to a greater or lesser extent, on one person. This subtly altered the balance of power between staff and management, the Executive Board and the Fund's shareholders, the national governments. For the first time it was possible to talk to one official in the Fund responsible for most lending decisions below the (rightly) Olympian figure of the Managing Director.

The Fund's management runs the Fund's day-to-day operations and for those operations the buck stops with the Managing Director. The management decides whether to recommend the Executive Board to lend or not to lend. By convention, the Executive Board of Directors always endorses the Management's recommendations. This approach may appear supine. In fact, it is essential to the smooth operation of the Fund. The government of a borrowing member would be in an untenable position if it publicly committed itself to a highly politically sensitive programme of economic reform, only for that programme to be subsequently overturned by the Executive Board. Even so, individual governments occasionally cast negative or abstaining votes against Fund management recommendations. While such votes are not successful in overturning the management's recommendations, they are not nugatory. They send signals to management about the content of subsequent programmes, either for the particular borrowing member or for future programmes generally.

The IMF staff

Below the four management figures, there is the Fund staff. The professional personnel are overwhelmingly macroeconomists. Most do not have direct experience of senior levels of government or of the financial markets. They are dedicated, high quality, long suffering and of great integrity, and the same can be said of the staff of the World Bank.

Sometimes governments seeking to borrow from the Fund accuse Fund staff of political naivety. Such accusations can usually be dismissed. Senior Fund officials are often more experienced in the politics of Fund programmes than ministers in the countries to whom they are lending. Such criticisms usually are evidence of unwillingness to accept lending conditions. Yet it would be wrong to deny that Fund staff have great influence and power. When the staff are on mission (that is, when they are visiting a member country to agree a lending programme or conduct an examination - 'surveillance' - of its economy), they operate under mandates approved by Fund management. But it is the staff who draft the negotiating mandates and implement them in the discussions and it is their judgement and advice on which the management relies for the crucial decisions. It is not sufficiently recognised that such judgements by the Fund's staff have often to be taken in a fog of uncertainty about the economic numbers and the ability of ministers with whom the Fund is negotiating to deliver their commitments. Sometimes too, Fund staff are not as well informed as they would wish on the workings of the member's economy, especially when the member has been unwilling over a considerable period to enter into dialogue about the prospects for its economy. Sometimes too, the Fund's involvement is delayed until the financial crisis is well underway, when time is of the essence and prudent due diligence of the economic programme is well nigh impossible. The job of Fund staff is a difficult one.

The Board of Executive Directors

The Executive Board is the third actor on the Fund's stage. The Board is composed of the Executive Directors (colloquially known as EDs). The Fund's Articles stipulate that there should be twenty Executive Directors. But there are, in fact, twenty-four. This increase is achieved by a vote every two years. This vote requires an 85 per cent majority and that majority requires the participation of the United States. This gives the United States a considerable contingent power over the Fund, though a power somewhat in the nature of an atomic bomb in its potential destructiveness. Blocking the periodic increases in Executive Directors would provoke an enormous crisis in the Fund, potentially uniting virtually the whole of the Fund membership against the United States.

The Executive Directors have a dual function. They represent national governments. Yet at the same time they owe loyalty to the Fund. This dichotomy need not cause problems in practice. Every Fund member, from the biggest to the smallest, shares a common interest in the maintenance of the Fund as an institution, for example in ensuring that its finances are solvent, loans are repaid on time and that salaries are adequate to retain staff.

The Executive Director is the principal link between his or her government and the Fund. Normally, but not invariably, Executive Directors come from finance ministries or central banks. This reflects the important fact, effectively endorsed in the Fund's Articles, that governments maintain their relationships with the Fund through those two institutions.[3] This is true for big and small members. This exclusive relationship is jealously prized by finance ministries, central banks and by the Fund itself. Foreign ministries are not formally involved, though it would be a foolish Executive Director from a major country who did not keep his foreign ministry broadly aware of developments. The Executive Director chooses his or her staff. They too usually come from national central banks and finance ministries. Finance ministries and central banks protect their exclusive role with the Fund partly for reasons of turf (which, unfortunately, is often a factor in international diplomacy). But the main reason is because it helps to safeguard the portion of their foreign exchange reserves that creditor countries pay over to the Fund to finance their contribution to Fund finances. If foreign ministries were heavily involved, such overt involvement would lead to pressure to adapt lending policies to political rather than economic ends. This could prejudice repayments and thus put at risk the foreign exchange reserves which members paid over to the Fund as their contributions to the Fund.

Because governments' relationships with the Fund are carried out through finance ministries and central banks, the Fund is, for good or ill, an institution that is heavily dominated by economics. There is a long-standing convention within the Executive Board that its language of debate should be the language of economics and finance and not of politics and inter-state relations. This helps to avoid wrangling on the most sensitive issues of international politics. But a skilful Executive Director can make a political point, within the conventions, through the use of economic language. The Chicago trained Argentinean Alternate Executive Director mounted a skilful and vigorous monetarist attack on British monetary policy during the Board's discussion of the UK economy in the aftermath of the Falklands conflict. In the 1980s, African Executive Directors mounted devastating attacks on 'structural impediments' in the South African labour market, thereby castigating the inefficiencies and inequalities of the apartheid system.

The dominance of economics in the Fund has not kept the lending decisions of the Fund (and the Bank) altogether immune from politics. During the Cold War, the Fund lent to 'clients' of some of its larger members to an extent that was disproportionate with the economic merits. Such egregious treatment is, hopefully, a thing of the past, though there are still occasions when strategically important members receive especial attention. Yet even in the case of these countries, reasons of global stability can be invoked for their treatment. This has not prevented complaints from some Asian countries that they have not received the generosity of treatment accorded, for example to Latin American countries. But whatever the merits of this debate, smaller, less strategically situated members with economic programmes deserving of support will receive that support. The hallowed principle of uniformity - the Fund's rules and practices apply equally to all its members - is by and large respected.

Constituencies and quotas

The Executive Directors are grouped into so-called 'constituencies'. The Articles provide for five appointed one-country constituencies, the United States, Japan, Germany, France and the United Kingdom. There are in addition three further one-country constituencies for large or rich countries (Saudi Arabia, China and Russia). The rest of the Executive Directors head multi-country constituencies. These constituencies group together disparate countries, often with a regional bias. The constituency leader, the Executive Director, assembles the constituency every two years. Often, this is only after some hard bargaining both to retain and attract new members into the constituency. Each director has a number of votes, comprising the total of the votes for all the countries in the constituency. The Executive Director has to cast his votes as a block. He cannot split them according to the views of the governments of the constituency members.

A Fund member's votes are closely related to, but are not exactly the same as, the sum of its contributions to the finances of the Fund, which are known in Fund jargon as 'the member's quota'. Quotas are calculated, usually every five years, according to an arcane formula broadly related to the wealth of a country and to its position in the world economy. So the wealthier a country, the greater its contribution to Fund finances and the more votes the country has in deciding how the Fund's resources are used. This system of weighted voting suggests that the Fund is more in the nature of a plutocracy rather than a democracy. This is perhaps inevitable given the fact the Fund is financed from contributions from members' foreign exchange reserves. These contributions would never be forthcoming unless the member could protect them through its voting power.

The same point applies in broad terms to the World Bank. Most of Bank lending is financed by borrowings from the capital market (or in the case of lending to the poorest countries from contributions largely provided from developed countries' aid budgets). This market borrowing is implicitly guaranteed by developed countries' formal undertakings to make further capital subscriptions to the Bank if the Bank's finances so require. These capital subscriptions determine Bank members' voting strength in the Bank. So naturally enough, developed countries in the Bank seek to ensure that Bank policy minimises the risk of calls for further capital subscriptions.

The arcane formula for calculating a Fund member's contribution gives considerable weight to past economic performance. So it was only in the 1990s that Britain surrendered its place as the second biggest shareholder in the Fund. Even that was achieved only as a result of an ad hoc calculation, which overrode the standard calculation and put Britain in fourth place in shareholder rankings, level with France and behind Germany and Japan with the United States as the largest shareholder. In March 2001, the United States had 17.16 per cent of total Fund votes, Japan 6.16 per cent, Germany 6.02 per cent and France and Britain equal with 4.97 per cent. The largest constituency in terms of members is the

Anglophone African constituency with twenty-one members, but only 3.23 per cent of Fund votes. This mismatch is due to the poverty, and therefore the low quota, of most of the constituency members. The constituency's Executive Director carries an enormous load in looking after his often troubled constituency members.

The constituency system is the key to the operation of the Fund's Board. It operates, in a very subtle way, to moderate opposing views in the Board. For example, East European countries are members of constituencies, which are lead by West European countries, such as the Netherlands and Belgium. Australia has within its constituency South Korea and New Zealand as well as some small South Sea islands. The constituency leaders know that they have to assemble a constituency every two years and this sensitively modifies the line, which they take on all matters of Fund business. But they do this in a way that still maintains their essential economic beliefs. This subtle process helps to maintain the balance in the Board and moves extremes to a central consensus.

There are increasing complaints that the system for calculating votes does not properly reflect the balance of global economic power - mainly for the reason that the backward looking quota system reflects past, not present, economic performance. Some critics argue that the system results in too many European Executive Directors - from France, Germany, the United Kingdom, Italy, Scandinavia, Belgium, Netherlands, Russia and Switzerland, over a third of the Executive Board.

This debate is not concluded. It may become associated with ideas occasionally mooted by some Member States of the European Union to consolidate their voting shares into a smaller number of constituencies, or even into one jumbo constituency. This would, it is argued, give greater coherence and presence to the views of European Union members, and especially to the views of members of the euro area. It would also provide an opportunity to tidy up some curiosities among the present constituency arrangements, Spain for example being in a South American constituency and Ireland in the Canadian constituency. But constituency change raises issues of national sovereignty and amour propre and is deeply controversial. So change will be neither easy nor quick. The more drastic forms of consolidation would probably require an amendment of the Fund's Articles. Amendments require a vote equivalent to 85 per cent of the votes of the Board of Governors. Such a majority requires the support of the United States, which no doubt would wish to reflect carefully before sanctioning the creation of a constituency with more votes than its own!

In fact, though simple majority votes govern individual lending decisions, the United States has a powerful grip on much, but not all, of the strategy of the Fund and the Bank. The voting arrangements in both the Boards of Governors and in the Executive Boards give the United States a veto on many strategic policy decisions. This, coupled with the geographical proximity of the US Treasury and the Fund and Bank buildings and the resources and expertise of the US Treasury and Federal Reserve, has permitted the United States to dominate the two institutions. While it is possible to take exception to particular decisions of the United States, successive Administrations' support for the institutions, often in the face of significant

Congressional opposition and public apathy if not hostility, has been an important factor in sustaining the global prosperity of the second half of the 20th century. Some Member States of the European Union have found United States' dominance of the Fund particularly irksome. The remedy is, in part, in the European Union's own hands - greater cooperation and cohesion in formulating and implementing Fund policies so as to provide the basis for a more equal partnership with the United States!

An effective Executive Board is crucial for the successful operation of the Fund. But the Board needs to be brought up to date. The IMF Board was once the place where policies were thrashed out and where contacts were made between governments. This is hardly the case today. Modern communications, e-mails, fax, easy and cheap telephone calls and air travel, have strengthened direct links between national capitals and senior officials resident in national capitals. Increasingly therefore, Fund policy, direction and decisions are discussed between national capitals or in groups of 'Deputies' (ie senior officials from capitals), such as the Group of Seven and Group of Twenty (G7 Deputies and G20 Deputies respectively), with the Executive Board left to filling out the details.

The authority of the Fund would be strengthened if this reality were recognised in the operation of the Executive Board. This could be accomplished if the Executive Director was the senior official responsible for Fund issues in national capitals. He, or she, would attend Washington, say once every six weeks, for two days for the major discussions, with the Alternate Executive Director, the Executive Director's second in command and resident in Washington, dealing with the day to day business. Such a change would be unpopular with many Executive Directors. But it would return power to the Board table in 19th Street in Washington.

The Board of Governors

The fourth actor in the International Monetary Fund is the Board of Governors. The Board comprises a representative from the governments of the 183 Fund members. The Fund's Articles give the Board power, among other matters, to amend the Articles, to change quotas, and to admit new members to the Fund. The Fund's (and Bank's) Board of Governors is not an effective policy-making body. It meets once a year in the early autumn at the so-called Annual Meetings. But its meetings are an empty shell. The national Governor reads his speech into a cavernous hall of aircraft hangar proportions, which for most of the time is at best a third full. This aspect of the Annual Meetings could be abolished with no loss.

The IMFC

The fifth actor on the Fund stage is the International Monetary and Financial Committee (IMFC), formerly the Interim Committee. It has, like the Executive Board, 24 members. It comprises a minister or the central banker from the country that provides the Executive Director on the IMF Board. It is an informal body with no legal power, but its communiqués effectively set the policy and direction of the Fund. Since 1999 Deputies (Ministers' nominated senior official representatives) have prepared its meetings, much to the chagrin of some of the Executive Directors who perhaps see this as a small step in the direction of the non-resident Board referred to earlier.

The Articles of the IMF provide an option, which if exercised would effectively convert the International Monetary and Financial Committee into a formal Council of the IMF. This is a proposal dear to French hearts but it has not been much liked by previous US governments who have a veto on its establishment under the Fund's voting rules. Most other countries have not expressed a view. But there does seem to be some value in the idea of a Council. It would give expression to the fundamental belief that the Fund is an instrument of government for which governments should take responsibility.

The G7

The sixth actor lurking in the wings is the G7 group of industrialised countries, meeting either as heads of state or government, or as G7 finance ministers and central bank governors. The G7 finance ministers and governors always meet, and usually issue a communiqué, before meetings of the IMFC. Their statements effectively set the agenda for discussion in the IMFC and provide the substance for its communiqué. This intensely annoys non-G7 countries, from the smaller Europeans to the larger Latin Americans. But the plain fact is that the G7 has, over the last few years, provided the lead for the development of IMF policies, for example, setting the substance of measures to improve the functioning of the international financial system, from poor country debt relief to the so-called international financial architecture.

The World Bank

The governance of the World Bank is radically different from that of the Fund.[4] It is modelled on the governance of an American corporation. Its top man is called a President and his immediate subordinates are Senior Vice Presidents and Vice Presidents. There is no distinction in the Bank equivalent to that in the Fund between management and staff. The Bank's Board appears as if it was intended to function rather like a US corporate board, keeping broad oversight over policy and leaving the direction to management. But it has never worked like that. This is not surprising given that the Executive Directors are hardly likely to be content with the non-executive status of a typical US corporate board member. Moreover, the Bank's work in a member country impacts on sometimes sensitive domestic policies and interest groups. Pressures from the home country are unlikely to allow the Executive Director, the Government's resident representative in Washington, to act in non-executive mode and to divorce him or herself from day to day operations of the institution. So it is not surprising that there have been periods of friction between President and Board.

It is said that Lord Keynes, the British architect of the Bretton Woods settlement, was aware of this potential conflict. He sought, according to the folk history, to deal with the conflict by making the Executive Directors 'non-resident'. But he lost the argument in the face of US opposition.[5] So he insisted that for

Britain the same person should hold the posts of British Executive Director at the Fund and at the Bank and of Economic Minister at the British Embassy. It is recounted that Keynes thought that this would prevent the Executive Director from succumbing to fussy interventionism in Bank and Fund business. This arrangement still persists in the case of the United Kingdom. One or two other constituencies have joint directors.

The Bank is a much harder institution to manage than the Fund. The Fund's activity is concentrated on its surveillance and on its lending programmes. Its staff broadly shares the same skills. To some extent, its success is observable, if not measurable. Fund surveillance of its members' economies is either effective or not effective and the lending programmes achieve or do not achieve their objectives. The Bank's activities are more diffuse and are spread over the entirety of a member's development programme, from governance issues to health policy, infrastructure design, financial sector reform and a host of other pressing needs. The results of such activities often appear, and sometimes are, diffuse and can take many years to become apparent. The Bank's activities can raise vociferous objections from, or on behalf of, groups that are geographically or politically concentrated. Bank staff too are drawn from many disciplines and their objectives can appear to conflict. If the Fund staff's leitmotiv is the somewhat austere concept of macroeconomic stability, that of Bank staff is the somewhat more sympathetic concept of poverty reduction. It is therefore not surprising that Fund staff recognise the adage, dear to finance ministry officials world wide, that they did not join their institution to be loved. Nor is it surprising that Bank personnel tend to become uncomfortable if they do not feel loved!

In the Bank, the distinction between developed and developing countries (Part I and Part II countries in Bank parlance) is more accentuated than in the Fund. Nor does the moderating force of the constituency system appear to be so powerful. This is perhaps because for many decades the Bank has lent only to developing countries. It does not exercise a 'universal' function over all its members akin to Fund surveillance. It is therefore unsurprising that in the Bank there is something of the attitude of 'them' and 'us' (the countries who provide the funds and the countries who borrow the funds). Executive Directors in the Bank from the developed countries are sometimes represented by officials from aid or development ministries and sometimes by officials from finance ministries (and occasionally by academics or business people). This can sometimes cause problems of coordination with governments delivering different messages in the Boards of the Bank and the Fund. Governments with joint directors, like the United Kingdom, avoid this problem.

There is considerable overlap between the work of the Fund and the Bank, which has lead to perennial problems of coordination and the occasional frictions between the two institutions. In 1984 the author proposed a long list of steps to deepen collaboration between the Bank and the Fund and obtained support significantly from the two other joint Fund and Bank directors (from France and Belgium).[6] But the rest of the Board was at best lukewarm and it took a further two years before there was any progress in the shape of limited joint working on policy towards low-income countries. Even so, complaints about poor cooperation still surfaced from time to time during the 1990s. As a result there has been some improvement recently in particular areas of work, notably work on financial sector reform and poor countries. But it is clear that if the institutions were being designed today, the distribution of functions between the institutions would be different.

The Challenges Ahead

The post-Cold War world, where capital and ideas flow almost instantaneously, presents a paradox for the Fund and the Bank. These forces have to some degree weakened the power of the national state. Yet the attraction of the national state as the basis for governmental organisation has never been so popular, as the burgeoning membership of the Fund and the Bank testifies. Those two institutions, together with the WTO and the economic agencies of the United Nations, can play a crucial role in defusing the tensions implicit in this paradox. They can provide the fora for debate, the instruments for rule-making and the political crucible in which the legitimacy and accountability of the system can be fashioned.

If the institutions do not succeed in this endeavour, the risks are clear. They are the establishment of a global economy without the appearance, let alone the actuality, of accountability, and a world economy that is prone to periodic crises, especially for its smaller and more vulnerable members with open economies. In short, back to the pre-Bretton Woods belief that mankind is subject to the dictates of forces, which are either random or deterministic, according to taste.

If the Bank and the Fund are to rise to the challenge, governments, at least in democratic societies, must have political backing in their own countries for their relationships with the institutions. Until recently, that political backing could be taken for granted in most developed countries, except perhaps in the United States where an active lobby has always been critical of the two institutions.[7] But in recent years, the institutions have been subject to much wider attack, and not only in the United States. This attack comes from environmentalists, anti-globalisation campaigners, human rights activists, labour organisations, those campaigning for debt relief and from some sections of the academic economic community.

Lurking beneath many of these criticisms are protectionist forces which run counter to the Fund's and the Bank's core beliefs. But some criticisms have force and the Fund and the Bank must respond to them. For example, they must provide stronger action to shield the poor from the rigours of economic adjustment programmes and give more help for the poor so that they can benefit from globalisation. They must acknowledge the need for greater openness, accountability and transparency, concentrate on their core tasks and avoid mission creep. Most senior officials in the Fund and the Bank would agree with these precepts and the institutions are working hard to respond to their critics.

Whatever the success of the two institutions in responding to their individual critics, they cannot by themselves meet the criticism that the governance of the international economy lacks coherence. The Fund, the Bank and the other international institutions active in the global economy, notably the World Trade Organization and various organs of the United Nations, are all effectively in the same business. They are helping to create a stable framework for the world economy and in particular are seeking to help the developing world prosper in that economy. The institutions have (mostly) the same shareholders, though the voting weight of the shareholders differs between the institutions. Yet each institution is perceived as ploughing its own furrow. Their chief executives, the Fund's Managing Director and the Bank's President, may meet from to time, but such meetings are ad hoc and informal. This may have been tolerable in the compartmentalised, pre-globalisation world of a decade or so ago. But it is not well suited to today's integrated international economy. It appears to many that the system is without governance and is at the mercy of massive, impersonal economic forces. It is therefore not surprising that some again are coming to believe that man is no longer master of his economic fate, but is subject to the dictates of fundamental, blind deterministic laws and forces.

One way of tackling this perception of lack of coherence and of governance of the international economy is to establish an overarching council - a World Economic Council. The council's role would be to seek to give coherence to often disparate initiatives - ensuring that the institutions are in fact cooperating towards common objectives - and to ensure that all that needs to be done to ensure the stability of the system is being done. It would not interfere with the governance of the individual institutions.   Its membership would consist of nominees of representative countries, perhaps based on the membership of the International Monetary and Financial Council, the Managing Director of the IMF, the President of the World Bank, the Director General of the WTO, the General Manager of the Bank for International Settlements (BIS) and the Secretary General of the United Nations. Properly presented and structured such an overarching council could be an important step in establishing confidence in the governance of the global economy.

The effectiveness of the IMF and the World Bank will be undermined if they are subject to constant attacks. If that happened on a large scale, we would have abandoned essential instruments that enable us to demonstrate that we are masters of our economic fate and are not subject to the dictates of some fundamental, blind deterministic laws and forces. That would set the world back almost sixty years.

Notes

1   A comprehensive treatment is in IMF Surveillance 1999, 'External Surveillance of Fund Surveillance: Report by a Group of Independent Experts', available on the Fund's website, www.imf.org, and found by searching for 'surveillance'.
2   For an excellent history of the IMF, see James 1996. Many relevant current papers are to be found on www.imf.org.
3   'Each member shall deal with the Fund only through its Treasury, central bank, stabilization fund, or other similar fiscal agency, and the Fund shall deal only with or through the same agencies'. *IMF Article V, section 1.*
4   The basic reference work on the World Bank is Kapur, Lewis and Webb 1997. Many relevant recent reports are on the Bank's website, www.worldbank.org.

5   See Gardner 1980, pp. 257-260.
6   See Kapur, Lewis and Webb 1997, vol. 2, p.500.
7   See, for example, Melzer 2000, with the reply in Gurria and Volcker 2000.

References

Gardner, R. (1980), *Sterling-Dollar Diplomacy in Current Perspective,* Columbia University Press, New York.
Gurria, R. and Volcker, P. (2000), *The Role of the Multilateral Development Banks in Emerging Market Economies,* available on the website of the Carnegie Endowment for International Peace, www.ceip,org.
IMF Surveillance (1999), *External Surveillance of Fund Surveillance: Report by a Group of Independent Experts,* available on www.imf.org under 'surveillance'.
James, H. (1996), *International Monetary Cooperation Since Bretton Woods,* IMF, Washington.
Kapur, R., Lewis, J. and Webb, S. (1997), *The World Bank: Its First Half Century,* Brookings Institution, Washington.
Melzer, A. (Chairman), (2000), *Report of the International Financial Institutions Advisory Commission,* United States Congress, Washington.

Chapter 17

The World Trading System

Richard Carden

This chapter[1] examines the issues that came to the fore in the world trading system in 2001, as the trauma of the failure of Seattle receded and negotiations over launching a new World Trade Round were gathering speed, in preparation for the WTO ministerial meeting in the autumn of that year. This is not an abstract analysis of the world trading system, but the observations of a practitioner, involved in those negotiations, standing back from the workface, and drawing out from recent experience some thoughts on the state of health of the world trading system and of the World Trade Organization (WTO) which polices that system, and on possible future developments.

The WTO, the Organization

Throughout the year 2000, all commentaries on world trade had started from Seattle. By early 2001, it seemed high time to break with that, to stop looking back, and start looking forward. But the failure of the WTO's ministerial meeting at Seattle had lessons for trade negotiators which they had certainly to keep in view. This chapter will not attempt a definitive analysis of what went wrong at Seattle, but it is clear that the conference failed for a combination of reasons.[2] The focus in this section is on the weaknesses that showed up at Seattle in the WTO as an organisation, and the need for change in the ways it works. There are three such ways, two of which are captured under the heading of 'transparency':

- First, the WTO needs to be open to the organisations that take an interest in what it does, and to the public at large.
- Secondly, it needs to be open with its own members. They need to be able to understand how decisions are being reached, and to participate and exert influence. This must embrace all the developed and developing country members, not just (as often in the past) an inner circle.
- Third, related to the previous point, the smaller and poorer member countries, those newly joined and/or those with only small administrations, need some help in building up their ability to take part in complex multinational negotiations. Efforts to achieve this go under the heading of *capacity building*.

Why the need for these reforms, and why was the need not diagnosed before, to save the débacle at Seattle? When the WTO in the year 2000 or 2001 is compared with GATT ten or twelve years previously, at the start of the Uruguay Round, it is striking how much changed in that time. The number of member countries of GATT in the late 1980s was around 90. The WTO in 2001 had more than 140 members. The GATT did not work in a transparent way. It had some mysterious processes for reaching decisions (eg 'Green Room') and for many years nobody seemed to set much store by keeping the wider membership or the outside world informed about what went on inside the decision-taking inner circle.

The WTO has a new generation of members, many of them developing countries, and some of the members of longer standing have advanced and diversified their economic interest since they first joined. They are, reasonably enough, on their guard against their interests being stitched up by a small core of developed countries. They want to know what is going on and they want a say.

Along with this there is lively and growing public interest in globalisation. It showed itself clearly on the streets of Seattle, and at a series of international conferences during 2000 and 2001, at Prague, Nice, and Davos, Gothenburg and Genoa. There was a call that trade negotiators could not miss hearing, and had not to ignore.

What then is being done to remedy those aspects of the WTO's functioning which have excited criticism? Moves were made in the wake of Seattle to:

- Give out more information more quickly about WTO proceedings (eg on the internet);
- Change the processes of decision-taking. There was much discussion in Geneva during 2000 and 2001, though the action taken on this fell short of formal changes, and left many critics uneasy;
- Build up the capacity of the smaller members through a variety of conferences, teach-ins and workshops in which the WTO staff, the European Commission and the UK Government all played their part.

Two other observations can be made about the WTO. First on the role of the Director-General and the way his responsibilities are defined. By comparison with the President of the European Commission or the Secretary General of the UN, the Director-General of the WTO is expected to play a strikingly more passive role. The WTO is defined as a member-driven organisation. This makes it difficult for the Director-General to take initiatives even when discussions are becalmed and initiative is badly needed. Directors-General over the years have stretched their role by stealth. It might be helpful if the role itself were redefined to let them exert initiative more openly.

Secondly, on the size of the staff. The range of work of the WTO expanded greatly as a result of the Uruguay Round and seems likely to expand again with the next Round. The staff are plainly at full stretch. The WTO has a staff of (in round terms) 500 people. For comparison OECD has around 1850. Governments might usefully take a hard look at whether their expectations have shifted from the OECD to the WTO, and whether the one should be trimmed and the other expanded, for a better match with current expectations.

The WTO itself seems in need of capacity building!

The World Trading System

Turning next to the system of rules which the WTO oversees - the rules of world trade - the system has been evolving. For convenience let us divide the rules on trade, and the focus of current discussions, into three categories here:

- *Traditional* GATT/WTO subjects: market access, tariffs, subsidies, anti-dumping, quantitative restrictions;
- *Newer* subjects - new with the Uruguay Round: agriculture, services, intellectual property (TRIPS);
- Subjects that are being labelled in current discussions the *'new issues'*: that is, issues not covered by existing multilateral rules on trade, which might be tackled in the next Round: investment (only partially covered by existing TRIMS rules), competition, trade facilitation, government procurement, environment, labour standards.

These topics all figure on the agenda for the next WTO Round. I aim here to draw out the underlying issues and prospects for change rather than going into the positions of the leading players or groups of players.

The traditional subjects

It is over 50 years since the first GATT Round, yet the work on the 'traditional' barriers to trade is not yet complete. These barriers have still not come down as far as they could.

- Reducing *tariffs* on industrial goods further could bring significant gains. A study for the Australian Government, for example, put the global welfare gains of a 50% cut in industrial tariffs at more than $66bn (£40bn) a year.[3]
- On *subsidies*, the rules were clarified in the Uruguay Round as to which kinds of subsidy are outlawed, and where action against subsidies is permissible; but even so many developing countries would like to reopen discussions.
- On *anti-dumping*, there is plenty of scope for tightening the rules. This would constrain the freedom with which developed countries can protect against exports from developing and transition economies, against whom a disproportionate number of anti-dumping cases are taken. It would also help stem a more recent trend: the increasing use of anti-dumping measures by developing countries themselves, often against other developing countries.

Conclusion: a Round which did nothing else but go over this traditional ground could result in quite large economic benefits.

The new-with-the-Uruguay-Round subjects

There is clearly further to go, for separate reasons, both on agriculture and services.

278 The New Economic Diplomacy

On *agriculture*, two opposing forces meet: countries, led by the Cairns Group, which reckon they gain from freer trade in food and agricultural commodities; and countries which, for a variety of reasons, see value in protecting their agriculture, this group including the EU, Japan, Norway and Switzerland but also, if less conspicuously, the United States.

In the Uruguay Round, the free traders succeeded in drawing the protectionists into serious negotiations about scaling down government support, with the long term aim of abolishing types of support that distort the market. The Cairns Group regarded the outcome of that Round as seriously disappointing. There is no doubt that the level of protection is still high. But it should be seen as a historic turning point that agriculture was drawn into the Uruguay Round and accepted for the first time then as a topic for multilateral negotiations aimed at liberalising trade. I have no doubt it will take tough negotiations to reach agreement on a second phase of market opening. That will be a central task for the next Round.

On *services*, there is more to do for a different reason. Trade in services was hardly significant when GATT started. There was little pressure for services to be tackled as an area for market opening. By 2001 it had become a very significant part of world trade. In 2000, global commercial services exports were $1435bn, accounting for nearly 20% of world trade. In value terms, services trade has grown seventeen-fold since 1970. Trade in conventional services such as banking, insurance, airlines and tourism, bulks large. Alongside this there is rapidly growing international commerce in electronic form (e-commerce) which some judge to be so different as to need some special rules of its own (though that is not the EU's position).

The Uruguay Round led to an agreement on services which, as with agriculture, was a first step. With services the objective in the next Round will be to take this further, to extend the range and depth of commitments to reduce barriers, and to explore the need for additional rules to cover the newly emerging services. For the UK there is a particularly strong economic interest in that the UK is the second largest exporter of services in the world, after the US.

Many developing countries, on the other hand, have fears that they could be pressed to open their markets to competition from highly developed companies based in the West before their own companies in the services sector have had time to acquire the expertise to compete. It is hard to judge how much strength there is in this, when you look, for example, at the speed with which India has grown the ability to compete in the IT area. But we do seem to need better information about the impact which the first steps in liberalising trade in services have had. There is work for economic analysts to do here.[4]

A case has been made also for looking again at *TRIPS*, the agreement on intellectual property rights such as patents and copyright. Commercially this has turned out to be a very important agreement, particularly for pharmaceuticals, the music industry and other knowledge-driven industries. But it has also turned out to be a highly controversial agreement, provoking protest from NGOs and some developing countries about the barriers to access to medicines needed for diseases (such as AIDS), which have a major impact in some developing countries, and about the patenting of life forms and more generally the alleged exploitation of local knowledge and resources. So there is no telling where a review of TRIPS might lead. The EU could hardly refuse pressure for a review of TRIPS in the next Round, since its position is precisely that the Round should encompass all members' concerns.

The 'New Issues'

These are the issues not subject to existing WTO rules - investment, competition, trade facilitation, public procurement, environment and labour - which were under discussion in 2001 as candidates for inclusion on the agenda for the next Round.

Taking the first two of these as a pair, there are not, at present, multilateral rules to protect *investment* made in one country by companies based in another, nor is there a uniform set of rules on *competition* to constrain monopolies and anti-competitive practices. The issue is whether there should be.

The EU view is that rules are desirable in both areas to provide a certain minimum level of assurance to investors, and to companies setting up operations in foreign markets. A case can also be made that this would be in the interest of developing countries that are trying to attract inward investment to build up their economies.

It remained unclear up to the time of the ministerial conference in November 2001 whether these subjects would be taken forward in the new Round.

Turning next to the *environment*, there is a general and a specific issue. There is a view held by some NGOs, and a sector of the public, that liberalisation of trade encourages economic growth in less developed countries that can be, and often is, damaging to the environment. The more specific issue is whether WTO rules on trade override, and can negate, the rules on protection of the environment made under various 'Multilateral Environment Agreements' or MEAs. This is a more technical question, but it is also an important practical issue which needs to be cleared up.

The arguments over WTO and the environment do not all run one way. When we look at agriculture, environmentalists have often criticised the high levels of support given by governments, particularly in Europe, as having caused intensification of farming with adverse impacts on landscape and biodiversity. WTO pressure to cut back government support for agriculture *might* reverse the trend.

These are some of the issues. There are two opposing views on whether to pursue these in the next Round. Broadly, there is a European view that environmental concerns must form part of the negotiations. That is the standpoint of governments which see themselves as under strong public pressure to show that further liberalisation of trade is compatible with long term care for the environment. Ranged against this are the majority of developing countries, deeply suspicious that talk by developed countries of concern for the environment in the context of trade negotiations is a cover for protectionism. This view runs deep.

With views so strongly divided, it was not clear, in advance of the ministerial conference in November 2001, whether there would be agreement on including the environment as a topic in its own right for the next Round.

Last of the 'new issues': *labour*. In short, the issue here is whether rules on trade should include respect for certain core standards in the treatment of people at work, and specifically bans on the exploitation of child labour, slavery and bondage. The US took the clearest position in favour of this view at the Seattle conference. On this issue as on the environment, the large majority of developing countries fear a new form of protectionism, and an attempt by developed countries with advanced economies to make them comply with standards which those countries did not themselves have to comply with when they were in the first stages of industrialisation. There is adamant resistance to the making of *WTO* rules on labour which would be backed by trade sanctions.

The EU, whose governments also attach importance to the elimination of practices such as child labour, suggested a way forward. This was that the making of rules, in this area, should remain where it is now, with the International Labour Organisation (ILO), whose rules do not have the force of law, and do not lead to trade sanctions; but that there should be joint working between WTO and ILO on how to tie together the liberalisation of trade and the economic advances which are expected from that with greater respect for core labour standards.

The Interests of Developing Countries

This chapter has made various references to the positions and interests of developing countries. There is much talk of the next WTO Round being a 'development Round'. What does this mean? There is clearly a strong case to be made on economic and development grounds for drawing developing countries more closely into the world trading system. That case runs through the UK Government's White Paper on International Development, published at the end of 2000, under the title: 'Eliminating World Poverty: Making Globalisation Work for the Poor' (DFID 2000).

On the practical level, much more attention is being given in WTO discussions now than previously to the interests and concerns of developing countries:

- Reform of the WTO (see above);
- Capacity building (see above);
- Steps to improve market access, most recently with the EU decision on 'Everything But Arms', a decision taken in February 2001 to open up to least developed countries progressively market access, free of tariffs and quota restrictions, for all products except weaponry;
- Discussion of LDCs' concerns about implementing the results of the Uruguay Round.

Along with this, the views of developing countries collectively as to what should and should not be on the agenda for the next Round and what the aims should be were constantly taken into the reckoning by the WTO membership as a whole during the discussions in 2000 and 2001.

The views of developing countries very clearly count now, in a way that they did not in any GATT Round in the past.

Multilateralism: Is There an Alternative?

Much of what has been said assumes that another round of liberalisation at world level would be desirable. Is that right? Even if it is, is the world bound to give priority to that path?

By way of answer to the first question, there is a large volume of data from respected sources indicating - at least at first sight - that there have been substantial gains worldwide from liberalisation of trade in goods up to now. The OECD put the gains from the Uruguay Round at over $200bn per year.[5] Studies by the European Commission and for the Australian Government suggest that an ambitious new Round could bring gains nearer $400bn,[6] while a recent study by the OECD suggests - more questionably - that elimination of all remaining tariffs globally could bring benefits up to three times larger than the Uruguay Round.[7]

But overall, liberalisation on the basis of multilateral rules, applying to all members of the world trading system, does appear to bring scope for gains to all members.

Is the world bound to give priority to the multilateral path? Even after Doha, this is not so clear. Many countries which belong to the WTO have been taking increasing interest in *regional* trading agreements, and many countries belong to one or more regional free trade areas as well as to the multilateral system. Many countries indeed have quite a number of regional agreements. The EU has more than most.

These are not mutually exclusive options: regional and multilateral agreements. But regional agreements are on the increase, countries with fewer see it as an objective to build up more, and those with many already are still extending their range - both US and EU are doing so. In a purely practical sense, the one can impede the other. Any country has limited resources to put into trade negotiations, and if their trade negotiators are actively engaged in working out new regional deals, less time and energy is left for work at the WTO level. Does this matter? The simple answer seems to me to be: yes. Regional agreements bring economic benefits but multilateral agreements almost by definition bring more. Certainly in practice the scope for benefits at that level seems greater. In multilateral negotiations with a wide range of subjects on the agenda governments have again and again proved more willing to give ground on issues they find difficult, in return for clear gains in other sectors of trade. A current illustration is that the US is refusing to negotiate on agriculture as part of the Free Trade Area of the Americas (FTAA) agreement, whereas it is keen to do so in a new WTO Round.

In addition, regional agreements *tend* to give advantages to developed countries over developing countries. A web of regional agreements with different rules applying in different areas, perhaps overlapping areas, is much more complex to understand than a single multilateral system. Large companies from advanced countries will find this easier to cope with than smaller companies in developing countries. There are also examples of developed countries writing into the rules of their regional and bilateral agreements rules, eg on labour standards, which developing countries see as imposing costs on them.

Last but not least, the past 50 years' growth in trade and world incomes has been based on the principle of non-discrimination. Regional arrangements undermine this key principle.

So I suggest it would *not* be to the good if the world turned its back on the multilateral trading system in favour of regional deal-making; and that it should be an objective of trade negotiators to head off any tendency that way.

The Outcome of the Doha Ministerial

Up to this point the analysis has related to the state of the world trading system in the aftermath of the failed Seattle conference, and the ideas for reform of the WTO and improvement of the world trading system on which member countries were concentrating as they prepared for the sequel to Seattle, the WTO's Fourth Ministerial conference, held at Doha (Qatar) in November 2001. Viewed against this background, the outcome of the Doha conference was a success.

First and foremost, agreement was reached to launch a new round of multilateral trade negotiations. Simply achieving this agreement seemed likely to have a positive impact on the world economy, much needed after the negative impact of the events of 11 September 2001. But next let us note that the negotiation launched at Doha is not (in contrast to past practice) being termed the Doha Round but the Doha Development Agenda. This signals the strong emphasis which is now being put on the needs and interests of the developing country members of the WTO.

In fact, close attention was paid throughout the Doha conference to the concerns of developing countries and several important decisions were taken which should bring results of benefit to them, well ahead of the deadline (January 2005) set for conclusion of negotiations on the 'Agenda':

- Access to medicines: agreement was reached to clarify the scope under the existing *TRIPS* rules for developing countries with public health emergencies to gain rapid access to patented medicines, and a commitment was given to find an early solution to the specific problems of countries with no capacity to manufacture such medicines for themselves;
- Fifty measures from the developing countries' list of problems with the outcome of the Uruguay Round were agreed, and commitments given to tackle the remainder as a priority in the new negotiation;
- Systematic attention is to be given to capacity building, with tighter coordination of action taken by the WTO, and the WTO's budget for capacity building and technical assistance measures has already been sharply increased for 2002.

Along with this, the developing countries, and others who were looking for the WTO to reform its ways of working, can take comfort from the fact that, despite the shortage of *formal* decisions on rule-changes, the Doha conference ran in several ways very differently from the conference at Seattle, with step by step checks with all members as discussions moved towards conclusions. Few complaints were heard on this occasion about the *process*, and its transparency or otherwise.

Other elements of the Doha conclusions matched up well to what other participants were looking for. Negotiations will cover the 'traditional' subjects noted above, and will give a new impulse to the talks (referred to earlier) aimed at greater liberalisation of trade in services and agriculture. On the latter, a careful compromise was found which, whilst not committing the EU or others to any particular outcome, gives a clear platform for a new drive to scale down the principal forms of subsidy and protection, including export subsidies which the Cairns Group have as their particular target.

Where the EU had aspirations (as noted earlier) to launch negotiations on several new issues, which a range of other countries treated with suspicion and some fear of protectionism, ways were found of agreeing to take work forward on all the topics concerned - investment, competition, trade facilitation, public procurement. But this will be done in phases, so that the process is to start with some further discussion of possible ways forward before (all being well) proceeding to serious negotiation of specifics. On the issue of the environment, where I would have rated the chances of reaching agreement as particularly low, a formula was agreed which opens the way to negotiation on a short list of topics, with the possibility of adding some others to this list after exploratory discussion.

The conference at Doha thus succeeded, where Seattle had failed, in laying the basis for a broad-based negotiation on further liberalisation of trade, with an agenda which appears to reflect well the interests of the full range of WTO members. This agreement and the process by which it was reached seems to bode well for the future of the WTO and the world trading system which it upholds, and to open up a prospect of gains for a very wide range of countries from the more liberal terms of trade which should in due course be the end result.

Notes

1   The comments in this chapter represent the views of the author and must not be taken as statements of UK government policy. All except the concluding paragraphs of the chapter are based on a lecture given at LSE in March 2001.
2   Bayne (2000) gives a convincing analysis.
3   The details are in Australian DFA (1999); see also note 6.
4   The LSE could possibly make a contribution to this analysis.
5   An OECD study (OECD 1993) estimated that a package of liberalisation measures similar to those agreed in the Uruguay Round could bring annual benefits of $274bn, by the year 2002. This was equivalent to less than 1% of projected world GDP in 2002.
6   The Australian and Commission studies (Australian DFA (1999) and Nagarajan (1999)) looked at the effects of 50% cut in protection in industrial products, agriculture and

(tentatively) services. The Commission put the gains at $385bn in 1995 prices (1.4% of GDP), while the Australian study put the gains at $400bn. It is difficult to interpret these numbers precisely, or compare them directly with results from earlier studies, because some important details of the calculations are not provided in the published reports.

7   The OECD Development Centre (Dessus and others (1999)) put the gains from full tariff liberalisation by developed and developing countries at 3.1% of world GDP in the year 2010. This is roughly equivalent to about $900bn in today's terms. Again, however, some important details are missing from the OECD study, making interpretation difficult. And the numbers themselves look suspiciously large given that the study does not cover services liberalisation.

References

Australian DFA (1999), *Global Trade Reform: Maintaining Momentum*, Australian Department of Foreign Affairs, Canberra.

Bayne, N. P. (2000b), 'Why Did Seattle Fail: Globalisation and the Politics of Trade', *Government and Opposition*, vol. 35, no. 2, pp. 132-151.

Dessus, S., Fukasaku, K. and Safadi, R. (1999), *Multilateral Tariff Liberalisation and the Developing Countries*, Policy Brief No. 18, OECD Development Centre, Paris.

DFID (2000), *Eliminating World Poverty: Making Globalisation Work for the Poor*, UK Government White Paper on International Development.

Nagarajan, N. (1999), *The Millennium Round: an Economic Appraisal*, Economic Papers No. 139, European Commission, Brussels.

OECD (1993), *Assessing the Effects of the Uruguay Round*, OECD, Paris.

CONCLUSIONS

Chapter 18

Economic Diplomacy in the 2000s

Nicholas Bayne and Stephen Woolcock

This final chapter is intended to pull together the record of economic diplomacy, as expounded in this book up to now. It will not offer a forecast on where economic diplomacy is going in the new millennium. Economic diplomacy constantly changes in unforeseen ways - it is very much a moving target. The aim is rather to pick out some of the dominant trends, which have emerged in the 1990s and the early 2000s and which justify speaking of 'The New Economic Diplomacy'. These trends will be illustrated from the case studies set out in the practitioner chapters.

This chapter returns to the analytical framework for economic diplomacy set out in Chapter 1, based on three tensions and eight associated questions. These are set out in Table 18.1 below, which repeats Table 1.1.

Table 18.1   Tensions and Questions in Economic Diplomacy

Tension Between Economics and Politics

1. How to reconcile economic and political objectives?
2. How to reconcile economic and political methods?

Tension between International and Domestic Pressures

3. How do governments reach common positions internally?
4. How can internally agreed positions be deployed internationally?
5. Which is better - voluntary cooperation or binding rules?
6. How to secure democratic accountability and legitimacy?

Tension between Governments and Other Forces

7. How do governments deal with private business?
8. How should governments respond to NGOs?

Economics and Politics

Reconciling international economics and international politics, covered by the first two questions in Table 18.1, is a constant objective of economic diplomacy. During much of the last 50 years this aim has been overshadowed by the other two objectives, which involve domestic pressures. Often the international incentives for economic cooperation are held in check by domestic constraints, both economic and political; this is why cooperation is so difficult. But on occasion the demands of international politics reinforce the arguments for economic cooperation so as to enable advances to be made. What are the prospects for this in the 2000s? History provides some clues.

It is clear that there was very successful interaction between international economics and politics in the years following World War II. The political *objective* of avoiding future wars and containing the spread of communism stimulated the creation of ambitious and durable economic institutions: the Bretton Woods twins, the GATT, the Marshall Plan and the European Community. This point was made by Nigel Wicks in his case study in Chapter 16 as well as in earlier chapters.

At that time, though the United States was the dominant, 'hegemonic' power, it did not impose its ideas on the rest of the world. Especially in the Marshall Plan, the United States required the Europeans to take responsibility - 'ownership' in current usage - for cooperation among themselves and was prepared to tolerate a degree of discrimination against its own interests. This proved a durable *method* of reconciling economics and politics.

Globalisation and the end of the Cold War

The end of the Cold War and the advance of globalisation created a new set of international political pressures at the start of the 1990s. The Western powers entered the decade with high ambitions to restore democracies and market economies in former communist countries. At the same time, the collapse of the centrally planned economies meant that the open competitive system prevailed worldwide, while international economic institutions became universal in membership. As argued in Chapter 5, this contributed to some striking achievements in economic diplomacy: the conclusion of the Uruguay Round and the creation of the WTO; and the harvest of environmental agreements associated with the UNCED conference at Rio.

But this early promise of 'a new world order' was not sustained. There was, in retrospect, too much of a tendency for the industrial West to impose its own ideas. Western donors were slow to give ex-communist countries a sense of 'ownership' of their new policies. More widely, the industrial countries still expected international institutions like the IMF, World Bank and WTO to operate for their own benefit, rather than for the entire worldwide membership. This approach received a rude shock at the Seattle meeting of the WTO. It became brutally clear that developing countries did not see the Uruguay Round and the WTO in the same positive light as the rich countries did.

Policy towards poor countries

This need for genuinely worldwide institutions is one of the consequences of advancing globalisation. Another is that globalisation's undoubted benefits are not equally spread. Many middle-income countries are using globalisation to catch up on the rich ones; but many of the poorest are falling further behind. Often this is because of policy mistakes. As noted in Chapter 5, the IMF said in 1997: "The pressures of globalisation . . . accentuate the benefits of good policies and the costs of bad policies".[1] But poor countries are inevitably more prone to policy mistakes than rich ones; and they have become sceptical about whether the international system can really work for their benefit, as Ivan Mbirimi explained in Chapter 15.

The poorest countries in general pose no threat to the economic system and offer few economic attractions. Policy towards them must be politically motivated and such motivation was largely lacking during the 1990s. The rich countries, taken together, provided increasing amounts of advice to poor ones but dwindling amounts of resources. For most poor countries, aid giving went down, private capital went elsewhere and their share of world trade shrank.[2]

The 2000s have opened, however, with a growing recognition of the need for change. More needs to be done to ensure that the poorest countries also benefit from globalisation. But the poor countries must have 'ownership' of their own development; it cannot be imposed from outside. This new approach was reflected in successive G8 summits - Cologne in 1999, Okinawa in 2000 and Genoa in 2001 - discussed by Colin Budd in Chapter 8. The measures proposed by the G8 at Cologne, to reduce the burden of debt on the poorest countries, were linked with moves to give these countries ownership of the poverty reduction strategies they agreed with the IMF and World Bank. The Africa Action Plan, commissioned at Genoa in 2001 and agreed at Kananaskis in 2002, promised G8 support for the measures the African leaders had themselves agreed to take as part of the New Partnership for Africa's Development (NEPAD). The African countries are clearly the owners of NEPAD and believe that by improving their standards of political and economic governance they will attract more foreign aid and investment. NEPAD and the Africa Action Plan, taken together, have clear parallels with the Marshall Plan.[3]

The fight against terrorism

A further political impetus has been provided by the terrorist attacks on the United States on 11 September 2001. The United States mobilised an impressive international coalition to fight against terrorism. It recognised that this must attack not just the symptoms of terrorism, but also its causes - which include poverty, disease and economic marginalisation. This means that the political campaign against terrorism in the 2000s, like the resistance to communism in the 1950s and 1960s, could be used to promote economic measures to ensure that all countries share in the benefits of globalisation and to enable even the poorest countries to catch up with the others.

The clearest example of this was seen in the successful outcome of the WTO meeting in Doha in November 2001, very soon after the terrorist attacks. This launched a new round of multilateral negotiations, as explained by Richard Carden in Chapter 17. The US and EU agreed to an agenda for the new round that responded to the interests and aspirations of developing countries, including the poorest, far more than what was on offer at Seattle two years before. It provided an opportunity for developing countries to regard the WTO as an institution that really works for them, not just for its richer members.

The fight against terrorism also motivated the unexpected American pledge of increased official aid in the context of the UN meeting on financial flows for developing countries held at Monterrey in March 2002. The US promised an extra $5 billion annually over five years, while comparable undertakings by the EU countries and Canada raised the total to $12 billion.[4] The G8's Africa Action Plan, whose economic provisions are linked with clear commitments to help Africans restore peace and security in troubled areas, recognises the danger of persistent conflict in states like Congo and Sudan.

But the political impulses generated by the fight against terrorism have also come up against serious obstacles provoked by domestic resistance. The Africans had hoped the G8 would provide more market access for their agricultural exports. Instead the United States is increasing subsidies for its farmers. The European Commission's proposals for reforming the CAP, which would reduce its distortion of trade, are being resisted by many Member States. These developments, as well as the new steel tariffs imposed by the US in 2002, will make it harder to get a good outcome to the Doha Round.

During the Marshall Plan, the United States accepted some economic damage by allowing European countries to discriminate against it, as the price of its political aims. There is little sign yet of G8 countries doing this for Africa. Even when international politics and economics combine, this is often too weak to overcome domestic constraints.

International and Domestic

The interaction of international and domestic pressures has become a standard feature of economic diplomacy. It emerges from many of the practitioner chapters, for example those by Matthew Goodman and Patrick Rabe, writing about the United States, Japan and Europe in Chapter 11 and Chapter 13. It is manifested in the great increase in the actors in economic diplomacy, both government departments and agencies and non-state actors. They are increasingly involved both in domestic economic decision-making at home and in international negotiations themselves. This increase in the intensity of economic diplomacy has led governments to adopt four new strategies in the 1990s, including the greater use of international institutions.

The next three questions from Table 18.1 are concerned with how to improve the *efficiency* of economic diplomacy. Questions 3 and 4, about domestic and international strategies, have been well documented already in this book. But there is more to be said about question 5 - the choice between voluntary cooperation and formal rules.

Voluntary cooperation or rule-based systems

The economic institutions created after World War II - the IMF, World Bank and GATT - were rule-based bodies, even if the detailed rules of the ITO were never adopted. By the 1970s, however, economic interdependence was well advanced, at least among industrial countries, while the post-war institutions were under severe strain. Governments reacted to the strains of interdependence by strengthening voluntary cooperation. Professor Robert Putnam's analysis of the Bonn G7 summit of 1978 was intended to show how much voluntary cooperation could achieve.[5]

With the globalisation of the 1990s, however, the balance shifted back to rule-making again. The WTO introduced rules for trade in agriculture and services, as well as legally binding dispute settlement. International commitments on climate change, biodiversity and protecting the ozone layer were embodied in formal UN treaties. As late as 1996 Harold James, the IMF's historian, could still write:

> The general evolution of the international monetary system has been away from rules and towards cooperation. Increased information has played the role previously occupied by a legal or quasi-legal framework.[6]

But the IMF and World Bank responded to the financial crises of 1997-8 by tightening its rules for supplying economic data, for conducting monetary and fiscal policy and for regulating financial institutions.

International rules have four clear advantages over voluntary cooperation, in conditions of globalisation:

- First, they are more *durable*. Voluntary cooperation will work while conditions favour it, but may well collapse under pressure. Rule-based systems are better able to survive bad times as well as good. It is like the difference between cohabitation and marriage.
- Second, rule-based systems are more *equitable*, since all are subject to the same rules and this protects the weaker members against the strong. Systems of voluntary cooperation are too easily dominated by the large and powerful.
- Third, voluntary cooperation can easily become elitist and non-transparent. Rule-based systems have to be *transparent* to some degree, otherwise no one will understand what the rules are.
- Fourth, as governments' relative power shrinks, they are prone to make voluntary commitments that they cannot deliver. There is much less risk of this with international rules.

These arguments carried much weight during the first half of the 1990s. But as the decade advanced, rule-making everywhere came under attack. Both developed and developing countries became discontented with the results of the

Uruguay Round. The WTO meeting in Seattle failed to launch a new rule-making round of trade negotiations and the WTO was criticised as lacking both equity and transparency. Meetings to agree new commitments under environmental agreements failed as often as they succeeded, as deep transatlantic differences emerged. The OECD's attempt to set new rules for investment came to nothing, while its efforts to discipline tax havens were bitterly resisted.

The trouble arose because the new international rules adopted in the 1990s went far beyond determining what happened **between** countries and began to dictate what happened **inside** countries. The WTO's agreements, for example, went further than the GATT, which had sought, rather ineffectively, to control national subsidy programmes and the abuse of technical regulations since the Tokyo Round of the 1970s. Increased interdependence of the world economy meant that international rules had to reach much deeper into domestic arrangements if open markets were to be guaranteed.

This deeper penetration created tensions between emerging international rules and domestic regimes. Some of these were long established. For example, efforts to create rules for financial services within the GATS created tensions with the US system of regulating financial services dating from, at least, the Glass-Steagal Act of the 1930s. In other cases the domestic regulatory regimes were just being reformed. In telecommunications, for example, the need to respond to technological change led to privatisation and regulatory reform. So the issue was whether the domestic regulatory regimes would be compatible with those being negotiated internationally in the GATS. In the environment, popular demands for greater environmental protection resulted in the introduction of domestic regulatory regimes in many developed countries. The strengthening of trade rules in the WTO was then perceived as threatening hard-fought-for environmental regulation.

A general challenge for economic diplomacy in the 2000s is therefore how to reconcile differing domestic regimes and make them internationally compatible.[7] Some of these regimes are deeply embedded in national legislation, regulatory practice and public expectations. Domestic vested interests generally have to be overcome, but when these have been knit into national (or sometimes European) regulatory regimes the process becomes that much harder. Economic diplomacy must deal not only with the economic interests involved, but also the regulatory agencies that have often been established to implement domestic regimes, such as financial regulators, environment agencies and food safety bodies. It also means dealing with the expectations and interests of civil society, consumers and environmental organisations, who have a stake in the domestic regimes.

It has thus become clear that operating a world-wide rules-based system is more demanding than governments have expected. During the 1990s the governments of developed countries persuaded themselves that the new rules amounted to no more than extending their existing domestic approaches to the international level. When it emerged that they were going to have to change their domestic policies, for example the EU on food safety or the US on greenhouse gas emissions, this often led to dispute or disagreement. Meanwhile developing countries, hoping for changes in their favour in the economic system, soon became disillusioned. If industrial countries, with their greater freedom of action, would not set a good example in accepting that international rules meant structural change, developing countries were reluctant to change domestic policies either.

Can the impetus towards the making and keeping of rules be revived in the 2000s? This will require governments to realise that, under globalisation, international rules will bite deep into their domestic policies. As the next section shows, this means ensuring that they have political backing for their international actions, not taking it for granted. The signs are that international rule-making will survive in the new decade, but the obstacles are severe and progress will be slow and painful.

In trade, the WTO's new round of negotiations, launched at Doha in November 2001, has a broad agenda. Many of the negotiating chapters - on agriculture, services, investment and competition - will take the WTO deeper into domestic policy. But progress since Doha has been halting and few now expect the round can be completed within its three-year deadline. In finance, the massive default by Argentina on its foreign debt at the end of 2001 has stimulated the search for better ways both to prevent and to treat such crises. The IMF is pursuing simultaneously a market-driven solution, involving changes in bond contracts, and a rule-based solution, embodied in a new international bankruptcy procedure. In the environment, the new US Administration's open opposition to the Kyoto Protocol on climate change was clearly a setback for rule-making. But the other parties to the climate change convention agreed during 2001, at Bonn and Marrakesh, commitments to implement the Kyoto Protocol, which should come into force in 2002 without the United States.[8]

Rule-making should therefore return to the centre of economic diplomacy. But it is a demanding technique, not to be pursued without realising the consequences. Failures in rules are worse than failures in voluntary cooperation, just as the break-up of a marriage causes more upheaval than the parting of a cohabiting couple.

Democratic Accountability and Legitimacy

Globalisation widens the range of actors in economic diplomacy. This increases the pressure on governments to make their economic diplomacy more accountable, which is the topic of question 6 on Table 18.1. While using institutions is intended to increase the *efficiency* of economic diplomacy, the other three new strategies adopted in the 1990s - involving ministers, engaging non-state actors and greater transparency - are meant to improve its *accountability*.

This brings us to a further issue at the centre of economic diplomacy at the beginning of the 21st century. On the one hand increased interdependence and globalisation calls for greater cooperation between states in order to ensure open markets and address potential market failures at an international level. On the other hand the existing means of providing democratic legitimacy to economic diplomacy remain national or at least 'domestic'.

In the past, governments - with perhaps the exception of the United States where the constitutional role of Congress for commercial policy meant the executive branch has only delegated powers - used to take the legitimisation of international economic decisions for granted. This has made the process of reaching international agreements easier by easing the domestic constraints under which negotiators have had to operate. Policies in the IMF, the GATT and WTO or in terms of other international economic issues have been decided within government. Political legitimacy has been provided by the fact that, whilst officials might deal with the uncontroversial issues, ministers have decided on the more sensitive questions. But consultation with national parliaments has not been very extensive and has often taken the form of a brief report from ministers on the course of negotiations.

In the United States, Congress has progressively tightened its grip over the policy process and reduced the discretion in the hands of executive branch negotiators or officials. Within the European Union the scope for discretion on the part of the European Commission negotiators in international trade negotiations is limited by the oversight of the national governments in the Council of Ministers or in specialist committees. But the role of national parliaments has been very limited and the 'democratic deficit' this represents has not yet been filled by the European Parliament. The pressure for increased transparency has also reduced the discretion available to negotiators, thus making it harder to find means of reconciling domestic and international objectives or rules.

Economic diplomacy has thus been largely shaped by negotiations between governments, with bureaucratic politics largely determining the scale of concessions that were acceptable in order to reach agreement. This prevailing model is now being challenged. Civil society does not see the established channels of democratic legitimisation, centred on elected ministers reporting to parliament, as sufficiently accountable and has therefore sought to engage directly in the policy process. Elected representatives have found it difficult to provide effective scrutiny of the negotiating process because of the often technical nature of the negotiations and the fact that they are conducted in different fora, eg in the EU and the WTO for the case of EU Member States. But opening economic diplomacy to the influence of civil society and or the views of national parliaments could render the task of finding international agreement much more difficult if not impossible.

One of the new strategies is the greater involvement in economic diplomacy of ministers and heads of government, who have much greater political accountability than bureaucrats. These politicians, as they become more active in economic diplomacy, should, in their turn, provide for more extensive debates in national parliaments. If national parliaments are to play a positive role in economic diplomacy, as opposed to a blocking negative role, they must be able to contribute to all stages of a negotiation, not just ratification. This will require more resources to enable specialist committees or working parties to monitor negotiations. If governments do not help to develop this form of effective scrutiny, national parliaments are likely to adopt a more negative approach and could end up vetoing the results of negotiations.

Governments and Other Actors

The last two questions in Table 18.1 are about forces outside government. Parliaments and legislatures, as already noted, make their impact on economic diplomacy overwhelmingly at the domestic level. What is striking about the new trends among business and NGOs is that they now operate at the international level as well.

Private business and markets

Globalisation is driven by the enterprise and innovation of private business. During the 1980s and early 1990s it was thought, at least in Britain and the United States, that business got things right, while government got things wrong. There was a general belief that the market could adjust to any potential failures and that public intervention to prevent market failures was likely to be flawed. Government surrendered many of its functions to the private sector and adopted business practices for much of what was retained. Business thus became more powerful, as government's relative powers dwindled.

In some areas, the private sector assumed a role as regulator in its own right, in what might be called the partial privatisation of economic diplomacy. The private sector has always played a role in developing standards, such as in the various national standards making bodies and the International Standards Organisation (ISO) and International Electrotechnical Committee (IEC). During the 1980s and 1990s, however, the growth of new technologies, especially in information technology and telecommunications, and the globalisation of business accelerated this trend. Because of the complexity of many technical areas, governments made greater use of delegation of regulatory authority to private or semi-public standard-setting bodies, which could shape access to markets. For example, governments were willing to let independent professional bodies shape accounting standards, both nationally and internationally.

Sometimes the private sector developed structures to enable firms to regulate themselves. At other times it resisted any form of regulation on the grounds of greater economic efficiency, arguing that the market should act as regulator. Electronic commerce and the Internet provided the clearest example of this. In the late 1990s IT firms argued that the rapid development and diffusion of this new technology for economic purposes was due to the absence of regulation; governments should therefore keep out.

By the early 2000s these arguments have been undermined by evidence that firms were much less good at regulation than they were at other things. The Asian financial crisis, the collapse of the 'dot-com' bubble and the Enron and WorldCom scandals showed that the private sector makes mistakes just as much as governments do. In short there remained a role of government and public regulation to anticipate and deal with market failures. Governments have therefore been re-asserting their right to regulate, for example to ensure data protection, fight against fraud, money-laundering and high-tech crime and look after the interests of consumers in general. They are strengthening public regulatory agencies, for example in financial services and food safety.

However, there remains a major constraint on governments in making regulatory policy; they have to think of the impact of their decisions on markets. Markets have become endogenous to the policy process to a far greater extent than had been the case in the 1960s or 1970s.[9] The policy areas in which markets impinge most upon policy-making are those which have a direct bearing on financial flows and foreign direct investment. The general liberalisation of capital markets worldwide means that government policies, which are not seen by markets to be credible in the longer run will lead to adverse market reactions, in which investors move money out of the economy concerned. Regulatory policies can also be influenced by markets. The experience of the Asian crisis showed clearly that poor financial market regulation was a factor. Regulation that does not match the expectations of investors can have an adverse impact on the capital account of a country. Finally, governments are now obliged to consider whether the policies they pursue are 'business friendly'. The globalisation of markets has not resulted in the demise of the state, but it has clearly resulted in governments being obliged to consider how policies impact upon the attractiveness of the country concerned to foreign investors.

NGOs

The rise of NGOs in the 1990s and early 2000s, to which Phil Evans referred in Chapter 9, has various causes. Partly they seek to counter the power of business, partly to promote action in areas that they think both government and business are neglecting. They have profited from the widespread popular anxiety about globalisation, which makes people feel vulnerable to forces outside their control. The extreme manifestations of anti-globalisation feeling have been the obstructive and often violent demonstrations at international meetings, mounting in intensity from Seattle in 1999 to the Genoa G8 summit in 2001.

The terrorist attacks of 11 September 2001 brought this violent progression to an abrupt halt. Public tolerance and understanding of anti-globalisation riots have dropped sharply. While many NGOs have also rejected violence.[10] But that does not mean that popular worries about globalisation have gone away. Responsible NGOs, with dedicated members and well-argued programmes and often substantial resources, will continue to gain support in industrial countries. They are likely to have a growing impact on the legislature, the media and the public generally and to be trusted as a source of informed opinion that is independent of government. But such NGOs will wish to make clear their broad-based support and distinguish themselves from small protest groups that exploit the internet to disseminate extreme views.

The influence exerted by NGOs will come less from public demonstrations and more from direct involvement both with business and with governments and international institutions. NGOs are targeting private firms to make them adopt programmes of corporate social responsibility. International firms are finding that greater power brings them not just more freedom of action, but also more responsibility towards public opinion. Governments and institutions often want to make use of NGOs' research capacities, their links with the wider public and their ability to generate new ideas.

This confronts many NGOs with a delicate choice. Those that are ready to work with others will find that both governments and business are keen to tap their expertise, while they can exert a healthy influence in making international institutions more transparent.[11] But NGOs will not want to forfeit their ability to take an independent position, in order to maintain their links with their grass-roots supporters. So all the parties concerned - NGOs, government and business - will be trying to work together while avoiding being captured by the others.

The picture is rather different in developing countries. One obstacle facing Western-based NGOs at the time of Seattle in 1999 was that they were regarded with suspicion in the developing countries that they professed to help. But that had changed by Doha in 2001. Especially because the successful joint campaign by Médécins sans Frontières and Brazil to promote better access to patented drugs and the use of generic alternatives, developing countries came to regard NGOs as more benign. In addition, many NGOs are building up local chapters and alliances in developing countries that can contribute, for example, to poverty-reduction strategies. This enables NGOs to represent themselves as a genuine source of alternative international opinion, which national governments cannot provide. It justifies speaking of NGOs collectively as 'global civil society'.

A Final Image

In economic diplomacy it does not make sense to think of states as impervious entities that can operate internationally while protecting their domestic regime completely. The last remaining country to try that, North Korea, is now emerging from its shell. Even the deplorable Taliban movement in Afghanistan relied heavily on revenues from the international drugs trade. But at the same time it makes no sense either to talk about 'a borderless world' or the end of the nation state. Physical borders are being removed, but regulatory borders are still in place. Governments have lost some of their powers, but their responsibilities remain. Only the nation state provides the basis for democratic legitimacy.

The borders that are disappearing, however, are the borders between international and domestic policies. This book about economic diplomacy has tried to show what that means for decision-making and negotiation, within governments, between governments and by governments in international institutions.

Economic diplomacy is like cookery. If the national economic pudding goes into the international steamer for too short a time, it comes out hard and unpalatable, however much brandy and raisins may be in it. But if it is left there too long, it dissolves into a tasteless mush. The skill is in the balance between ingredients, timing and intensity of cooking. There are all sorts of different types of cuisine in economic diplomacy, as this book has shown. The authors of the practitioner chapters, like practising chefs, have explained how different dishes are prepared. But in the end, the proof of the pudding is in the eating.

Notes

1 See IMF (1997), p. 72.
2 This emerges from World Bank (2001), which distinguishes between about twenty 'more globalised' poor countries (including populous China and India) and a larger number of 'less globalised' poor countries.
3 A valuable analysis of NEPAD and its links with the G8 is in De Waal 2002. There are other useful articles on Africa and NEPAD in the same issue of *International Affairs* - vol. 78, no. 3.
4 Japan, however, has had to cut back its aid by 10%, because of its economic difficulties.
5 See Putnam and Henning (1989), especially p. 98.
6 See James (1996), p. 586.
7 As noted above the international level includes regional, plurilateral as well as multilateral agreements. When reconciliation of domestic regimes at the multilateral level looks impractical, governments can be expected to seek to conclude regional or plurilateral agreements. This could be seen as one factor behind the continued growth of regional agreements since the completion of the Uruguay Round and the efforts to reach plurilateral agreements such as in the 'Multilateral' Agreement on Investment. For a discussion of regional agreements covering such regulatory policies see Sampson and Woolcock forthcoming.
8 A useful and compact summary of the treatment of the environment and development, including climate change, between the UNCED conference at Rio in 1992 and the World Summit on Sustainable Development at Johannesburg in 2002 is in Brack 2002.
9 Odell (2000) provides an analytical framework for including markets in decision-making and provides a number of examples of how governments have been obliged to think about markets.
10 This is well documented in Green and Griffith 2002.
11 For example, both NGOs and private firms were much involved in the preparation and follow-up to the Genoa G8 summit - see Bayne 2001.

References

Bayne, N. (2001), 'G8 Decision Making and the Genoa Summit', *International Spectator*, vol. XXXVI, no. 3, pp. 69-75.
Brack, D. (2002), Sustainable Development: We will Have to Do Better', *The World Today*, vol. 58, no. 8/9, pp. 5-7.
De Waal, A. (2002), 'What's New in the "New Partnership for Africa's Development"?', *International Affairs*, vol. 78, no. 3, pp. 463-476.

Green, D. and Griffith, M. (2002), 'Globalisation and its Discontents', *International Affairs*, vol. 78, no. 1, pp. 49-68.

International Monetary Fund (IMF), (1997), *World Economic Outlook, May 1997*, IMF, Washington.

James, H. (1996), *International Monetary Cooperation Since Bretton Woods*, IMF, Washington.

Odell, J. (2000), *Negotiating the World Economy*, Cornell University Press, Ithaca and London.

Putnam, R. D. and Henning, C. R. (1989), 'The Bonn Summit of 1978: A Case Study in Coordination', in Cooper, R. N. and others (eds.), *Can Nations Agree? Issues in International Economic Cooperation*, the Brookings Institution, Washington.

Sampson, G. and Woolcock, S. (eds.) (forthcoming), *Multilateralism, Regionalism and Economic Integration: the Evidence So Far*, UN University Press, Tokyo.

World Bank (2001), *Globalization, Growth and Poverty*, Policy Research Report, World Bank, Washington.

Bibliography

Aberbach, J., Putnam, R. D. and Rockman, B. (1981), *Bureaucrats and Politicians in Western Democracies*, Harvard University Press, Cambridge, Massachusetts and London.

Australian DFA (1999), *Global Trade Reform: Maintaining Momentum*, Australian Department of Foreign Affairs, Canberra.

Baldwin, D. A. (1985), *Economic Statecraft*, Princeton University Press, Princeton.

Barston, R. P. (1997), *Modern Diplomacy*, 2nd edition, Longmans, London and New York.

Bayne, N. (1987), 'Making Sense of Western Economic Policies: the Role of the OECD', *The World Today*, vol. 43, no.1, pp. 4-11.

Bayne, N. (1994), 'International Economic Relations After the Cold War', *Government and Opposition*, vol. 30, no. 4, pp. 492-509.

Bayne, N. (1997), 'What Governments Want From International Institutions and How They Get It', *Government and Opposition*, vol. 32, no. 2, pp. 361-379.

Bayne, N. (1998), 'Britain, the G8 and the Commonwealth: Lessons of the Birmingham Summit', *The Round Table*, no. 348, pp. 445-457.

Bayne, N. (2000a), *Hanging In There: the G7 and G8 Summit in Maturity and Renewal*, Ashgate, Aldershot.

Bayne, N. (2000b), 'Why Did Seattle Fail: Globalisation and the Politics of Trade', *Government and Opposition*, vol. 35, no. 2, pp. 131-151.

Bayne, N. (2001), 'G8 Decision Making and the Genoa Summit', *International Spectator*, vol. XXXVI, no. 3, pp. 69-75.

Bayne, N. (forthcoming), 'Are World Leaders Puppets or Puppeteers? The Sherpas of the G7/G8 System', in Reinalda, B. and Verbeek, B. (eds.), *Decision Making within International Organisations*, Routledge, London.

Benedict, R. (1954), *The Chrysanthemum and the Sword*, Charles E. Tuttle & Company, Inc., Tokyo.

Bhagwati, J. (1992), 'The Threats to the World Trading System', *The World Economy*, vol. 15, no. 4.

Bhagwati, J. (2001), 'After Seattle: Free Trade and the WTO', *International Affairs*, vol. 77, no. 1, pp. 15-30.

Bhagwati, J. and Kreuger, A. (1995), *The Dangerous Drift to Preferential Trade*, American Enterprise Institute, Washington.

Bhagwati, J. and Patrick, H. (eds.) (1991), *Aggressive Unilateralism: America's 301 Trade Policy and the World Trading System*, University of Michigan Press, Ann Arbor.

Bhagwati, J. and Srinvasan, T. (1982), 'The Welfare Consequences of Directly Unproductive Profit-seeking (DUP) Lobbying Activities: Price *Versus* Quality Distortions', *Journal of International Economics*, vol. 13, no. 1, pp. 33-44.

Blair, D. (1993), *Trade Negotiations in the OECD: Structures, Institutions and States*, Kegan Paul International, London and New York.

Bourgeois, J. (1987), 'The Common Commercial Policy: Scope and Nature of the Powers' in E. L. M. Völker (ed.), *Protectionism and the European Community*,

Kluwer Law and Taxation Publishers, Deventer, pp. 1-16.

Brack, D. (2002), 'Sustainable Development: We Will Have to Do Better', *The World Today,* vol. 58, no. 8/9, pp. 5-7.

Brundtland, G. H. (Chairman) (1987), *Our Common Future,* Report of the World Commission on Environment and Development, Oxford University Press, Oxford.

Brusasco-Mackenzie, M. (1997), 'The Earth Summit + 5: The United Nations General Assembly Special Session, June 13-27 1997; the Role of the European Union', *European Foreign Affairs Review,* vol. 3, no. 2, pp. 197ff.

Bull, H. (1977/1995), *The Anarchical Society: A Study of Order in World Politics,* 1st edition 1977, 2nd edition 1995, Macmillan, London and Basingstoke.

Cable, V. (1999), *Globalisation and Global Governance,* Royal Institute for International Affairs, London.

Carson, R. (1962), *The Silent Spring,* Penguin Books Ltd, London.

Christopher, W. (1998), *In the Stream of History,* Stanford University Press, Stanford.

Cohn, T. (2002), *Governing Global Trade: International Institutions in Conflict and Convergence,* Ashgate, Aldershot.

Cooper, R. N. (1972), 'Economic Interdependence and Foreign Policy in the Seventies', *World Politics,* vol. 24, no. 2, pp. 159-181.

Croome, J. (1995), *Reshaping the World Trading System: A History of the Uruguay Round,* World Trade Organization, Geneva.

Curtis, G. (1988), *The Japanese Way of Politics,* Columbia University Press, New York.

De Clercq, W. (1995), 'Introduction' in Bourgeois J., Berrod, F. and Gippini Fourier, E. (eds.), *The Uruguay Round Results: a European Lawyer's Perspective,* European Interuniversity Press, Brussels.

De Menil, G. and Solomon, A. M. (1983), *Economic Summitry,* Council on Foreign Relations, New York.

Desai, M. (1996), 'Organising the Only Game in Town' in *The World Today,* vol. 52, no. 12, pp. 310-312.

Dessus, S., Fukasaku, K. and Safadi, R. (1999), *Multilateral Tariff Liberalisation and the Developing Countries,* Policy Brief No. 18, OECD Development Centre, Paris.

De Waal, A. (2002), 'What's New in the "New Partnership for Africa's Development"?', *International Affairs,* vol. 78, no.3, pp. 463-476.

DFID (2000), *Eliminating World Poverty: Making Globalisation Work for the Poor,* White Paper on International Development Presented to Parliament by the Secretary of State for International Development, Stationery Office, London.

Diebold, W. (1952), *The End of the ITO, Essays in International Finance* No 16, Princeton University Press, Princeton.

Doi, T. (1981), *The Anatomy of Dependence,* Kodansha, Tokyo.

Eichengreen, B. (1999), *Towards a New International Financial Architecture,* Institute for International Economics, Washington.

Evans, H. (2000), *Plumbers and Architects,* FSA Occasional Papers, Financial

Services Authority, London.

Evans, P., Jacobsen, H. K. and Putnam, R.D. (eds.) (1993), *Double-Edged Diplomacy: International Bargaining and Domestic Politics,* University of California Press, Berkeley.

Fallows, J. (1989), *More Like Us: Making America Great Again,* Houghton Mifflin Company, Boston.

Featherstone, K. and Ginsburg, R. (1996), *The United States and the European Union in the 1990s: Partners in Transition,* 2nd edition, Macmillan, London.

Feldstein, M. (1998), 'Refocusing the IMF', *Foreign Affairs,* vol. 77, no. 2, pp. 20-33.

Fischer, S. (1998), In Defence of the IMF', *Foreign Affairs,* vol. 77, no. 4, pp. 103-106.

Frieden, J. and Lake, D. A. (eds.) (2000), *International Political Economy: Perspectives on Global Power and Wealth,* 4th edition, Routledge, London and New York.

Frost, E. (1999), *Transatlantic Trade: A Strategic Agenda,* International Institute for Economics, Washington.

Gardner, R. (1980), *Sterling-Dollar Diplomacy in Current Perspective,* Columbia University Press, New York.

Gilpin, R. (2001), *Global Political Economy: Understanding the International Economic Order,* Princeton University Press, Princeton and Oxford.

Goldstein, J. (1988), 'Ideas, Interests, and American Trade Policy', *International Organization,* vol. 42, no. 1, pp. 179-217.

Gowa, J. (1994), *Allies, Adversaries and International Trade,* Princeton University Press, Princeton.

Green, D. and Griffith, M. (2002), 'Globalisation and its Discontents', *International Affairs,* vol. 78, no. 1, pp. 49-68.

Grieco, J. (1990), *Cooperation Among Nations; Europe, America and Non-Tariff Barriers to Trade,* Cornell University Press, Ithaca and London.

Grubb, M. with Vrolijk, C. and Brack, D. (1999), *The Kyoto Protocol: A Guide and Assessment,* Royal Institute of International Affairs/Earthscan, London.

Gurria, R. and Volcker, P. (2000), *The Role of the Multilateral Development Banks in Emerging Market Economies,* available on website of the Carnegie Endowment for International Peace, www.ceip,org.

Haas, P. (1997), *Knowledge, Power and International Policy Coordination,* University of South Carolina Press, Columbia, SC. See also *International Organization,* vol. 46, no. 1 (1992).

Haass, R. N. (ed.) (1998), *Economic Sanctions and American Diplomacy,* Council on Foreign Relations, New York.

Hanson, P. (1988), *Western Economic Statecraft in East-West Relations: Embargoes, Sanctions, Linkage, Economic Warfare and Détente,* Royal Institute of International Affairs, London.

Hayes, J. P. (1993), *Making Trade Policy in the European Community,* Macmillan, Basingstoke.

Held, D., McGrew, A., Goldblatt, D. and Perraton, J. (1999), *Global Transformations: Politics, Economics and Culture,* Polity Press, Cambridge.

Henderson, P. D. (1993), 'International Economic Cooperation Revisited', *Government and Opposition*, vol. 28, no. 1.

Henderson, P. D. (1999), *The MAI Affair: A Story and its Lessons*, Royal Institute of International Affairs, London.

Hirst, P. and Thompson, G. (1999), *Globalisation in Question*, 2nd edition, Polity Press, Cambridge.

Howe, G. (1994), *Conflict of Loyalty*, Macmillan, London.

Ikenberry, G. J., Lake, D. A. and Mastanduno, M. (eds.) (1988), *The State and American Foreign Economic Diplomacy*, Cornell University Press, Ithaca and London. See also *International Organization*, vol. 42, no. 1.

IMF (1997), *World Economic Outlook, May 1997*, International Monetary Fund, Washington.

IMF Surveillance (1999), External Surveillance of Fund Surveillance: Report by a Group of Independent Experts, available on www.imf.org under 'surveillance'.

Jackson, J. H. (1990), *Restructuring the GATT System*, Royal Institute of International Affairs, London.

Jackson, J. H. (1998), *The World Trade Organization: Constitution and Jurisprudence*, Royal Institute of International Affairs, London.

James, H. (1996), *International Monetary Cooperation Since Bretton Woods*, IMF, Washington.

Johnson, M. (1998), *European Community Trade Policy and the Article 113 Committee*, Royal Institute of International Affairs, London.

Kapur, R., Lewis, J. and Webb, S. (1997), *The World Bank: Its First Half Century*, Brookings Institution, Washington.

Katzenstein, P. (1978), *Between Power and Plenty: Foreign Economic Policies in Advanced Capitalist States*, University of Wisconsin Press, Madison and London.

Kenen, P. B. (ed.) (1994), *Managing the World Economy: Fifty Years After Bretton Woods*, Institute for International Economics, Washington.

Kenen, P. (2001), *The International Financial Architecture: What's New? What's Missing?*, Institute for International Economics, Washington.

Keohane, R. O. (1984), *After Hegemony: Co-operation and Discord in the World Economy*, Princeton University Press, Princeton.

Killick, T. (1995), *IMF Programmes in Developing Countries: Design and Impact*, Routledge, London and New York.

Killick, T. (1998), *Aid and the Political Economy of Policy Change*, Routledge, London and New York.

Kissinger, H. (1982), *Years of Upheaval*, Weidenfeld and Nicholson, London.

Klein, N. (2000), *No Logo*, Vintage Canada, Toronto.

Krasner, S. (1983), *International Regimes*, Cornell University Press, Ithaca and London.

Lawrence, R. (1993), *Regionalism, Multilateralism, and Deeper Integration*, Brookings Papers on Economic Activities, The Brookings Institution, Washington.

Lincoln, E. J. (1999), *Troubled Times: US-Japan Trade Relations in the 1990s*, The Brookings Institution, Washington.

Macleod, I., Hendy, I.D. and Hyatt, S. (1997), *The External Relations of the European Communities: a Manual of Law and Practice*, Clarendon Press, Oxford.

Mansfield, E. and Milner, H. (eds.) (1997), *The Political Economy of Regionalism*, Columbia University Press, New York.

Maresceau, M. (1994), *The EC's Commercial Policy after 1992: the Legal Dimension*, Nijoff, Dordrecht.

Marjolin, R. (1989), *Architect of European Unity: Memoirs 1911-1986*, Weidenfield and Nicholson, London, translated by William Hall from *Le Travail d'une Vie*, Robert Laffont, Paris 1986.

Marks, G. and Hooghe, L. (2001), *Multilevel Governance and European Integration*, Rowman and Littlefield, Boulder, Colorado.

Marshall, P. (1999), *Positive Diplomacy*, Palgrave, Basingstoke.

Meltzer, A. (Chairman) (2000), *Report of the International Financial Institutions Advisory Commission*, United States Congress, Washington.

Meunier, S. and Nicholaidis, K. (1999), 'Who Speaks for Europe? The Delegation of Trade Authority in the European Union', *Journal of Common Market Studies*, vol. 37, no. 3, pp. 477-501.

Milner, H. (1997), *Interests, Institutions and Information: Domestic Politics and International Relations*, Princeton University Press, Princeton.

Milner, H. (1998), 'Rationalizing Politics: The Emerging Synthesis of International, American and Comparative Politics', *International Organization*, vol. 52, no. 4, pp. 759-786.

Moravscik, A. (1993), 'Introduction' in Evans, P, Jacobsen, H. K. and Putnam, R.D. (eds), *Double Edged Diplomacy: International Bargaining and Domestic Politics*, University of California Press, Berkeley.

Murphy, R. T. (1996), *The Weight of the Yen: How Denial Imperils America's Future and Ruins an Alliance*, W.W. Norton & Company, Inc., New York.

Nagarajan, N. (1999), *The Millennium Round: an Economic Appraisal*, Economic Papers No. 139, European Commission, Brussels.

O'Brien, R., Goetz, A. M., Scholte, J. A. and Williams, M. (2000), *Contesting Global Governance: Multilateral Economic Institutions and Global Social Movements*, Cambridge University Press, Cambridge.

Odell, J. (2000), *Negotiating the World Economy*, Cornell University Press, Ithaca and London.

Odell, J. and Eichengreen, B. (2000), 'Changing Domestic Institutions and Ratifying Regime Agreements' in Odell, J. *Negotiating the World Economy*, Cornell University Press, Ithaca and London.

OECD (1993), *Assessing the Effects of the Uruguay Round*, OECD, Paris.

Ohmae, K. (1992), *The Borderless World: Power and Strategy in the Interlinked Economy*, Routledge, London.

Ohmae, K. (1995), *The End of the Nation State*, HarperCollins, London.

Ostry, S. (1997), *The Post-Cold War Trading System: Who's On First?* University of Chicago Press, Chicago and London.

Paarlberg, R. (1995), *Leadership Begins at Home: US Foreign Economic Policy after the Cold War*, The Brookings Institution, Washington.

Pape, R. A. (1997), 'Why Economic Sanctions Do Not Work', *International Security,* vol. 22, no. 2, pp. 90-136.

Patrick, H. and Rosovsky, H. (1976), *Asia's New Giant: How the Japanese Economy Works,* The Brookings Institution, Washington.

Pelkmans, J. and Winters, L. with Wallace, H. (1988), *Europe's Domestic Market,* Routledge for Royal Institute for International Affairs, London.

Persaud, B. (2001), 'OECD Curbs on Offshore Financial Centres: A Major Issue for Small States', *The Round Table,* no. 359, pp. 199-212.

Peterson, J. (1996), *Europe and America in the 1990s: Prospects for Partnership,* Routledge, London.

Preeg, E. (1995), *Traders in a Brave New World: the Uruguay Round and the Future of the International Trading System,* University of Chicago Press, Chicago.

Putnam, R. D. (1988), 'Diplomacy and Domestic Politics: the Logic of Two-Level Games', *International Organization,* vol. 42, no. 3, pp. 427-460.

Putnam, R. D. and Bayne, N. (1987), *Hanging Together: Cooperation and Conflict in the Seven-Power Summits,* SAGE, London.

Putnam, R. D. and Henning, C. R. (1989), 'The Bonn Summit of 1978: A Case Study in Coordination', in R. N. Cooper and others (eds.), *Can Nations Agree? Issues in International Economic Cooperation,* the Brookings Institution, Washington.

Ray, J. E. (1995), *Managing Official Export Credit: the Quest for a Global Regime,* Institute for International Economics, Washington.

Reinalda, B. and Verbeek, B. (eds.) (1998), *Autonomous Policy Making by International Organisations,* Routledge, London and New York.

Rodrik, D. (1997), *Has Globalization Gone Too Far?,* Institute for International Economics, Washington.

Rodrik, D. (1999), *The New Global Economy and Developing Countries: Making Openness Work,* Overseas Development Council, Washington.

Rosenau, J. (1969), *Linkage Politics: Essays on the Convergence of National and International Systems,* Free Press, New York.

Ruggie, J. G. (1982), 'International Regimes, Transactions and Change: Embedded Liberalism in the Postwar Economic Order', *International Organization,* vol. 36, no. 2, pp. 379-415.

Sachs, J. (1999), 'Helping the World's Poorest', *The Economist,* 14 August 1999.

Sampson, G. and Woolcock, S. (eds.) (forthcoming), *Multilateralism, Regionalism and Economic Integration: the Evidence So Far,* UN University Press, Tokyo.

Scholte, J. A. (2001), 'Global Civil Society' in Woods, N. (ed.), *The Political Economy of Globalisation,* St Martin's Press, New York.

Schoppa, L. J. (1997), *Bargaining with Japan: What American Pressure Can and Cannot Do,* Columbia University Press, New York.

Schott, J. (1994), *The Uruguay Round: An Assessment,* Institute of International Economics, Washington.

Sherifis, R. F. and Astraldi, V. (2001), *The G7/G8 from Rambouillet to Genoa,* FrancoAngeli, Milan.

Smith, M. and Woolcock, S. (1993), *The United States and the European*

Community in a Transformed World, Pinter for Royal Institute of International Affairs, London.

Spero, J. and Hart, M. (1997), *The Politics of International Economic Relations*, 5th edition, St Martin's Press, New York.

Stiglitz, J. (2002), *Globalisation and its Discontents*, Allen Lane, London.

Stokes, B. (2000), *A New Beginning: Recasting the US-Japan Economic Relationship*, Council on Foreign Relations, Washington.

Strange, S. (1988), *States and Markets: an Introduction to Political Economy*, Pinter, London.

Strange, S. (1996), *The Retreat of the State: the Diffusion of Power in the World Economy*, Cambridge University Press, Cambridge.

Thatcher, M. (1993), *The Downing Street Years*, HarperCollins, London.

Van Bergeik, P. (1994), *Economic Diplomacy, Trade and Commercial Policy; Positive and Negative Sanctions in a New World Order*, Edward Elgar, Aldershot and Brookfield, Virginia.

Van Scherpenberg, J. and Thiel, E. (eds.) (1998), *Towards Rival Regionalism? US and EU Economic Integration and the Risk of a Transatlantic Rift*, Stiftung Wissenschaft und Politik, Eberhausen.

Van Wolferen, K. (1989), *The Enigma of Japanese Power*, Alfred A. Knopf, New York.

Viner, J. (1950), *The Customs Union Issue*, Stevens and Sons, London.

Wechsler, W. (2001), 'Follow the Money', *Foreign Affairs*, vol. 80, no. 4, pp.40-57.

Wilson, J. Q, (ed.) (1980), *The Politics of Regulation*, Basic Books, London.

Winham, G. L. (1986), *International Trade and the Tokyo Round Negotiations*, Princeton University Press, Princeton.

Winham, G. L. (1992), *The Evolution of International Trade Agreements*, University of Toronto Press, Toronto and London.

Woods, N. (ed.) (2001), *The Political Economy of Globalisation*, St Martin's Press, New York.

Woolcock, S. (1998), 'European and American Approaches to Regulation; Continuing Divergence?' in Van Scherpenberg, J. and Thiel, E, (eds.), *Towards Rival Regionalism? US and EU Economic Integration and the Risk of Transatlantic Regulatory Rift*, Stiftung Wissenschaft und Politik, Eberhausen.

Woolcock, S. (1999), 'The United States and Europe in the Global Economy' in Burwell F. G. and Daalder, I. H. (eds.), *The United States and Europe in the Global Arena*, Macmillan, London, and St Martin's Press, New York, pp. 177-207.

Woolcock, S. (2000), 'European Trade Policy' in Wallace H. and Wallace W., (eds.), *Policy-Making in the European Union*, 4th edition, Oxford University Press, Oxford.

Woolcock, S. and Hodges, M. (1997), 'The European Union in the Uruguay Round: The Story Behind the Headlines' in Wallace, H. and Wallace, W. (eds.) *Policy-Making in the European Union*, 3rd Edition, Oxford University Press, Oxford.

World Bank (2001), *Globalization, Growth and Poverty,* Policy Research Report, World Bank, Washington.

WTO (2000), *Inventory of Non-Tariff Provisions in Regional Trade Agreements,* Background Note by the Secretariat, WT/REG/26 5 May 1998, World Trade Organization, Geneva.

Zajac, E. E. (1995), *Political Economy of Fairness,* MIT Press, Cambridge, Massachusetts.

Index

This index covers people, places and institutions. Where places are associated with international agreements, the agreement is named, eg Kyoto Protocol *and* Maastricht Treaty. *Where they are associated with international meetings, only the place is given, eg* Genoa *and* Gothenburg, *not Genoa summit or Gothenburg European Council.*

A

Acheson, Dean, 108
ACP (African, Caribbean and Pacific), 199, 222, 257
Actionaid, 57
Administration, US, 29, 34-36, 38, 40, 49, 72, 76, 91, 107, 109, 110, 112, 142, 151, 153, 175-177, 182-186, 191, 192, 201, 210, 225, 293
Afghanistan, 40, 297
Africa, 26, 87, 88, 92, 93, 97, 133, 176, 177, 198, 199, 219, 220, 222, 252, 254, 256, 257, 262, 266, 268, 289, 290
AIDS, 92, 143, 278
Amsterdam Treaty, 203, 208, 216
APEC (Asia-Pacific Economic Cooperation), 95-97, 171, 172, 175, 182, 198, 233, 235
Argentina, 57, 89, 90, 108, 167, 201, 221, 231, 254, 266, 293
Article 133 Committee, 48, 152, 202-208, 210
ASEAN (Association of South East Asian Nations), 97, 198, 200
Asia, 19, 86, 88, 89, 90, 92, 95, 97, 122, 133, 143, 144, 181, 182, 186, 193, 198, 199, 220, 231, 245, 266, 295, 296
Atlantic Charter, 103, 108
Australia, 51, 55, 68, 109, 110, 171, 198, 220, 238, 268, 277, 281
Austria, 116, 198

B

Baldwin, David, 7
Balkans, 144, 199, 200
Baltic States, 84
Bangladesh, 242

Barre, Raymond, 128
Barshefsky, Charlene, 233
Beijing, 96
Belgium, 35, 110, 268, 271
Berlin, 74, 83
Bhagwati, Jagdish, 148
BIAC (Business and Industry Advisory Council), 59, 239
Birmingham, 78, 139, 141, 143-145
BIS (Bank for International Settlements), 182, 273
Blair House Agreement, 176, 210
Blair, Tony, 71, 79, 80, 95, 134, 141, 142, 226
Bonn, 125-127, 130-134, 291, 293
Brazil, 19, 88, 108, 110, 169, 201, 219, 252, 254, 297
Bretton Woods, 7, 27, 32, 62, 109, 110, 112, 121, 169, 170, 225, 261, 270, 272, 288
Britain — *see* United Kingdom
Brown, Gordon, 143
Brundtland, Gro Harlem, 219
Brussels, 29, 54, 56, 74, 207, 217, 257
Bush, George, US President (1989-1992), 36, 185, 219
Bush, George, US President (2001-), 79, 91, 164, 172, 173, 175-177, 226

C

Cabinet Office, UK, 69-71, 109, 113
Cairns Group, 234, 278, 283
Callaghan, James, 127
Camdessus, Michel, 264
Canada, 7, 18, 24, 51, 66, 68, 69, 78, 91, 93, 95, 107, 109, 110, 123, 124, 156, 163, 164, 173-175, 198, 220, 235, 238, 240-242, 268, 290
CAP (Common Agricultural Policy of the EC), 50, 91, 97, 109, 255, 290

F

G

H

I